ASN.1 Complete

ASN.1 Complete

by

Professor John Larmouth

Morgan
Kaufmann

ACADEMIC PRESS, A Harcourt Science and Technology Company

San Diego San Francisco New York Boston
London Sydney Tokyo

Academic Press
A Harcourt Science and Technology Company
525 B Street, Suite 1900, San Diego, CA 92101-4495
http://www.apnet.com

Academic Press
24-28 Oval Road, London NW1 7DX United Kingdom
http://www.hbuk.co.uk/ap/

Morgan Kaufmann Publishers
A Harcourt Science and Technology Company
340 Pine Street, Sixth Floor, San Francisco, CA 94104-3205
http://www.mkp.com

Library of Congress Catalog Number: 99-66138
International Standard Book Number: 0-12-233435-3

Printed in the United States of America
99 00 01 02 03 IP 9 8 7 6 5 4 3 2 1

Dedication

This book is dedicated to the girls at Withington Girls' School, who are there with my daughter Sarah-Jayne, and to the boys at The Manchester Grammar School, who are there with my son James, in the hope that it may one day be of use to some of them!

Contents

Foreword

This text is written primarily for those involved in protocol specification or in the implementation of ASN.1-based protocols. It is expected, however, that it will be of interest and use to a wider audience including managers, students, and simply the intellectually curious.

The Introduction that follows should be at least scanned by all readers, and ends with a discussion of the structure of the text. Thereafter, readers generally have a reasonable degree of freedom to take sections and chapters in any order they choose, and to omit some (or many) of them, although for those with little knowledge about ASN.1 it would be sensible to read the whole of Section I first, in the order presented.

Here is a rough guide to what the different types of reader might want to tackle:

- **Managers**: Those responsible for making decisions related to possible use of ASN.1 as a notation for protocol specification, or responsible for managing teams implementing protocols defined using ASN.1, should read Section I (ASN.1 Overview), and need read no further, although Section IV (History and Applications) might also be of interest. This would also apply to those curious about ASN.1 and wanting a short and fairly readable introduction to it.

- **Protocol specifiers**: For those designing and specifying protocols, much of Section I (ASN.1 Overview) and Section IV (History and Applications) should be scanned in order to determine whether or not to use ASN.1 as a specification language, but Section II (Further Details) is very important for this group.

- **Implementors using an ASN.1 tool**: For this group, Section I (ASN.1 Overview) and Section II (Further Details) will suffice.

- **Implementors doing hand-encodings**: (or those who may be developing ASN.1 tools) must supplement the preceding sections by a careful reading of

Section III (Encodings) and indeed of the actual ITU-T Recommendations/ISO Standards for ASN.1.

- **Students on courses covering protocol specification techniques**: Undergraduate and postgraduate courses aiming to give their students an understanding of the abstract syntax approach to protocol specification (and perhaps of ASN.1 itself) should place the early parts of Section I (ASN.1 Overview) and some of Section IV (History and Applications) on the reading list for the course.

- **The intellectually curious**: Perhaps this group will read the whole text from front to back and find it interesting and stimulating! Attempts have been made wherever possible to keep the text light and readable—go to it!

There is an electronic version of this text available, and a list of further ASN.1-related resources, at the URL given in Appendix 5. **And importantly, errata sheets will be provided at this site for downloading.**

The examples have all been verified using the "OSS ASN.1 Tools" package produced and marketed by Open Systems Solutions (OSS), a U.S. company that has (since 1986) developed and marketed tools to assist in the implementation of protocols defined using ASN.1. I am grateful to OSS for much support in the production of this book, and for the provision of their tool for this purpose. While OSS has given support and encouragement in many forms, and has provided a number of reviewers of the text who have made very valued comments on early drafts, the views expressed in this text are those of the author alone.

John Larmouth
(«hyperlink mailto:j.larmouth@salford.ac.uk »)
May 1999

Introduction

Summary

This introduction

- describes the problem ASN.1 addresses,

- briefly says what ASN.1 is, and

- explains why it is useful.

1 The Global Communications Infrastructure

We are in a period of rapid advance in the collaboration of computer systems to perform a wider range of activity than ever before. Traditional computer communications to support human-driven remote logon, e-mail, file-transfer, and latterly the World Wide Web (WWW) are being supplemented by new applications requiring increasingly complex exchanges of information both between computer systems and between appliances with embedded computer chips.

Some of these exchanges of information continue to be human-initiated, such as bidding at auctions, money wallet transfers, electronic transactions, voting support, or interactive video. Others are designed for automatic and autonomous computer-to-computer communication in support of such diverse activities as cellular telephones (and other telephony applications), meter reading, pollution recording, air traffic control, control of power distribution, and applications in the home for control of appliances.

In all cases there is a requirement for the detailed specification of the exchanges the computers are to perform, and for the implementation of software to support those exchanges.

The most basic support for many of these exchanges today is provided by the use of TCP/IP and the Internet, but other carrier protocols are still in use, particularly in the telecommunications area. However, the specification of the data formats for messages that are to be passed using TCP (or other carriers) requires the design and clear specification of **application protocols,** followed by (or in parallel with) implementation of those protocols.

For communication to be possible between applications and devices produced by different vendors, standards are needed for these application protocols. The standards may be produced by recognized international bodies such as the International Telecommunications Union Telecommunications Standards Sector (ITU-T), the International Standards Organization (ISO), or the Internet Engineering Task Force (IETF), or by industrial associations or collaborative groups and consortia such as the International Civil Aviation Organization (ICAO), the Open Management Group (OMG) or the Secure Electronic Transactions (SET) consortium, or by individual multinational organizations such as Reuters or IBM.

These different groups have various approaches to the task of specifying the communications standards, but in many cases ASN.1 plays a key role by enabling

- rapid and precise specification of computer exchanges by a standardization body, and

- easy and bug-free implementation of the resulting standard by those producing products to support the application.

In a number of industrial sectors, but particularly in the telecommunications sector, in security-related exchanges, and in multimedia exchanges, ASN.1 is the dominant means of specifying application protocols. (The only other major contender is the character-based approach often used by IETF, but which is less suitable for complex structures, and which usually produces a much less compact set of encodings.) A description of some of the applications where ASN.1 has been used as the specification language is given in Chapter 20.

2 What Exactly Is ASN.1?

The term "TCP/IP" can be used to describe two protocol specifications (Transmission Control Protocol—TCP, and Internet Protocol—IP), or more broadly to describe the complete set of protocols and supporting software that are based around TCP/IP. Similarly, the term "ASN.1" can be used narrowly to describe a notation or language called "Abstract Syntax Notation One", or can be used more broadly to describe the notation, the associated encoding rules, and the software tools that assist in its use.

The things that make ASN.1 important and unique include the following:

- It is an internationally standardized, vendor-independent, platform-independent, and language-independent notation for specifying data-structures at a high level of abstraction. (The notation is described in Sections I and II.)

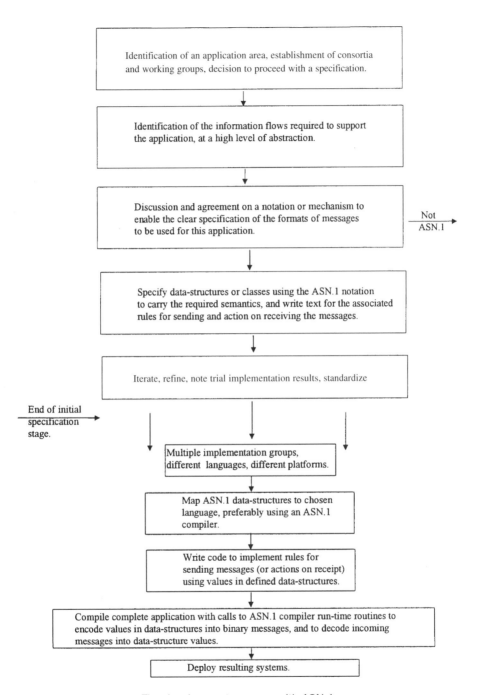

The development process with ASN.1.

- It is supported by rules that determine the precise bit-patterns (again plat-form-independent and language-independent) to represent values of these data-structures when they have to be transferred over a computer network, using encodings that are not unnecessarily verbose. (The encoding rules are described in Section III.)

- It is supported by tools available for most platforms and several program-ming languages that map the ASN.1 notation into data-structure definitions in a computer programming language of choice, and which support the automatic conversion between values of those data-structures in memory and the defined bit-patterns for transfer over a communications line. (The tools are described in Chapter 6.)

There are a number of other subtle features of ASN.1 that are important and are dis-cussed later in this text. Some of these are

- It addresses the problem of, and provides support for, interworking between deployed "version-1" systems and "version-2" systems that are designed and deployed many years apart. (This is called "extensibility".)

- It provides mechanisms to enable partial or generic specification by one standards group, with other standards groups developing (perhaps in very different ways) specific specifications.

- It recognizes the potential for interworking problems between large sys-tems capable of handling long strings, large integer values, large iterative structures, and small systems that may have a lesser capability.

- It provides a range of data-structures that is generally much richer than that of normal programming languages, such as the size of integers, naming structures, and character string types. This enables precision in the specifi-cation of the range of values that need to be transferred, and hence pro-duction of more optimal encodings.

3 The Development Process with ASN.1

The flow diagram on page xxv illustrates the development process from inception to deployment of initial systems.

(But it must be remembered that this process is frequently an iterative one, with both early revisions by the standardization group to "get it right" and with more substantial revisions some years later when a "version-2" standard is produced.)

Some key points to note from the diagram included

- The decision to employ ASN.1 as the notation for defining a standard is a key one. It requires a good understanding of the ASN.1 notation by the standardization group, but provides a rich set of facilities for a clear specification. Alternative means of protocol specification are discussed in Chapter 1.

- There is no need for the standardization group (or implementors) to be concerned with the detailed bit-patterns to be used to communicate the desired semantics: details of encoding are "hidden" in the ASN.1 encoding rule specifications and in the run-time support provided by the ASN.1 tools.

- The implementation task is a simple one: the only code that needs to be written (and debugged and tested) is the code to perform the semantic actions required of the application. There is no need to write and debug complex parsing or encoding code.

4 Structure of the Text

Section I covers the most commonly encountered features of the ASN.1 notation. It also briefly introduces all other aspects of the notation, with full coverage in Section II. It is intended that those who are not primarily responsible for writing specifications using ASN.1 or for coding implementations, but who need a basic understanding to assist in or to manage development (of standards or implementations), will obtain all that they need from Section I. Those with primary responsibility for writing or coding will need Section II also.

Section III describes the principles behind the ASN.1 encoding rules, and much of the detail. However, this text is really only for the curious! There is no need for standards writers or coders to know about these encodings (provided that a tool is used for the implementation).

Section IV completes the text (apart from various supporting appendices) by giving some details of the history of ASN.1, and of the applications that have been specified using it.

A detailed treatment of ASN.1 is a fairly "heavy" subject, but I have tried to inject just a little lightness and humor where possible. Skip what you wish, read what interests you, but please, **enjoy!**

ASN.1 Overview

## CHAPTER 1

Specification of Protocols
(Or: Simply Saying Simply What Has To Be Said!)

Summary

This chapter

- introduces the concept of a "protocol" and its specification,

- provides an early introduction to the concepts of
    - layering,
    - extensibility,
    - abstract and transfer syntaxes,

- discusses means of protocol specification, and

- describes common problems that arise in designing specification mechanisms and notations.

(Readers involved in protocol specification should be familiar with
much of the early "concepts" material in this chapter, but may find
that it provides a new and perhaps illuminating perspective on
some of the things they have been trying to do.)

1.1 What Is a Protocol?

A computer protocol can be defined as

> A well-defined set of **messages** (bit-patterns or—increasingly today—
> octet strings), each of which carries a defined meaning (**semantics**),
> together with the **rules** governing when a particular message can be sent.

However, a protocol rarely stands alone. Rather, it is commonly part of a "protocol
stack", in which several separate specifications work together to determine the
complete message emitted by a sender, with some parts of that message destined
for action by intermediate (switching) nodes, and some parts intended for the
remote end system.

In this "layered" protocol technique

- One specification determines the form and meaning of the outer part of the message, with a "hole" in the middle. It provides a "carrier service" (or just "service") to convey any material that is placed in this "hole".

> **What Is a Protocol?**
>
> A well-defined set of messages, each of which carries a defined meaning, and,
>
> the rules governing when a particular message can be sent, and
>
> explicit assumptions about the nature of the service used to transfer the messages, which themselves either support a single-end application or provide a richer carrier service.

- A second specification defines the contents of the "hole", perhaps leaving a further hole for another layer of specification, and so on.

Figure 1.1 illustrates a TCP/IP stack, where real networks provide the basic carrier mechanism, with the IP protocol carried in the "hole" they provide, and with IP acting as a carrier for TCP (or the less well-known User Datagram Protocol—UDP), forming another protocol layer, and

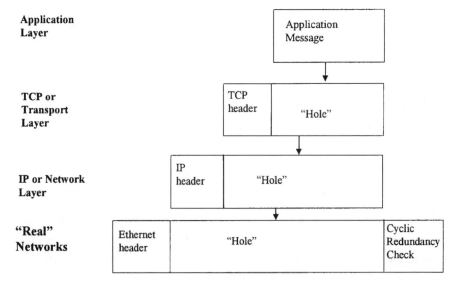

Figure 1.1   Sample protocol stack—TCP/IP.

with a (typically for TCP/IP) monolithic application layer—a single specification completing the final "hole".

The precise nature of the "service" provided by a lower layer—lossy, secure, reliable—and of any parameters controlling that service, need to be known before the next layer up can make appropriate use of that service.

We usually refer to each of these individual specification layers as "a protocol", and hence we can enhance our definition.

Note that in Figure 1.1, the "hole" provided by the IP carrier can contain either a TCP message or a UDP message—two very different protocols with different properties (and themselves providing a further carrier service). Thus one of the advantages of "layering" is in reusability of the carrier service to support a wide range of higher level protocols, many perhaps that were never thought of when the lower-layer protocols were developed.

When multiple different protocols can occupy a hole in the layer below (or provide carrier services for the layer above), this is frequently illustrated by the layering diagram shown in Figure 1.2.

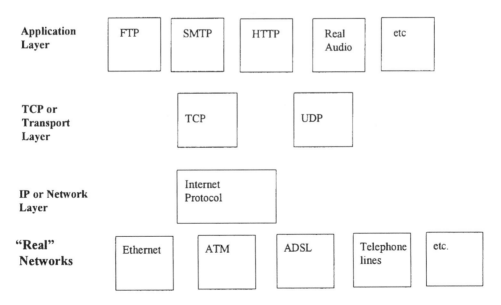

Figure 1.2   Layered protocols—TCP/IP.

1.2 Protocol Specification: Some Basic Concepts

Protocols can be (and historically have been) specified in many ways. One fundamental distinction is between *character-based specification* vs. *binary-based specification*.

Character-based specification   The "protocol" is defined as a series of lines of ASCII encoded text.

Binary-based specification   The "protocol" is defined as a string of octets or of bits.

For binary-based specification, approaches vary from various picture-based methods to use of a separately defined notation with associated application-independent encoding rules.

The latter is called the "**abstract syntax**" approach. This is the approach taken with ASN.1. It has the advantage that it enables designers to produce specifications without undue concern with the encoding issues, and also permits application-independent tools to be provided to support the easy implementation of protocols specified in this way. Moreover, because application-specific implementation code is independent of encoding code, it makes it easy to migrate to improved encodings as they are developed.

1.2.1 Layering and Protocol "Holes"

The layering concept is perhaps most commonly associated with the International Standards Organization (ISO) and International Telecommunications Union (ITU) "architecture" or "7-layer model" for Open Systems Interconnection; (OSI) shown in Figure 1.3.

While many of the protocols developed within this framework are not greatly used today, it remains an interesting academic study for approaches to protocol specification. In the original OSI concept in the late 1970s, there would be just 6 layers providing (progressively richer) carrier services, with a final "application layer" where each specification supported a single end-application, with no "holes".

However, over the next decade it became apparent that even in the "application layer" people wanted to leave "holes" in their specification for later extensions, or to provide a means of tailoring their protocol to specific needs. For example, one of the more recent and important protocols—Secure Electronic Transactions (SET)—contains a wealth of fully defined message semantics, but also provides for

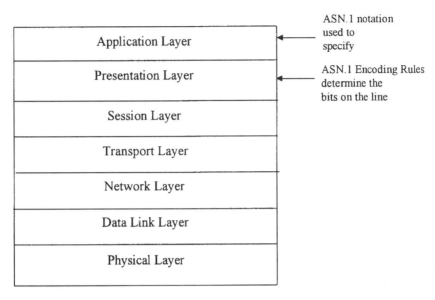

Figure 1.3   OSI layers and ASN.1.

a number of "holes" that can transfer "merchant details" not specified in the SET specification itself. So we have basic messages for purchase requests and responses, inquiry requests and responses, authorization requests and responses, and so on, but within those messages there are "holes" for "message extensions"—additional information specific to a particular merchant.

It is thus important that any mechanism or notation for specifying a protocol should be able to cater well for the inclusion of "holes". This has been

> **Hole**
>
> Part of a specification left undefined to carry material defined by others.

one of the more important developments in ASN.1 in the last decade, and will be a subject of much further discussion in this book.

"Catering well" for the inclusion of "holes" implies that the notation must have defined mechanisms (preferably uniformly applied to all specifications written using that notation) to identify the contents of a hole at communications time. (In lower layers, this is sometimes referred to as the "protocol id" problem.) Equally important, however, are notational means to identify clearly that a specification **is** incomplete (contains a hole), together with well-defined mechanisms to relate the (perhaps later in time) specification of the contents of holes to the location of the holes themselves.

1.2.2 Early Developments of Layering

The very earliest protocols operated over a single link (called, surprisingly, "LINK" protocols!) were specified in a single monolithic specification in which different physical signals (usually voltage or current) were used to signal specific events related to the application. (An example is the "off-hook" signal in early telephony systems.) If you wanted to run a different application, you redefined and rebuilt your electronics!

This illustrates the major advantage of "layering"—it enables reusability of carrier mechanisms to support a range of different higher-layer protocols or applications, as illustrated in Figure 1.2.

Nobody today would dream of providing a single monolithic specification similar to the old "LINK" protocols; perhaps the single most important step in computer communication technology was to agree that current, voltage, sound, and light signaling systems would do nothing more than transfer a two-item alphabet—a zero or a one—and that applications would build on that. Another important step was to provide another "layer" of protocol to turn this continuous flow of bits into delimited or "framed" messages with error detection, enabling higher layer protocols to talk about "sending a message" (which may get lost, may get through, but the unit of discussion is the message).

But this is far too low a level of discussion for a book on ASN.1! Between these electrical levels and the normal carriers that ASN.1 operates with we have layers of protocol concerned with both addressing and routing through the Internet or a telecoms network and with recovery from lost messages.

At the ASN.1 level, we assume that an application on one machine can "talk" to an application on another machine by reliably sending octet strings between themselves. (Note that all ASN.1-defined messages **are** an integral multiple of 8-bits—an octet string, not a general bit string.) This is illustrated in Figure 1.4.

Nonetheless, many ASN.1-defined applications are still specified by first specifying a basic "carrier" service, with additional specifications (perhaps provided differently by different groups) to fill in the holes. This is illustrated in Figure 1.5. As we will see later, there are many mechanisms in ASN.1 to support the use of "holes" or of "layering".

People have sometimes described the OSI 7-layer model as "layering gone mad". Layering **can** be an important tool in promoting reusability of specifications (and code), and in enabling parts of the total specification (a low or a high layer), to be later improved, extended (or just mended!) without affecting the other parts of the

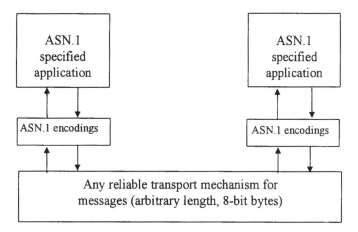

Figure 1.4   Application communication with ASN.1.

total specification. This desirable feature will, of course, only be achieved if the means for linking the different parts of the specification together to form the complete whole are sufficiently rich.

1.2.3 The Disadvantages of Layering: Keep It Simple!

Layering clearly carries important advantages in reusability, but it also carries the major disadvantage that in order to implement completely some given application, many different documents may have to be consulted, and the "glue" for linking these together may not always be precise enough to ensure that implementations by different vendors interwork.

It is important, therefore, in designing protocols that the desire for generality and long-life be tempered by an equal desire to keep the total specification simple. This is again a theme that we will return to later—ASN.1 makes it possible to write very simple and clear specifications very easily and quickly. But it also contains powerful features to support layering and "extensibility" (see following text). The decision to use or not to use such features must be one for the designer. There are circumstances where their use is essential for a good long-lasting specification. There are other cases where the added complexity (and sometimes implementation size) does not justify the use of advanced features.

1.2.4 Extensibility

A remark was made earlier that layering enables "later improvement" of one of the layers without affecting the specification of layers above and below. This concept

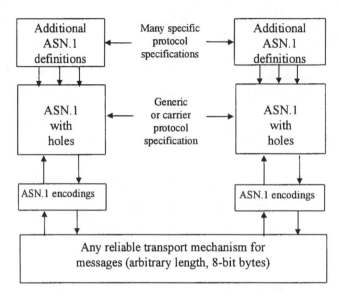

Figure 1.5   Generic and specific protocols with ASN.1.

of "later improvement" is a key phrase, and has importance beyond any discussion of layering. One of the important aspects of protocol specification recognized in the 1980s is that a protocol specification is rarely (probably never!) completed on date xyz, implemented, deployed, and left unchanged.

> **Extensibility Provision**
>
> Part of a version 1 specification designed to make it easy for future version 2 (extended) systems to interwork with deployed version 1 systems.

There is **always** a "version 2". And implementations of version 2 need to have a ready means of interworking with the already-deployed implementations of "version 1", preferably without having to include in version 2 systems a complete implementation of both version 1 and version 2 (sometimes called "dual-stacks"). Mechanisms enabling version 1 and version 2 exchanges are sometimes called a "migration" or "interworking strategy" between the new and the earlier versions. In the transition from IPv4 to IPv6 (the "IP" part of "TCP/IP"), it has perhaps taken as much work to solve migration problems as it took to design IPv6 itself! (An exaggeration of course, but the point is an important one—interworking with deployed version 1 systems matters.)

It turns out that provided you make plans for version 2 when you write your version 1 specification, you can make the task of "migration" or of defining an "interworking strategy" much easier.

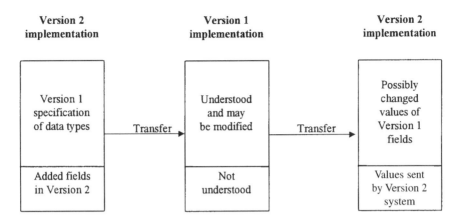

Figure 1.6   Version 1 and Version 2 interworking.

We can define **extensibility provision** as

- elements of a version 1 specification that allow the encapsulation of unknown material at certain points in the version 1 messages, and

- specification of the actions to be taken by the version 1 system if such material is present in a message.

Provision for extensibility in ASN.1 is an important aspect, which will be discussed further later in this book, and is illustrated in Figure 1.6.

Extensibility was present in early work in ITU-T and ISO by use of a very formalized means of transferring parameters in messages, a concept called "TLV"—Type, Length, Value, in which all pieces of information in a message are encoded with a type field identifying the nature of that piece of information, a length field delimiting the value, and then the value itself, an encoding that determines the information being sent. This is illustrated in Figure 1.7 for parameters and for groups of parameters. The approach is generalized in the ASN.1 Basic Encoding Rules (BER) to cover groups of groups, and so on, to any depth.

Note that the encoding used for the value only needs to unambiguously identify application information within the context of the parameter identified by the type field. This concept of distinct octet strings that identify information within the context of some explicit "class" or "type" identifier is an important one that will be returned to later.

By requiring in the version 1 specification that parameters that are "unrecognized"—added in version 2—should be silently ignored, the designers of version 2 have a

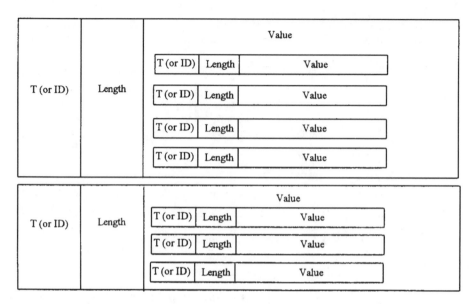

Figure 1.7 The "TLV" approach for parameters and groups.

predictable basis for interworking with deployed version 1 systems. Of course, any other well-specified behavior could be used, but "silently ignore" was a common specification. ASN.1 provides a notation for defining the form of messages, together with "encoding rules" that specify the actual bits on the line for any message that can be defined using the notation. The "TLV" described above was incorporated into the earliest ASN.1 encoding rules (the **Basic Encoding Rules**; or **BER**) and provides very good support for extensibility due to the presence in every element of the "T" and the "L", enabling "foreign" (version 2) material to be easily identified and skipped (or relayed). It does, however, suffer from encoding identification and length fields that are often unnecessary apart from their use in promoting extensibility. For a long time it was thought that this verbosity was an essential feature of extensibility, and it was a major achievement in encoding rule design when the ASN.1 **Packed Encoding Rules (PER)** provided good support for extensibility with little additional overhead on the line.

1.2.5 Abstract and Transfer Syntax

The terms abstract and transfer syntax were primarily developed within the OSI work, and are variously used in other related computer disciplines. The use of these terms in ASN.1 (and in this book) is almost identical to their use in OSI, but does not of course make ASN.1 in any way dependent on OSI.

The following steps are necessary when specifying the messages forming a protocol (see Figure 1.8):

- The determination of the information that needs to be transferred in each message; this is a "business-level" decision. We refer here to this as the **semantics** associated with the message.

- The design of some form of data-structure (at about the level of generality of a high-level programming language, and using a defined notation) capable of carrying the required semantics. The set of values of this data-structure are called the **abstract syntax** of the messages or application. We call the notation we use to define this data structure or set of values the **abstract syntax notation** for our messages; ASN.1 is just one of many possible abstract syntax notations, but is probably the one most commonly used.

- The crafting of a set of rules for encoding messages such that, given any message defined using the abstract syntax notation, the actual bits on the line to carry the semantics of that message are determined by an algorithm specified once and once only (independent of the application). We call such rules **encoding rules**, and we say that the result of applying them to the set of (abstract syntax) messages for a given application defines a **transfer syntax** for that application. A transfer syntax is the set of bit-patterns to be used to represent the abstract values in the abstract syntax, with each bit-pattern representing just one abstract value. (In ASN.1, the bit-patterns in a transfer syntax are always a multiple of 8 bits, for easy carriage in a wide range of carrier protocols.)

We saw that early LINK protocols did not clearly separate electrical signaling from application semantics, and similarly today, some protocol specifications do not clearly separate the specification of an abstract syntax from the specification of the bits on the line (the transfer syntax). It is still common to specify directly the bit-patterns to be used (the transfer syntax), and the semantics associated with each bit-pattern. However, as will become clear later, failure to clearly separate abstract from transfer syntax has important implications for reusability and for the use of common tools. With ASN.1 the separation is complete.

1.2.6 Command Line or Statement-Based Approaches

Another important approach to protocol design (not the approach taken in ASN.1) is to focus not on a general-purpose data-structure to hold the information to be

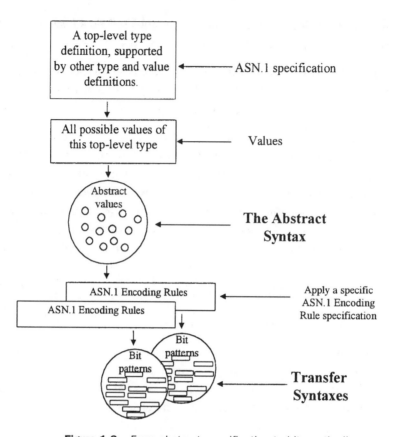

Figure 1.8   From abstract specification to bits-on-the-line.

transferred, but rather to design a series of lines of text each of which can be thought of as a command or a statement, with textual parameters (frequently comma separated) within each command or statement. This approach predated the use of ASN.1, but is still frequently employed today, more commonly in Internet-defined protocols (for example, the Internet Hyper-Text Transfer Protocol—HTTP—that supports the World Wide Web) than in ITU-T/ISO-defined protocols. A further discussion of this approach is given in 1.5.4.

1.2.7 Use of an Interface Definition Language

The use of an Interface Definition Language (IDL) is very similar to the abstract syntax approach of ASN.1. Here, however, the model is of objects interacting over a network through defined interfaces that enable the functions or methods of an object to be invoked, and its results to be returned. The model is supported by an

Interface Definition Language that enables the data-structures that are passed across each interface to be specified at a high-level of abstraction.

Probably the most important IDL today is the Common Object Request Broker Architecture (CORBA) IDL. In CORBA, the IDL is supported by a wealth of specifications and tools including encoding rules for the IDL, and means of transfer of messages to access interfaces across networks.

A detailed comparison of ASN.1 and CORBA goes beyond this text, and remarks made here should be taken as this author's perception in mid 1999. In essence, CORBA is a complete architecture and message passing specification in which the IDL and corresponding encodings form only a relatively small (but important) part. The CORBA IDL is simpler and less powerful than the ASN.1 notation, and as a result encodings are generally much more verbose than the Packed Encoding Rule (PER) encodings of ASN.1. ASN.1 is generally used in protocol specifications where very general and flexible exchange of messages is needed between communicating partners, whereas CORBA encourages a much more stylized "invocation and response" approach, and generally needs a much more substantial supporting infrastructure.

1.3 More on Abstract and Transfer Syntaxes

1.3.1 Abstract Values and Types

Most programming languages involve the concept of types or classes (and notation to define a more complex type by reference to built-in types and "construction mechanisms"), with the concept of a value of a type or class (and notation to specify values). ASN.1 is no different.

So, for example, in C we can define a new type "My-type" as:

```
typedef struct My-type {
        short        first-item;
        boolean      second-item} My-type;
```

The equivalent definition in ASN.1 appears below.

In ASN.1 we also have the concept of values of basic types or of more complex structures. These are often called **abstract values** (see Figure 1.8 again), to emphasize that we are considering them without any concern for how they might be represented in a computer or on a communications line. For convenience, these abstract values are grouped together into types. For example, we have the ASN.1 type notation

```
INTEGER
```

that references the integer type, with abstract values from (more or less) minus infinity to plus infinity. We also have the ASN.1 type notation

```
BOOLEAN
```

that references the boolean type with just two abstract values "TRUE" and "FALSE."

We can define a type of our own:

```
My-type ::= SEQUENCE
              {first-item   INTEGER,
               second-item  BOOLEAN}
```

each of whose abstract values is a pair of values, one "integer" and one "boolean". The important point, however, is that for many purposes, we do not care about (or discuss) any internal structure of the values in "My-type". Just like "integer" and "boolean", it is simply a convenient means of referencing a set of abstract values.

1.3.2 Encoding Abstract Values

So (to summarize the above discussion) for any type that can be defined using ASN.1, we say that it contains (represents) a set of abstract values. (See Figure 1.8 again.)

But now for the important part:

> **When any (correct!) set of encoding rules is applied to the abstract values in any given ASN.1 type, they will produce bit-patterns (actually octet-strings) for each value such that any given octet string corresponds to precisely one abstract value.**

Note that the reverse is not necessarily true—there may be more than one octet string for a given abstract value. This is another way of saying that there may be **options** in the encoding rules. (ASN.1 requires all conforming decoders to handle any encodings that a conforming encoder is allowed to use.)

If we restrict encoder options so that for any given abstract value in the type there is precisely one encoding, we say that the encoding rules are **canonical**. Further discussion of canonical encoding rules appears in Section III.

Now let us consider a designer who wants to specify the messages of a protocol using ASN.1. It would be possible to define a set of ASN.1 types (one for each different sort of message), and to say that the set of abstract values to be transmitted in protocol exchanges (and hence needing encoding) is the set of all the abstract values of all those ASN.1 types. The observant reader (some people will not like me saying that!)

> **Abstract Syntax**
>
> The set of abstract values of the top-level type for the application.

will have spotted that the preceding requirement on a correct set of encoding rules is not sufficient for unambiguous communication of the abstract values, because two abstract values in separate but similar ASN.1 types could have the same octet-string representation. (Both types might be a sequence of two integers, but they could carry very different semantics.)

It is therefore an important requirement in designing protocols using ASN.1 to specify the total set of abstract values that will be used in an application as the set of abstract values **of a single ASN.1 type**. This set of abstract values is often referred to simply as **the abstract syntax of the application**, and the corresponding set of octet strings after applying some set of encoding rules is referred to as a possible **transfer syntax for that application**. Thus the application of the ASN.1 Basic Encoding Rules (as in Figure 1.8) to an ASN.1 type definition produces a transfer syntax (for the abstract syntax) which is a set of bit patterns that can be used to represent these abstract values unambiguously during transfer.

> **Transfer Syntax**
>
> A set of unambiguous octet strings used to represent a value from an abstract syntax during transfer.

Note that in some other areas, where the emphasis is on storage of data rather than its transfer over a network, the concept of abstract syntax is still used to represent the set of abstract values, but the term **concrete syntax** is sometimes employed for a particular bit-pattern representation of the material on a disk. Thus some authors will talk about "concrete transfer syntax" rather than just "transfer syntax", but this term is not used in this book.

We will see later how, if we have distinct ASN.1 types for different sorts of messages, we can easily combine them into a single ASN.1 type to use to define our abstract syntax (and hence our transfer syntax). There is specific notation in the post-1994 version of ASN.1 to identify this "top-level" type clearly. All other ASN.1 type definitions in the specification are there solely to give support to this top-level type, and if they are not referenced by it (directly or indirectly), their definition is superfluous and a distracting irrelevance! Most people **don't** retain superfluous type definitions in published specifications, but sometimes for historical reasons (or through sloppy editing or both!) you may encounter such material.

In summary then—ASN.1 encoding rules provide unambiguous octet strings to represent the abstract values in any ASN.1 type; the set of abstract values in the top-level type for an application is called the abstract syntax for that application; and the corresponding octet-strings representing those abstract values unambiguously (by the use of any given set of encoding rules) is called a transfer syntax for that application.

Note that where there are several different encoding rule specifications available (as there are for ASN.1) there can in general be several different transfer syntaxes (with different verbosity and extensibility—etc.—properties) available for a particular application, as shown in Figure 1.8.

In the OSI world, it was considered appropriate to allow run-time negotiation of which transfer syntax to use. Today, we would more usually expect the application designer to make a selection based on the general nature and requirements of the application.

1.4 Evaluative Discussion

1.4.1 There Are Many Ways of Skinning a Cat: Does It Matter?

While the clear separation of abstract syntax specification (with associated semantics) from specification of a transfer syntax is clearly "clean" in a purist sort of way, does it matter? Is there value in having multiple transfer syntaxes for a given application? The ASN.1 approach to protocol design provides a common notation for defining the abstract syntax of any number of different applications, with common specification text and common implementation code for deriving the transfer syntax from this. Does this really provide advantages over the character line approach discussed earlier? Both approaches have certainly been employed with success. Different experts hold different views on this subject, and as with so much of protocol design, the approach you prefer is more likely to depend on the culture you are working within than on any rational arguments. Indeed, there are undoubted advantages and disadvantages to both approaches, so that a decision becomes more one based on which criteria you consider the most important, rather than on any absolute judgment. So here (as in a number of parts of this book) Figure 999: *Readers take warning* (modified—"Smoking"

> **Government Health Warning**
>
> This discussion can damage your health!
>
> **Figure 999:** Readers take warning.

replaced by "This discussion"—from text that appears on all UK cigarette packets!) applies. (I will refer back to Figure 999 whenever a remark appears in this book that may be somewhat contentious.)

1.4.2 Early Work with Multiple Transfer Syntaxes

Even before the concepts of abstract and transfer syntax were spelled out and the terms defined, protocol specifiers recognized the concepts and supplied multiple transfer syntaxes in their specifications.

Thus in the Computer Graphics Metafile (CGM) standard, the body of the standard defines the functionality represented by a CGM file (the abstract syntax), with three additional sections defining a "binary encoding", a "character encoding", and a "clear-text encoding". The "binary encoding" was the least verbose, was hard for a human to read (or debug), was not easy to produce with a simple program, and required a storage or transfer medium that was 8-bit transparent. The "character encoding" used two-character mnemonics for "commands" and parameters, and was in principle capable of being produced by a text editor. It was more human readable, but importantly mapped to octets via printing ASCII characters and hence was more robust in the storage and transfer media it could use (but was more verbose). The "clear-text" encoding was also ASCII-based, but was designed to be very human-readable, and very suitable for production by a human being using a suitable text editor, or for viewing by a human being for debugging purposes. It could be employed before any graphical interface tools for CGM became available, but was irrelevant thereafter.

These alternative encodings are appropriate in different circumstances, with the compactness of the "binary encoding" giving it the market edge as the technology matured and tools were developed.

1.4.3 Benefits

Some of the benefits that arise when a notation for abstract syntax definition is employed are identified here, with counterarguments where appropriate.

1.4.3.1 Efficient Use of Local Representations

Suppose you have an application using large quantities of material, which is stored on machine-type-A in a machine-specific format—say with the most significant octet of each 16-bit integer at the lower address byte. On machine-type-B, however, because of differing hardware, the same abstract values are represented and stored with the most significant octet of each 16-bit integer at the higher address byte. (There are usually further differences in the machine-A/machine-B representations, but this so-called "big-endian/little-endian" representation of integers is often the most severe problem.)

When transferring between machine-type-A and machine-type-B, it is clearly necessary for one or both parties (and if we are to be even-handed it should be both!) to spend CPU cycles converting into and out of some agreed machine-independent transfer syntax. But if we are transferring between two separate machines both of machine-type-A, it clearly makes more sense to use a transfer syntax closely related to the storage format on those machines.

This issue is generally more important for applications involving the transfer of large quantities of highly structured information, rather than for small headers negotiating parameters for later bulk transfer. An example where it would be relevant is the Office Document Architecture (ODA) specification. This is an ISO Standard and ITU-T Recommendation for a large structure capable of representing a complete service manual for (for example) a Boeing aircraft, so the application data can be extremely large.

1.4.3.2 Improved Representations over Time

It is often the case that the early encodings produced for a protocol are inefficient, partly because of the desire to be "protective", or to have encodings that are easy to debug, in the early stages of deployment of the application, partly from simple time pressures. It can also be because insufficient effort is put into the "boring" task of determining a "good" set of "bits-on-the-line" for this application.

Once again, if the bulk of the protocol is small compared with some "bulk-data" that it is transferring, as is the case—for most messages—with the Internet's Hyper-Text Transfer Protocol (HTTP) or File Transfer Protocol (FTP), then efficiency of the main protocol itself becomes relatively unimportant.

1.4.3.3 Reuse of Encoding Schemes

If we have a clear separation of the concept of abstract syntax definition from transfer syntax definition, and have available a notation for abstract syntax definition (such as ASN.1) that is independent of any application, then specification and implementation benefits immediately accrue. The task of generating "good" encoding rules for that notation can be done once, and these rules can be referenced by any application that uses that notation to define its abstract syntax. This not only saves much effort if a new application is to be specified, but it also provides a specification of a transfer syntax that has already been argued over, agreed, and gotten debugged!

This approach also ensures a common "look-and-feel" to the resulting transfer syntaxes over a number of different applications, with well-understood characteristics and familiarity for implementors. It also makes possible the emergence of tools, as discussed here.

The advantage extends to the implementation. Where there is a clear notation and well-defined encoding rules that are application-independent, it becomes possible to provide a set of generic encode/decode routines that can be used by any application. This significantly reduces implementation effort and residual bugs. Figure 1.9 illustrates this situation, where the greyed-out text describes effort that is not required due to the reuse of existing material.

1.4.3.4 Structuring of Code

If the specification of the encodings is kept clearly separate from the abstract syntax specification, and if the latter can be easily (by a tool or otherwise) mapped into

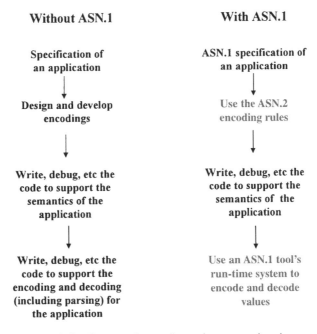

Figure 1.9   Re-use of encoding schemes and code.

data-structures in the implementation language, this encourages (but of course does not require) a modular approach to implementation design in which the code responsible for performing the encodings of the data is kept clearly separate from the code responsible for the semantics of the application.

1.4.3.5 Reuse of Code and Common Tools

This is perhaps the major advantage that can be obtained from the separation of abstract and transfer syntax specification, which is characteristic of ASN.1.

By the use of so-called ASN.1 "compilers" (dealt with more fully in Chapter 7 and which are application-independent), any abstract syntax definition in ASN.1 can be mapped into the (abstract) data-structure model of any given programming language, through the textual representation of data-types in that language. Implementors can then provide code to support the application using that (abstract) data-structure model with which they are familiar, and can call an application-independent piece of code to produce encodings of values of that data-structure for transmission (and similarly to decode on reception).

It is very important at this point for the reader to understand why "(abstract)" was included in the preceding text. All programming languages (from C to Java) present to their users a "memory-model" by which users define, access, and manipulate structures. Such models are platform independent, and generally provide some level of portability of any associated code. However, in mapping through compilers and run-time libraries into real computer memory (concrete representation of the abstract data-structures), specific features of different platforms intrude, and the precise representation in memory differs from machine-type to machine-type (see the "big-endian/little-endian" discussion in Chapter 18).

A tool-vendor can provide (possibly platform-specific, but certainly application-independent) run-time routines to encode/decode values of the abstract data-structures used by the implementor, and the implementor can continue to be blissfully unaware of the detailed nature of the underlying hardware, but can still efficiently produce machine-independent transfer syntaxes from values stored in variables of the implementation language.

As with any discussion of code structure, reusability, and tools, real benefits arise only when there are multiple applications to be implemented. It is sometimes worthwhile building a general-purpose tool to support a single implementation, but more often than not it is not. Tools are of benefit if they can be used for multiple implementations, either by the same implementors or by a range of implementors.

Tools for ASN.1 have only really emerged and matured because ASN.1 has become the specification language of choice for a wide range of applications.

1.4.3.6 Testing and Line Monitor Tools

The use of a common notation to define the syntax of messages makes it possible to automate many aspects of total protocol support that go beyond the simple implementation of a protocol. For example, it becomes possible to automatically generate test sequences, and to provide generic line-monitors or "sniffers".

1.4.3.7 Multiple Documents Require "Glue"

Separation of abstract and transfer syntax specification, while distinct from layering, has some common aspects. It promotes reusability of specifications and code, but it means that more than one document has to be obtained and read before it is possible to implement the application. It also means that unless the "glue" between the two parts of the total specification is well defined, there is scope for errors.

In the case of ASN.1, the "glue" is the ASN.1 notation itself, and there have been almost no instances of the "glue" coming "unstuck" for normal use. However, when we come to the question of canonical encoding rules—where there has to be a distinct bit-pattern, but only one, for each abstract value, the "glue" has to include a very clear definition of **exactly** what are the abstract values in any given ASN.1 type. During the first decade in which ASN.1 specifications were used this caused some problems and debate when it came to some theoretically possible (but never used) constructions! (But for all real-world applications, it never proved a problem.)

Another disadvantage arises if specification documents, particularly of the "glue"—the ASN.1 notation, are not freely (without cost) available to anyone who wants them. This has been theoretically a problem with ASN.1 over the last decade and a half, but I suspect that almost everyone who was unable to afford ITU-T/ISO prices for the ASN.1 documents has managed to get them one way or another!

1.4.3.8 The "Tools" Business

Expressing an abstract syntax in a high-level application-independent notation such as ASN.1 **enables**, but does not itself require, the use of tools, and it was some five years after the first specifications using ASN.1 were produced that "ASN.1 tools" began to show up on the market.

Today a new business area of "ASN.1 tools" for the notation and its encoding rules has been generated, with a commercial advantage for those who can justify the cost of acquiring a tool to help their implementation task.

1.5 Protocol Specification and Implementation: A Series of Case Studies

This section completes this chapter with discussion of a number of approaches to protocol specification and implementation, ending with a simple presentation of the approach that is adopted when ASN.1 is used.

1.5.1 Octet Sequences and Fields within Octets

Protocols for which all or much of the information can be expressed as fixed-length fields, which are all required to be present, have traditionally been specified by drawing diagrams such as the one shown in Figure 1.10—*Traditional approach*.

Figure 1.10 is part of the Internet Protocol Header (the Internet Protocol is the IP protocol of the TCP/IP stack illustrated in Figure 1.2). A similar picture is used in X.25 level 2 to define the header fields.

This approach was very popular in the early days, when implementations were performed using assembler language or languages such as BCPL or later C, allowing the implementor close contact with the raw byte array of a computer memory.

It was relatively easy for the implementor to read in octets from the communications line to a given place in memory, and then to hardwire into the implementation code access to the different fields (as shown in the diagram) as necessary (similarly for transmission). In this approach the terms "encoding" and "decoding" were not usually used.

The approach worked well in the mid 1970s, with the only spectacular failures arising (in one case) from a lack of clarity in the specification of which end of the octets (given in the diagram) was the most significant when interpreting the octet as a numerical value, and which end of the octets (given in the diagram) was to be transmitted first on a serial line. The need for a very clear specification of these bit-orders in binary-based protocol specification is well understood today, and in particular is handled within the ASN.1 specification, and can be ignored by a designer or implementor of an ASN.1-based specification.

1.5.2 The TLV Approach

Even the simplest protocols found the need for variable length "parameters" of messages, and for parameters that could be optionally omitted. This was briefly described earlier (see Figure 1.7) in 1.2.4.

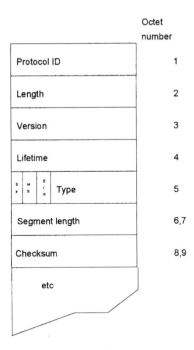

Figure 1.10   Traditional approach.

In this case, the specification would normally identify some fixed-length mandatory header fields, followed by a "parameter field" (often terminated by a length count). The "parameter field" would be a series of one or more parameters, each encoded with an identification field, a length field, and then the parameter value. The length field was always present, even for a fixed-length parameter, and the identification field even for a mandatory parameter. This ensured that the basic "TLV" structure was maintained, and enabled "extensibility" text to be written for version 1 systems to skip parameters they did not recognize.

An implementor would now write some fairly general-purpose code to scan the input stream and to place the parameters into a linked list of buffers in memory, with the application-specific code then processing the linked buffers. Note, however, that while this approach was quite common in several specifications, the precise details of length encoding (restricted to a count of 255 or unrestricted, for example), varied from specification to specification, so any code to handle these parameters tended to be application-specific and not easily reusable for other applications.

As protocols became more complicated, designers found the need to have complete groups of parameters that were either present or omitted, with all the parameters in a given group collected together in the parameter field. This was the approach taken in the Teletex (and later the OSI Session Layer) specifications, and gave rise to a second level of TLV with an outer identifier for a parameter group, a length field pointing to the end of that group, and then the TLV for each parameter in the group (revisit Figure 1.7).

This approach was also very appropriate for information that required a variable number of repetitions of a given parameter value.

At the implementation level, the code to "parse" an input octet string is now a little more complex, and the resulting data-structure to be passed to the application-specific code becomes a two-level tree-structure rather than a simple linked list, with level 1 nodes being parameter groups, and level 2 nodes parameters.

This approach has been presented here in a very "pure" form, but in fact it was rarely so pure! The Teletex and Session Protocols actually mixed together at the top level parameter group TLVs and parameter TLVs!

Those who already have some familiarity with the ASN.1 Basic Encoding Rules (BER) (to be described in much more detail later), will recognize that this TLV approach was generalized to form the basic (application-independent) encoding used by BER. For BER, the entire message is wrapped up with an identifier (that distinguishes it from any other message type in the same abstract syntax) and a length field pointing to the end of the message. The body is then, in general, a sequence of further TLV triplets, with the "V" part of each triplet being either further TLV triplets (etc., to any depth), or a "primitive" field such as an integer or a character string. This gives complete support for the power of normal programming language data-structure definitions to define groupings of types and repetitions of types to any depth, as well as providing support at all levels for both optional elements and extensibility.

1.5.3 The EDIFACT Graphical Syntax

This approach comes closest to ASN.1, with a clear (graphical) notation for abstract syntax specification, and a separate encoding rule specification. An example of the Electronic Data Interchange For Administration, Commerce and Transport (EDIFACT) graphical syntax is given in Figure 1.11, *EDIFACT graphical syntax*. As with ASN.1, the definition of the total message can be done in conveniently sized chunks using reference names for the chunks, then those chunks are combined to define the complete message. So in Figure 1.11 we have the message fragment (defined earlier or later) "UNH", which is mandatorily present once, similarly "AAA", then "BBB", which is conditional and is present zero to ten times, then "CCC" similarly, then up to 200 repetitions of a composite structure consisting of one "DDD" followed by up to ten "EEE", etc.

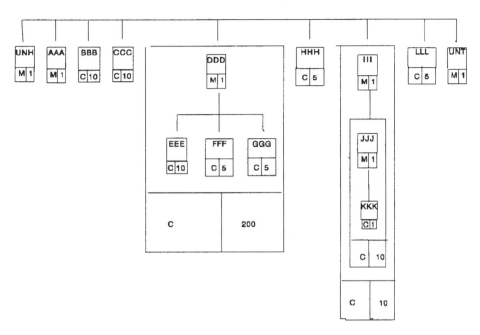

Figure 1.11   EDIFACT graphical syntax.

The actual encoding rules were, as with ASN.1, specified separately, but were based on character encoding of all fields. The graphical notation is less powerful than the ASN.1 notation, and the range of primitive types much smaller. The encoding rules also rely on the application designer to ensure that a type following a repeated sequence is distinct from the type in that repeated sequence, otherwise ambiguity occurs. This is a problem avoided in ASN.1, where any legal piece of ASN.1 produces unambiguous encodings.

At the implementation level, it would be possible to map the EDIFACT definition into a data-structure for the implementation language, but I am not aware of any tools that currently do this.

1.5.4 Use of BNF to Specify a Character-Based Syntax

This approach was briefly described earlier, and is common in many Internet protocols.

Where this character-based approach is employed, the precise set of lines of text permitted for each message has to be clearly specified. This specification is akin to the definition of an abstract syntax, but with more focus on the representation of the information on the line than would be present in an ASN.1 definition of an abstract syntax.

The notation used to define this syntax is usually some variation of a notation frequently used to define the syntax of programming languages (and indeed used to define the syntax of ASN.1 itself), something called Bacchus-Naur Form (BNF), named after its original inventors.

For example, in ASN.1, the BNF statements:

```
EnumeratedType ::= ENUMERATED { Enumeration }
Enumeration ::= NamedNumber |
                    Enumeration , NamedNumber
NamedNumber ::= identifier(SignedNumber)
SignedNumber ::= number | - number
```

are used to specify that one of the constructs of the language consists of the word "ENUMERATED", followed, in curly brackets, by a comma-separated list with each item being an identifier followed by a number (possibly preceded by a minus sign) in round brackets.

Unfortunately, there are many variations of BNF in use today, and most applications employing it find it necessary to define their own particular BNF notation. This makes it more difficult than it should be to use common tools to support BNF-based specifications.

BNF is a relatively low-level notational support tool. It is very powerful for defining arbitrary syntactic structures, but it does not in itself determine how variable length items are to be delimited or iteration counts determined. Even where the same BNF notation is employed, the "look-and-feel" of two protocols defined in this way can still be very different, as the means of terminating strings (quotation marks, reserved characters, reserved characters with escapes) or of variable length repetitions of items, have to be written into the specific application using the BNF notation for this definition.

Of course, as with any tool, if the design is a good one, a good result can follow. Many of the Internet protocol designs take this approach, and the best designers ensure that the way in which length and iteration terminations are achieved follows as closely as possible the approach taken in other related specifications, and is consistent for different fields and commands within that application.

Software tools to support BNF-based specifications are usually restricted to lexical analysis of an incoming string, and generally result in the application-specific code and encoding matters being more closely intertwined than would normally be the case if an ASN.1 tool was used.

Identification fields for lines in the messages tend to be relatively long names, and "enumerations" also tend to use long lists of names, so the resulting protocol can be quite verbose. In these approaches, length fields are normally replaced by reserved-character delimiters, or by end-of-line, often with some form of escape or extension mechanism to allow continuation over several lines (again these mechanisms are not always the same for different fields or for different applications).

In recent years there has been an attempt to use exactly the same BNF notation to define the syntax for several Internet protocols, but variations still ensue.

At implementation-time, a sending implementation will typically hardwire the encoding as a series of "PRINT" statements to print the character information directly onto the line or into a buffer. On reception, a general-purpose tool would normally be employed that could be presented with the BNF specification and that would parse the input string into the main lexical items. Such tools are available without charge for Unix systems, making it easy for implementations of protocols defined in this way to be set as tasks for Computer Science students (particularly as the protocol specifications tend also to be available without charge!).

In summary then, this approach can work well if the information to be transferred fits naturally into a two-level structure (lines of text, with an identifier and a list of comma-separated text parameters on each line), but can become complex when a greater depth of nesting of variable numbers of iterated items becomes necessary, and when escape characters are needed to permit commas as part of a parameter. The approach also tends to produce a much more verbose encoding than the binary approach of ASN.1 BER, and a very much more verbose encoding than the ASN.1 Packed Encoding Rules (PER).

1.5.5 Specification and Implementation Using ASN.1: Early 1980s

ASN.1 was first developed to support the definition of the set of X.400 Message Handling Systems CCITT (the International Telegraph and Telephone Consultative Committee, later to be renamed ITU-T) Recommendations, although the basic ideas were taken from the Xerox Courier Specification.

X.400 was developed by people with a strong application interest in getting the semantics of the information flows for electronic messaging right, but with relatively little interest in worrying about the bit-level encoding of messages. It was clear that they needed more or less the power of data-structure definition in a high-level programming language to support their specification work, and ASN.1 was designed to provide this.

Of course, notation closer to an actual programming language could have been used, but this would not have made the application easy to implement for those who might be forced (for platform reasons) to use a different language. Moreover, while using an existing language might solve the notational problem, there would still be work needed to define encodings, as in-memory representations of data structures from even the same language on the same platform differed (and still differ today) from compiler-writer to compiler-writer.

So ASN.1 was produced, and was heavily used by X.400 and by many other ITU-T and ISO specifications, where its power and the freedom it gave to designers to concentrate on what mattered—the application semantics—was much appreciated. Later, ASN.1 became used in many telecommunications applications, and applications in specific business sectors (and most recently for Secure Electronic Transactions—SET).

In the early 1980s, the only ASN.1 tools around were simple syntax checkers to help the designers get the specification right. The encoding rules were the TLV-based BER described earlier, and implementation architectures tended to be similar to those used for the character command-line approach described earlier. That is to say, some routines were produced to generate the "T" and the "L" part of an encoding (and the "V" part for the primitive types such as integer and boolean), and the structure of the message was hard-wired into the implementation by repeated calls to these subroutines to generate T and L parts for transmission down the line. On reception, quite simple (and application-independent) parsing code could be written to take the input stream of nested TLV encodings and to produce a tree-structure in memory with the leaves of the tree containing encodings of primitive items like integers, booleans, character strings, etc. The application code would then "tree-walk" this structure to obtain the input values.

Thus in these early days, the ASN.1 notation

- Provided a powerful, clear and easy to use way of specifying information content of messages.

- Freed application designers from concerns over encoding.

- Provided application-independent encoding making development of reusable code and sophisticated tools possible, although not instantly realized.

- Gave implementors a set of encoding rules to implement that were not as verbose as the BNF-based approach, and no harder (but no easier either) to implement.

1.5.6 Specification and Implementation Using ASN.1: 1990s

It is of course still possible to produce an implementation of an ASN.1-based protocol without tools. What was done in the 1980s can still be done today. However, there is great pressure today to reduce the "time-to-market" for implementations, and to ensure that residual bugs are at a minimum. Use of tools can be very important in this respect.

Today there are two main families of ASN.1 encoding rules, the original (unchanged) BER, and the more recent (standardized 1994) Packed Encoding Rules (PER). The PER encoding rules specification is more complex than that of BER, but produces very much more compact encodings. (For example, the encoding of a boolean value in PER uses only a single bit, but the TLV structure of BER produces at least 24 bits!)

There seems to be a "conventional wisdom" emerging that while encoding/decoding without a tool for BER is an acceptable thing to do if you have the time to spare, it is likely to result in implementation bugs if PER is being employed. The reader should again refer to Figure 999: *Readers take warning!*. This author would contend that there are implementation strategies that make PER encoding/decoding without tools a very viable proposition. Certainly much more care at the design stage is needed to identify correctly the field-widths to be used to encode various elements, and when padding bits are to be added (this comment will be better understood after reading Chapter 17 on PER), but once that is done,

> **ASN.1 Allows**
>
> designers to concentrate on application semantics,
>
> design without encoding-related bugs and with compact encodings available,
>
> implementors to write minimum code to support the application— fast development, and
>
> bug-free encode/decode with absence of interworking problems.

hardwiring a PER encode/decode into application code is still (this author would contend) possible.

Nonetheless, today, good tools, called "ASN.1 compilers", **do** exist, and for any commercial development they provide good value for money and are widely used. How would you implement an ASN.1 specification using a tool? This is covered more fully (with examples based on the "OSS ASN.1 Tools" package) in Chapter 7. However, the basic outline is as follows (see Figure 1.12).

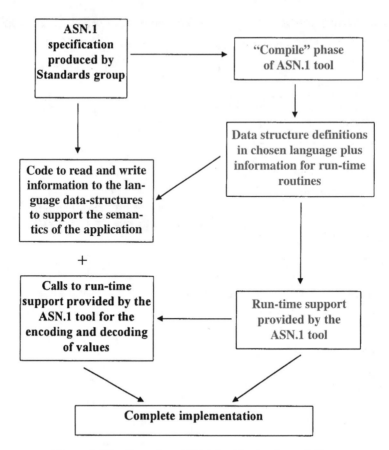

Figure 1.12 Use of an ASN.1 tool for implementation.

The ASN.1 produced by the application designer is fed into the "compile phase" of the tool. This maps the ASN.1 into a language data-structure definition in any one of a wide range of supported languages (and platforms), including C, C++, and Java. The application code is then written to read and write values from these data-structures, concentrating solely on the required semantics of the application.

When an encode is needed, a run-time routine is called that uses information provided by the compile phase about certain aspects of the ASN.1 definition, and which "understands" the way in which information is represented in memory on this platform. The run-time routine encodes the entire message, and returns the resulting octet string. A similar process is used for decoding. Any issues of big-endian or little-endian byte order (see 18.2.3), or most-significant bits of a byte, are completely hidden within the encode/decode routines, as are all other details of the encoding rule specifications.

Of course, without using a tool, a similar approach of mapping ASN.1 to a language data-structure and having separate code to encode and decode that data-structure is possible, but is likely to be more work (and more error prone) than the more "hardwired" approach outlined here. But with a tool to provide the mapping and the encode/decode routines, this is an extremely simple and fast means of producing an implementation of an ASN.1-based application.

In conclusion then, using a tool, ASN.1 today:

- Provides a powerful, clear and easy to use way for protocol designers to specify the information content of messages.

- Frees application designers from concerns over encoding, identification of optional elements, termination of lists, etc.

- Is supported by tools mapping the ASN.1 structures to those of the main computer languages in use today.

- Enables implementors to concentrate solely on the application semantics without any concern with encoding/decoding, using application-independent run-time encode/decode routines to produce bug-free encodings for all the ASN.1 encoding rules.

## CHAPTER 2

Introduction to ASN.1

(Or: Read Before You Write!)

Summary

The best way of learning any language or notation is to read some of it. This chapter presents a small example of ASN.1 type definitions and introduces the main concepts of

- built-in key-words,

- construction mechanisms,

- user-defined types with type-reference-names,

- identifiers or "field-names", and

- alternatives.

There is a reference to "tagging", which is discussed in more detail in Section II.

This chapter is intended for beginners in ASN.1, and can be skipped by those who have already been exposed to the notation.

2.1 Introduction

Look at Figure 2.1. The aim here is simply to make sense of the data-structure it is defining—the information that transmission of a value of this structure would convey.

Figure 2.1 is an "artificial" example designed to illustrate the features of ASN.1. It does not necessarily represent the best "business solution" to the problem it appears to be addressing, but the interested reader could try to invent a plausible rationale for some of its more curious features. For example, why have different "details" been used for "uk" and for "overseas" when the "overseas" case can hold any information the "uk" case can? Plausible answer, the "uk" case was in version 1, and the "overseas" was added later when the business expanded, and the designer wanted to keep the same bits-on-the-line for the "uk" case.

This example is built-on as this book proceeds, and the scenario for this "Wineco protocol" appears in Appendix 1 with the complete protocol in Appendix 2.

ASN.1 is not, of course, normally published in multiple fonts, but rather in just one font (Courier very often). We will return to that point later!

2.2 The Example

Refer to Figure 2.1 constantly! Note that the lines of four dots are **not** part of the ASN.1 syntax—they just mean that I have not completed that part of the specification.

```
Order-for-stock ::= SEQUENCE
    {order-no        INTEGER,
    name-address     BranchIdentification,
    details          SEQUENCE OF
                      SEQUENCE
                 {item      OBJECT IDENTIFIER,
                 cases      INTEGER},
    urgency          ENUMERATED
                 {tomorrow(0),
                 three-day(1),
                 week(2)}  DEFAULT week,
    authenticator Security-Type}

....

....

BranchIdentification ::= SET
        {unique-id  OBJECT IDENTIFIER,
         details    CHOICE
            {uk   [0] SEQUENCE
                  {name       VisibleString,
                   type       OutletType,
                   location   Address},
              overseas [1] SEQUENCE
                  {name     UTF8String,
                   type     OutletType,
                   location Address},
              warehouse [2] CHOICE
                  {northern  [0] NULL,
                   southern  [1] NULL} } }

....

....

Security-Type ::=   SET
        { ....
           ....
           .... }
```

Figure 2.1   An (artificial) example of ASN.1.

2.2.1 The Top-Level Type

There is nothing in the example (other than that it appears first) to tell the reader clearly that "Order-for-stock" is the top-level type, the type whose values form the abstract syntax, the type that when encoded provides the messages that are transmitted by this application. In a real ASN.1 specification, you would discover this from human-readable text associated with the specification, or in post-1994 ASN.1 by finding a statement:

```
my-abstract-syntax ABSTRACT-SYNTAX ::=
 {Order-for-stock IDENTIFIED BY
   {joint-iso-itu-t international-organization(23) set(42) set-vendors(9)
    wineco(43) abstract-syntax (1)}}
```

This simply says that we are naming the abstract syntax "my-abstract-syntax", that it consists of all the values of the type "Order-for-stock", and that if it were

> **Top-Level Type**
>
> All application specifications contain a (single) ASN.1 type that defines the messages for that application. It will often (but need not) appear first in the specification, and is a good place to start reading!

necessary to identify this abstract syntax in an instance of computer communication, the value given in the third line would be used. This is your first encounter with a piece of ASN.1 called "an OBJECT IDENTIFIER value" (which you will frequently find in ASN.1 specifications). The whole of that third line is actually just equivalent to writing a string of numbers:

```
{2 23 42 9 43 1}
```

But for now, we will ignore the OBJECT IDENTIFIER value and go back to the main example in Figure 2.1.

2.2.2 Bold Is What Matters!

The parts in bold are the heart of the ASN.1 language. They are reserved words (note that they are mainly all uppercase—case **does** matter in ASN.1), and reference built-in types or construction mechanisms. A later chapter goes through each and every built-in type and construction mechanism!

2.2.3 Names in Italics Are Used to Tie Things Together

The parts in italic are names that the writer has freely chosen to name the application types. They usually carry a good hint to a human reader about the sort of information that type is intended to carry, but for a computer, their sole purpose is to link together different parts of the specification.

So, for example, we have the type-reference-name *"BranchIdentification"* appearing in the third line of *"Order-for-stock"*. This is legal if and only if somewhere else in the specification (in this case further down, but it could have been earlier) there is precisely one "type assignment" giving a type for *"BranchIdentification"*. As far as a computer is concerned, the whole of the text following

```
BranchIdentification ::=
```

starting with "SET", and up to the closing curly bracket matching the one following "**SET**", can be used to textually replace the type-reference-name *"BranchIdentification"* wherever it appears. The resulting ASN.1 would be unchanged. Of course, if *"BranchIdentification"* is referenced in many different places, we would then have multiple copies of the text of the associated type, which would be very error prone, and would make the specification hard to read, so use of type-reference-names in such cases is a "good thing". But that is a matter of style and will be dealt with in a later chapter.

> **Most Names Present in a Specification Are Either**
> - names of built-in types or other built-in keywords (usually all uppercase), or
> - type-reference-names (mixed case, starting upper), or
> - names of elements or alternatives in more complex types (mixed case, starting lower), or
> - (less commonly seen) value-reference-names (mixed case, starting lower), or
> - names of enumerations (mixed case starting lower).

2.2.4 Names in Normal Font Are the Names of Fields/Elements/Items

The names in normal font are again chosen arbitrarily by the application designer, and again are irrelevant to a computer, but help a human reader to understand the specification. They also provide a "handle" for human-readable text to specify clearly the semantics associated with the corresponding part of the specification.

It may be helpful initially to think of the normal font words as the names of fields of a record structure, with the following bold or italic word giving the type of that field. The correct ASN.1 terminology is to say that the normal font words are either

- naming elements of a sequence,

- naming elements of a set,

- naming alternatives of a choice, or

- (in one case only) naming enumerations.

If an ASN.1 tool is used to map the ASN.1 specification to a data-structure definition in a programming language, these normal font names are mapped to identifiers in the chosen language, and the application code can set or read values of the corresponding parts of the data-structure using these names.

The alert reader—again!—will immediately wonder about the length of these names, and the characters permitted in them, and ask about any corresponding problems in doing a mapping to a given programming language. These are good questions, but will be ignored for now, except to say that all ASN.1 names can be arbitrarily long, and are distinct even if they differ only in their hundredth character, or even their thousandth (or later)! Quite long names are fairly common in ASN.1 specifications.

2.2.5 Back to the Example!

So, . . . what information does a value of the type "*Order-for-stock*" carry when it is sent down the line?

"*Order-for-stock*" is a structure with a sequence of fields or "elements" (an ordered list of types whose values will be sent down the line, in the given order). The first field or element is called "order-no", and holds an integer value. The second is called "name-address" and is itself a fairly complex type to be defined later, with a lot of internal structure. The next top-level field is called "details", and is also a fairly complex structured field, but this time the designer, purely as a matter of style, has chosen to write out the type "in-line" rather than using another type-reference-name.

This field is a "**SEQUENCE OF**", that is to say, an arbitrary number of repetitions of what follows the "**SEQUENCE OF**" (could be zero). There is ASN.1 notation to require a minimum or maximum number of repetitions, but that is not often encountered and is left until later.

What follows is another **"SEQUENCE"**, binding together an **"OBJECT IDENTI-FIER"** field called "item" and an **"INTEGER"** field called "cases". (Remember, we are ordering stocks—cases—of wine!) So the whole of "details" is arbitrarily many repetitions of a pair of elements—an object identifier value and an integer value.

You already met object identifier values when we discussed identification of the abstract syntax for this application. Object identifiers are world-wide unambiguous names. Anybody can (fairly!) easily get a bit of the object identifier name space, and these identifiers are frequently used in ASN.1-based applications to name a whole variety of objects. In the case of this example, we use names of this form to iden-tify an "item" (in this case, the "item" is probably some stock item—identification of a particular wine). We also see later that the application designer has chosen to use identifications of this same form in "BranchIdentification" to provide a "unique-id" for a branch.

Following the "details" top-level field, we have a field called "urgency", that is of the built-in type **"ENUMERATED"**. Use of this type name **requires** that it be fol-lowed by a list of names for the enumerations (the possible values of the type). In ASN.1, but not in most programming languages, you will usually find the name followed by a number in round brackets, as in this example. These numbers were required to be present up to 1994, but can now be automatically assigned if the application-designer so desires. They provide the actual values that are transmit-ted down the line to identify each enumeration, so if the "urgency" is "deliver it tomorrow", what is sent down the line in this field position is a zero. (The reason for requiring the numbers to be assigned by the designer in the early ASN.1 specifica-tions is discussed later, but basically has to do with trying to avoid inter-working problems if a version 1 spec-ification has an extra enumeration added in version 2—extensibility again!)

> Keyword DEFAULT: Identifies a default value for an element of a SEQUENCE or SET, to be assumed if a value for that ele-ment is not included.
>
> Keyword OPTIONAL: Identifies an element for which a value can be omitted. Omission carries dif-ferent semantics from any nor-mal value of the element.

Again, the "urgency" field has a feature not found in programming language data-structure definition. We see the keyword **"DEFAULT"**. What this means for the Basic Encoding Rules (BER—the original ASN.1 Encoding Rules) is that, as a sender's option, that field need not be transmitted if the intended value is the value following the word "**DEFAULT**"—in this case "week". This is an example in which there is more than one bit-pattern corresponding to a single abstract value—it is an encoder's option to choose whether or not to encode a "**DEFAULT**" value. For the later Packed Encoding Rules, the encoder is **required** to omit this simple field if the value is "week", and the decoder assumes that value. (If "urgency" had been a more complex data type the situation would be slightly different, but that is a matter for Section III.)

There is another ASN.1 keyword similar to "**DEFAULT**", namely, "**OPTIONAL**" (not included in the example in Figure 2.1). Again, the meaning is fairly obvious: the field can be omitted, but there is no presumption of any default value. The keyword might be associated, for example, with a field/element whose name was "additional-information".

Just to return briefly to the question of "What are the precise set of abstract values in the type?", the answer is that the presence of **DEFAULT** does not change the number of abstract values, it merely affects encoding options, but the presence of **OPTIONAL does** increase the number of abstract values—an abstract value with an optional field absent is distinct from any abstract value where it is present with some value, and can have different application semantics associated with it.

Finally, in "*Order-for-stock*", the last element is called "authenticator" and is of some (possibly quite complex) type called "*Security-Type*" defined by the application designer either before or after its use in "Order-for-stock". It is shown in Figure 2.1 as a "**SET**", with the contents not specified in the example (in a real specification, of course, the contents of the "**SET**" would be fully defined). "SET" is very similar to "**SEQUENCE**". In BER (the original ASN.1 encoding rules), it again signals a sender's (encoder's) option. The top-level elements (fields) of the **SET**, instead of being transmitted in the order given in the text (as they are for **SEQUENCE**) are transmitted in any order that is convenient for the sender/encoder. Today, it is recognized that encoder options are a "BAD THING" for both security reasons and for the extra cost they impose on receivers and particularly for exhaustive testing, and there are many who would argue that "**SET**" (and the corresponding "**SET OF**") should never be used by application designers, and should be withdrawn from ASN.1! But please refer to Figure 999 again!

Figure 2.1 shows "*Security-Type*" being defined later in the specification, but actually, this is precisely the sort of type that is more likely to be **imported** by an application designer from some more specialized ASN.1 specification that defines types (and their semantics) designed to support security features.

There are mechanisms in ASN.1 (discussed later) to enable a designer to reference definitions appearing in other specifications, and these mechanisms are often used. You will, however, also find that **some** application designers will **copy** definitions from other specifications, partly to make their own text complete without the need for an implementor to obtain (perhaps purchase!) additional texts, and partly to ensure control over and "ownership" of the definition. If you are using this book with a colleague or as part of some course, you can have an interesting debate over whether it is a good thing to do this or not!

2.2.6 The BranchIdentification Type

Now let us look briefly at the "*BranchIdentification*" type, which illustrates a few additional features of the ASN.1 notation. (For now, please completely ignore the numbers in square brackets in this definition. These are called "tags", and are discussed at the end of this chapter.)

This time it has been defined as a "SET", so in BER the elements are transmitted in any order, but we will take them in textual order.

As an aside (but an important aside), we have already mentioned in Chapter 1 that BER uses a TLV type of encoding for all elements. Clearly, if the sender is able to transmit the elements of a "**SET**" in any order, the value used for the "T" in the TLV of each element has to be different. (This would not be necessary for **SEQUENCE**, unless there are **OPTIONAL** or **DEFAULT** elements whose presence or absence had to be detected.) It is this requirement that gives rise to the "tag" concept to be introduced briefly below, and covered more fully later.

The first listed element is "unique-id", an "**OBJECT IDENTIFIER**" value, which has already been discussed. The only other element is "details." Notice that the name "details" was also used in "*Order-for-Stock*". This is quite normal and perfectly legal—the contexts are different.

It is usual for application designers to use distinct names for top-level elements in a **SEQUENCE** or **SET**, but it was not actually a requirement prior to 1994. It **is** now a requirement to have distinct names for the elements of both "**SEQUENCE**" and "**SET**" (and for the alternatives of a "**CHOICE**"—see later text). The requirement was added partly because it made good sense, but mainly because

> ### Names of Elements and Alternatives
> Should all be distinct within any given SEQUENCE, SET, or CHOICE (a requirement post-1994).

the ASN.1 notation for the values of a type could in some circumstances be ambiguous if this rule was not followed.

Looking at "details": This is a "**CHOICE**", meaning that what goes in this field-position is one of a number of possible alternatives. In this case there are three possibilities, the "uk", "overseas", and "warehouse" alternatives. (Again, the alert reader will recognize that with the TLV approach used in BER, the "T" assigned to each of these alternatives has to be distinct if the receiver/decoder is to determine correctly which one is being transmitted.)

The "uk" alternative is a "**SEQUENCE**" of three elements, a "name", a "type", and a "location." The latter two elements have type names in italics that are therefore presumably fairly complex, and will be defined earlier or later in the specification. They are not discussed further here. The "name" is a "**VisibleString**". This is one of a rather long list (about a dozen) of ASN.1 types that are "character strings"—strings of characters from some specified character repertoire. The names of these types are all mixed upper-lowercase, and are one of the few exceptions (the types carrying calendar date and time are the other main exception) to the rule that built-in types in ASN.1 (names that cannot be redefined by the user) are always entirely uppercase (such as "**INTEGER**", "**BOOLEAN**", etc.).

> ASN.1 has many character string types providing support ranging from pure ASCII text to text containing characters from any language in the world.

Values of the "**VisibleString**" type are strings of **printing** ASCII characters, plus "space". Thus they are fine for UK or USA names, but would not cope well with other European countries, and very badly with names from other parts of the world!

By contrast, the "name" element for the "overseas" alternative has a type "**UTF8String**". If you are into character encoding schemes, you will have heard of UNICODE (and/or ISO 10646!) and UTF8! If you are not, the area will be discussed more fully later. Suffice it to say that "**UTF8String**" can contain characters from any of the languages of the world, but with the interesting property that if the characters just happen to be ASCII characters, the encoding is precisely ASCII.

The UTF8 encoding scheme for characters is relatively new, and was only added to ASN.1 in 1998. It can legally only be used if the application designer references the 1998 (or later) ASN.1 specification.

However, we have already noted that some restrictions were added in 1994 (names of elements of a "**SEQUENCE**", "**SET**" etc. were required to be distinct, for example). Suppose you can not be bothered to upgrade your (300 pages long!) specification to conform to 1994 or later, but still want to use **UTF8String** in a new version? Well, legally, you **can not.** ("Oh yeah?", you say, "What government has passed that law?" "Which enforcement agency will punish me if I break it?" I remain silent!) But as an implementor/reader, and if you see it happening, you will know what it means. Of course, as part of an application design team, you would make absolutely sure it did not happen in **your** specifications, wouldn't you?

Back to Figure 2.1. The third alternative in the "details" is "warehouse", and this itself is another "**CHOICE**", with just two alternatives—"northern" and "southern," each with a type "**NULL**". What is "**NULL**"? "**NULL**" formally is a type with just a single value (which is itself perhaps confusingly called "**NULL**"). It is used where we need to have a type, but where there is no additional information to include. It is sometimes called a "placeholder." Note that in the "warehouse" case, we could just as well have used a **BOOLEAN** to decide "northern" vs. "southern", or an **ENUMERATED**. Just as a matter of style (and to illustrate use of "**NULL**"!) we chose to do it as a choice of **NULLs**.

2.2.7 Those Tags

Now we will discuss the numbers in square brackets—the "tags". In post-1994 ASN.1, it is **never** necessary to include these numbers. If they would have been required pre-1994, you can (post-1994) ask for them to be automatically generated (called AUTOMATIC TAGGING), and need never actually include them. However, in existing published specifications, you will frequently encounter tags, and should have some understanding of them.

In some of the very oldest ASN.1-based application specifications you

| **Tags** |
| Numbers in square brackets, not needed post-1994, are there to ensure unambiguous encodings. They do not affect the information that can be carried by the values of an ASN.1 type. |

will frequently find the keyword "IMPLICIT" following the tag, and occasionally today the opposite keyword "EXPLICIT". These qualify the meaning of the tag, and are fully described in Chapter 3.

Why do we have tags? Remember the basic structure of BER, for a "SEQUENCE", there is a TLV for each element of the sequence; these are placed end-to-end to form the "V" part of an outer-level TLV. By default the "T" part of the TLV for any basic ASN.1 type such as "INTEGER" or "BOOLEAN" has a value that is specified in the ASN.1 specification itself, and the "T" part of the outer-level TLV for a "SEQUENCE" again has a value that is specified in the ASN.1 specification.

This means that by default, the encoding of the "northern" "NULL" and of the "southern" "NULL" will be identical—the receiver/decoder would not know which was sent. The encoding has violated the necessary and obvious rule that for each alternative of a "CHOICE" the "T" used for each alternative should be different. **The purpose of the tag is to override the default "T" value with a value specified in the tag.** So with the example as written, the "northern" "T" contains zero, and the "southern" "T" contains one. Similarly, it is important to override the default tag on the outer-level "T" for at least one of the "uk" and "overseas" "SEQUENCE" encodings. (As a matter of style, we chose to override both.)

A later section fully explains the rules about when tags have to be inserted. (Pre-1994, Figure 2.1 would be illegal without at least some of the numbers in square brackets—the tags.) The rules are "the minimum necessary to avoid ambiguity," and once that is understood, the reader will be able to remember the detailed rules easily enough. However, there is (normally) no penalty in overriding a default tag, and as a matter of style and of a "don't think about it, just do it!" philosophy, it is quite common to see (as in Figure 2.1) tags sequentially assigned to each of the elements of every "CHOICE" construction, whether strictly necessary or not. Similarly (but not done in Figure 2.1), it is also quite common (pre-1994) to see tags applied with sequential tag numbers to all elements of "SEQUENCE" and of "SET" constructions.

A final introductory comment—earlier text has implied that tags are just plain old numbers. In fact, the tag name-space, the value encoded in the "T" part of a TLV, is slightly more complicated than that. You will sometimes find the keywords "APPLICATION" or "PRIVATE" or "UNIVERSAL" after the opening square bracket, for example:

```
Tagged-type ::= [APPLICATION 1] Order-For-Stock
```

These keywords define the "class" of the tag. In their absence, the "class" is so-called "context-specific", which is by far the most common class of tag that is applied. Full details of tagging appear in Chapter 11.

2.3 Getting Rid of the Different Fonts

Suppose you have a normal ASN.1-based application specification using a single font. How do you apply fonts as in Figure 2.1?

First, in principle, you need to know what are the reserved words in the language, including the names of the character string and the date/time types, and you make sure these become bold! In practice, you can make a good guess that any name that is all uppercase goes to bold, but this is not a requirement. The *"Address"* type-reference-name in Figure 1.4 could have been *"ADDRESS"*, and provided that change was made everywhere in the specification, the result is an identical and totally legal specification. But as a matter of style, all uppercase for type reference names is rarely used.

Any other name that begins with an initial uppercase letter you set to italics—it is a type-reference-name. Type-reference-names are **required** to begin with an upper-case letter. After that they can contain uppercase or lowercase interchangeably.

You will see in Figure 2.1 a mixture of two distinct styles. In one case a type-reference-name (*"Order-for-stock"*) made up of three words separates the words by a hyphen. In another case a type-reference-name (*"OutletType"*) uses another uppercase letter to separate the words, and does not use the hyphen. *"Security-Type"* uses both!

You normally don't see a mix of these three styles in a single specification, but all are perfectly legal. Hyphens (but not two in adjacent positions, to avoid ambiguity with comment—see later text) have been allowed in names right from the first approved ASN.1 specification, but were not allowed by drafts prior to that first approved specification, so early writers had no choice, and used the *"OutletType"* style. Of course, nobody ever reads the ASN.1 specification itself—they just copy what everybody else does! So that style is still the most common today. It is, how-ever, just that—a matter of style, and an unimportant one at that—all three forms are legal and it is a personal preference which you think looks neater or clearer.

And finally, the normal font, most names starting with a lowercase letter are names of elements or alternatives ("order-no", "urgency", etc.), and again such names are **required** to start with an initial lowercase letter, but can thereafter contain either uppercase or lowercase.

Names beginning with lowercase are also required for the names of **values**. A sim-ple example is the value "week" for the "urgency".

Application specifications can contain not only type assignment statements such as those appearing in Figure 2.1 (and which generally form the bulk of most application specifications), but can also contain statements assigning values to "value-reference-names". The general form of a value reference assignment is illustrated below:

```
my-default-cases INTEGER ::= 20
```

which is defining the value-reference-name "my-default-cases", of type "**INTEGER**" to reference the integer value "20". It could then be used in the "cases" element in Figure 2.1 as, for example:

```
cases INTEGER DEFAULT my-default-cases
```

2.4 Tying Up Some Loose Ends

2.4.1 Summary of Type and Value Assignments

First, let us summarize what we have seen so far. ASN.1 specifies a number of pieces of notation (type-notation) that define an ASN.1 type. Some are very simple, such as "BOOLEAN", others are more complex such as that used to define an enumerated type or a sequence type. **A type-reference-name is also a piece of type-notation that can be used wherever ASN.1 requires a piece of type-notation.**

> An application specification contains lots of type assignment statements and occasionally (but rarely) some value assignment statements.

Similarly, ASN.1 specifies a number of pieces of value-notation (any type you can write with ASN.1 has a defined value-notation for all of its values).

Again, some notations for values are very simple, such as "20" for integer values; others are more complex, such as the notation for object identifier values that you saw at the start of this chapter, or the notation for values of sequence types. **Again, wherever ASN.1 requires value-notation, a value-reference-name can be used** (provided it has been assigned a value somewhere).

The general form of a type assignment is:

```
type-reference-name   ::=   type-notation
```

and of a value assignment is:

```
value-reference-name type-notation ::= value-notation
```

where the value-notation has to be the "correct" value-notation for the type identified by the type-notation. This is an important concept. Anywhere in ASN.1 where you can use type-notation (for example to define the type of an element of a "SET" or "SEQUENCE", you can use **any** legal type-notation. However, where value-notation is allowed (for example, in value assignments or after DEFAULT), there is always a corresponding type-notation called the **governor** (which might be a type-reference-name) that restricts the syntax of the value-notation to that which is permitted for the type identified by the type-notation.

So far, you have seen value notation used in the "IDENTIFIED BY" at the start of the chapter, and following the word DEFAULT. There are other uses that will be described later, but it remains the case that value-notation is used much less often than type-notation.

2.4.2 The Form of Names

All names in ASN.1 are mixed upper/lowercase letters and digits and hyphens (but not two adjacent or one at the end, to avoid confusion with comment), starting with either an uppercase letter or with a lowercase letter, depending on what the name is being used for. (As you will have guessed by now, they cannot contain the space character!) In every case of naming in ASN.1, the case of the first letter is fixed. If an uppercase letter is legal, a lowercase letter will not be, and vice versa. Names can be arbitrarily long, and are different names if they differ in either content or case at any position in the name.

Note that because names can contain only letters and digits and hyphens, a name that is followed by any other character (such as an opening curly bracket or a comma), can have the following character adjacent to it with no space or new-line, or as a matter of purely personal style, one or more spaces or new-lines can be inserted.

> **Names and Layout**
>
> Names contain letters, digits, or hyphens. They are arbitrarily long. Case is significant. Layout is free format. Comment starts with a pair of adjacent hyphens and ends with a pair of adjacent hyphens or a new-line.

2.4.3 Layout and Comment

Layout is "free-format"—anywhere you can put a space you can put a new-line. Anywhere you have a new-line you can remove it and just leave a space. So a complete application specification can appear as a single line of text, and indeed that is basically the way a computer sees it.

As a matter of style, **everybody** puts a new line between each type or value assignment statement, and generally between each element of a set or sequence and the alternatives of a choice. The layout style shown in Figure 2.1 is that preferred by this author, as it makes the pairing of curly brackets very clear, but a perhaps slightly more common layout style is to include the opening curly bracket after "SEQUENCE" on the same line as the keyword "SEQUENCE", for example:

```
SEQUENCE  {
    items   OBJECT IDENTIFIER,
    cases   INTEGER   }
```

Still other authors (less common) will put the closing curly bracket on a line of its own and align it vertically with its matching opening bracket. All pure (and utterly unimportant!) stylistic matters.

On a slightly more serious vein, there was pre-1994 value notation for the "CHOICE" type in the "BranchIdentification" that would allow:

```
details   warehouse   northern   value-ref
```

as a piece of value notation (where "value-ref" is a value reference name for the "NULL" value). Remember that ASN.1 allows names to be used before they are assigned in a type or value assignment, and a poor dumb computer can be hit at the start of the specification with something looking like:

```
joe Fred ::= jack jill joseph Mary ::= etc etc
```

In this case, it cannot determine where the first assignment ends—after "jack" or after "jill" or after "joseph"—it depends on the actual type of "Fred"—defined later). This can give a computer a hard time! Some of the early tool vendors could not cope with this (even though it probably never actually occurred!), and asked for the "semicolon" character to be used as a statement separator in ASN.1. To this day, if you use these tools, you will need to put in semicolons between all your type assignments. (The "OSS ASN.1 Tools" package does **not** impose this requirement.) The requirement to insert semicolons in ASN.1 specifications was resisted, but to assist tool vendors a "colon" was introduced into the value notation for "CHOICE", so that post-1994 the above value notation would be written:

```
details : warehouse : northern : value-ref
```

(With or without the spaces, but with the colon.) And (for example):

```
joe Fred ::= jack : jill joseph Mary ::= etc etc
```

has the end of the first assignment after "jill", while:

```
joe Fred ::= jack : jill: joseph Mary ::= etc etc
```

has the end of the first assignment after "joseph". This is another small area where the 1994 specification imposed additional requirements not present before then.

Comment can be inserted wherever spaces and new-lines are allowed. Comment begins with a pair of hyphens (with **no** space between them), and ends **either** on the first new-line **or** with another pair of hyphens. (This is the only case where "new-line" is different from other forms of white space.)

This is a perfectly good and consistent rule, but is not quite the same as that used for a certain well-known programming language, so take care! If you want a block of comment spread over several lines, you need a pair of hyphens at the start of each line.

2.5 So What Else Do You Need to Know?

Really, you are now pretty well able to go away and read ASN.1 specifications! But as you have taken the trouble to obtain (perhaps you've even **paid for!**) this text, you will expect it to go on a bit further.

In the next few chapters we look at the outer-level structure of an ASN.1-based application specification, and go through the various built-in types and construction mechanisms (like "SEQUENCE"), and the associated value notations. That text is boring! You will need to read it quickly!

This will complete all you need to read. Most of the ASN.1 that was produced prior to 1994, with the exception of a few less commonly used "advanced" features like subtyping and mechanisms for "holes", which are left to Section II, used only what is covered in Section I. Section II also contains most of the discussion of the "new" features that were introduced in 1994.

Section I ends with a more detailed discussion of how to produce implementations using "ASN.1 compilers", and some further guidelines related to implementation.

## CHAPTER 3

Structuring an ASN.1 Specification

(Or: The Walls, Floors, Doorways and Elevators, with Some Environmental Considerations!)

Summary

ASN.1-based application specifications consist mainly of type definitions as illustrated in Chapter 2, but these are normally (and are formally **required to be**) grouped into collections called *modules*.

This chapter

- introduces the module structure,

- describes the form of module headers,

- shows how to identify modules, and

- describes how to export and import type definitions between modules.

The chapter also discusses

- some issues of publication format for a complete application specification, and

- the importance of making machine-readable copy of the ASN.1 parts available.

Part of the definition of a module is the establishment of

- a *tagging environment*, and

- an *extensibility environment*

for the type-notations appearing in that specification. The meaning and importance of these terms is discussed in this chapter, with final details in Section II.

3.1 An Example

The example we gave in Figure 2.1 had one top-level type ("Order-for-stock"), and a number of supporting types, most of which we left incomplete. We will still leave the supporting types incomplete (and, indeed, will use three lines of four dots for the body of all the types to avoid repetition), but will now otherwise turn the example in Figure 2.1 into a complete ASN.1 specification that follows the rules of the language, and that could be fed into an ASN.1 compiler tool.

The complete specification is shown in Figure 3.1.

```
Wineco-ordering-protocol
   {joint-iso-itu-t internationalRA(23) set(42) set-vendors(9)
   wineco(43) modules(2) ordering(1)}
DEFINITIONS
        AUTOMATIC TAGS ::=
BEGIN

        Order-for-stock ::=   SEQUENCE
                { ....
                  ....
                  ....}

        BranchIdentification ::= SET
                { ....
                  ....
                  ....}

        Security-Type ::= SET
                { ....
                  ....
                  ....}

        OutletType ::= SEQUENCE
                { ....
                  ....
                  ....}

        Address ::= SEQUENCE
                { ....
                  ....
                  ....}

END
```

Figure 3.1 A complete single-module ASN.1 specification.

This example forms what is called an *ASN.1 module* consisting of a six-line (in this—simple!—case) module header, a set of type (or value) assignment statements, and an "END" statement. This is the smallest legal piece of ASN.1 specification, and many early specifications were of this form—a single module. Today, it is more common for a complex protocol to be presented in a number of ASN.1 modules (usually within a single physical publication or set of Web pages). This is discussed further later.

Modules

All ASN.1 type and value assignments are required to appear within a `module`, starting with a module header and ending with "END".

It is very common in a real publication for the module header to appear at the start of a page, for there then to be up to 10 or more pages of type assignments (with the occasional value assignment perhaps), and then the END statement, which terminates the module. Normally there would be a page-break after the END statement in a printed specification, whether followed by another module or not.

However, Figure 3.1 is typical of early ASN.1 specifications, where the total protocol specification was probably only a few pages of ASN.1, and a single self-contained module was used for the entire specification.

Note that while the use of new-lines and indentation at the start of this example is what is commonly used, the normal ASN.1 rule that white-space and new-lines are interchangeable applies here too—the module header could be on a single line.

We will look in detail at the different elements of the module header later in this chapter, but first we discuss a little more about publication style.

3.2 Publication Style for ASN.1 Specifications

Over the years, different groups have taken different approaches to the presentation of their ASN.1 specifications in published documents. Problems and variations stem from conflicting desires:

NOTE

The use of three lines of four dots in Figures 2.1 and 3.1 is not legal ASN.1! It is used in this book out of sheer laziness! In a real specification there would be a complete list of named and fully specified (directly or by type-reference-names) elements. In Figure 3.1, it is assumed that no further type-reference-names are used in the body of these types—they use only the built-in types of the language such as INTEGER, BOOLEAN, VisibleString, etc.

a. A wish to introduce the various ASN.1 types that form the total specification gradually (often in a "bottom-up" fashion), within normal human-readable text that explains the semantics of the different types and fields.

> You may want to consider adding line-numbers to your ASN.1 to help references and cross-references . . . but these are not part of the language!

b. A wish to have in the specification a complete piece of ASN.1 that conforms to the ASN.1 syntax and is ready to feed into an ASN.1 tool, with the type definitions in either alphabetical order of type-reference-name, or in a "top-down" order.

c. The desire not to repeat text, in order to avoid unintended differences, and questions of which text takes precedence if differences remain in the final product.

There is no one perfect approach—application designers must make their own decisions in these areas, but the following two subsections discuss some common approaches.

3.2.1 Use of Line Numbers

One approach is to give line numbers sequentially to the entire ASN.1 specification, as partly shown in Figure 3.2 (again, lines of four dots are used to indicate pieces of the specification that have been left out).

It is important to note that if this specification is fed into an ASN.1 tool, the line numbers have to be removed—they are not part of the ASN.1 syntax, and the writer knows of no tool that provides a directive to ignore them.

If you have tools to assist in producing it (and they exist), this line-numbered approach also makes it possible to provide a cross-reference at the end of the specification that gives, for each type-reference-name, the line number of the type assignment where it is given a type, followed by all the line numbers where that reference is used. **For a large specification, this approach is VERY useful to readers.** If you don't do this, then you may wish to reorder your definitions into alphabetical order.

Once you decide to use line numbers, there are two main possibilities. You can

*   put the ASN.1 in only one place, as a complete specification (usually at the end), and use the line-numbers to reference the ASN.1 text from within the normal human-readable text that specifies the semantics, or

```
001 Wineco-ordering-protocol
002  { joint-iso-itu-t internationalRA(23) set(42) set-vendors(9)
003   wineco(43) modules(2) ordering(1)}
004 DEFINITIONS
005        AUTOMATIC TAGS ::=
006 BEGIN
007
008        Order-for-stock ::=  SEQUENCE
009              {order-no        INTEGER,
010               name-address  BranchIdentification,

....


....


159              digest    OCTET STRING}
160
161 END
```

Figure 3.2   Module with line numbers.

- break the line-numbered ASN.1 into a series of "figures" and embed them in the appropriate place in the human-readable text, again using the line-numbers for more specific references.

The latter approach only works well if the order in which you have the type definitions (in the total specification) is the same as the order in which you wish to introduce and discuss them in the main text.

3.2.2 Duplicating the ASN.1 Text

A number of specifications have chosen to duplicate the ASN.1 text (usually but not necessarily without using line numbers). In this case the types are introduced with fragments of ASN.1 embedded in the human-readable text, and the full module specification with the module header and the "END" are presented as either the last clause of the document, or in an Appendix.

> You may choose to repeat your ASN.1 text, fragmented in the body of your specification and complete in an annex—but be careful the texts are the same!

Note that where ASN.1 text is embedded in normal human-readable text, it is highly desirable for it to be given a distinctive font. This is particularly important where the individual names of ASN.1 types or sequence (or set) elements or choice alternatives are embedded in a sentence. Where a distinctive font is not possible, then use of italics or of quotation marks is common for such cases. (Quotation marks are generally used in this text.)

If ASN.1 text appears in more than one place, then it used to be common to say that the collected text in the Appendix "took precedence if there were differences". Today it is more common to say that "if differences are found in the two texts, this is a bug in the specification and should be reported as such".

3.2.3 Providing Machine-Readable Copy

An annex collecting together the entire ASN.1 is clearly better than having it totally fragmented within many pages of printed text, no matter how implementation is to be tackled.

Prior to the existence of ASN.1 tools, the ASN.1 specification was there to tell an implementor what to code up, and would rarely need to be fed into a computer, so printed text sufficed.

> If your implementors use tools, they will want machine-readable copy: consider how to provide this, and to tell them where it is!

With the coming of ASN.1 compilers, which enable a major part of the implementation to be automatically generated directly from a machine-readable version of the ASN.1 specification, some attention is needed to the provision of such material.

Even if the "published" specification is in electronic form, it may not be easy for a user to extract the formal ASN.1 definition because of the format used for publication, or because of the need to remove the line numbers discussed in earlier text, or to extract the material from "figures".

Wherever possible, the "published" specification should identify an authoritative source of machine-readable text for the complete specification. This should currently (1998) be ASCII encoded, with only spaces and new-lines as formatting characters, and using character names (see Chapter 9) for any non-ASCII characters in value notations. It is, however, likely that the so-called UTF8 encodings (again see Chapter 9), allowing direct representation of any character, will become increasingly acceptable, indeed, preferable.

It is unfortunate that many early ASN.1 specifications were published by ISO and ITU-T. These organizations had a history of making money from sales of hard-copy specifications and did not in the early days provide machine-readable material.

However, a number of Editors of the corresponding Standards and Recommendations did obtain permission to circulate (usually without charge) a machine-readable copy of the ASN.1 (usually as ASCII text), but the availability of such material was not always widely publicized.

It is unfortunate that many ASN.1 specifications have had to be rekeyed from printed copies for use in tools, with all the errors this can cause. The better tool vendors have built up over time a stock of machine-readable specifications (either obtained from Editors or by rekeying themselves) for the most common protocols, and will supply these to their customers on request. (The URL in Appendix 5 provides a link to a list of many ASN.1-based specifications, and in some cases to sources of machine-readable specifications where these are known to exist.)

3.3 Returning to the Module Header!

3.3.1 Syntactic Discussion

Figure 3.3 repeats the module header lines (with line numbers).

Let us take the items in turn. The first line contains the *module name*, and is any ASN.1 name beginning with a capital letter. It is intended to identify the module and its contents for human beings, and would normally be distinct from any other module name in the same application specification. This is not, however, a requirement, as ASN.1 has no actual concept of a complete application specification (only of a complete and legal module). We return later to the question of a "complete specification".

> **The Module Header Provides**
>
> · a module name;
>
> · a unique module identification;
>
> · definition of the tagging environment; and
>
> · definition of the extensibility environment.

The second/third line is called the *module identifier*, and is another case of an object identifier value. This name-form **is** required to be distinct from that of any other module—not just from those in the same application specification, but from any ASN.1 module ever-written or ever to-be-written, world-wide! (Including—though some might say Figure 999 on page 19 applies—any later version of this module.)

Strictly speaking, you do not need to include this second/third line. It was introduced into ASN.1 in about 1988, and was left optional partly for reasons of back-

```
001 Wineco-ordering-protocol
002  {joint-iso-itu-t internationalRA(23) set(42) set-vendors(9)
003    wineco(43) modules(2) ordering(1)}
004 DEFINITIONS
005        AUTOMATIC TAGS ::=
006 BEGIN
007
008        Order-for-stock ::=  SEQUENCE
009              {order-no       INTEGER,
010               name-address  BranchIdentification,

. . . .
```

Figure 3.3 The module header.

wards compatibility and partly to take account of those who had difficulty in obtaining (or were too lazy to try to obtain!) a bit of the object identifier name-space.

It is relatively easy today to get some object identifier name-space to enable you to give world-wide unambiguous names to any modules that you write, but we defer a discussion of how to go about this (and of the detailed form of an object identifier value) to Section II. Suffice it to say that the object identifier values used in this book are "legitimate", and are distinct from others (legally!) used to name any other ASN.1 module in the world. If name-space can be obtained for this relatively unimportant book. . . !

The fourth and the sixth lines are "boiler-plate". They say nothing, but have to be there! No alternative syntax is possible. (The same applies to the "END" statement at the end of the module.)

The fifth line is one of several possibilities, and determines the "environment" of the module that affects the detailed interpretation of the type-notation (but not of type-reference-names) textually appearing within the body of the module.

Designers please note—Not only is it illegal ASN.1 to write a specification without a module header and an "END" statement, it can also be very ambiguous because the "environment" of the type-notation has not been determined.

So, what aspects of the "environment" can be specified, and what syntax is possible in this fifth line?

There are two aspects to the "environment", called (in this book) "the tagging environment" and "the extensibility environment". The reader will note that these both contain terms that we have briefly mentioned before, but have never properly explained. Please do not be disappointed, but the explanation here is again going to be partial—for a full discussion of these concepts you will need to go to Section II.

The tagging environment (with the string used in line 4 to specify it given in parentheses) is one of the following:

- an environment of explicit tagging (EXPLICIT TAGS);

- an environment of implicit tagging (IMPLICIT TAGS); and

- an environment of automatic tagging (AUTOMATIC TAGS).

Omission of all of these **implies** an environment of **explicit** tagging. (This is for historical reasons, as an environment of explicit tagging was the only available tagging environment up to the 1988 specification.)

The extensibility environment (with the string used in line 4 to specify it given in parentheses) is one of the following:

- an environment requiring explicit extensibility markers (no mention of extensibility in line 4); and

- an environment of implied extensibility markers (EXTENSIBILITY IMPLIED).

We discuss these environments below. If both a tagging and an extensibility environment are being specified, the text for either one can come first.

3.3.2 The Tagging Environment

The treatment here leans heavily on the effect of tagging in a TLV-style encoding, and on BER in particular. It was to assist in such an encoding scheme that tagging was introduced into ASN.1. A more abstract treatment of tagging applicable to **any** encoding rules is given in Section II.

> **Three Tagging Environments**
> - explicit tagging
> - implicit tagging
> - automatic tagging

To look more closely at the effects of tagging, let us review a section from Figure 2.1, repeated in Figure 3.4.

We have already noted that in BER a SEQUENCE is encoded as a TLV, with the "V" part being a series of TLVs, one for each element of the sequence. Thus the "overseas" element is a TLV, with the "V" part consisting of three TLVs, one for each of the three elements. We have also stated that the tag "[1]" overrides the tag value in the outermost "T" for the "overseas" sequence.

Similarly, we have noted that the tag [0] and the tag [1] on the NULLs override the default tag on the TLV for each NULL. In this case, the encoding no longer contains

. . . .

```
overseas [1] SEQUENCE
        {name      UTF8String,
         type      OutletType,
         location Address},
warehouse [2] CHOICE
        {northern  [0] NULL,
         southern [1] NULL}
```

. . . .

Figure 3.4   A fragment of Figure 2.1.

the default tag for NULL, and the fact that this TLV does actually represent a NULL (or in other cases an INTEGER or a BOOLEAN, etc.) is now only **implied** by the tag in the "T" part—you need to know the type definition to recognize that [0] is in this case referring to a NULL. We say that we have "implicitly tagged the NULL". Similarly, the "overseas" "SEQUENCE" was implicitly tagged with tag "[1]".

But what about the tag we have placed on the "warehouse" "CHOICE"? There is a superficial similarity between "CHOICE" and "SEQUENCE" (they have almost the same following syntax), but in fact they are **very** different in their BER encoding. With "SEQUENCE", following elements are wrapped up in an outer-level TLV wrapper as described earlier, but with "CHOICE", we merely take any one of the TLV encodings for one of the alternatives of the "CHOICE", and we use that as the entire encoding (the TLV) for the "CHOICE" itself.

Where does that leave the tagging of "warehouse"? Well, at first sight, it will override the tag of the TLV for the "CHOICE" (which is either "[0]" or "[1]" depending on which alternative was selected) with the tag "[2]". **Think for a bit, and then recognize that this would be a BUST specification!** The alternatives were specifically given (by tagging the NULLs) distinct tags precisely so as to be able to know which was being sent down the line in an instance of communication, but now we are overriding **both** with a common value ("[2]")! This cannot be allowed.

To cut a long story short—two forms of tagging are available in ASN.1.

- **Implicit tagging**—(this is what has been described so far), where the new tag overrides the old tag and type information which was carried by the old tag is now only **implicit** in the encoding; **this cannot be allowed for a "CHOICE" type**; and

- **Explicit tagging**—we add a new TLV wrapper specifically to carry the new tag in the "T" part of this wrapper, and carry the entire original TLV (with the old tag) in the "V" part of this wrapper; clearly this is OK for "CHOICE".

While implicit tagging is forbidden for "CHOICE" types (it is an illegal ASN.1 specification to ask for it), both implicit and explicit tagging can be applied to any other type. However, while explicit tagging retains maximum type information, and might help a dumb line monitor to produce a sensible display, it is clearly more verbose than implicit tagging.

> Implicit tagging: overrides the "T" part
>
> Explicit tagging: adds an extra TLV wrapper

Now, what do the different tagging environments mean?

3.3.2.1 An Environment of Explicit Tagging

With an *environment of explicit tagging*, all tags produce explicit tagging unless the tag (number in square brackets) is immediately followed by the keyword "IMPLICIT."

An environment of explicit tagging was the only one available in the early ASN.1 specifications, so it was common to see the word "IMPLICIT" almost everywhere, reducing readability. Of course, it was—and is—illegal to put "IMPLICIT" on a tag that is applied to a "CHOICE" type-notation, **or to a type-reference-name for such notation**.

3.3.2.2 An Environment of Implicit Tagging

> An environment of implicit tagging only produces implicit tagging where it is legal—there is no need to say "EXPLICIT" on a "CHOICE".

With an *environment of implicit tagging*, all tags are applied as implicit tagging unless one (or both) of the following apply:

- The tag is being applied to a "CHOICE" type-notation or to a type-reference-name for such notation; or

- The keyword "EXPLICIT" follows the tag notation.

In the preceding cases, tagging is still explicit tagging. In practice most specifications written between about 1986 and 1995 specified an environment of implicit tagging in their module headers, and it was unusual to see either the keyword

"IMPLICIT" or the keyword "EXPLICIT" after a tag. Occasionally, EXPLICIT was used for reinforcement, and occasionally (mainly in the security world to guarantee an extra TLV wrapper) on specific types within an environment of implicit tagging.

3.3.2.3 An Environment of Automatic Tagging

The rules about explicit and implicit tagging add to what is already a complicated set of rules on when tagging is needed, and in the 1994 specification, partly to simplify things for the

> **Automatic Tagging**
>
> Set up this environment and forget about tags!

application designer, and partly because the new Packed Encoding Rules (PER) were not TLV-based and made little use of tags, the ability to specify an *environment of automatic tagging* was added.

In this case, tags are automatically added to all elements of each sequence (or set) and to each alternative of a choice, sequentially from "[0]" onwards (separately for each "SEQUENCE", "SET", or "CHOICE" construction). They are added in an environment of implicit tagging EXCEPT that if tag-notation is present on any one of the elements of a particular "SEQUENCE" (or "SET") element or "CHOICE" alternative, then it is assumed that the designer has taken control, and there will be NO automatic application of tags. (The tag-notation that **is** present is interpreted in an environment of implicit tagging in this case.)

It is generally recommended today that "AUTOMATIC TAGS" be placed in the module header, and the designer can then forget about tags altogether. However (refer back to Figure 999 please!), there is a counterargument that "AUTOMATIC TAGS" can be more verbose than necessary in BER, and can give more scope for errors of implementation if ASN.1 tools are not used. You take your choice; I know what mine would be!

> **The Extensibility Marker**
>
> An ellipsis (or a pair) that identifies an insertion point where version 2 material can be added without affecting a version 1 system's ability to decode version 2 encodings.

3.3.3 The Extensibility Environment

We have already discussed the power of a TLV-style of encoding to allow additions of elements in version 2, with version 1 specifications able to skip and to ignore such additional elements. (This extensibility concept actually generalizes to things other than sequences and sets, but these are sufficient for now.)

If we are to retain some extensibility capability in ASN.1 **and** we are to introduce encoding rules that are less verbose than the TLV of BER (such as the new PER), then a designer's requirements for extensibility in his application specification have to be made explicit.

We also need to make sure not only that encoding rules will allow a version 1 system to find the end of (and perhaps ignore) added version 2 material, but also that the application designer clearly specifies the actions expected of a version 1 system if it receives such material.

To make this possible, the 1994 specification introduced an *extensibility marker* into the ASN.1 notation. In the simplest use of this, the type-notation "Order-for-stock" could be written as in Figure 3.5.

Here we are identifying that we require encoding rules to permit the later addition of outer-level elements between "urgency" and "authenticator", and additional enumerations, in version 2, without ill-effect if they get sent to version 1 systems. (Full details are in Section II.) (Should we have been happy to add the version 2 elements at the end after "authenticator", then a single ellipsis would have sufficed.)

The place where the ellipses are placed, and where new version 2 material can be safely inserted without upsetting deployed version 1 systems is called (surprise, surprise!) the *insertion point*. You are only allowed to have one insertion point in any given sequence, set, choice, etc.

The alert reader (you should be getting used to that phrase by now, but it is probably still annoying—sorry!) will recognize that in addition to warning encoding rules to make provision, it is also necessary to tell the version 1 systems what to do with added

```
Order-for-stock ::= SEQUENCE
    {order-no        INTEGER,
     name-address    BranchIdentification,
     details         SEQUENCE OF
                       SEQUENCE
                     {item    OBJECT IDENTIFIER,
                      cases   INTEGER},
     urgency         ENUMERATED
                     {tomorrow(0),
                      three-day(1),
                      week(2), ... }  DEFAULT week,
                      ... ,
                      ... ,
     authenticator Security-Type}
```

Figure 3.5 Order-for-stock with extensibility markers.

material. In the case of new outer-level elements, it may appear "obvious" that the required action would be to silently ignore the added elements. But what should a version 1 system do if it receives an "urgency" value that it does not know about? There is a further piece of notation (see Section II, again, I am afraid, if you want details!) called the *exception specification*, which can be added immediately after the extensibility ellipsis. (The exception specification starts with an exclamation mark, so you will know it when you see it!).

Application designers are encouraged to provide exception specifications when they use extensibility markers, although this has not been made mandatory.

> **Exception Specification**
>
> Specification of the behavior of a version 1 system in the presence of added version 2 elements or values.

In an *environment requiring explicit extensibility markers*, the ellipsis, and any implications on encoding rules and version 1 behavior that stem from the presence of an ellipsis, only occurs if the ellipsis is textually present in the specification wherever it is required.

In an *environment of implied extensibility markers*, all type-notations in this environment that do not already contain an extensibility marker in constructions where such markers are permitted automatically have one added **at the end of the construction**.

Thus if the type-notation of Figure 3.5 was in an environment of implied extensibility, an additional extension marker would be automatically inserted at the end of the "SEQUENCE{....}" construction in the "details" "SEQUENCE OF".

> Environment of implied extensibility markers: an environment where any construction without an extensibility marker (and which is allowed one) has one added (at its end).

At the time of writing this text, extension markers are being extensively used, but few designers have chosen to specify an environment of implied extensibility markers, even though the cost of having additional, perhaps unnecessary, insertion points for the insertion of version 2 material is low in terms of bits on the line.

The problem probably stems from three problems with using this environment.

- The insertion point is always at the end—you have no control over its position.

- When producing the version 2 specification, you have to actually insert the ellipses explicitly before your added elements—and you might forget!

- There is no provision (when this environment is used) for the presence of an exception specification with the extension marker, so all rules for the required behavior of version 1 systems in the presence of version 2 elements or values have to be generic to the entire specification.

Concluding advice: Think carefully about where you want extension markers and about the handling you want version 1 systems to give to version 2 elements and values (using exception specifications to localize and make explicit those decisions), but do not attempt a blanket solution using an environment of implied extensibility.

3.4 Exports/Imports Statements

It has taken more text to describe the effects of a six-line header than is contained in the ASN.1 Standard/Recommendation! And we are not yet done!

> **Exports/Imports Statements**
>
> A pair of optional statements at the head of a module that specify the use of types defined in other modules (import), or that make available to other modules types defined in this module (export).

Following the sixth line ("BEGIN") and (only) before any type or value assignment statements, we can include an *exports statement* (first) and/or an *imports statement*. These are usually regarded as part of the module header.

At this point it is important to highlight what has been only hinted at earlier: There is more in the ASN.1 repertoire of things that have reference names than just types and values, although these are by far the most important (or at least, the most prolific!) in most specifications.

Pre-1994 (only) we add *macro names*, and post-1994 we add names of *information object classes*, *information objects*, and *information object sets*. These can all appear in an export or an import statement, but for now we concentrate only on type-reference-names and value-reference-names.

An exports statement is relatively simple, and is illustrated in Figure 3.6, where we have taken our type definitions for "OutletType" and "Address", put them into a module of commonly used types, and exported them, that is to say, made them available for use in another module.

```
Wineco-common-types
      { joint-iso-itu-t internationalRA(23) set(42) set-vendors(9)
wineco(43) modules(2) common(3)}
   DEFINITIONS
       AUTOMATIC TAGS ::=
   BEGIN

   EXPORTS  OutletType, Address;

   OutletType ::=  SEQUENCE
       {  ....
          ....
          .... }

   Address ::= SEQUENCE
       {  ....
          ....
          .... }

   .....

   END
```

Figure 3.6 The common types module (first attempt).

In reality there would be more supporting types in "Wineco-common-types" that we are choosing not to export—they are not available for use in other modules. There would probably also be rather more types exported.

Note the presence of the semicolon as a statement terminator for the "EXPORTS" statement. We will see this also being used to terminate the "IMPORTS" statement. These are the only two cases where ASN.1 has a statement terminator.

> Absence of an EXPORTS statement means "exports EVERYTHING." The statement "EXPORTS;" means "exports NOTHING".

Note also that for historical reasons ("EXPORTS" was only added in 1988) the omission of an "EXPORTS" statement has the semantics "everything is available for import by another module", while:

```
   EXPORTS ;
```

has the semantics "nothing is available for import by another module".

Next we are going to assume that the "Security-Type", which we first used in Figure 2.1, is being imported from the Secure Electronic Transactions (SET) specification

```
Wineco-common-types
       { joint-iso-itu-t internationalRA(23) set(42) set-vendors(9)
         wineco(43) modules(2) common(3)}
     DEFINITIONS
         AUTOMATIC TAGS ::=
     BEGIN

     EXPORTS  OutletType, Address, Security-Type;

     IMPORTS Security-Type FROM
           SET-module
         {joint-iso-itu-t internationalRA(23) set(42) module(6) 0};

     OutletType ::=  SEQUENCE
         { ....
           ....
           .... }

     Address ::= SEQUENCE
         { ....
           ....
           .... }

     .....

     END
```

Figure 3.7   The common types module (enhanced).

(a totally separate publication), and will be used in our "Wineco-common-types" module but also in our other modules. We import this for use in the "Wineco-common-types" module, but also export it again to make the imports clauses of our other modules simpler (they merely need to import from "Wineco-common-types"). This "relaying" of type definitions is legal.

This changes Figure 3.6 to Figure 3.7.

As with EXPORTS, the text between "IMPORTS" and "FROM" is a comma separated list of reference names. We will see how to import from more than one other module in the next figure.

Note at this point that if a type is imported from a module with a particular tagging or extensibility environment into a module with a different tagging or extensibility environment, the type-notation for that imported type continues to be interpreted with the environment of the module in which it was originally defined. This may seem obvious from the way in which the environment concept was presented, but it is worth reinforcing the point—what is being imported is in some sense the "abstract type" that the type-notation defines, **not** the text of the type-notation.

3.5 Refining Our Structure

Now we are going to make quite a few changes. We will add a second top-level message (and make provision for more) called "Return-of-sales" defined in another module, and we will now include the "ABSTRACT-SYNTAX" statement (mentioned in Chapter 2) to define our new top-level type in yet another module. We will put that module first.

We will do a few more cosmetic changes to this top-level module, to illustrate some slightly more advanced features. We will

> **The Final Example**
>
> We now use several modules; we have a CHOICE as our top-level type, and we clearly identify it as our top-level type. We use an object identifier value-reference-name, we use APPLICATION class tags, we handle invalid encodings, we have extensibility at the top-level with exception handling. We are getting quite sophisticated in our use of ASN.1!

- use "APPLICATION" class tags for our top-level messages. This is not necessary, but is often done (see later discussion of tag classes),

- assign the first part of our long object identifiers to the value-reference-name "wineco-OID" and use that as the start of our object identifiers, a commonly used feature of ASN.1, and

- add text to "ABSTRACT-SYNTAX" to make clear that if the decoder detects an invalid encoding of incoming material our text will specify exactly how the system is to behave.

The final result is shown in Figure 3.8, which is assumed to be followed by the text of Figure 3.7. Have a good look at Figure 3.8, and then read the following text that "talks you through it".

Lines 001 to 006 are nothing new. Note that in lines 10 and 13 we will use "wineco-OID" (defined in lines 015 and 016) to shorten our object identifier value, but we are not allowed to use this in the module header, as it is not yet within scope, and the object identifier value must be written out in full.

Line 007 simply says that nothing is available for reference from other modules.

```
001    Wineco-common-top-level
002        { joint-iso-itu-t internationalRA(23) set(42) set-vendors(9)
003          wineco(43) modules(2) top(0)}
004    DEFINITIONS
005        AUTOMATIC TAGS ::=
006    BEGIN
007    EXPORTS ;
008    IMPORTS Order-for-stock FROM
009         Wineco-ordering-protocol
010       {wineco-OID modules(2) ordering(1)}
011          Return-of-sales FROM
012       Wineco-returns-protocol
013       {wineco-OID modules(2) returns(2)};
014
015    wineco-OID OBJECT IDENTIFIER ::=
016          { joint-iso-itu-t internationalRA(23)
017                   set(42) set-vendors(9) wineco(43)}
018    wineco-abstract-syntax  ABSTRACT-SYNTAX ::=
019             {Wineco-Protocol IDENTIFIED BY
020                          {wineco-OID abstract-syntax(1)}
021                          HAS PROPERTY
022                          {handles-invalid-encodings}
023                          --See clause 45.6 --    }
024
025    Wineco-Protocol ::= CHOICE
026        {ordering   [APPLICATION 1] Order-for-stock,
027         sales      [APPLICATION 2] Return-of-sales,
028         ... ! PrintableString : "See clause 45.7"
029         }
030
031    END
—New page in published spec.
032    Wineco-ordering-protocol
033    { joint-iso-itu-t internationalRA(23) set(42) set-vendors(9)
034      wineco(43) modules(2) ordering(1)}
035    DEFINITIONS
036        AUTOMATIC TAGS ::=
037    BEGIN
038    EXPORTS Order-for-stock;
039    IMPORTS OutletType, Address, Security-Type FROM
040                 Wineco-common-types
041            {wineco-OID modules(2) common (3)};
042
043    wineco-OID OBJECT IDENTIFIER ::=
044          { joint-iso-itu-t internationalRA(23)
045                   set(42) set-vendors(9) wineco(43)}
046
047    Order-for-stock ::=  SEQUENCE
048              { ....
....              ....
....              .... }
....
```

```
070     BranchIdentification ::= SET
071             { ....
....            ....
....            ....}
....
....    ....
....
101     END
--New page in published spec.
102     Wineco-returns-protocol
103     { joint-iso-itu-t internationalRA(23) set(42)
104       set-vendors(9) wineco(43) modules(2) returns(2)}
105     DEFINITIONS
106         AUTOMATIC TAGS ::=
107     BEGIN
108     EXPORTS Return-of-sales;
109     IMPORTS OutletType, Address, Security-Type FROM
110                 Wineco-common-types
111             {wineco-OID modules(2) common (3)};
112
113     wineco-OID OBJECT IDENTIFIER ::=
114         {iso identified-organization icd-wineco(10)}
115
116     Return-of-sales ::=  SEQUENCE
117             { ....
....            ....
....            .... }
....
....    ....
....
139     END
```

Figure 3.8   (Last figure of this Chapter.)

Lines 008 to 013 are the imports we were expecting from our other two modules. Note the syntax here: If we had more types being imported from the same module, there would be a comma separated list as in line 039, but when we import from two different modules lines 011 to 013 just run on from lines 008 and 010 with no separator.

Lines 015 and 017 provide our object identifier value-reference-name with a value assignment. It is a (very useful!) curiosity of the value notation for object identifiers that it can begin with an object identifier value-reference-name, which "expands" into the initial part of a full object identifier value, and is then added to, as we see in lines 010, 013, and 020. If you are interested and want to jump ahead, the OID tree is more fully described in Chapter 8.

Lines 018 to 023 are the "piece of magic" syntax that defines the top-level type, names the abstract syntax, and assigns an object identifier value to it—something which in older specifications would be done in human-readable text. In fact, this syntax is not ad hoc, it is an example of an *information object assignment statement* that will be discussed in Section II.

The "HAS PROPERTY" with lines 22 to 23 is the only "property" that can be specified at present. The inclusion of this syntax is partly to counter an old OSI viewpoint that decoding was a separate layer from the application, and that if decoding failed to produce a recognized abstract value, all you could do was abort the connection! (Do check Figure 999 again!) Stupid idea! But including lines 20 to 23 reassures the reader that the specification does indeed contain (in clause 45.6) text to cover what to do in this case.

Lines 025 to 029 define the single-ASN.1-type that we need for our top-level messages to ensure that each encoding (of either or our main message types) is unambiguous. If we simply applied BER to the two types "Order-for-stock" and "Return-of-sales-data", we could (and probably would) get a bit-pattern used for a value of one type also being used as an encoding for a value of the other type. By forming a new CHOICE type, the rules for tag uniqueness of a CHOICE type solve this problem. Notice that we have used "AUTOMATIC TAGS" in line 005, so there was no need to add any tags in lines 026 and 027, but as a matter of personal preference and style, we chose to take complete control of the "T" value in the outermost TLV of our messages and make one an encoding of "[APPLICATION 0]" and the other of "[APPLICATION 1]", no matter what the original tags were. Some designers argue that this is helpful for hand-encoders—it is certainly irrelevant to those using a tool. Notice that the presence of tags in lines 026 and 027 disables automatic tagging for the CHOICE in line 025, temporarily replacing the tagging environment with an environment of implicit tagging.

Line 028 tells us that in version 2 we suspect we may need more outer-level messages, and that encoding rules must ensure that adding such messages does not prevent version 1 systems from correctly receiving messages that were in version 1. The exclamation mark and following material (the exception specification—described in detail in Section II) in line 028 tells us that clause 45.7 details the actions that a version 1 system should take if it receives messages added in version 2 (or later).

Lines 032 to 101 are our second module (the development of the original Figure 2.1), and contain nothing new. Note, however, that lines 043 and 045 are a repetition of 015 to 017, and this might seem undesirable. It would have been possible to define "wineco-OID" in yet another module (with lots of other value-reference-names we might need), and to import that name from that module. However, we would not (for obvious "infinite recursion") reasons be allowed to use "wineco-OID" in the "FROM" for that import, so we would end up writing out as much text (and repeating it in each module where we wish to do the import) as we have written in lines 015 to 017 and 043 to 045. What we have is about as minimal as we can get.

Lines 102 to 139 are our third module, structurally the same as 032 to 101, and introducing nothing new. The whole specification then concludes with the text of Figure 3.7, giving our "common-type" module, which we have already discussed.

3.6 Complete Specifications

As was stated earlier, there is no concept in ASN.1 of a "complete specification", only of correct (complete) modules, some of which may include an "ABSTRACT-SYNTAX" statement to identify a top-level type (or which may contain a top-level type identified in human-readable text).

In many cases if a module imports a type from some other module, the two modules will be in the same publication (loosely, part of the same specification), but this is not a requirement. Types can be imported from any module anywhere.

Suppose we take a top-level type in some module, and follow the chain of all the type-reference-names it uses (directly or indirectly) within its own module, and through import and export links (again chained to any depth) to types in other modules. This will give us the complete set of types that form the "complete specification" for the application for which this is the top-level type, and the specifications of all these types have (of course) to be available to any implementor of that application **and to any ASN.1 compiler tool assisting in the implementation.** Purely for the purposes of the final part of this chapter of this book, this tree of type definitions will be called the *application-required types*.

It is important advice to any application designer to make it very clear early in the text of any application specification precisely which additional (physical) documents are required to obtain the definitions of all the application-required types.

But suppose we now consider the set of modules in which these application-required types were defined. (Again, purely for the next few paragraphs, we will call these the *application-required modules*).

In general, the module textually containing the top-level type **probably** does not contain any types other than those that are application-required types (although there is no requirement that this be so). But as soon as we start importing, particularly from modules in other publications that were perhaps produced to satisfy more general requirements, then there are likely to be some types defined in application-required modules that are not application-required types.

As we shall see later, tools vary in their intelligence. There are some tools that require you to physically extract referenced types and put everything into the same module with the top-level type first. This is at the extreme bad end, and can give real problems if the tagging or extensibility environments of the different modules are different.

The best tools will allow you to present them with machine-readable text (perhaps in several files) that contains all the application-required modules (and a directive identifying the top-level type), and will extract from those modules **only** the application-required types, mapping only those to data structures in your chosen programming language. (This keeps the memory requirement for the implementation to a minimum.)

Remember the discussion you had with yourself earlier (as a potential application designer) about the pros and cons of referencing (importing) or textually copying types from other modules? You may want to reopen that discussion.

3.7 Conclusion

We have come a long way from our simple type assignments in Figure 2.1.

The high-level structure of an ASN.1-based application specification has been described and explored, and most of the important concepts have now been introduced.

But a word of caution: The simple protocol we have used here for illustration would probably be better structured as the single-ASN.1-module outlined in Figure 3.1. The additional power (but complexity) of multiple modules with export/import **is** important for large specifications, but should not be used unnecessarily—keep it as simple as possible. If the Figure 3.1 structure will do, stay with Figure 3.1.

It now remains to complete the discussion of the ASN.1 type and value notations for the simple built-in types and the construction mechanisms (this is done in the next chapter), and (in Section II—with an introduction in Chapter 5) to give a fuller treatment of the more advanced concepts we have mentioned, and to discuss more of the features added in 1994.

The reader should, however, now be able to read and to understand the bulk of most real ASN.1 specifications produced before 1994, and to recognize the use of some features introduced in the 1994 ASN.1. Read on!

The Basic Data Types and Construction Mechanisms: Closure

(Or: You Need Bricks of Various Shapes and Sizes!)

Summary

There are a number of types that are predefined in ASN.1, such as

- INTEGER,

- BOOLEAN, and

- UTF8String.

These are used to build more complex user-defined types with construction mechanisms such as

- SEQUENCE,

- SET,

- CHOICE,

- SEQUENCE OF,

- SET OF, and

- etc.

Many of these construction mechanisms have appeared in the examples and illustrations of earlier chapters.

This chapter completes the detailed presentation of all the basic ASN.1 types, giving in each case a clear description of

- the type-notation for the type,

- the set of abstract values in the type, and

- the value-notation for values of that type.

Additional pieces of type/value-related notation are also covered, largely completing the discussion of syntax commonly used in pre-1994 specifications.

The chapter ends with a list of additional concepts whose treatment is deferred to either the next chapter or to Section II.

4.1 Illustration by Example

> Figure 4.1 has been carefully constructed to complete your introduction to all the basic ASN.1 types—that's it folks!

In order to illustrate some of the type and value notations, we will define our Return-of-Sales message as in Figure 4.1. Figure 4.1 has been designed to include all the basic ASN.1 types apart from NULL, and provides the hook for further discussion of these types.

```
Return-of-sales ::= SEQUENCE
    {version         BIT STRING
               {version1 (0), version2 (1)} DEFAULT {version1},
    no-of-days-reported-on  INTEGER
          {week(7), month (28), maximum (56)} (1..56) DEFAULT week,
    time-and-date-of-report  CHOICE
               {two-digit-year  UTCTime,
                four-digit-year GeneralizedTime},
          -- If the system clock provides a four-digit year,
          -- the second alternative shall be used.  With the
          -- first alternative the time shall be interpreted
          -- as a sliding window.
    reason-for-delay  ENUMERATED
          {computer-failure, network-failure, other} OPTIONAL,
          -- Include this field if and only if the
          -- no-of-days-reported-on exceeds seven.
    additional-information  SEQUENCE OF PrintableString OPTIONAL,
          -- Include this field if and only if the
          -- reason-for-delay is "other".
    sales-data  SET OF Report-item,
    ... ! PrintableString : "See wineco manual chapter 15"}
```

Figure 4.1 (Part 1) Illustration of the use of basic ASN.1 types.

```
Report-item ::= SEQUENCE
    {item                   OBJECT IDENTIFIER,
     item-description       ObjectDescriptor OPTIONAL,
        -- To be included for any newly-stocked item.
     bar-code-data          OCTET STRING,
        -- Represents the bar-code for the item as specified
        -- in the wineco manual chapter 29.
     ran-out-of-stock   BOOLEAN DEFAULT FALSE,
        -- Send TRUE if stock for item became exhausted at any
        -- time during the period reported on.
     min-stock-level        REAL,
     max-stock-level        REAL,
     average-stock-level    REAL
        -- Give minimum, maximum, and average levels during the
        -- period as a percentage of normal target stock-level-- }

wineco-items OBJECT IDENTIFIER ::=
    { joint-iso-itu-t internationalRA(23) set(42) set-vendors(9)
wineco(43) stock-items (0)}
```

Figure 4.1 (Part 2)   Illustration of the use of basic ASN.1 types.

Have a good look at Figure 4.1. It should by now be fairly easy for you to understand its meaning. If you have no problems with it, you can probably skip the rest of this chapter, unless you want to understand ASN.1 well enough to write a book, or to deliver a course, on it! (We included wineco-items in Figure 4.1 to reduce the verbosity of the object identifier values in Figure 4.2 later.)

4.2 Discussion of the Built-In Types

4.2.1 The BOOLEAN Type

(See "ran-out-of-stock" in Figure 4.1). There is nothing to add here. A "BOOLEAN" type has the obvious two abstract values, true and false, but notice that the value-notation is the words "TRUE" or "FALSE" (**all in capital letters**). You can regard the use of capitals as either consistent with the fact that (almost) all the built-in names in ASN.1 are all uppercase, or as inconsistent with the fact that ASN.1 **requires** value-reference-names to begin with a lowercase letter! ASN.1 does not always obey its own rules!

4.2.2 The INTEGER Type

(See "number-of-days-reported-on" in Figure 4.1). This example is a little more complicated than the simple use of "INTEGER" that we saw in Figure 2.1. The example here contains what are called *distinguished values*. In some early ASN.1 specifications (ENUMERATED was not added until around 1988) people would sometimes use the "INTEGER" type with a list of distinguished values, whereas today they would use "ENUMERATED". In fact, the syntax can look quite similar, so we can write the equivalent of the example in Figure 2.1 as:

```
urgency   INTEGER
              {tomorrow (0),
               three-day (1),
               week (2)}   DEFAULT week
```

It is, however, important here to notice some important differences. The presence of the list following "INTEGER" is entirely optional (for "ENUMERATED" it is required), and the presence of the list in no way affects the set of abstract values in the type.

The following two definitions are **almost** equivalent:

```
My-integer ::= INTEGER {tomorrow(0), three-day (1), week(2) }
```

and

```
My-integer ::= INTEGER
tomorrow My-integer ::= 0
three-day My-integer ::= 1
week My-integer ::= 2
```

The Integer Type

- Just the word INTEGER, nice and simple!; and/or,

- Add a distinguished value list; and/or,

- Add a range specification (subtyping); then,

- Put an extension marker and exception specification in the range specification. (Getting complicated again!)

The difference lies in ASN.1 scope rules. In the second example, the names "tomorrow" etc. are value-reference-names that can be assigned only once within the module, can be used anywhere within that module where an integer value is needed (even, in fact, as the number on an enumeration or in another distinguished value list or in a tag—but all these uses would be unusual!), and can appear in an EXPORTS statement at the head of the module. On the other hand, in the first example, the names "tomorrow" etc. cannot be exported, can appear (with the same or different values) in other distinguished value lists, or indeed as value-reference names for a value of some totally different type. The name "tomorrow" in the first example has the meaning of identifying the zero value of "My-integer" ONLY when it appears in value notation that is governed by the type "My-integer", such as when it is used as the "DEFAULT" value for a sequence element of that type.

Notice also that although we have been using numbers in distinguished value lists in ascending order, there is no requirement for this; the order is irrelevant, and does not affect the resulting definitions.

We have seen that a decimal number can be used as value notation for a positive integer value. Negative values are, for example:

```
minus-two INTEGER ::= -2
```

but you are not allowed to write "-0", nor is any form of binary or hex notation valid as value notation for the "INTEGER" type.

What are the set of abstract values for "INTEGER"? An early draft of the ASN.1 specification actually stated the maximum and minimum values of ASN.1 integers, based on restrictions imposed by BER encodings. However, a calculation showed that with a communications line running at a terabit a second, it would take approximately 100 million years to transmit the largest or smallest value! ASN.1 integers are "effectively unbounded". (And in the more recent PER encodings, there is no limit on the size of an integer value.)

This raises the beginnings of a discussion that more properly belongs in a later chapter—do you really have to write your implementation code to handle arbitrarily large integers? If we look again at "no-of-days-reported-on" in Figure 4.1, we see the text "(1..56)" following the distinguished value list. (This can be present whether we have a distinguished value list or not). This is our first example of a *subtype constraint*—a notation that restricts the range of our integer, or subsets it. In this case it is saying that the only values a conforming sender is permitted to send are values in the range from 1 to 56, and it is clear that an implementor need only allocate one byte for this field. A fuller discussion of subtype notation (for other types as well as for the integer type) appears later, but this simple restriction of the range of an integer is by far the most common use of this notation. **Application designers are encouraged to place a range constraint such as this on "INTEGER" types whenever they can do so, and to state explicitly in comment if they expect implementors to truly handle arbitrarily large integers.** However, as an implementor, if you see simply "INTEGER", with no range constraint and no clarifying text, it is usually a safe assumption that a four-octet integer value will be the largest you will receive.

One final point: The similarity of the syntax for defining distinguished values to that for defining enumerations can be confusing. As the definition of distinguished values does not change in any way the set of abstract values in the type or the way they are encoded, there is never any "extensibility" question in moving to version 2—if additional distinguished values are added, this is simply a notational convenience and does not affect the bits on the line. So the ellipsis extensibility marker (available for the list in the enumerated type), is neither needed nor allowed in the list of distinguished values (although it can appear in a range constraint, as we will see later).

Enumerated

Can have an extension marker.

Numbers for encodings needed pre–1994, optional post–1994.

4.2.3 The ENUMERATED Type

(See "urgency" in Figure 2.1 and "reason-for-delay" in Figure 4.1). There is little to add to our earlier discussions. The numbers in round brackets were required pre-1994, and are optional post-1994. The type consists precisely and only of values corresponding to each of the listed names.

The numbers were originally present to avoid extensibility problems; if version 2 added a new enumeration, it was important that this should not affect the values used (in encodings) to denote original enumerations, and the easiest way to ensure this was to let the application designer list the numbers to be used. Post-1994, extensibility is more explicit, and we might see:

```
Urgency-type ::= ENUMERATED
        {tomorrow,
         three-day,
         week,
         ...,
          -- Version 1 systems should assume any other value
          -- means "week".
         month}
```

Here "month" was added in version 2, although the requirement placed on version 1 systems when version 1 was first specified actually means that such deployed systems will treat "month" as "week". This illustrates the importance of thinking hard about the exception handling you want from version 1 systems. If instead the version 1 spec had said "treat any unknown enumeration as **tomorrow**", then the effect of adding "month" in version 2 might have been less satisfying. Notice that in this case we chose to give the exception-handling behavior in comment after the ellipsis, rather than using an exception specification; this is quite satisfactory, particularly if the exception handling is peculiar to this field. Selection of appropriate exception handling is discussed further in 7.2.6 on page 141.

Finally, if you want to be really weird, you can put numbers in for some enumerations and not for others—if you are lucky, the result will still be legal! Read the ASN.1 specification if you want to do daft things like this, because this book will not help you!

4.2.4 The REAL Type

(See "min-stock-level" etc. in Figure 4.1). The type-notation for the "REAL" type is given in Figure 4.1. This is the only option.

REAL

Two sets of abstract values, base 10 and base 2, are distinct even if mathematically equal. The value notation is a comma separated list of integers for the mantissa, the base (2 or 10), and the exponent. Also PLUS-INFINITY and MINUS-INFINITY.

The value notation is slightly curious. Here are examples of some pieces of value notation for the real type:

```
v1 REAL ::= {mantissa 314159, base 10, exponent -5}

v2 REAL ::= {mantissa 3141590, base 10, exponent -6}

v3 REAL ::= {mantissa 1, base 2, exponent -1}

v4 REAL ::= {mantissa 5, base 10, exponent -1}

v5 REAL ::= 0

v6 REAL ::= {mantissa 0, base 2, exponent 100}

v7 REAL ::= {mantissa 0, base 10, exponent 100}
```

Notice that apart from v5, these are all comma-separated lists of three numbers. (Comma-separated lists occur frequently in ASN.1 value notation and were chosen for type REAL because an ASN.1 tool may encounter the value notation when the governor is a type-reference name that has not yet been defined, and the tool needs a simple means of finding the end of the notation). The mathematical value being identified by {mantissa x, base y, exponent z} is (x times (y to the power z)), but y is allowed to take **only** the values 2 and 10.

There are also explicitly included (and encoded specially) two values with the following value notation:

```
PLUS-INFINITY

MINUS-INFINITY
```

Again, all uppercase letters. When "REAL" was first introduced, there was discussion of adding additional special "values" such as "OVERFLOW", or even "PI" etc., but this never happened.

That is really all you need to know, as the "REAL" type is infrequently used in actual application specifications. The rest of the discussion of the "REAL" type is a bit academic, and you can omit it without any "real" damage. However, if you want to know which of v1 to v7 represent the same abstract value and which different ones, read on!

You might expect from the name that the abstract values are (mathematical) real numbers, but for those of a mathematical bent, only the rationals are included.

Formally, the type contains two sets of abstract values, one set comprising all the numbers with a finite representation using base 10, and the other set comprising all the numbers with a finite representation base 2. (Notice that from a purely mathematical point of view, the latter values are a strict subset of the former, but the former contains values that are not in the latter set). In all ASN.1 encoding rules, there are *binary encodings* for "REAL", and there are also *decimal encodings* as specified in the ISO standard 6093. This standard specifies a character string to represent the value, which is then encoded using ASCII. An example of these encodings is:

```
56.5E+3
```

but ISO 6093 contains many options!

It is possible (post-1994) to restrict the set of abstract values in "REAL" to be only the base 10 or only the base 2 set, effectively giving the application designer control over whether the binary or the decimal encoding is to be used. Where the type is unrestricted, it is theoretically possible to put different application semantics on a base 10 value from that on the mathematically equal base 2 value, but probably no one would do so! (Actually, "REAL" is not used much anyway in real protocols.)

To wrap this discussion up—looking at the forementioned values v1 to v7, we can observe that the value-reference-names listed on the same line below are value notation for the same abstract value, and those on different lines are names for different abstract values:

```
v1, v2
v3
v4
v5, v6
v7
```

(v5 equals v6 because v5 is defined to represent the base2 value zero.)

4.2.5 The BIT STRING Type

(See "version" in Figure 4.1). There are two main uses of the BIT STRING type. The first is that given for "version", where we have a list of *named bits* associated with the type. The second and simplest is the type-notation:

```
BIT STRING
```

> BIT STRING is often used with named bits to support a bit-map for version negotiation.

Note that, as we would expect, this is all uppercase, but as we might not expect, the name of the type (effectively a type-reference-name) contains a space. The space is not merely permitted, it is **required**! Again ASN.1 breaks its own rules!

We will return to Figure 4.1 in a moment. Let us take the simpler case where there is no list of named bits.

If a field of a sequence (say) is defined as simply "BIT STRING", then this can be a sign of an inadequately specified protocol, as semantics need to be applied to any field in a protocol. "BIT STRING" with no further explanation is one of several ways in which "holes" can legally be left in ASN.1 specifications, but to the detriment of the specification as a whole.

We will see later that where any "hole" is left, it is important to provide fields that will clearly identify the content of the hole in an instance of communication, and to either ensure that all communicating partners will understand all identifications (and the resulting contents of the hole), or will know what action to take on an unknown identifier. ASN.1 makes provision for such "holes" and the associated identification and it is not a good idea to use "BIT STRING" to grow your own "holes" (but some people do)!

So, BIT STRING without named bits has a legitimate use to carry encodings produced by well-identified algorithms, and in particular to carry encryptions for either concealment or signature purposes. But even in this case, there is usually a need to clearly identify the security algorithm to be applied, and perhaps to indirectly reference specific keys that are in use. The BIT STRING data type is (legitimately) an important building block for those providing security enhancements to protocols, but further data is usually carried with it.

> BIT STRING without named bits is also frequently used as part of a more complex structure to carry encrypted information.

The use of BIT STRING with named bits as for "version" in Figure 4.1 is common. The names in curly brackets simply provide names for the bits of the BIT STRING and the associated bit number. It is important to note that the presence of a named bit list (as with distinguished values for integers), does not affect the type. The list in no way constrains the possible length of the BIT STRING, nor do bits have to be named in order.

ASN.1 talks about "the leading bit" as "bit zero", down to the "trailing bit". Encoding rules map the "leading bit" to the "trailing bit" of a bit-string type into octets when encoding.

(BER—arbitrarily, it could have chosen the opposite rule—specifies that the leading bit be placed in the most significant bit of the first octet of the encoding, and so on.)

How are these names of bits used? As usual, they can provide a handle for reference to specific bits by the human-readable text. They can also, however, be used in the value notation.

The obvious (and simplest) value notation for a BIT STRING is to specify the value in binary, for example:

```
'101100110001'B
```

If the value is a multiple of four bits, it is also permissible to use hexadecimal:

```
'B31'H
```

(Note that in ASN.1 hexadecimal notation, only uppercase letters are allowed.)

If, however, there are named bits available, then an additional value notation is available, which is a comma-separated list of bit-names within curly brackets (see, for example, the "DEFAULT" value of "version" in Figure 4.1). The value being defined is one in which **the bit for every listed bit-name is set to one, and all other bits are set to zero.**

The alert reader (I have done it again!) will spot that this statement is not sufficient to define a BIT STRING value, as it leaves undetermined how many (if any) trailing zero bits are present in the value. So, the use of such a "value-notation" if the length of the BIT STRING is not constrained does not really define a value at all—it defines a set of values! All those with the same one bits, but zero to infinity trailing zero bits.

The ASN.1 specifications post-1986 (or so) circumvent this problem with some "weasel" words (slightly changed in different versions): "If a named bit list is present, trailing zero bits shall have no semantic significance"; augmented later by "encoding rules are free to add (or remove) trailing zero bits to (or from) values that are being encoded!"

This issue is not a big one for normal BER, where it does not matter if there is doubt over whether some value exactly matches the "DEFAULT" value, but it matters much more in the canonical encoding rules to be described later.

The most common use for named bits is as a "version" map, as illustrated in Figure 4.1. Here an implementation would be instructed to set the bits corresponding to the versions that it is capable of supporting, and—typically—there would be some reply message in which the receiver would set precisely one bit (one of those set in the original message), or would send some sort of rejection message.

4.2.5.1 Formal/Advanced Discussion

N O T E — Most readers should skip this next bit! Go on to OCTET STRING, which has fewer problems! If you insist on reading on, **please** read Figure 999 again!

There have been many different texts in the ASN.1 specifications over the last 15 years associated with "BIT STRING" definitions with named bits. Most have been constrained by the desire:

    a.   not **really** to change what was being specified, or at least, not to break current deployed implementations; and

b.   not to add a large amount of text that would seem to imply a) even if it did not really do it!

The result is that you as an alert and intelligent reader (!) may well be able to take issue with what follows, depending on the vintage of the specification you are reading, and/or on whether people insist on calling you an "ASN.1 Expert!"

The ASN.1 Standard seems to imply that the presence of a named bit list (and the extent of such a list) has no impact on the set of abstract values in the type being defined. However, abstract values are there to enable application designers to associate different application semantics with them, with the assurance that each value will have a distinct encoding, and with the equal assurance that for canonical encodings there will be precisely one encoding for each value.

> BIT STRING with named bits raises interesting issues about what is the precise set of abstract values of such a type:
>
> IGNORE SUCH QUESTIONS, they don't matter!

(Controversial remark follows!) The specification states that "application designers should ensure that different (application) semantics are not associated with ... values (of types with named bits) which differ only in the number of trailing zero bits." What this is actually saying is that such **apparently distinct** abstract values are actually **a single abstract value**.

The only remaining issue is how such abstract BIT STRING values should be represented by encoding rules. The standard gives guidance: "encoding rules are free to add (or remove) arbitrarily many trailing zero bits to (or from) values that are being encoded or decoded." Perhaps not the best way of expressing it, but the principles are clear:

- when a named bit list is present, we have just one abstract value corresponding to different bit-patterns that differ only in the number of their trailing zero bits;

- encoding rules are (of course!) free to represent this abstract value as they like, but one option is to encode any one of those bit patterns that differ only in their trailing zero bits.

For BER, which does not claim to provide a single encoding for each abstract value, the rules permit arbitrarily many trailing zero bits in the encoding. (The decision to allow this was necessary to avoid breaking existing implementations when this rather abstract(!) problem was first understood.) Existing BER implementations will frequently include trailing zero bits in the encoding of a value of a BIT STRING type with a named-bit list.

For canonical encoding rules, however, including PER, a single encoding is necessary, and at first sight saying that such encoding rules never have trailing bits in the encoding looks like a good solution.

But the choice of encoding (and indeed the selection of the precise abstract BIT STRING value—from the set of abstract values with the same semantics—that is to be used for encoding) is complicated if there are **length constraints** at the abstract level on the bit-string type.

The matter is further complicated because in BER-related encoding rules, length constraints are "not visible" that is, they do not affect the encoding. In PER, they may or may not be visible.

The upshot of all this is that in the canonical versions of BER **trailing zero bits are never transmitted in an encoding**, but the value delivered to the application is required to have sufficient zero bits added (the minimum necessary) to enable it to satisfy any length constraints that might have been applied. (Such constraints are assumed to be visible to the application and to the Application Program Interface (API) code, whether they are visible to—affect—the encoding rules or not.)

However, PER, where (some) length constraints are PER-visible, changes this slightly: What is transmitted is always consistent with PER-visible constraints, so (the minimum number of) trailing zero bits are present in transfer if they are needed to satisfy a length constraint. The encoding can thus be delivered to the application unchanged, provided there are no not-PER-visible constraints applied, otherwise the canonical BER rules would apply; the application gets a value that is permitted by the constraints and carries the same application semantics as that derived directly from the transmitted encoding.

And if you have read this far, I bet you wish you hadn't! It kind of all works, but it is **not** simple!

Issues like this do not affect the normal application designer—just do the obvious things and it will all work; nor do they affect the normal implementor who obeys the well-known rules: encode the obvious encoding; and be **liberal** in your decoding.

These issues **are**, however, of importance to tool vendors who provide an option for "strict diagnostics" if incoming material is perceived to be erroneous. In such cases a very precise statement of what is "erroneous" is required!

4.2.6 The OCTET STRING Type

(See "bar-code-data" in Figure 4.1). Once again, a space is needed between "OCTET" and "STRING"! And once again, an OCTET STRING is a tempting candidate to "carry anything"—a delimited hole. (But do not be tempted!) Yet again, it is not appropriate unless supported by identification fields and exception handling. ASN.1 provides better mechanisms to support "holes".

In the case shown in Figure 4.1, the precise contents of the OCTET STRING are (hopefully!) well-specified in "Chapter 29 of the Wineco manual". However, this specification is not very general. The intent is clearly to provide a container for additional identification information, using some encoding outside of ASN.1. In general, and over time, there may be a number of different encodings of various forms of identification that the designer may wish to carry in this OCTET STRING, and again we see the need for additional identification fields saying "this is a bar-code version 1"—or something else, and "this is how it is encoded today," rather than hardwiring these decisions into "Chapter 29". Once again, we are discussing "holes".

> The OCTET STRING type is simple—but don't use it! It usually represents a poorly supported "hole", and it is better to use a prefabricated "hole"—see later!

In summary (but see Figure 999 again!) it is probably a BAD THING to have OCTET STRING or BIT STRING (other than for version bit maps) fields in application specifications unless you really know what you are doing and really want to "dig your own hole". But of course, perhaps you do!

The value notation for OCTET STRING is always hexadecimal or binary as illustrated earlier for bit string. If the result is not an integral multiple of eight bits, then zero bits are added at the end.

4.2.7 The NULL Type

(See "warehouse" in Figure 2.1). Formally, NULL is a type that has just one value. The value notation for this value is rather confusingly:

```
NULL
```

again, all uppercase, where one might expect an initial lowercase letter.

The normal use is very much as in Figure 2.1, where we need a type to provide a TLV (whose presence or absence carries some semantics), but

> For NULL, you know it all—a placeholder: no problems.

where there is no additional information to be carried with the type. NULL is often referred to as a "placeholder" in ASN.1 courses.

4.2.8 Some Character String Types

(See "additional-information" in Figure 4.1 and "name" (twice) in Figure 2.1). In the examples so far, you have met "PrintableString" (present in the earliest ASN.1 drafts), "VisibleString" (deprecated synonym "ISO646String"), and "UTF8String" (added in 1998). There are several others.

Despite not being all-uppercase, these (and the other character string type names) have been reserved words (names you may not use for your own types) since about 1988/90. The early designers of ASN.1 felt (rightly!) that the character string types and their names were a bit ad hoc, and gave them a somewhat reduced status!

Actually, in the earliest ASN.1 specification, there was the concept of "Useful Types", that is, types that were defined using the ASN.1 notation rather than pure human language, and these all used mixed upper/lowercase. The character string types were originally included as "Useful types", and were defined as a tagged OCTET STRING. Today (since about 1990 when they became reserved words) they are regarded as fairly fundamental types with a status more or less equal to that of INTEGER or BOOLEAN.

The set of characters in "PrintableString" values is "hardwired" into ASN.1, and is roughly the old **telex** character set, plus lowercase letters. The BER encoding in the "V" part of the TLV is the ASCII encoding, so the reduced character set over "VisibleString" (following) is not really useful, although a number of application specifications do use "PrintableString".

The set of characters in "VisibleString" values is simply the printing ASCII characters plus "space". The BER encoding in the "V" part of the TLV is, of course, ASCII.

The set of characters in "UTF8String" is any character—from Egyptian hieroglyphs to things carved in wood in the deepest Amazon jungle to things that we will in due course find on Mars—that has been properly researched and documented (including the ASCII control characters). The BER (and PER if the type is not constrained to a reduced character set) encoding per character is variable length, and has the "nice" property that for ASCII characters the encoding per character is one octet, stretching to three octets for all characters researched and documented so far, and going to at most seven octets per character once we have all the languages of the galaxy in there! Those who are "into" character set stuff may recognize the name "Unicode". UTF8 is an encoding scheme covering the whole of Unicode (and more) that is becoming (circa 1999) extremely popular for communication and storage of character information. (**Advice**: If you are designing a new protocol, use UTF8String for your character string fields unless you have a **very** good reason not to do so.)

4.2.9 The OBJECT IDENTIFIER Type

(See "item" and "wineco-items" in Figure 4.1, and module identifiers in Figure 3.8.) Values of the object identifier type have been used and introduced from the start of this book. But we are still going to postpone to a later chapter a detailed discussion of this type.

> OBJECT IDENTIFIER—Perhaps used more than any other basic ASN.1 type—you can get some name-space in lots of ways, but you don't really need it!

The OBJECT IDENTIFIER type may well lay claim to being the most used of all the ASN.1 types (excluding the constructors SEQUENCE, SET, and CHOICE, of course). Wherever world-wide unambiguous identification is needed in an ASN.1-based specification, the object identifier type is used.

Despite the apparent verbosity of the value-notation, the encoding of values of type object identifier is actually very compact (the human-readable names present in the value notation do not appear in the encoding). For the early components of an object identifier value, the mapping of names to integer values is "well-known", and for later components in any value-notation, the corresponding integer value is present (usually in round brackets).

The basic name space is a hierarchically allocated tree-structure, with global authorities responsible for allocation of top-level arcs, and progressively more local authorities responsible for the lower-level arcs.

For you (as an application designer) to be able to allocate values from the object identifier name space, you merely need to "get hung" from this tree. It really does not matter where you are "hung" from (although encodings of your values will be shorter the nearer you are to the top, and international organizations tend to be sensitive about where they are "hung"!).

For a standards-making group, or a private company, or even an individual, there is a range of mechanisms for getting some of this name-space, most of which require no administrative effort (you probably have an allocation already). These mechanisms are described later, although such is the proliferation of branches of the OID tree (as it is often described) that it is hard to describe all the finer parts.

It has been a criticism of ASN.1 that you need to get some OID space to be able to write: ASN.1 modules. This is actually not true—the module identifier is **not** required. However, most people producing ASN.1 modules **do** (successfully) try to get a piece of the OID space and **do** identify their modules with OID values. But, if this provides you with problems, it is **not** a requirement.

4.2.10 The ObjectDescriptor Type

(See "item-description" in Figure 4.1). The type-notation for the ObjectDescriptor type is:

```
ObjectDescriptor
```

without a space, and using mixed uppercase and lowercase! This is largely a historical accident. This type was formally defined as a tagged "GraphicString" (another character string type capable of carrying most of the world's languages, but regarded as obsolete today). Because its definition was by an ASN.1 type-assignment statement, it was deemed originally to be merely a "Useful Type", and was given a mixed upper/lowercase name with no space. Today, the term "Useful Type" is not used in the ASN.1 specification, and the use of mixed case for this built-in type is a bit of an anachronism.

> **ObjectDescriptor**
>
> Yes, mixed case! You will never see it in a specification, and you are unlikely to want to use it—ignore this text!

The existence of the type stems from arguments over the form of the OBJECT IDENTIFIER type. There were those who (successfully) argued for an identification mechanism that produced short, numerical identifiers when encoded on the line. There were others who argued (unsuccessfully) for an identification mechanism that was "human-friendly", and contained a lot of text (for example, something like a simple ASCII encoding of the value notation we have met earlier), and perhaps no numbers. As the debate developed, a sort of compromise was reached that involved the introduction of the "OBJECT IDENTIFIER" type—short, numerical, guaranteed to be unambiguous world-wide, but supplemented by an additional type "ObjectDescriptor" that provided an indefinitely long (but usually around 80 characters) string of characters plus space to "describe" an object. The "ObjectDescriptor" value is not in any way guaranteed to be unambiguous world-wide (the string is arbitrarily chosen by each designer wishing to describe an object), but because of the length of the string, usually it **is** unambiguous.

There is a strong recommendation in the ASN.1 specification that whenever an object identifier value is allocated to identify an object, an object descriptor value should also be allocated to describe it. It is then left for application designers to include in their protocol (when referring to some object) either an "OBJECT IDENTIFIER" element only, or both an "OBJECT IDENTIFIER" and an "ObjectDescriptor", perhaps making the inclusion of the latter "OPTIONAL".

In practice (apart from the artificial example of Figure 4.1) you will never encounter an "ObjectDescriptor" in an application specification! Designers have chosen not to use it. Moreover, the rule that whenever an object identifier value is allocated for some object, an object descriptor value should also be assigned, is frequently broken.

Take the most visible use of object identifier values—in the header of an ASN.1 module: What is the corresponding object descriptor value? It is not explicitly stated, but most people would say that the **module name** appearing immediately before the object identifier in the header forms the corresponding object descriptor. Well—OK!

But there are other object identifier values originally assigned in the ASN.1 specification itself, such as:

```
{iso standard 8571}
```

This identifies the numbered standard (which is actually a multipart standard), and also gives object identifier name-space to those responsible for that standard. There is, however, no corresponding object descriptor value assigned.

4.2.11 The Two ASN.1 Date/Time Types

Yes, you did indeed interpret Figure 4.1 correctly—UTCTime is a date/time type that carries only a two-digit year!

You will also notice that both "UTCTime" and "GeneralizedTime" are again mixed upper/lowercase. Again this is a historical accident: They were defined using an ASN.1 type-assignment statement as a tagged "VisibleString", and were originally listed as "Useful Types".

Why both? Was GeneralizedTime added later? Yes and no! In the early drafts in 1982, UTCTime was all that was present, and contained the specification of the character string to be used to represent dates and times "hardwired" into the ASN.1 specification, that is to say, the complete text defining this type was present in the ASN.1 specification.

GeneralizedTime was added before the first ASN.1 specification was published in 1984, but did not contain the full specification; it referred to what was then a new ISO Standard (ISO 8601). However, early users of ASN.1

> **UTCTime and GeneralizedTime**
>
> Simple in concept, easy to use, but not without their problems!

were already finalizing their texts based on use of UTCTime, and it was left in the ASN.1 specification. The fact that UTCTime only used a two-digit year and GeneralizedTime a four-digit year was not even a subject of discussion in 1982! (The other difference between the two types was in the precision of the time—at best a precision of a second for UTCTime, more for GeneralizedTime.)

Slightly less forgivable was the Directory work, which was not published until 1988, but also used UTCTime! It is possible that the attraction of a "hardwired" specification—you do not need to seek out another publication in order to see what you are getting—was an influence in encouraging designers to use UTCTime (rather than GeneralizedTime) during the 1980s.

The comment in Figure 4.1 about interpreting a UTCTime value as a "sliding window" is one of three varying recommendations often made for two-digit year fields:

- (DEFAULT in the past). Interpret as a year between 1900 and 1999—the default setting, and certainly the intent in 1982, but a bad idea today.

- (SIMPLE proposal for now). Interpret as a year between 1950 and 2049—simple, and it buys us another 50 years!

- (SLIDING WINDOW—works forever!) Interpret any two-digit year that matches the bottom two digits of the current year as the current year. Interpret all other values as years within a window from the current year minus 50 years to the current year plus 49 years (or minus 49 to plus 50—a matter of choice—but it should be clearly defined). This means that on December 31st each year, the interpretation of dates 50 years in the past changes to an interpretation as a date 50 years in the future. If there never are dates in your system that are 50 years in the past (and no need to refer to any that are more than 49 years in the future), this system clearly works, and allows two-digit years to be used indefinitely. A neat solution!

What does "UTC" stand for? It comes from the Consultative Committee on International Radio (CCIR) and stands for "Coordinated Universal Time" (the curious order of the initials comes from the name in other languages). In fact, despite the different name, "GeneralizedTime" also records Coordinated Universal Time. What is this time standard? Basically, it is Greenwich Mean Time, but for strict accuracy, Greenwich Mean Time is based on the stars and there is a separate time standard based on an atomic clock in Paris. Coordinated Universal Time has individual "ticks" based on the atomic clock, but from time to time it inserts a "leap-second" at the end of a year (or at the end of June), or removes a second, to ensure that time on a global basis remains aligned with the earth's position in its orbit around the sun. This is, however, unlikely to affect any ASN.1 protocol!

What is the exact set of values of UTCTime? The values of the type are character strings of the following form:

```
yymmddhhmmZ
yymmddhhmmssZ
yymmddhhmm+hhmm
yymmddhhmm-hhmm
yymmddhhmmss+hhmm
yymmddhhmmss-hhmm
```

"yymmdd" is year (00 to 99), month (01 to 12), day (01 to 31), and "hhmmss" is hours (00 to 23), minutes (00 to 59), seconds (00 to 59).

The "Z" is a commonly used suffix on time values to indicate "Greenwich Mean Time" (or UTC time), others being "A" for one hour ahead, "Y" for one hour behind, etc., but these are **NOT** used in ASN.1.

If the "+hhmm" or "-hhmm" forms are used (called a *time differential*), then the first part of the value expresses **local** time, with UTC time obtained by **subtracting** the "hhmm" for "+hhmm", and **adding** it for "-hhmm". The ASN.1 specification contains the following example (another example, added in 1994 shows a "yy" of "01" representing 2001!):

```
If local time is 7am on 2 January 1982 and coordinated universal time
is 12 noon on 2 January 1982, the value of UTCTime is either of
```

```
"8201021200Z"

or

"8201020700-0500".
```

GeneralizedTime is the same overall format, but has a four-digit year, and allows "any of the precisions specified in ISO 8601".

GeneralizedTime is not without its problems, however. ISO Standards undergo revision from time to time, and referencing them from within another specification can allow things to change under your feet. It became clear in the mid-1990s that many people had implemented GeneralizedTime assuming that the maximum available precision for seconds was three digits after the decimal point (a millisecond). On closer inspection of ISO 8601 (current version), it is clear that **unlimited** precision is permitted—there is no restriction on the number of digits after the decimal point. It was an uncompleted homework task for the author to try to find earlier versions (and in particular the version current in 1982) of ISO 8601 to determine for how long an arbitrary precision had been permitted. Perhaps a reviewer will undertake the research? Otherwise it is left as another small exercise for the reader!

Another issue arising with both UTCTime and GeneralizedTime relates to canonical encodings: Should the different precisions be regarded as different encodings for the same abstract value (a given time) where trailing zeros are present ("8202021200Z" vs. "820202120000Z"), or as different abstract values (because precision is a part of the abstract information conveyed)? A similar question occurs with the time differential. It actually does not matter much which approach is taken, so long as those using canonical encoding rules know the answer. The current text says that the precision and time differential are different ways of encoding a time (a single abstract value), and that in canonical encoding rules, the time differential shall not be present (and the "Z" shall), and that there shall be no trailing zeros in the precision, so the example "8202022120000Z" is not legal in the canonical encoding rules. This is another area where arguments can continue over the precise set of abstract values of this type.

4.3 Additional Notational Constructs

4.3.1 The Selection-Type Notation

There is no example in Figure 4.1. I have seen "selection types" used in only one application specification.

The ASN.1 specification talks about "The selection type", but the heading in this clause is more accurate—this is a piece of notation more akin to "IMPORTS" than to a type definition and it references an existing definition.

> The SELECTION TYPE nota-
> tion—you are unlikely ever to
> see this—forget it!

The selection-type notation takes the following form:

```
identifier-of-a-choice-alternative < Type-notation-for-a-CHOICE
```

For example, given:

```
Example-choice ::= CHOICE
    {alt1    Type1,
     alt2    Type2,
     alt3    Type3}
```

then the following type-notation can be used wherever type-notation is required within the scope (module) in which "Example-choice" is available:

```
        alt1 < Example-choice
or      alt2 < Example-choice
or      alt3 < Example-choice
```

This notation references the type defined as the named alternative of the identified choice type, and should be seen as another form of type-reference-name. Notice that if the selection-type notation is in a module different from that in which "Example-choice" was originally defined, any tagging or extensibility environment applied to the referenced type is that of the module containing the original definition of Example-choice, **not** that of the selection-type notation.

Value notation for "a selection type" is just the value notation for the selected type.

In other words, for the type-notation "alt3 < Example-choice", the value-notation is the value-notation for "Type3". (The identifier "alt3" does not appear in the value-notation for the "selection type", nor are there any colons present.)

4.3.2 The COMPONENTS OF Notation

This is another example of a rarely used piece of notation that references the inner part of a sequence or set. The only reason to use it is that you can avoid an extra TLV wrapper in BER. It is not illustrated in Figure 4.1.

What follows is described in relation to "SEQUENCE", but applies equally to "SET". However, a "COMPONENTS OF" in a "SEQUENCE" must be followed by type-notation for a sequence-type (which remember may, and usually will, be a type-reference-name), and similarly for SET.

> The COMPONENTS OF nota-
> tion—you won't often see this
> either, so forget this too!

Suppose we have a collection of elements (identifiers and type-notation) that we want to include in quite a few of the sequence types in our application specification. Clearly we do not want to write them out several times, for all the obvious reasons. We could, of course, define a type:

```
Common-elements ::= SEQUENCE
    {element1    Type1,
     element2    Type2,
     ....
     element23   Type23}
```

and include that type as the first (or last) element of each of our "actual" sequences:

```
First-actual-sequence ::=  SEQUENCE
    {used-by-all   Common-elements,
     next-element Some-special-type,
     next-again    Special2,
     etc           The-last}
```

We do the same for all the sequences in which these common elements are needed. That is fine (and with PER it really **is** fine!). But with BER, if you recall the way it works, we get an outer-level TLV for "First-actual-sequence", and in the "V" part a TLV for each of its elements, and in particular a TLV for the "used-by-all" element. Within the "V" part of that we get the TLVs for the elements of "Common-elements". But if we had textually **copied** the body of "Common-elements" into "First-actual-sequence", there would be no TLV for "Common-elements"—we would have saved (with BER) two or three, perhaps even four, octets!

If we use "COMPONENTS OF", we can write:

```
First-actual-sequence ::=  SEQUENCE
    {              COMPONENTS OF Common-elements,
     next-element Some-special-type,
     next-again    Special2,
     etc           The-last}
```

The "COMPONENTS OF" notation provides for such copying without textually copying, it "unwraps" the sequence type it references.

Note that there is no identifier on the "COMPONENTS OF element". This is not optional—the "identifier" **must** be omitted. The "COMPONENTS OF" is not really an element of the SEQUENCE, it is a piece of notation that extracts or unwraps the elements. It is often referred to as "textual substitution", but that is not quite correct (alert reader!) because the tagging and extensibility environment for the extracted elements remains that of the module where they were originally defined.

There is some complexity if automatic tagging is applied and COMPONENTS OF is used. The reader has two choices: just forget it and note that it all works (unless you are a hand-coding implementor, in which case see the next option!), or as a good exercise (none are formally set in this book!) go to the ASN.1 specification and work out the answer!

> An application designer can generally choose to use SEQUENCE or SET more or less arbitrarily. Read this text then use SEQUENCE always!

4.3.3 SEQUENCE or SET?

The type-notation for SEQUENCE, SET, SEQUENCE OF and SET OF has been well illustrated in earlier text and examples, together with the use of "DEFAULT" and "OPTIONAL". Remember that in BER (not CER/DER/PER), the default value is essentially advisory. An encoder is permitted to encode explicitly a default value, or to omit the corresponding TLV, entirely as an encoder's option.

We have already discussed briefly the differences between

```
    SEQUENCE { .... }    and    SET { .... }
```

from an encoding point of view in BER (the TLVs are in textual order for SEQUENCE, in an order chosen by the encoder for SET), and also from the more theoretical standpoint that "order is not semantically significant" in SET.

The problem is that if we regard the abstract value as a collection of unordered information, and we want a single bit pattern to represent that in an encoding, we have to invent some more or less arbitrary criteria to order the collection in order to form a single bit-pattern encoding. This can make for expensive (in CPU and perhaps also in memory terms) encoding rules. In the case of SET { .... }, if we want to remove encoder options, it is possible to use either textual order (not really a good idea) or tag order (tags are required to be distinct among the elements in a SET) to provide the ordering as a static decision. However, in the case of "SET OF", no one has found a way of providing a single bit pattern for a complete SET OF value without doing a run-time sort of the encodings of each element. This can be expensive!

We will return to this point when we discuss the canonical (CER) and distinguished (DER) encoding rules in Section III, but advice today (but see figure 999!) would be: Best to keep off "SET {", and avoid "SET OF" like the plague!

One very small detail to mention here: the default tag provided for "SET {" and for "SET OF" is **the same**. It is different from that provided for "SEQUENCE {" and for "SEQUENCE OF", but these are also the same. This only matters if you are carefully applying tags within CHOICEs and SETs etc. with the minimal application of tags. In this case you will have studied and be happy with later text on tagging, and will carefully check the ASN.1 specification to determine the default tag for all types! If you are a normal mortal, however, you will routinely apply tags to everything (pre-1994), or will use "AUTOMATIC TAGS" (post-1994), and the fact that the default tag for "SEQUENCE {" is the same as that for "SEQUENCE OF" will not worry you in either case!

4.3.4 SEQUENCE, SET, and CHOICE (Etc.) Value-Notation

We have used the type notation for these constructions almost from the first page of this book, but now we need to look at their value-notation. (Actually, you will never encounter this except in courses or an illustrative annex to the ASN.1 specification, but it reinforces the point that for any type you can define with ASN.1 there is a well-defined notation for all of its values.)

To say it simply: value notation for "SET {" and "SEQUENCE {" is a pair of curly braces containing a comma-separated list. Each item in the list is the identifier for an element of the "SEQUENCE {" (taken in order) or

> **SEQUENCE, SET, CHOICE, Etc. Value-Notation**
>
> You won't ever need to write it, and will only ever read it in courses and ASN.1 tutorials and books like this, but here it is. It is good to complete your education!

"SET {" (in any order), followed by value-notation for a value of that element. Of course this rule is recursively applied if there are nested "SEQUENCE {" constructs.

For "SET OF" and "SEQUENCE OF" we again get a pair of curly braces containing a comma-separated list, with each item being the value notation for a value of the type-notation following the "OF".

Finally, for "CHOICE" it is NOT what you might expect, there are no curly braces! Instead you get the identifier of one of the alternatives, then a colon (:), then value

```
todays-return Return-of-sales ::=
     {version                  {version2},
      no-of-days-reported-on   8,
      time-and-date-of-report
                    two-digit-year:"9901022359Z",
      reason-for-delay  {network-failure},
          -- additional-information not included
      sales-data
          {--Report-item 1:
           {item                   {wineco-items  special-tiop (112)},
            item-description     "Special Reserve Purchase Tio Pepe",
            -- A newly-stocked item.
            bar-code-data         'A0B98764934174CDF'H,
            -- ran-out-of-stock is defaulted to FALSE.
            min-stock-level      {mantissa 2056, base 10, exponent -2},
            max-stock-level      {mantissa 100, base 10, exponent 0},
            average-stock-level  {mantissa 7025, base 10, exponent -2} }

           --Report-item 2:
           {item                   {wineco-items own-dry-sherry (19)},
            bar-code-data         'A0B897632910DFE974'H,
            ran-out-of-stock      TRUE,
            min-stock-level      {mantissa 0, base 10, exponent 1},
            max-stock-level      {mantissa 105, base 10, exponent 0},
            average-stock-level  {mantissa 5032, base 10, exponent -2}  }
      --Only two report items in this illustration
                                          }     }
```

Figure 4.2   A value for "return-of-sales".

notation for a value of that alternative. There is no value notation for any occurrence of tags, nor for extensibility markers or exception specifications. The colon in choice values was not present prior to the 1994 ASN.1 Standards.

This should be sufficient for the reader to work through Figure 4.2, which is cast as "todays-return" a (random) value for the type "Return-of-sales" given in Figure 4.1.

4.4 What Else Is in X.680/ISO 8824-1?

This chapter has attempted to cover "Basic ASN.1"—the material present in the first of the four documents specifying the ASN.1 notation, and in common use in specifications today. There is, however, some additional material in this first of the ASN.1 documents that has been deferred to later chapters. For completeness of this chapter, this is briefly mentioned here.

The additional areas include:

- **Extensibility and version brackets:** This is a big subject, touched on briefly already, and first introduced in 1994. (Exception specifications are a related subject, but do not appear in X.680; they are in X.682 and are also treated later.)

- **Tagging:** Touched on briefly already. This was important in the past, but with the introduction of automatic tagging in 1994 is much less important now.

- **The object identifier type:** This was fully covered in X.680/ISO 8824-1 pre-1998, but parts of the material are now split off into another Recommendation/Standard. Previous chapters of this book produced a lot of introductory material, but the discussion remains incomplete!

- **Hole types:** This term is used for the more formal ASN.1 terms EXTERNAL, EMBEDDED PDV, CHARACTER STRING, and "Open Types" (post-1994). And dare we mention ANY and ANY DEFINED BY (pre-1994)? If you have never heard of ANY or ANY DEFINED BY, that is a good thing. But you will have to be sullied by later text—sorry!

- **The character string types:** There are about a dozen different types for carrying strings of characters from various world-wide character sets. So far we have met PrintableString, VisibleString, GraphicString, and UTF8String, and discussed them briefly. There is a lot more to say!

- **Subtyping, or constrained types:** This is a big area, with treatment split between X.680/ISO 8824-1 and X.682/ISO 8824-3. We have already seen an example of it with the range constraint "(1..56)" on "no-of-days-reported-on" in Figure 4.1. This form is the one you will most commonly encounter or want to use, but there are many other powerful notations available if you have need of them.

- **Macros:** We have to end this chapter on an obscenity! Some reviewers said, "Don't dirty the book with this word!" But macros were **very** important (and valued) in ASN.1 up to the late 1980s, and will still be frequently encountered today. But I hope none of you will be driven to writing one! Sections I and II will not tell you much more about macros, but the historical material in Section IV discusses their introduction and development over the life of ASN.1. It is a fascinating story.

Additionally, there are a number of new concepts and notations that appear in X.681/ISO 8824-2, X.682/ISO 8824-3, and X.683/ISO 8824-4 (published in 1994). These are: information object classes (including information object definition and information object sets); and parameterization.

Where the preceding items have already been introduced (in this chapter or earlier), their detailed treatment is left to a chapter of Section II. Where they have not yet been discussed, a brief introduction appears in the following short chapter.

## CHAPTER 5

Reference to More Complex Areas

(Or: There Is Always More to Learn!)

Summary

This chapter provides an introduction to concepts and notation that are treated more fully in Section II. Some of these features have been briefly mentioned already, but without a full treatment. This includes

- Object identifiers,

- Character string types,

- Subtyping,

- Tagging, and

- Extensibility, exceptions, and version brackets.

Other topics that are introduced here for the first time are

- Hole types,

- Macros,

- Information object classes and objects and object sets,

- Other types of constraint,

- Parameterization, and

- The ASN.1 semantic model.

An introduction is provided here for the reader who wishes to ignore Section II. **As of mid-1999, there are no areas or concepts concerned with the ASN.1 notation that have not been at least introduced by the end of this chapter.**

The aim of the text in this chapter is

- to describe the concept and the problem that is being addressed,

- to illustrate where necessary key aspects of the notational support so that the presence of these features in a published protocol can be easily recognized, and

- to summarize the additional text available in Section II.

If further detail is needed on a particular topic (if something takes the reader's interest), then the appropriate chapter in Section II can be consulted. The chapter in Section II provides "closure" on all items mentioned in this chapter unless otherwise stated.

5.1 Object Identifiers

The OBJECT IDENTIFIER type was briefly introduced in Chapter 4 (4.2.9), where the broad purpose and use of this type was explained (with the type notation). Examples of its value notation have appeared throughout the text, although these have not completely illustrated all possible forms of this value notation.

A more detailed discussion of the form of the object identifier tree (the name-space) is given in Chapter 8 together with a full treatment of the possible forms of OJECT IDENTIFIER value notation.

Earlier text has given enough for a normal understanding of this type and the ability to read existing specifications. It is only if you feel you need some object identifier name-space and do not know how to go about getting some that the "Further Details" material will be useful. This material also contains some discussion about the (legal) object identifier value notation that omits all names and uses numbers only, and about the (contentious) value notation where different names are associated with components, depending on where the value is being published and/or the nature of lower arcs.

> OBJECT IDENTIFIERs have a simple type notation, and a value notation that has already been seen. The "Further Details" chapter tells you about the form of the name-space and how to get some, and provides discussion of the value notation.

5.2 Character String Types

The names of types whose values are strings of characters from some particular character repertoire have appeared throughout the earlier text, and Chapter 4 (4.2.8) discussed in some detail the type notations

```
PrintableString

 isibleString

ISO646String

UTF8String
```

although the treatment introduced terms such as "Unicode" that may be unfamiliar to some readers.

> There are many more character string types than you have met so far, and mechanisms for constructing custom types and types where the character repertoire is not defined until run-time. The value notation provides both a simple "quoted string" mechanism and a more complex mechanism to deal with "funny" characters.

There has also been little treatment so far of the value notation for these types, nor has the precise set of characters in each repertoire been identified fully.

Chapter 9 provides a full treatment of the value notation and provides references to the precise definitions of the character repertoires for all character string types. Chapter 9 describes the following additional character string types that you will encounter in published specifications (all the character string types are used in at least one published specification):

```
NumericString

IA5String

TeletexString

T61String

 ideotexString

GraphicString

GeneralString

UniversalString

BMPString

UTF8String
```

The simplest value notation for the character string types is simply the actual characters enclosed in quotation marks (the ASCII character QUOTATION MARK, usually represented as two vertical lines in the upper quartile of the character glyph).

For example,

```
"This is an example character string value"
```

The (alert—I hope we still have some!) reader will ask four questions:

- How do I express characters appearing in character string values that are not in the character set repertoire used to publish the ASN.1 specification? (Publication of ASN.1 specifications as ASCII text is common.)

- How do I include the ASCII QUOTATION MARK character (") in a character string value?

- Can I split long character string values across several lines in a published specification?

- How do I define precisely the white-space characters and control characters in a character string value?

These are topics addressed in the "Further Details" section.

In summary:

- A QUOTATION MARK character is included by the presence of adjacent quotation marks (a very common technique in programming languages).

- ASN.1 provides (by reference to character set standards), names for all the characters in the world (the names of these characters use only ASCII characters), and a value notation that allows the use of these names.

- Cell references are also available for ISO 646 and for ISO 10646 to provide precise specification of the different forms of white-space and of control characters appearing in ASCII.

An example of a more complex piece of character string value notation described in the "Further Details" is,

```
{ nul, {0,0,4,29}, cyrillicCapitalLetterIe, "ABC"}
```

go to "Further Details" if you want to know what that represents!

The preceding provision is, however, not the end of the story. If UniversalString or BMPString or UTF8String are used, then ASN.1 has built-in names (again defined by reference to character set standards) for about 80 so-called "collections" of characters. Here are the names of some of these collections:

```
BasicLatin

BasicGreek

Cyrillic

Katakana

IpaExtensions

MathematicalOperators

ControlPictures

Dingbats
```

Formally, these collections are subsets (subtypes—see 5.3) of the BMPString type, and it is possible to build custom character string types using combinations of these pre-defined types.

Chapter 9 provides full coverage of these features, but a more detailed discussion of the form and historical progression of character set standardization is presented in Section IV ("History and Applications"). Readers interested in gaining a full understanding of this area may wish to read the relevant chapter in Section IV before reading the Section II chapter.

Finally, ASN.1 also includes the type:

```
CHARACTER STRING
```

that can be included in a SEQUENCE or SET (for example) to denote a field that will contain a character string, but without (at this stage) determining either the character repertoire or the encoding.

This is an incomplete specification or "hole", and is covered in Chapter 14. If this character string type is used, both the repertoire and the encoding are determined by announcement (or if the OSI stack is in use, by negotiation) at run-time, but can be constrained by additional specification using "constraints" (see 5.9), either at primary specification time, or by "profiles" (additional specifications produced by some group that reduces options in a base standard).

5.3 Subtyping

There has been little discussion of this subject so far. We have seen an example of:

```
INTEGER (1..56)
```

to specify an integer type containing only a subset of the integer values—those in the range from 1 to 56 inclusive. This is called "simple subtyping" and was provided in the ASN.1 Specifications from about 1986 onward.

Simple subtyping enables a subset of the values of any ASN.1 type to be selected to define a new type, using a variety of quite powerful mechanisms. Note that an abstract syntax (the set of abstract values that can be communicated) for a "Full Class" protocol is normally defined as the set of values of a single ASN.1 type (see

> From simple subtyping through to relational constraints. ASN.1 provides powerful mechanisms for selecting a subset of the values of an ASN.1 type, and (in PER) for encoding that selected subset in a very efficient manner.

1.21, 1.2.3, 1.3, and 3.4). If a "Basic Class" protocol is needed, then this can conveniently be defined as a subset of those values. The "simple subtyping" mechanisms described in Chapter 10 contain enough power to enable such a specification to be formally provided using the ASN.1 notation.

An example of a more complex form of subtyping would be:

```
Basic-Ordering-Class  ::=  Wineco-Protocol
    (WITH COMPONENTS
        ordering (Basic-Order) PRESENT,
        sales                  ABSENT } )
```

Note that all subtyping (and application of constraints—see the next paragraph) is done by syntax which is enclosed in round parentheses and follows some piece of type notation (frequently a type reference name).

It is, however, possible to also view the notation

```
INTEGER (1..56)
```

as putting a **constraint** on the integer field, and this gives rise to considerations of what is to be done if the constraint is violated in received material. (This should normally only occur if the sender has implemented a later version of the protocol where the constraint has been relaxed. This is covered in Chapter 12 and introduced in 5.5 following.

A number of other forms of constraint were introduced into ASN.1 in 1994 related to constraining what can fill in a "hole", or to relating the contents of that "hole" to the value of some other field. These other forms of constraint are covered in Chapter 13.

5.4 Tagging

Earlier text has dipped in and out of tagging, but has never given a full treatment. The TLV concept (which underlies tagging) was introduced in 1.5.2 and further text on ASN.1 tagging appeared in 2.2.7 and 3.3.2, where tagging was described entirely in relation to the TLV encoding philosophy, and the concepts of "implicit tagging" and "explicit tagging" were introduced.

Some mention has also been made of different "classes" of tag, with syntactic constructs such as

```
[3] INTEGER

My-Useful-Type ::= [APPLICATION 4] SEQUENCE { .... }

[PRI ATE 4] INTEGER

[UNI ERSAL 25] GraphicString
```

Up to 1994, getting your tags right was fundamental to writing a correct specification. Post-1994, AUTOMATIC TAGS in the module header enables them to be forgotten. So details are relegated to Section II. If you want to read and understand a specification (or even to implement one), you already know enough about the tag concept, but if you want to take control of your tags (as you had to pre-1994), you will need the Section II material.

Chapter 11

- gives a full treatment of the different classes of tag,

- provides an abstract model of types and values that makes the concepts of explicit and implicit tagging meaningful, even if encoding rules are being employed that are not TLV-based,

- discusses matters of style in the choice of tag-class used in a specification, and

- gives the detailed rules on when tags on different elements of sets and sequences or alternatives of choices are required to be distinct.

5.5 Extensibility, Exceptions, and Version Brackets

The first two terms—extensibility and exceptions—have been mentioned in several places already.

Clause 2 of the Introduction defined "extensibility" as the means of providing interworking between deployed "version 1" systems and "version 2" systems that are designed and deployed many years later.

If a very great provision is made for extensibility, then almost every element in an encoding has to be "wrapped up" with a length field and an identification, even when both parties (if they know the full specification) are perfectly aware that

> You will recognize the use of extensibility provision by an ellipsis (three dots), of exception specification by the use of an exclamation mark (!), and of version brackets by the use of an adjacent pair of open square brackets with a matching adjacent pair of closing square brackets.

these are fixed values. In other words, we are forced into a "TLV" (see 1.5.2) style of encoding. If, however, we restrict the places where a version 2 specification can add new material (and wrap up only the new version 2 material), we can produce a much more efficient encoding. This is provided by the Packed Encoding Rules (PER).

The extension marker was briefly introduced in 3.3.3, page 61, together with the exception specification that identifies actions that version 1 systems should take with any added material.

Chapter 12

- expands on the Chapter 3 text,

- describes all the places where extension markers can be placed,

- illustrates the exception specification, and

- introduces and describes the concept of "version brackets".

When extensibility provision was first introduced into ASN.1, every added sequence or set element was "wrapped up", but later it became apparent that this was not necessary—all that needed "wrapping up" was the totality of the material added in this place in the new version. Hence we have the concept of bracketing

```
SEQUENCE
    {field1   TypeA,
     field2   TypeB,
     ... ! PrintableString : "See clause 59",
     -- The following is handled by old systems
     -- as specified in clause 59.
     [[ v2-field1   Type2A,
        v2-field2   Type2B ]],
     [[ v3-field1   Type3A,
        v3-field2   Type3B ]],
     ... ,
     -- The following is version 1 material.
            field3   TypeC}
```

Figure 5.1   Illustration of extensibility markers and version brackets.

this material together with so-called "version brackets". This is illustrated in Figure 5.1, which is repeated and described more fully in Chapter 12.

Notice that it is not mandatory to include version brackets. If they are absent the effect is as if each element of the sequence had been added separately in a succession of versions.

Note also that if there is no further version 1 material ("field3 TypeC" in Figure 5.1 is not present), then the final ellipsis is not required, and will frequently be omitted.

5.6 Hole Types

Clause 2.2.1 introduced the concept of "holes": parts of a specification left undefined to allow other groups to "customize" the specification to their needs, or to provide a carrier mechanism for a wide variety of other types of material.

> You can leave a hole by using one of several ASN.1 types, but it may be better to use Information Object Classes instead!

In general, specifiers can insert in their protocols any ASN.1 type and leave the semantics to be associated with values of that type undefined. This would constitute a "hole". Thus "holes" can in principle be provided using INTEGER or PrintableString! But usually when specifiers leave a "hole", they want the container to be capable of carrying an arbitrary bit-pattern. Thus using OCTET STRING or BIT STRING to form a "hole" would be more common. This is generally not recommended, as there are specific ASN.1 types that are introduced to clearly identify the presence of a hole, and in some cases to provide an associated identification field that will identify the material in the "hole".

Provision for "holes" has been progressively enriched during the life of ASN.1, and some of the early mechanisms are disparaged now. The following are the types normally regarded as "hole" types, and are described fully in Chapter 14:

```
ANY (removed in 1994)

ANY DEFINED BY (removed in 1994)

EXTERNAL (deprecated)

EMBEDDED PDV

CHARACTER STRING
```

5.7 Macros

ASN.1 contained (from 1984 to 1994) a very complex piece of syntax called "the macro notation". It was removed in 1994, with equivalent (but much improved) facilities provided by the "Information Object Class" and related concepts (see below).

Many languages, graphics packages, and word processors have a macro facility. The name "macro" is very respectable. However, the use of this term in ASN.1 bears very little relationship to its use in these other packages. Section IV says a little more about what macros are all about. You

There is much controversy surrounding macros. They were part of ASN.1 for its first decade, but produced many problems, and were replaced by Information Object Classes in 1994. You will not often see text defining a macro (and should certainly not write any today), but you may still see in older specifications text whose form depends on a macro definition imported into a module.

are unlikely to meet the definition of a macro (use of the macro notation) in specifications that you read, but Figure 5.2 illustrates the general structure (the four dots representing further text whose form is defined by the macro notation specification).

```
MY-MACRO MACRO ::=
         BEGIN
                 TYPE NOTATION ::= ....
                 ....
                 VALUE NOTATION ::= ....
                 ....
         END
```

Figure 5.2 The structure of a macro definition.

This piece of syntax can appear anywhere in a module where a type reference assignment can occur, and the name of the macro (conventionally always in uppercase) can be (and usually is) exported from the module for use in other modules.

The macro notation is the only part of ASN.1 that is not covered fully in this book! Readers of this book should NEVER write macros! However, you will encounter modules that **import** a macro name and then have syntax that is an invocation of that macro. Again, a macro invocation can appear anywhere that a type definition can appear.

One standard that contains a lot of "holes" is called "Remote Operations Service Element (ROSE)." ROSE defines (and exports) a macro called the OPERATION macro to enable its users to provide sets of information to complete the ROSE protocol. A typical piece of syntax that uses the OPERATION macro would look like Figure 5.3 (but most real examples are much longer).

To fully understand this you need some knowledge of ROSE. A brief description of ROSE is given in Chapter 14, partly because of its widespread use, but mainly because it provides good illustrations of macro use, Information Object Class specification, and exception handling.

The OPERATION macro definition was replaced in the 1994 ROSE specification by specification of an OPERATION Information Object Class, and specifications including syntax like Figure 5.3 are gradually being changed to make use of the OPERATION Information Object Class instead.

5.8 Information Object Classes and Objects and Object Sets

When protocol specifiers leave "holes" in their specification, frequently there are several such holes, and the users of the specification need to provide information of a specified nature to fill in these holes. Most of the uses of the macro notation were to enable these users to have a notation to specify this additional information.

```
lookup   OPERATION
            ARGUMENT  IA5String
            RESULT   OCTET STRING
            ERRORS  {invalidName, nameNotFound}
                  ::= 1
```

Figure 5.3   An example of use of the ROSE OPERATION macro.

The Information Object Class concept recognizes that specifiers leaving "holes" need to clearly identify where these holes are, but more particularly to be able to list the information required to complete the "hole". In the simplest case, the information needed will be a set of ASN.1 types (with their associated semantics) that can fill the hole, together with either an integer or an object identifier value that is associated with that type and its semantics. The identifier will be carried in the carrier protocol, as well as a value of the type.

> Information Object Classes (with objects and object sets) was the main addition to the ASN.1 notation in 1994, replacing macros with a much enhanced functionality.
>
> Details in these areas are given in Section II, but an increasing number of old specifications are being revised to use this notation, and most new specifications use it.
>
> These areas are important!

ASN.1 provides a syntax for defining the form of information to be collected. This is illustrated in Figure 5.4.

Note the use of the "&" character. This is the only place that "&" is used in ASN.1, and its presence is a clear indication that you need to read the Section II material on Information Object Classes! (See Chapter 8, beginning on page 157.)

> Table constraints, relational constraints—the way to constrain holes in a manner consistent with the definition of an Information Object Set. Go to Section II.
>
> User-defined constraints—a catch-all for any other constraint that you need!

Once a specifier has defined an Information Object Class (and typically exported the reference name), users can then define sets of objects of that class, and link them into the base protocol. This is amplified and illustrated in Section II.

5.9 Other Types of Constraint

There are forms of constraint that are a little more complex than the simple

```
MY-CLASS ::= CLASS
        {&Type-to-fill-hole,
         &identifier  INTEGER}
```

Figure 5.4 Notation to define an Information Object Class.

subtyping discussed earlier. They are called "table constraints", "relational constraints", and "user-defined" constraints. The first two are closely related to the use of a defined set of information objects to fill in holes in a consistent manner. The latter relates to specification of hole contents that cannot be done in a wholly formal manner within the ASN.1 notation. Like simple subtyping, these constraints always appear in round brackets following a type name (or a hole specification). They are illustrated and described in Section II.

5.10 Parameterization

The ability to parameterize an ASN.1 specification is a very simple but extremely powerful mechanism. It was introduced in 1994. The concept of dummy parameters of functions or methods in a programming language is quite common, with actual parameters being supplied when the function or method is invoked.

In a similar way, an ASN.1 type reference name can be given dummy parameters, with actual parameters being supplied when that type is used.

For example,

```
My-Type {INTEGER:dummy1, Dummy2} ::=
        SEQUENCE
            {first-field  Dummy2,
             second-field  INTEGER (1..dummy1) }
```

Parameterization—very simple but very powerful. All ASN.1 reference names can have a dummy parameter list; actual parameters are supplied when they are used.

Here "My-Type" has two dummy parameters—the first an integer used to provide a bound on "second-field," and a second that provides the type for the first field. Typically, My-Type will be used in several different places in the total specification, with different actual parameters in each case.

Parameterization is an important tool to enable the linking of Information Object Sets defined by user groups into the holes left by the original specifier, although its use is wider than this.

5.11 The ASN.1 Semantic Model

There are many places in ASN.1 where the phrase "must be of the same type as" appears. For example, if a dummy parameter is the value of some type, then the actual parameter "must be of the same type as the dummy parameter". A value following DEFAULT "must be of the same type as the type preceding the word DEFAULT". It is clear that if the types in question are the same type-reference name, then they "are the same type". But suppose the two types in question are specified with textually distinct but identical text? Or textually distinct but with some minor variations in the text? Are they still "the same type"? What "minor variations" might be permit-

> Abstractions, abstractions, models, models. Everybody has their own.
>
> But sometimes they need to be explicit in order to express clearly what is legal and what is not.

ted? ASN.1 text up to 1999 had little to say to clarify these questions! Fortunately, difficult cases rarely appear in real specifications, but writers of ASN.1 tools do need to know what is legal and what is not (or to make assumptions themselves)!

An attempt was made in 1990 to remove all such phrases and provide more rigor in these areas, but it proved impossible to get agreement on satisfactory text in time, and at the last minute text for the 1994 specification reverted back to the original "must be of the same type".

Work in this area, however, continued. It was recognized that to solve the problem there needed to be a well-defined "abstract model" or "mental model" or "semantic model" (the latter term was eventually chosen) to define the underlying abstractions that were represented by a piece of ASN.1 text, with the starting point being the concept of a type as a container of a set of abstract values as first described in Chapter 1 (1.3.1).

At the time of this writing (early 1999), the work is complete and agreement reached; and publication is expected later in 1999.

5.12 Conclusion

This completes the discussion of the ASN.1 notation for Section I "ASN.1 Overview" (the remaining chapters discuss ASN.1 tools and management and design issues). If more detail is needed on any of the topics that have not been fully described in this section, then the appropriate chapter of Section II should be consulted. These are largely independent, and can be taken in any order.

For more details about Encoding Rules, see Section III, and for a history of the development of ASN.1 and some of its applications, see Section IV.

## CHAPTER 6

Using an ASN.1 Compiler

(Or: What It Is All About: Producing the Bits on the Line!)

Summary

This chapter

- describes approaches to implementation of ASN.1-defined protocols,

- briefly describes what needs to be done if an ASN.1 compiler is not available,

- describes in detail the concept and operation of an ASN.1 compiler,

- illustrates the implementation process (when using an ASN.1 compiler), with examples of programming language structures produced by the "OSS ASN.1 Tools" product, and

- discusses what to look for when seeking a "best buy" in an ASN.1 compiler.

This chapter discusses implementation architectures, strategy, and so on. Therefore, it is inevitably incomplete and partial. The issues discussed are not standardized, and different implementors will produce different approaches. It is also the case that what is "best" on one platform may well not be "best" on a different platform.

This chapter also gives an insight into the implementation of protocols specified using ASN.1, but much of the detail depends on knowledge of programming languages such as C and Java, and knowledge of BER encodings that are covered in Section III. Nonetheless, those without such knowledge can still gain useful information from this chapter. But if you are not a programmer, read 6.1 then skip the rest completely!

6.1 The Route to an Implementation

We discussed in Chapter 1 (1.5.6) (and illustrated it in Figure 1.12) the implementation process using an ASN.1 compiler. Before reading this chapter, you may wish to review that material. You simply "compile" your ASN.1 into a programming language of your choice, include the compiler output with application code that deals with the semantics of

> It's all so simple with a compiler!

the application, (really) compile and link. Your own code reads/writes language data-structures, and you call ENCODE/DECODE run-time routines provided by the ASN.1 compiler vendor when necessary (and provide an interface to your lower-layer APIs.)

That is actually all you need to know, but if you want some more detail, read on!

6.2 What Is an ASN.1 Compiler?

We all know what "a compiler" normally means—a program that reads in the text of a program written in a high-level language and turns it into instructions that can be loaded into computer memory and obeyed by some particular computer hardware, usually involving a further linking-loader stage to incorporate run-time libraries.

> What does it mean to "compile" a data-structure definition?

But ASN.1 is not a programming language. It is a language for defining data structures, so how can you "compile" ASN.1?

The term compiler is a little bit of a misnomer, but was first used to distinguish very advanced tools supporting the implementation of ASN.1-defined protocols from early tools that provided little more than a syntax-checking and pretty-print capability. In the rest of this chapter, we will use the term "ASN.1-compiler-tool", rather than "compiler".

There are several ways of implementing a protocol defined using ASN.1. The three main options are discussed in the following text.

- Write all necessary code to encode and decode values in an ad hoc way. This is only suitable for the very simplest ASN.1 specifications, and leaves you with the full responsibility for debugging your encoding code, and for ensuring that you have the ability to handle all options on decoding. (The same statement would apply to character-based protocols defined using BNF, where there are some tools to help you, but they do not provide anything like as much support as an ASN.1-compiler-tool with an ASN.1-based specification.) We will not discuss this option further.

- Use a pre-built and pre-tested set of general-purpose library routines with invocations such as

```
encode_untagged_int (int_val, output_buffer)
```

However, the above is just about the simplest invocation you will get. In most cases you will also want to provide an implicit or explicit tag (of one of three possible classes), and for constructed types such as SEQUENCE, support in this way can become quite complex. This approach also only really works well with BER, where constraints are irrelevant and there is a relatively rigid encoding of tags and lengths. This approach pre-dated the development of ASN.1-compiler-tools, and is discussed a little further later.

- Use an ASN.1-compiler-tool that lets you put values into a programming language data-structure corresponding to your ASN.1 type (and generated by the ASN.1-compiler-tool automatically from your ASN.1 type). Then make a single invocation of "encode" when you have all your values in place, to produce a complete encoding of the value of that type. This provides the simplest implementation, with the least constraints on the structure of the application code, and is the approach discussed most in this chapter. It works equally well for PER, DER and CER as it does for BER, and makes maximum use of tested and debugged code for all aspects of encoding.

However, remember that we usually have to decode as well as to encode. In the case of the third option (use of an ASN.1-compiler-tool), decoding is no more difficult than encoding. Run-time routines provided by the ASN.1-compiler-tool will take an encoding of the value of an ASN.1 type and set all the fields of the programming language data-structure corresponding to that type.

With the middle option, encoding is basically a series of invocations of appropriate library routines, but for decoding there is the further problem of parsing the received bit-string into a tree structure of primitive values, and then tree-walking this parse tree to find the primitive values. Again, this is more easily possible with BER than with PER, because with BER the parse tree can be constructed without knowledge of the type of the value being decoded.

The use of a library of encode routines and of a parse tree are discussed (briefly), but this chapter concentrates mainly on the use of an ASN.1-compiler-tool, as this provides a simple approach to implementation of ASN.1-based specifications, with effectively a 100% guarantee (assuming the ASN.1-compiler-tool is bug-free!) that

- only correct encodings of values will be produced, and

- no correct encoding will "blow" the decoder, with values being correctly extracted from all possible correct encodings.

As an illustration of what ASN.1-compiler-tools produce, we will use a part of our wineco specification, that for "Return-of-sales", which references "Report-item". These were shown first in Figure 4.1 (part 2) in Chapter 4, and are repeated here without the comments. The C and Java structures and classes produced by the "OSS ASN.1 Tools" product (a good example of an ASN.1-compiler-tool product) are given in Appendices 3 and 4, and those familiar with C and Java may wish to compare these structures and classes with Figure 6.1. (The "OSS ASN.1 Tools" product also provides mappings to C++, but we do not illustrate that in this book—it is too big already!)

```
Return-of-sales ::= SEQUENCE
   {version        BIT STRING
         {version1 (0), version2 (1)} DEFAULT {version1},
    no-of-days-reported-on   INTEGER
         {week(7), month (28), maximum (56)} (1..56)
         DEFAULT week,
    time-and-date-of-report   CHOICE
         {two-digit-year   UTCTime,
          four-digit-year GeneralizedTime},
    reason-for-delay   ENUMERATED
      {computer-failure, network-failure, other} OPTIONAL,
    additional-information
            SEQUENCE OF PrintableString OPTIONAL,
    sales-data  SET OF Report-item,
    ... ! PrintableString : "See wineco manual chapter 15" }
Report-item ::= SEQUENCE
   {item                 OBJECT IDENTIFIER,
    item-description      ObjectDescriptor OPTIONAL,
    bar-code-data         OCTET STRING,
    ran-out-of-stock      BOOLEAN DEFAULT FALSE,
    min-stock-level       REAL,
    max-stock-level       REAL,
    average-stock-level REAL}
```

Figure 6.1 An example to be implemented.

6.3 The Overall Features of an ASN.1-Compiler-Tool

An ASN.1-compiler-tool is composed of a "compiler", application-independent programming language text to be included with your implementation (for C, this is .H and .C files), and libraries to be linked into your final executable. For some platforms, the compiler may also emit text that has to be compiled to produce a DLL that will be used at run-time.

> This does it all. Take your ASN.1 type. "Compile" it into a language data-structure. Populate it with values. Call ENCODE. Done! Decoding is just as easy.

The overall pattern is that the "compiler" phase takes in ASN.1 modules, and produces two main outputs. These are

- data-structure definitions (for the language you have chosen) that correspond to the ASN.1 type, and

- source text (for the language you have chosen), which will eventually produce either tables or code that the run-time routines in the supplied libraries can use to perform encode/decode operations, given only pointers to this information and to the in-core representation of the values to be encoded (and a handle for the buffer to encode into). This text includes all details of tagging in your ASN.1 types, so you never need to worry about tags in your implementation code.

For some platforms, the situation can be just a bit more complex. The compiler may output text that you must compile to produce a DLL for use by your application.

The next section examines the use of a simple library of encode/decode routines, and describes the output from the "compiler" part of the "OSS ASN.1 Tools" compiler, and then the use of that tool.

> A library of encode/decode routines (one for each ASN.1 type) is better than nothing. But complications arise in the handling of nested SEQUENCE types etc., particularly in relation to length fields.

6.4 Use of a Simple Library of Encode/Decode Routines

The earliest support for ASN.1 implementations (after simple syntax checkers and "pretty print" programs had been produced) was a library of routines that helped in the generation of BER tag (identifier) fields, BER length fields, and the encoding of BER primitive types.

Some implementations today still use this approach. It is better than doing everything from scratch!

The approach is described in terms of a BER encoding. For a PER encoding it tends to work rather less well, and the ASN.1-compiler-tool approach would be more appropriate here.

6.4.1 Encoding

Encoding of untagged primitive items is trivial, but add tagging and add constructed types with nesting of SEQUENCE OF within SEQUENCE within another SEQUENCE OF (etc.), and . . . well, life is not quite so simple if all you have available is a library that only does identifier and length encodings for you (and encodings of primitive values).

> Encoding using a library of routines can get messy, because you often need to know the length of an encoding before you encode it!

Before the emergence of ASN.1-compiler-tools, a common approach to encoding a sequence such as "Report-item" (see Figure 6.1) would be to have code looking something like that in Figure 6.2 (using pseudo-code).

Here we assume we have routines available in a library we have purchased that will take a value of any given ASN.1 primitive type (using some datatype in the language capable of supporting that primitive type) and returning an encoding in a buffer. Finally, we call another library routine that will put all the buffers together (note the copying that is involved here) and will generate the "T" and the "L" for a SEQUENCE (assuming we are using BER), returning the final coding in buffer_y.

Clearly, if we have more complex nested structures in our ASN.1, this can become quite messy unless we are using a programming language that allows full recursion. We have effectively hardwired the ASN.1 structure into the structure of our code, making possible changes to version 2 of the protocol more difficult.

There are some things that can be done to eliminate some of the copying. Part of the problem is that we cannot generate the BER octets for the length octets of a SEQUENCE until we have encoded all the elements of that sequence and counted the length of that encoding.

```
Get value for "item" into x1
encode-oid (x1 , buffer_x[1] )
Get value for "item-description" into x2
encode_obje_desc ( x2, buffer_x[2] )
Get "bar-code-data" into x3
encode_octet_str ( x3, buffer_x[3] )
Get "ran-out-stock" value into x4
IF x4 is true THEN
encode_boolean ( true, buffer_x[4] )
ELSE
Set buffer_x[4] to an empty string
END IF
....
etc, encoding the last item into buffer_x[7] say.
....
encode-sequence (buffer_x, 1, 7, buffer_y)
-- This encodes the contents of buffer_x from 1 to 7
-- into buffer_y with a "SEQUENCE" wrapper.
-- Note that in practice the SEQUENCE may be tagged
-- resulting in a more complicated calling sequence
Pass buffer_y to lower layers for transmission.
Clear buffer_x, buffer_y
```

Figure 6.2   Pseudo-code to encode "Report-item".

For encoding a SEQUENCE there are (at least!) four ways to reduce/eliminate this problem of having to copy encodings from one buffer to another. These are:

- Do a "trial encoding" which just does enough to determine the length of each element of the sequence (this really needs to be a recursive call if our structure involves many levels of SEQUENCE or SEQUENCE OF), then generate the SEQUENCE header into the final buffer, then encode each of the SEQUENCE elements into that buffer.

- Use the indefinite length form, in which case we can generate the sequence header into our final buffer and then encode into that buffer each of the elements of the sequence, with a pair of zeros at the end.

- Use the "trick" of allocating space for a long-form length encoding that is a length of length equal to 2, followed by two blank octets that we will fill in later once the length is known, and then encode each element into the same final buffer.

- Use (assuming it is available!) a "gather" capability in the interface to lower-layer software that enables you to pass a chain of buffers to that software, rather than a single contiguous piece of memory.

These approaches have been shown to work well for BER, but for CER/DER/PER, they can be either not possible (CER/DER demands minimum octets for length encoding) or more difficult/complex.

6.4.2 Decoding

Decoding using library routines is not quite so easy. You need a general-purpose parser—relatively easy for BER (less easy for PER), tree-walking code, and then the basic decode routines for primitive types. This rather parallels what you have to do with character-based encodings—but with character-based encodings you need a quite sophisticated tool to split the incoming character string (based on input of the BNF) into a tree-structure of "leaf" components for processing. Producing a parse tree of BER is rather easier.

In general, use of a simple library of encode-decode routines with ASN.1 is neither complex nor more simple than use of parsers for character-based protocols defined using BNF,

> For decoding you need a general-purpose parser, then you tree-walk. The library approach is easier with BER than with PER as the TLV structure is independent of the data-type.

although it is arguable that the original ASN.1 definition is more readable to a "layman" than a BNF description of a character-based protocol.

It is also the case that parsing an incoming BER encoding into a tree-structure (where each leaf is a primitive type) is a great deal easier than producing a syntax tree from a character-based encoding defined using BNF.

Decode implementations for BER can take advantage of the use of bit 6 of the identifier octets to identify whether the following "V" part is constructed, enabling application-independent code to produce a tree-structure with primitive types at the leaves. That tree-structure is then "walked" by the application-specific code to determine the values that have been received.

This "library of useful routines" approach is certainly better than doing everything from scratch! But things are so much simpler with an ASN.1-compiler-tool as described below.

6.5 Using an ASN.1-Compiler-Tool
6.5.1 Basic Considerations

An ASN.1-compiler-tool makes everything much more of a one-step process (for the user of the tool). All the decisions on how to encode (copying buffers, doing trial encodings, using indefinite length, using long-form definite length with a length of two) are buried in the run-time support of the ASN.1-compiler-tool, as are the mechanisms for parsing an incoming encoding into components that can then be placed into memory in a form that matches a programming-language data-structure.

> With an ASN.1-compiler-tool, life gets quite a bit simpler! How simple can you make it? Not much more, given that ASN.1 does not address semantics in the formal notation.

ASN.1-compiler-tools are specific to a given platform (meaning hardware, operating system, programming language, and perhaps even development environment) and you will need to find one that is available for the platform that you are using. If you are using C, C++, or Java, on commonly used hardware and operating systems you will have no problem, but if you are locked into some rather archaic language (sorry if I sound rude!), life may be more difficult.

A particular product may support several of these languages in one software package, using "compiler directives", or you may have to pay for several versions of a product if you want support for multiple platforms (C and Java, say). In some cases "cross-compilation" (which some ASN.1-compiler-tools support) can provide implementation support on older platforms. Basically, you need to "filter" available tools according to whether they can support directly or through cross-compilation the platform you want/need to use, then choose the "best" (see 6.7 for what "best" might be).

"Want/need" is important here. Sometimes the implementation platform is fixed and almost impossible to change for either historical reasons or for reasons of company policy, but more often, there are costs associated with the use of different platforms (procurement of hardware which is not "in-company", training costs of programmers, etc., etc.) which must be balanced against the "quality" (and cost) of available tools for these platforms.

6.5.2 What Do Tool Designers Have to Decide?

There are three very critical decisions in the design of a good ASN.1-compiler-tool—how to map ASN.1 data-structures to programming-language data-structures, how to make CPU/memory tradeoffs in the overall run-time support, and how to handle memory allocation and buffer management during encode/decode operations. But other important decisions are how much user control, options, and flexibility to provide in these areas. All of these factors contribute to the "quality" of any particular tool.

The designers of the ASN.1-compiler-tool will have made some important decisions. We will see later that the quality of these decisions very much affects the quality of the ASN.1-

> How to map to the programming language, CPU/memory trade-offs, memory allocation and buffer management, and user control—these are the main issues.

compiler-tool (and the ease and flexibility with which you can use it to help you to produce protocol implementations).

The most important areas tool designers have had to address (and which affect the quality of the resulting ASN.1-compiler-tool) are the following.

- How to map ASN.1 into programming-language data-structures?

- What are the right tradeoffs between run-time encoding/decoding speed and memory requirements?

- How to handle memory allocation when performing encode and decode operations?

- How much user control should be provided (and how—global directives or local control) on the behavior of the tool for mappings and for run-time operation?

These decisions are not easy, but the best tools will provide some degree of user control in all these areas, through the use of "compiler directives", ideally both in terms of global default settings as well as specific local overrides (for example, for two-octet, four-octet, or truly indefinite-length integers).

6.5.3 The Mapping to a Programming-Language Data Structure

The designers of the ASN.1-compiler-tool will have determined a **mapping** from any arbitrarily complicated set of ASN.1 types into a related (and similarly complicated) set of data-types in your chosen language. And they will have written a program (this is the bit that is usually called the "compiler") that will take in the text of an ASN.1 module (or several modules linked by EXPORTS and IMPORTS) and will process the module(s) to generate as output the mapping of the types in those modules into the chosen target language.

How does that help you? Well, your pseudo-code for encoding "Report- item" now looks more like Figure 6.3.

This is perhaps the most impor-tant design decision. It is often called "defining the API for ASN.1", and in the case of C++ there is an X-Open standard for this. Get that wrong and there will be some abstract values of the ASN.1 type that cannot be repre-sented by values of the program-ming-language data-structure. Or perhaps the programming-lan-guage data-structure generated will just produce programming-lan-guage-compiler error messages when you try to use it!

Note that regardless of how compli-cated a nested structure of types or repetitions of SEQUENCE OF there are, there is just one call of "Encode" at the end to encode your complete message from the values you have set in your programming language data-structure.

For incoming messages, the process is reversed. Your own code does no parsing, and no tree-walking. It merely accesses the fields of the pro-gramming-language data-structure that the "compiler" part of the tool generated for you.

"CompilerInfo" in the call of "Encode" is information passed from the "com-piler" part of the tool to the run-time routines. This passes (inter alia) the tagging to be applied for BER. Although largely invisible to you (you do not need to under-stand the form of this information), it is absolutely essential to enable the run-time routines to provide their encode/decode functions.

6.5.4 Memory and CPU Tradeoffs at Run-Time

What is this parameter "CompilerInfo"? This is a vital magic ingredient! This is pro-duced by the compiler, and contains the "recipe" for taking the contents of memory

```
Get value for "item" into Report-item.item
Get value for "item-description" into
Report-item.item-description
Get "bar-code-data" into Report-item.bar-code-data
Get "ran-out-of-stock" value into
Report-item.ran-out-of-stock
...
etc, setting all the fields of Report-item
...
Call Encode (CompilerInfo, Report-item, Buffer)
Pass Buffer to lower layers for transmission
Clear Buffer
```

Figure 6.3 Pseudo-code to encode using an ASN.1-compiler-tool.

pointed to by "Return-of-sales" (for example), finding from that memory the actual values for the ASN.1 type, and encoding those values with correct tags, correct use of DEFAULT, etc. It essentially contains the entire information present in the ASN.1-type definition.

There are (at least!) two forms this "CompilerInfo" can take:

> Interpretation of tables is a pretty compact way of performing a task, but open code is faster! With the best tools you choose.

- It can be a very compact set of tables that are used in an interpretive fashion by "Encode" to determine how to encode the contents of the memory containing a value of (e.g.) "Return-of-sales" (and similarly for "decode").

- It can be (rather more verbose, but faster) actual code to pick up the value of each field in turn to do the encoding of that field (and to merge the pieces together into larger SEQUENCE, SEQUENCE OF, etc. structures). In general, open code is probably more appropriate for PER than for BER, as tags and lengths are often omitted in PER, whereas a table-driven approach, defining the tags to be encoded and letting the interpreter generate the lengths, may be more appropriate for BER. The best approach depends on the circumstances, or as they would say in England, it is horses for courses!

Just as there are many different implementation architectures for hand-encoding, so there are many different possible architectures for the design of tools. With implementation architectures, all that matters is that the bits-on-the-line are correct. And similarly with an ASN.1-compiler-tool, all that really matters is that it produces a programming-language data-structure that can represent all abstract values of the ASN.1 type, and that it efficiently produces correct encodings for values placed in that data-structure (with similar remarks concerning decoding). I do not know exactly how the "OSS ASN.1 Tools" product goes about producing an encoding (or decodes), but it does produce the right results!

6.5.5 Control of a Tool

There are a host of options that can be incorporated into an ASN.1-compiler-tool (and/or the run-time libraries that support it). For example,

> Inevitably there are options you want to leave to the user. How best to do that?

- the language or platform to "compile" for,

- how to represent ASN.1 INTEGER types in the programming-language data-structures,

- whether to use arrays or linked-list structures in the mapping from ASN.1 to your programming-language (for example, for "SEQUENCE OF"),

- which encoding rules to use for encoding (and to assume for decoding),

- (slightly more subtle) which encoding rules can be selected at run-time—all or only a subset? (This affects the library routines that are included, and hence the size of the executable.)

- which encodings to use in the noncanonical encoding rules.

- whether the user prefers the fastest possible encode/decode or the smallest executable,

- (fairly unimportant) the names of the directories and files that will be used at both compile-time and run-time, and

- many others.

The control by the user can be expressed by a global configuration file, by command-line directives, by an "options" button in a Windows-based product, by "compiler directives" embedded in the ASN.1 source, or by run-time call parameters, or by several of these, with one providing a global default and another overriding that default locally. With the "OSS ASN.1 Tools" product, compiler directives are included after a type definition (where a subtype specification might go) as a specialized form of comment. For example:

```
SET --<LINKED>-- OF INTEGER
```

6.6 Use of the "OSS ASN.1 Tools" Product

Here we describe how to encode values with one particular tool. The process with other ASN.1-compiler-tools is similar.

When you use the "OSS ASN.1 Tools" product to support an application written using the C programming language, you input an ASN.1 specification (and identify the top-level type that forms the abstract syntax, or PDU, to the compiler via a compiler directive). This can be defined using a single module or several modules. There are four outputs (but only the last two are important for correct ASN.1 input). These are

- a "pretty-print" listing (not really very important),

- error and warning messages if your ASN.1 is a bit "funny,"

> Put your values in the language data-structure and call ENCODE. That is all there is to it! More or less!

- a ".h" header file that contains the mapping of your ASN.1 types into C language data-structures, and

- a ".c" control file that conveys information from the compiler to the run-time routines that you will invoke to encode and decode.

The latter is pretty incomprehensible (but vitally important), and you ignore it, other than to compile it with your C compiler and link in the resulting object file as part of your application.

The ".h" file is included with your own code, and compiled to form the main part of your application, which will include calls to "encode" and "decode". You also link in a run-time library. At this stage you may wish to look at Appendices 3 and 4, which have not been included in this chapter due to their bulk.

Appendix 3 gives most of the ".h" file for "Return-of-sales" and "Report-item" for the C language implementation (and some parts of relevant "include" files). Appendix 4 gives the equivalent for a Java implementation.

I offer no explanation or discussion of these appendices—if you are a C or Java programmer, the text (and its relation to the ASN.1 definitions) will be quite understandable. If you are not, just ignore them!

And there you have it! Of course, the original application standard could have been published in "pseudo-C" or in Java instead of using ASN.1, but would that really have been a good idea? For once I will express an opinion—NO! Ask the same question in 1982 to 1984 and it would have been COBOL or Pascal (or perhaps Modula) that we would have been talking about. And even if you define your structures in "pseudo-C", you still have to make statements about the encoding of those structures, the most important being about the order of the bytes in an integer when transmitted down the line, about the flattening of any tree structures you create, about the size of integers and of pointers, and so on. It really is rather simpler with ASN.1—let the ASN.1-compiler-tool take the strain!

The appendices are **not** of course the entire compiler output. There is also the control information used by the run-time routines to perform the encode/decode, but the implementor need never look at that, and it is not shown here.

6.7 What Makes One ASN.1-Compiler-Tool Better than Another?

There are many dimensions on which the quality of a tool can be judged. The major areas to be looked at are

- the extent of support for the full ASN.1 notation,

- the mappings to programming-language data-structures,

- run-time memory/CPU tradeoffs,

- memory allocation mechanisms, and

- the degree of user control over options.

We have already had some discussion of most of these areas when we discussed the sorts of decisions a tool vendor needs to make. Here we highlight a few points of detail. **It is, however, important to recognize that with the best tools, absolutely none of the problems listed below will arise.** Indeed, many of the problems occurred only in early tools before they were fully developed.

> OK. So you want to buy an ASN.1-compiler-tool? What to look for in a best buy? It is not as easy as buying a washing machine! Here are some things you might want to look for or to be wary of.

Some early tools provided no support for ASN.1 value notation, so you needed to remove all value assignments from your module and replace "DEFAULT" with "OPTIONAL", handling the default value in your application code.

Other early tools could only handle a single module (no support for IMPORTS and EXPORTS), so you had to physically copy text to produce a single module. The better tools today will handle multiple modules, and (once you have identified your top-level message to them) will extract from those modules precisely and only those types that are needed to support your top-level message.

Another issue is whether you can use the ASN.1 definition as published, or whether you have to help the parser in the tool by adding a semicolon to the end of each of the assignment statements in your module.

There are other tools that are designed simply to support one particular protocol, and will recognize only the types that appear in that protocol. If that protocol is extended in version 2 to use more types, you may have to wait for an upgrade to your tool before you can implement version 2!

There is also the issue of the 1994 extensions to ASN.1—Information Object Classes etc., described in Section II. This is probably the area where you are most likely still to find lack of support in some tools.

The mapping to the programming-language data-structure is a very critical area. If this is done wrong you may not be able to set all the values you should be able to!

Note also that ASN.1 allows arbitrary length names for identifiers (with all characters significant), and is case sensitive. In some programming languages, characters after, for example, the 31st are simply discarded. Does the tool ensure that long names (which are quite common in ASN.1) are mapped into distinct programming language names in an ergonomic way that you can understand?

What about INTEGER types? A good tool will give you control (usually through either global directives or directives you embed into the ASN.1 text against a particular type) over the mapping of INTEGER types, for example, into a short, normal, long, or huge (represented as a string) integer.

There are also efficiency considerations in the mappings. On some platforms there is the concept of "native" integer types. Mapping directly into these can be much more efficient than proceeding in a more generic (platform-independent) manner.

It is important here to remember that the mappings from ASN.1 to a programming language (usually called an "ASN.1 Application Programme Interface (API)" are in general not standardized, so each tool vendor does his or her own thing. (Work was done within X-Open on standardization of the mapping to C++—called the ASN.1/C++ API—but I am not sure whether the document was finally ratified. If you want to use C++ as your implementation language, you may want to ask your tool vendor whether they use that mapping or not.)

We discussed earlier the option of a largely interpretative table-driven approach (using little memory) vs. an approach based on generated code (taking more memory but faster) to run-time encoding and decoding. This is one area where you will probably be looking for options in the use of the tool that will enable you to choose for each application or platform which approach you want taken.

And finally, we discussed earlier the means of providing user control over tool options and the range of such options that can be controlled.

All these factors contribute to the "quality" of a tool, but you will certainly want to look at the cost as well! Most tool vendors charge a license fee that gets you just one copy of the ASN.1-compiler-tool, but unlimited copies of the run-time support (which you clearly need if you are to distribute your resulting application!).

6.8 Conclusion

This chapter has discussed how to build an actual implementation for a protocol that has been defined using ASN.1. It is followed by some discussion of management and design issues for consideration by managers, specifiers, and implementors, to complete Section I of this book.

Management and Design Issues for ASN.1 Specification and Implementation

(Or: Things You Need to Think About!)

Summary

This chapter

- collects together many of the issues and "style" decisions mentioned elsewhere in the text,

- identifies some global issues for management decisions,

- identifies matters that specifiers need to consider, and

- identifies matters that implementors need to consider.

The section on management decisions should be understandable to anyone who has read Section I. **The remaining sections will require a knowledge of material covered in Section II, assume a quite detailed knowledge of ASN.1, and cover some fairly abstruse areas.**

A word of caution: I am not a believer in management gurus and elaborate "methodologies". Most of the headings below have the word "issues" in them. The following text is designed to give the reader some idea of the options, and things they should consider. At the end of the day you make the decisions, not me! I try as much as possible to suggest areas you should think about, rather than to tell you what I think you should do. If occasionally I move toward the latter, I apologize and please feel free to ignore my advice!

Much of what is being said in this chapter is opinion (Figure 999 again!), not fact, and there are others who may well have different and perhaps opposite views to some of the suggestions made here.

7.1 Global Issues for Management Decisions

7.1.1 Specification

7.1.1.1 To Use ASN.1 or Not!

This was well discussed in Chapter 1, wherein a variety of techniques for defining protocols were described. This of course is the number 1 decision, but may be more conditioned by the culture within which the protocol specification is being made, or on the specification notation that has been used for other related protocols.

> If you have read this far, and you are able to influence the specification language used for a protocol, then I am sure you will ensure that ASN.1 is seriously considered. Go on to 7.2!

By now, you should have a clear view of the ease of producing a specification using ASN.1, and of the ease of implementing such a protocol provided an ASN.1 tool is available.

The counterargument is that, simply because of its ease of use, ASN.1 does not force you to keep your specification simple (but of course does not prevent you from doing so), and the more complex the protocol becomes, the more your implementors will need tool support, and tools do cost money!

However, if you are expecting your protocol to be implemented by commercial firms, with perhaps ten to twenty man-years of effort going into the implementation, the cost of purchasing a tool becomes totally insignificant. Paying money for a professionally developed, supported, and robust tool is often more effective in the long run than use of a "freebie". (The main counterargument to this is probably the Apache Web server—probably the most popular Web server in use today, and it is free! But there is an English saying, "the exception proves the rule.")

7.1.1.2 To Copy or Not?

If you need an ASN.1 type defined in (and exported by) another standard, there is a clear argument for importing that type into your own module(s). This is commonly

> Copying is wrong, yes? You may be able to get permission, and it may be the better solution. Look at the issues here.

done for ROSE data-types and object classes, and for X.500 Directory Names and for X.509 certificates. In this case you would, of course, also include a clear reference to the source that you were importing from.

There is, however, another option that has been taken by some specifiers. That is to simply copy a type definition into your own specification (of course also giving the semantics related to the fields). This is arguably in violation of the copyright laws, or at least of intellectual property rights, unless your specification is to be published by the same standards body as the one from which you are copying, but it has occurred in a number of specifications, even when the caveat does not apply!

There are three main reasons for copying (embedding) rather than importing and referencing:

- It gives you control over the material, preventing problems and confusion if the referenced material is changed in a later version in a way that is not compatible with your own specification.

- It means that your implementors only need to obtain your documents— your specification is complete and self-contained.

- You want only a simplified version of the copied material (this is often the reason why you find copies of the ROSE material in other specifications, rather than direct use of IMPORT).

Decisions on this issue are not easy, and should be made consciously after appropriate discussion.

There are no other real management issues related to specification (but many more details for specifiers are discussed in what follows), so we now turn to issues related to implementation.

7.1.2 Implementation: Setting the Budget

Any commercial project needs detailed costings, but it can be easy to overlook some of the hidden costs (or opportunities to spend money wisely) when undertaking an implementation of an ASN.1-based specification. Some of these are mentioned in the following text.

> Just a few things you should not forget about when doing your costings. . .

7.1.2.1 Getting the Specs

There are two sets of specifications that you need—those for the protocol you are implementing, and those for ASN.1 itself.

In most cases you will want to use the latest versions of both the protocol specification and the ASN.1 specifications, but occasionally there may be some industry or community of interest agreement on use of older versions. (The ASN.1 1990 issue is discussed in Chapter 19). Be careful, too, to look out for corrigenda and addenda to the specifications. The place you obtained your specifications from should be able to

> Of course, you need the specification for your protocol. But also for ASN.1, and possibly for anything either of these reference.

alert you to this. In some cases there may be **draft** corrigenda or addenda in circulation. In this latter case, you may need to investigate further and perhaps try to contact the chairman or rapporteur or editor of the standards to discover the stability of these documents. Draft corrigenda and draft addenda do not always become approved corrigenda or addenda (at least not without sometimes substantial change).

Note that ITU-T now has a Web site from which (provided you have set up an account) you can purchase all ITU-T specifications and download copies over the Web. The European Telecommunications Standards Institute (ETSI) has a similar site, but ETSI standards are free! Many of these use ASN.1 as their specification language. Links to these sites can be obtained via Appendix 5.

In the case of your protocol specifications (but not the ASN.1 specifications themselves) it will be important to try to get hold of an electronic copy of the ASN.1 parts of the specification if you are going to use a tool, otherwise you will have the tedious and error-prone task of keying in that text.

The vendor of your tool is likely to be able to help you here, and electronic copies of ASN.1 specifications usually circulate without charge and are sometimes on the Web. Another source of an electronic copy is the Editor of the protocol specification, who will usually be happy to provide one provided that there are no commercial vendors of electronic versions and provided he or she knows you have bought the printed version of the specifications.

You will need to get these specifications in a timely manner for your project, and in both cases (ASN.1 specs and your protocol specs) you will probably find you need some supporting specifications as well, and these need to be identified early in the project.

In the case of the ASN.1 specifications, full details of the encoding of REAL, of GeneralizedTime and of most of the character set types require reference to additional separate specifications, so if these types are used in your protocol specification, you will need to obtain these other specifications as well.

It is ISO advice that when one Standard references another, you should always use the latest version of the referenced Standard. This can, however, sometimes be dangerous, and it is always well to check publication dates to see which version of a referenced Standard was current at the time of publication of the referencing Standard, and see what impact the changes made might have on your protocol.

7.1.2.2 Training Courses, Tutorials, and Consultants

Another cost that is easily overlooked (and time for it not included in the project plan) is training time and the cost of courses for your implementation team.

A "theory only" course on ASN.1 (covering more or less the same technical material as this book, but without the sorts of discussions that are appearing in this chapter and in a few other

> Commercial courses are commercial! (But your tool vendor may have a bundle that includes some courses and tutorial material for you.)

places) will take about two days. A course with some hands-on work writing ASN.1 specifications and using a tool could be as long as four days.

You may also want to supplement such courses with purchases of this book! (Or of the companion volume by Olivier Dubuisson—available in both French and English. See Appendix 5 for a link.)

Similarly, there are commercial courses available giving a good introduction to many of the protocols that are specified using ASN.1, and if these are available for the protocol you are implementing, you will probably want to use them. Frequently the speaker/trainer/presenter will be active in standardization of that protocol, and can alert you to the state of any addenda and corrigenda that may be circulating.

Finally, there are a (small) number of people who advertise themselves as "ASN.1 consultants". They will give implementation advice, or will take an outline of a protocol you want written and produce the ASN.1 for you. But you pay consultancy prices!

7.1.3 Implementation Platform and Tools

You may have no choice on the implementation platform (hardware, operating system, programming language), due to the need to extend an existing system, or to your firm's global policies, or simply due to the operating system and programming language experience of your employees.

But if you do have a choice, a decision on the platform should be made along with the decision on whether to use a tool, and if so which one. (Aspects of the "quality" of a tool were discussed in the previous chapter, and should be considered here.)

At least one tool vendor will provide his or her tool for any platform, provided a C-compiler or a C-cross-compiler exists for that platform. Tools supporting programming in C, C++, and Java are all available.

> There are many factors involved in making decisions on implementation platforms, but there can be interactions between tool choice and platform choice.

7.2 Issues for Specifiers

This clause discusses a number of points that those involved in protocol specification using ASN.1 should consider.

7.2.1 Guiding Principles

There are four (four?, surely it should be the magic sever, or perhaps three, or just one!) main principles to keep in mind (some apply to all protocol design, whether or not ASN.1 is used). These principles may sound very obvious, but they are often overlooked.

- **Simplicity:** Keep it as simple as possible, while being as general and flexible as necessary.

- **Unambiguous and complete:** Make absolutely sure you have left no ambiguities in your specification, and no implementation dependence in your specification unless you consciously decide to do so. In the latter case, make sure that such dependencies are clearly stated, not just implied or hidden, and that you consider the full interworking problems of such dependencies.

- **Avoid options:** Try to avoid encoder options unless there is a very good reason for them, as this reduces decoder implementation costs and testing costs. Allowing options on what parts of the total specification need be implemented is also dangerous, and unless done carefully can seriously limit interworking (but is often done!). A detailed application of this principle says "Don't use SET or SET OF, always use SEQUENCE or SEQUENCE OF instead."

- **Think about the next version:** There always will be a next version if your protocol takes off. How might it differ? How do you want added material to be handled by version 1 systems?

7.2.2 Decisions on Style

The best advice is for you to look at as many different specifications as you can and make a conscious decision on the various style issues.

Some simple things to consider as follows.

- **Fonts:** Use of different fonts to distinguish formal material from English text.

- **Order of definitions:** Top-down listing of type definitions or alphabetical listing?

- **Module structure:** Grouping of related definitions into modules and the order and overall structure of modules.

> A good style makes the specification easy to read and follow, a bad one makes it hard. The actual bits on the line may be just the same!

- **Line numbers and indexes:** Possible use of line numbering and provision of an index (showing where defined and where used for each reference name) for the specification.

- **Lengths of reference names:** Long names can be clearer, but can clutter a specification. Do not rely on the name alone to define (imply) the associated semantics.

- **Duplicated text:** Try not to duplicate text where several messages have common elements, but where this is clearer than (for example) using parameterization, do not be afraid of it if it makes the specification simpler.

- **Number of parameters:** If you have a large number of parameters in a reference name definition, consider defining an Information Object Class to bundle them into a single parameter, as described in Chapter 14.

- **Web publication:** There are many standards that now have their ASN.1 (or even the complete specification) on the Web. An approach some take is to provide hyper-text links from every use of a reference name to the definition of that name, but of course you need an ASN.1 tool to generate the HTML for you in this case, or it would be too tedious and error prone to produce. You also still need to provide the "ASCII" text of your specification for input to an ASN.1 compiler-tool.

Other issues are a little more than "style", or warrant a longer discussion than can be provided in a bullet. These are discussed in the following text.

7.2.3 Your Top-Level Type

You need to very clearly specify what is the top-level type that defines your messages. This should be a single type, and will almost always be an extensible CHOICE type.

> This is your set of messages. Give it the importance and prominence it deserves. All other types are simply there to support this type.

Include in this CHOICE all and only those types that define one of your complete outer-level messages, not types that might be used in constraints on open types, for example.

You may use the ABSTRACT-SYNTAX notation to identify this top-level type, or you can simply make it very clear by English text and by placing it in a conspicuous position—perhaps in a module of its own.

ABSTRACT-SYNTAX is not often used in current specifications, partly because it was added to ASN.1 at a relatively late date, and partly because the associated object identifier value is needed in communications only if the full OSI stack is being used, but it provides a very clear way of identifying your top-level types.

As with all cases where you use the extensibility marker, you should think about, and specify clearly, what you want version 1 systems to do if they receive messages that have been added in version 2. If you leave this undefined (implementation-dependent), you have violated one of the four previously mentioned principles, and it will probably end up biting you!

7.2.4 Integer Sizes and Bounds

> Think about sizes and bounds. In most cases you don't intend infinity!

This is a detailed issue, and relates not just to the size of integers but also to the length of strings and to iterations of SEQUENCE OF and SET OF.

If you are using PER, then it is very important that bounds be formally expressed using the sub-type notation, as tools will perform encodings according to the bounds. If you are using BER, then the issue is not one of encoding, but concerns the following.

- What size integer should be used in the internal processing of these fields? (How should they be mapped into your chosen programming language?)

- If you fail to give any specification, one implementation may map to (and encode and transmit) 4-octet integers, and another may only support 2-octet integers. Still others may increase implementation costs significantly by making strenuous but unnecessary efforts to handle arbitrarily large integers or arbitrarily long strings.

These are, of course, issues with PER as well, but if you have placed bounds on INTEGER types, the implementor can deduce the appropriate size of integer to use internally.

If a specification is littered with bounds, particularly if these are set in a single module and imported, or passed as parameters, it can make the specification (while totally clear to a computer!) less readable by a human being. An alternative can be to define your own type INTEGER4, but then this has to be exported and imported to wherever you want to use it.

ASN.1 tools generally permit global statements on the size of programming language integers that the ASN.1 INTEGER type is to be mapped into. Thus a clear statement in ordinary English that unless otherwise stated, INTEGER fields are expected to be implemented as 4-octet integers, can suffice.

Notice that there is a certain tension here between specification of bounds to ensure the smallest possible number of bits on the line when using PER encodings, vs. guidance on what to use for mapping to programming language integers and internal processing.

What is absolutely vital, however, is to make it clear when very large integers (such as those that appear in signatures in X.509 certificates) have to be supported for the ASN.1 INTEGER type.

We have concentrated mainly on INTEGER in the preceding text, but remember that there are bounds issues related to all of the following.

- INTEGER values.
- Lengths of BIT STRING, OCTET STRING, character string types, and GeneralizedTime.
- Number of iterations of each SEQUENCE OF and SET OF.

And in each case, you have the two main issues raised in the preceding discussion, namely, ensuring optimum PER encodings, and ensuring interworking. The latter is arguably the more important.

As is pointed out in Chapter 14, if you really **do** decide to leave some bounds (or anything else) as implementation-dependent, then inclusion of a parameter of the abstract syntax clearly flags this, and you can then include an exception marker on the bound to specify what a receiver should do if the two implementation choices are not the same. If you **do** take this route, it would be as well to clearly explain in English text what you intend, your reasons for leaving implementation-dependence, and when you expect it (or do not expect it) to cause interworking problems.

7.2.5 Extensibility Issues

We have already mentioned the importance of considering what extensions you are likely to require in version 2, and the importance of inclusion of an ellipsis at appropriate points.

Most people do not use EXTENSIBILITY IMPLIED in the module header, preferring to explicitly include the ellipsis wherever necessary rather than have overkill. This is probably clearer, and does allow separate exception handling in each case if this is desired (see the following text).

> Extensibility is important and will work for you—but only if you obey the rules when you write version 2!

It is important to recognize what changes you can and can not make in your version-2 specification if you want interworking with deployed version-1 systems to be possible without some separate version negotiation or requiring version-2 implementors to support "dual stacks".

You can only add material where you have put your ellipses in version 1. Unless you originally wrote "EXTENSIBILITY IMPLIED", you cannot add new ellipses in version 2 (except in new types you add as extensions, of course), nor can you remove ellipses. And you cannot change existing types, for example, from

```
INTEGER
```

to

```
CHOICE { INTEGER , OBJECT IDENTIFIER }
```

A last addition to "what you cannot do" (but of course this list is not exhaustive!) is optionality. You cannot add or remove OPTIONAL or DEFAULT from existing elements (although you can, if you wish, add another mandatory element at your ellipsis with the same type as an earlier OPTIONAL element).

7.2.6 Exception Handling

7.2.6.1 The Requirement

It is absolutely vital that when you use ellipsis you give a clear statement of what behavior you expect

> Version 1 must be told what to do when hit by version 2—and you must remember what you told it to do when you write version 2!

- from version-1 systems if they receive added material, and

- how version-2 systems, where mandatory fields have been added, are to handle messages from version-1 systems.

The former is the more common case, as version-2 additions tend usually to be marked OPTIONAL.

> Not even an exhaustive list of options. Certainly not telling you what to do! But perhaps enough to get you thinking.

7.2.6.2 Common Forms of Exception Handling

7.2.6.2.1 SEQUENCE and SET

Consider first added elements in a SEQUENCE or SET. It is extremely common here to specify that these are to be silently ignored by version-1 systems (you then need to consider the implications of this in your version-2 protocol).

ASN.1 tools are likely to support the removal of such material within the

> The simplest cases first—silently ignore.

decode routines. Thus the application code is never even aware that it has been hit by a version-2 message, unless action is taken to specifically indicate to the tool that such material has to be passed up (for example, for relaying).

7.2.6.2.2 CHOICE

In the case of CHOICE, the situation is more difficult, and will depend on the precise interactions that occur within your protocol.

> A bit trickier. And the top-level CHOICE is often a bit special.

The simplest case is your top-level CHOICE, where there is probably some defined responses to top-level messages from an initiator of an exchange, and you can make provision in those responses for some form of "Sorry, I have not implemented that, I am just a version-1 system" indication. (Such provision needs to be made in the version-1 response messages, of course.)

Consider now the case where an extensible CHOICE is embedded in a sequence, and perhaps is an extensible choice of some character string types, which in version-2 has new types added.

It would be possible for a version-1 system receiving a version-2 value of such a type to treat that value as an empty string—effectively to ignore it, and to say in subsequent processing "No value available for this field". Of course, many other actions are possible, depending on your detailed protocol and the importance of the CHOICE field. Only you can decide what would be appropriate.

7.2.6.2.3 INTEGER and ENUMERATED

For extensible ranges on INTEGER, or for extensible ENUMERATIONS, the situation is not clearcut. One option can be to define (in version 1) a mapping of any new version-2 value into a specific version-1 value, and specify the processing of that value as version-1 behavior.

> Another difficult one. Is there a version-1 value that all version-2 values can be mapped to without causing too many problems? Otherwise you need to look at just how the integer or enumeration is going to affect subsequent processing.

You need to try to think (when writing version-1) why you might be making the extension in version-2, and whether this behavior would work out OK. You need to revisit that discussion when you do eventually make version-2 additions!

Mapping to a version-1 value will not always be right, and the presence of a version-2 value may need to be carried as an "unknown value" through several stages of further processing (perhaps even into a database), and its effect on later code which is processing that value should be fully determined in version-1.

7.2.6.2.4 Extensible Strings

The next case we need to consider are strings that had a limited (but extensible) maximum size in version 1, and the size in version 2 was increased.

Here again we see a conflict between the need to use constraints to get a tight PER encoding, and what we really want implementors to support in subsequent processing.

It would be possible in this case to say (in version 1) that the constraint determines the maximum for version-1 senders (it is all that is considered necessary at present), but that version-1 receivers should be capable of handling in their implementation sizes up to, say, twice the version-1 limit—and perhaps truncate after that.

But again, depending on the subsequent use and processing of the string field, options such as treating a version-2 value as "unknown value" can also be appropriate.

> Two main options, both obvious: Require version 1 to support longer strings at the processing level or truncate.

7.2.6.2.5 Extensible Bounds on SET OF and SEQUENCE OF

This situation is very similar to the situation with bounds on strings.

It is clearly possible to require version-1 systems to support greater iterations on receipt. It is also possible to specify that they process the iterated material up to some limit of iterations, and then ignore the rest of the material (equivalent to truncating a string), possibly with some form of error return.

> Very similar to strings, as you would expect.

Bounds on SET OF and SEQUENCE OF iterations are, however, relatively uncommon (with or without extension markers), so this case does not often arise. But the reader will be aware from earlier discussion that this means potential interworking problems or expensive implementations; few implementations will truly support an unlimited number of iterations unless told that they are required to do so.

The problem, however, is that real implementation limits are more likely to be on the total size of the iterated material when mapped into an implementation programming language data structure rather than on the number of iterations per se. This perhaps explains why bounds on iteration counts are often left unspecified.

7.2.6.2.6 Use of Extensible Object Sets in Constraints

Finally, we consider the case where an extensible Information Object Set is used as a table or relational constraint, as in ROSE. Here it would be common to have some form of error response such as the ROSE REJECT message if a version-2 object is received.

> Our last example, both the most complex and the simplest!

But in other cases the option of silently ignoring (perhaps linked to an additional "criticality" field) the version-2 object, or to treat it as a version-1 object, can also be possibilities.

7.2.6.2.7 Summary

In the earlier text we have used six main mechanisms. They are

- silently ignore,

- give some form of error response,

- map to a version-1 value or object,

- include a special "unknown value" in version-1 and specify its processing,

- take the added material or unknown choice or value and relay it on unchanged, and

- process as much as possible then truncate (silently or with some form of error response).

> Six mechanisms were described earlier—someone please find another one and we will have the magic seven!

Depending on the actual extensible construct, where that construct is used, the semantics associated with it, and how it affects later (perhaps much later) processing, we can choose one of these behaviors—or perhaps determine that another application-specific handling is more appropriate.

7.2.6.3 ASN.1-Specified Default Exception Handling

ASN.1 has been criticized for not specifying default exception handling behavior, but I hope the earlier discussion of options makes it clear that good and appropri-

> "I don't want to mess with this stuff—why can't I just put in the ellipsis and invoke default exception handling procedures?" "Sorry, it goes with the job—you have to be responsible for (and about) exception handling!"

ate exception handling must be related to the needs of a specific protocol, and will frequently differ in different places in the protocol.

It would be positively dangerous to allow specifiers to insert ellipses without thinking through the implications of different sorts of version-1 exception handling behavior.

Ellipsis is not an easy option. It was introduced originally to ensure that the efficient PER encodings were such that some interworking would still be possible between version-1 and version-2 systems, but even with BER, if version-2 additions are made without a clear (earlier) specification of version-1 behavior, serious problems result.

It may be difficult, and it may be a chore, but giving serious consideration to extensibility issues and the associated exception handling is part of the job of a protocol specifier—the job is more than simply defining a few data structures!

Unfortunately, if a bad job is done on exception handling in version-1, it is quite possibly a wholly new (and innocent!) group of specifiers producing version-2 that will suffer from the bad version-1 design. But I am afraid that is life.

7.2.6.4 Use of the Formal Exception Specification Notation

Before leaving this discussion of extensibility, we must make some mention of the use of the formal exception specification notation (the notation that starts with "!").

The important thing (emphasized in 7.2.6.3) is that exception handling should be stated very clearly, and the places in the protocol where particular handling is to be used are clearly identified. If there are relatively few uses of ellipsis, and particularly if the required exception handling is the same for all of them, then there is no real gain in including the formal exception specification notation, and English language text can suffice. (This might be the case if the only ellipses are at the end of SEQUENCE constructs, and the required behavior in all cases is to silently ignore added material.)

> To say it formally or not? Well, why not?

(Actually, that is not quite true—inclusion of the formal notation tells a reader that exception handling **has** been considered, and that somewhere in the text there **are** details of required behavior, and it is my own personal view that there should be formal exception specification notation wherever extensibility occurs, but I know that there are others who disagree with me!)

In a protocol with perhaps four or five different exception-handling procedures specified (to be used with different instances of ellipsis, each behavior applying to several instances of ellipsis), use of the formal notation (perhaps simply using "!1", "!2", etc.) on each ellipsis can be a simple and convenient way of identifying clearly which behavior applies to which. Something similar to this is done very effectively in the ROSE protocol (using value reference names for "1", "2", etc.), as described in Chapter 13.

7.2.7 Parameterization Issues

Parameterization is powerful and can be the only way of achieving certain "reusability" goals, particularly where one group provides a carrier protocol and several other groups fill in the holes in different ways to produce a complete specification.

But if a parameterized type is instantiated only a limited number of times within a single specification, then it may be that parameterization is unnecessary, and that the same effect can be achieved more clearly by using different (but similar) type or value definitions.

> Just a repetition of what has been said elsewhere in this book.

Object Set parameters of the abstract syntax are a very good way of providing precise specifications of "must implement all, but can add" vs. "can implement a subset, but can't add" vs. "this is a guide, add or subtract," but are currently unfamiliar to many readers of ASN.1, and should be accompanied by explanatory text.

Integer parameters of the abstract syntax (used in bounds) are also a very good way of clearly indicating that (for whatever reason), you have chosen to leave implementation-dependent features in your specification.

But in both these cases, it is essential that exception-handling procedures be fully specified, as discussed earlier.

The use of the {...} notation is a form of parameterization, declaring that the object set to be used is implementation dependent, and is generally a less clear and precise notation than parameterization (but there are those who would disagree).

It is important if this notation is used, that text clearly specifies how it is intended (by whom and where) for the specification to be completed, what implications there are on interworking, and what exception handling is to be applied. If that is done, this notation can produce a less cluttered specification than many different parameters (object sets of various classes) being passed from the top-level type all the way down to where they are being used as a constraint.

Finally, remember (Chapter 14) that if you have many parameters of a parameterized type (or other form of reference name), you can reduce them to a single object set parameter by defining a suitable Information Object Class whose objects carry the complete set of information for each parameter. This can be a very useful simplification and reduction of verbosity in your text.

7.2.8 Unconstrained Open Types

Unconstrained open types—elements of sequences, for example,

```
OPERATION.&Type
```

are syntactically allowed in ASN.1 as part of the Seoul (see Chapter 19) introduction of the Information Object Class concept, but that was largely in response to a perceived need to provide syntax that was semantically equivalent to the old "raw ANY", and I hope the reader (at least those who have read Section II) by now appreciates that a "raw ANY" (and hence an unconstrained open type) is a BAD THING.

> There is only one thing to say—
> DON'T!

All that a tool can deliver for this construct is an octet string. And even the implementor of the application has no clear indication of where to look to determine the possible types that can occur in this element, the semantics associated with those types, and which type has actually appeared in a given instance of communication, that is, how to decode and interpret the octet string.

As a specifier in the years 2000 onward, **please** do not use this form, even though you are allowed to! Look at the ROSE chapter (Chapter 13) to see how to give a more precise and implementable specification of these sorts of constructs. I suspect that if ASN.1 is still going strong in 2010, forbidding this unconstrained construct may become possible (I am likely to campaign for it), provided no one shouts "1990, 1990!" (again, see Chapter 19).

7.2.9 Tagging Issues

If you are writing a new specification, you should use AUTOMATIC TAGS (and—as an aside—not specify enumeration values for enumerations). But if you are adding to an existing specification, life can be more complicated.

Remember that a textually present tag construct automatically disables automatic tagging in a CHOICE, SEQUENCE, or SET—you are back in control (with IMPLICIT tagging).

> There is only one thing to say:
> use AUTOMATIC TAGS.

If you have good reasons not to use AUTOMATIC TAGS, then you need to have a much greater understanding of tagging, but you should then always use IMPLICIT TAGS in your module header. Using an explicit tagging environment in modern specifications would be confusing, and you would either have a very verbose protocol (with BER), or a specification that was littered with the word IMPLICIT.

If you choose to specify that certain tags are EXPLICIT, the reasons for this will be obscure to most readers, and you should indicate in your text why this was done.

There are usually two possible reasons. In an implicit tagging environment, tags on a choice type do in fact become explicit tags. It can help people implementing without a tool if this is made clear in the specification by writing in the word EXPLICIT (it is redundant to a computer, but may help a human being).

The other reason is some desire to essentially associate some semantics or categorization with particular tag values, and to ensure that (in BER) there is a length wrapper round the actual type being identified. A similar motivation comes from use of a type constraint on an open type when PER is used. Both of these (rather obscure) devices appear in some security specifications.

Of course, all the preceding discussion on tagging assumes you have written your type definitions within the defined ASN.1 module framework, not just written it standalone! I am sure that readers of this book would never do that!

7.2.10 Keeping It Simple

ASN.1 has a number of powerful mechanisms for providing clear specifications, but you will often find people recommending that some of them not be used in the interests of a simpler specification.

> This is Figure 999 stuff again—others would have a different list of what is "not simple," and make different recommendations!

There can sometimes be justification for this, but what appears simple tends very much to depend on what has been frequently encountered in the past, and new notational constructs may take a little time to gain a ready acceptance and recognition. Once understood and recognized, they can provide a clearer (and hence simpler) specification than the alternative of English text.

There is a second reason sometimes advanced for not using certain constructs, which is that some current-day tools will accept those constructs, but make no use of them, instead relying on so-called "compiler directives" (usually a specialized form of ASN.1 comment) that provide the same effect (and which in some cases pre-date the introduction of the notation into ASN.1).

Notations that fall into this category for either or both reasons are (in no particular order)

- use of ABSTRACT-SYNTAX,

- use of parameters of the abstract syntax (variable constraints),

- use of a type constraint on an Open Type,

- use of the {...} notation, and

- use of the ! exception specification notation.

I would **not** recommend avoidance of any of these, but I would caution that where these constructs (or of any other construct that is not—yet—widely used) **are** used, it can be sensible to include an ASN.1 comment, or introductory text in the main body of the specification, saying how and why the constructs are being used and their precise meaning for this protocol. That way, such constructs will become familiar to all, and become "simple"!

7.3 Issues for Implementors

This section is slightly shorter than the "issues for specifiers," but quite a few of the earlier topics recur here. The difference is that you (the implementor) are on the receiving end, and if the specifiers have produced ambiguities or left implementation dependencies, you have to sort them out! (Implementors would also be well advised to read carefully the two earlier parts of this chapter, as well, of course, as the whole of Section II.)

7.3.1 Guiding Principles

Principles for Internet implementors are often stated as follows.

- Strictly confirm to the specification in what you send.

- Be forgiving in what you receive.

That sounds like good advice, and it is often possible to write code that understands and processes things that are strictly invalid.

This situation arises more often in Internet protocols than in ASN.1-based protocols. This is because the use of a text-based format often introduces more redundancy, and

> Actually, I am not sure I want to give any! Implementation is a very detailed and messy task, particularly if you don't use a tool!

hence scope for "understanding" formally incorrect encodings, and also because most Internet protocols rely on this principle to provide for interworking between version 1 and version 2 of a specification. The situation will rarely arise with PER, which has almost no redundancy, and an explicit extensions bit!

With BER you could decide to be forgiving if you got a universal class 16 tag (SEQUENCE) with the primitive/constructor bit set to "primitive". Or you could be accidentally forbidding by just not bothering to write the code to check that bit once you had detected universal class 16!

But if you are forgiving of errors (a primitive sequence, or say, integers exceeding stated bounds), you should consider carefully the effect of being forgiving. This issue is related very strongly to extensibility—what you have got is implied extensibility (that you yourself have decided to introduce), and you are on your own to define the best exception-handling procedures.

I would recommend that in the case of ASN.1-based protocols it is rarely a good idea to silently ignore and process incorrect encodings that you are able to give meaning to (your own extensions). You may well choose to continue processing, but the error (with details of the sender) should at least be logged somewhere, and if the protocol permits it, sent back to the sender in some form of error message.

7.3.2 Know Your Tool

In any development environment there are an immense number of features in the tool chosen that can make an implementor's life easier. It is important to become familiar with those features/options/parameters of the tool.

> You'll know this already!

Part of the "quality" aspects of a tool is the ease with which you can acquire an understanding of the functions it provides, and the detailed syntax needed to obtain those functions. Of course, you may regard the actual functions it provides as more important, but functions that are not obvious in associated documentation or help files are almost as bad as missing functions.

7.3.3 Sizes of Integers

This issue has been discussed extensively in the section for specifiers (which is also relevant to implementors). Tools will often give you control over the length of integer they map to on a global basis (usually by command-line parameters), but will also give an override for individual fields, usually by "compiler directives"—special forms of ASN.1 comment.

The better tools will also allow you to specify that certain integer fields are to be treated as strings to allow them to be arbitrarily large (using dynamic memory allocation) subject to available memory.

> You need to know exactly what was intended. With luck, the specification will tell you. Otherwise a good guess is four octets! But if you guess, cover your back—raise it as an issue in your implementation team.

You have the following two problems,

- interpreting the intent of the specifier of the protocol, and

- getting your tool to do what you want, if what you want is not part of the formal specification or contradicts it!

The latter depends on the quality of the tool. So if your protocol specification says that a field is "INTEGER (0..7)", but you want it (for ease of programming and/or writing to a database) to be mapped to a 4-octet integer rather than a 2- or 1-octet integer in the programming language of your choice, are you able to do it?

> Everyone working on protocol specification, particularly in ISO and ITU-T, are well skilled at producing specifications that is not ambiguous, and that have no hidden implementation dependencies!

The former can be the more difficult problem! If specifiers have obeyed the guidelines/exhortions in this area given earlier in this chapter, you should have no problem, but otherwise you may need to try to guess (from knowledge of the application and from other parts of the specification, or by enquiry from others), just what the intention was, or how others are interpreting it.

7.3.4 Ambiguities and Implementation-Dependencies in Specifications

Don't believe the box! It is hard to write a specification that is completely clean (particularly in the first published specification), and that has totally specified the bits on the line that the implementation is required to produce under all circumstances. (I hate to say it, but if done well, the specifier's job is harder than the implementor's, but in the specifier's case it is a lot easier to do the job badly and not be found out!

The most important advice to implementors—and this is very important—is that if you find things that are not said, **raise them as an issue,** at least within your team, but preferably with the specifiers themselves through some appropriate mailing list or group.

Some of you will have heard of the Alternating Bit Protocol. A very similar protocol was specified for use over a particular LAN (no names, no pack drill!) in the late 1970s, but the specification did not say what the behavior was to be when an ACK with the wrong number was received. The implementors decided that the "right" action was to immediately retransmit the last message (with the same sequence number), trusting the receiver to discard duplicates. Result: parasitic transmissions. Throughput dropped to half until the load backed off, with every packet being transmitted twice!

If there is one clear duty for implementors, it is not to take their own decisions when specifications are unclear!

7.3.5 Corrigenda

Implementors need to be as much aware as those in a more managerial capacity of what corrigenda are around, their status, and how they might impact the implementation in the future.

> Just read the advice given at the start of this chapter on management issues—worry about corrigenda!

If you know something is coming, its arrival can be a lot less painful if plans have been made for it!

7.3.6 Extensibility and Exception Handling

This text is getting repetitive! If you are told clearly what the bits on the wire should be (and what you do in response to them), and how you are to handle unknown stuff coming in, and if your decoding tool is sufficiently good and flexible, then there are no problems.

> With a good spec and a good tool, you have no problems!

Otherwise worry!

7.3.7 Care with Hand Encodings

If, for whatever reason, you do not even have access to a well-debugged library of routines to encode simple types like INTEGER, etc., let alone access to a fully fledged ASN.1 compiler, then you deserve sympathy!

Producing ASN.1 encodings from scratch, by hand, is not impossible, and in one sense, not even difficult. (But it is probably easier to get it right the first time with BER than with PER, unfortunately, due to the large number of optimizations in PER.) It is simply time-consuming and error prone.

First of all, you need to read Section III more carefully than you otherwise would! Then you need to spend a lot of time with the actual ASN.1 encoding specification that you will be using.

Second, you will need some sort of ad hoc "line monitor" tool to display what you are producing in a format that will make it easy for you to check that you are producing what you intended.

> No tool? Life will be hard. Be careful. (You have lost the option to be good!)

And, lastly, you really need an ASN.1 tool! Not one that necessarily runs on your platform (the lack of that is presumably why you are not using a tool), but one that can run on some other communicating platform, take your output, and display the values it thinks you are transmitting.

Well, that was almost last! There is nothing like final interoperability testing with a totally different complete implementation, particularly if it (and you!) have good error logging of things you think are erroneous about what you are receiving.

7.3.8 Mailing Lists

There is a mailing list you can use for general ASN.1 enquiries (see Appendix 5 for a link to this), and

> Get tapped in!

many protocol specifications today are supported by mailing lists, news groups, Web pages, etc.

These resources can be very valuable to you. (As can people who give ASN.1 and specific protocol courses, who are usually willing to leave their e-mail addresses with you and to answer queries subsequent to their courses.)

7.3.9 Good Engineering: Version 2 **Will** Come!

Any protocol you implement will have a version-2 specification that you or your descendants (teamwise) will have to implement.

> Extensibility is not just for specifiers.

All the usual good engineering principles apply to make sure that your code and documentation enable others to modify your implementation to support the version-2 specification as and when this is produced.

You will obtain some hints in the extensibility provisions of version 1 of what areas the specifiers expect to change. This can help you to engineer the structure of your implementation to be easily able to accommodate those changes when they arrive.

Just as getting exception handling as correct as possible is a challenge for specifiers, obtaining an implementation architecture that enables extensions to be easily handled (and providing correct exception handling in version 1 when there are as yet no version-2 systems around to test against) is the challenge for the implementor. As for specifiers—this is part of your job, get it right!

7.4 Conclusion

This completes the first section of the book. Many of you will be leaving us at this point (although you may find some parts of Section IV interesting). I hope you have found it useful. The more technically minded will no doubt be proceeding to Sections II and III—read on!

Further Details

## CHAPTER 8

The Object Identifier Type
(Or: What's in a Name?)

Summary

The object identifier type, and its associated hierarchical name-space is heavily used by protocol specifiers that use ASN.1. It provides a world-wide unambiguous naming scheme that anyone can use, and has been used to name a very wide range of "things".

Object identifiers are used to identify

a. ASN.1 modules,

b. Abstract and transfer syntaxes,

c. Managed objects and their attributes,

d. Components of Directory (X.500) names,

e. Headers of MHS messages (X.400) and MHS Body Types,

f. Banks and Merchants in Secure Electronic Transactions,

g. Character Repertoires and their encodings,

h. Parcels being tracked by courier firms, and

i. Many other "things" or "information objects".

8.1 Introduction

Final discussion of the object identifier type has been deferred to this "Further Details" section but as a type notation it is as simple as BOOLEAN. You just write:

```
OBJECT IDENTIFIER
```

all uppercase. The complexity arises with the set of values of this type, and with the value notation.

First, we should note that the set of values is dynamically changing on a daily basis, and that no one computer system (or human being) is expected to know what all the legal values are. The value notation

> Object identifiers were intro-
> duced into ASN.1 in 1986 to
> meet a growing need for a
> name-space with globally
> unique short identifiers, which
> permitted easy acquisition of
> name-space by anybody.

has a structure, and each object identifier value can be mapped onto a sequence of simple integer values, but these structures do not matter. Treated as an atomic entity, an object identifier value (and its associated semantics) is either known to an implementation, or not known. This is all that matters.

When this type is used in a computer protocol, it is almost always used in circumstances where there is (or should be!) a clear specification of the exception handling that is required if a received object identifier value does not match a known value.

Note that all current ASN.1 encoding rules provide a canonical encoding of object identifier values (no encoder options), which is the same for all encoding rules and is also an integral multiple of eight bits (an octet string). So storing those object identifier values for which the semantics is known as simple octet strings containing the ASN.1 encoding, and comparing incoming encodings with these, is a viable implementation option.

We have already met values of the type as a way of identifying modules, and have seen some of the value notation. We now discuss the model underlying such values and the allocation of object identifier name-space.

8.2 The Object Identifier Tree

The underlying concept for object identifiers is a tree-structure, usually drawn as in Figure 8.1. Each object identifier value corresponds to precisely one path from the root down to a leaf (or possibly an internal node), with each component of the value notation identifying one of the arcs traversed on this path.

The tree has a single root (usually drawn at the top as is the usual way with trees in computing), and a number of arcs to the next level (all arcs go just to the next level), providing nodes at that level. Each node at the next level has arcs down to nodes at the next level below, and so on. **Both the depth of the tree and the number of arcs from each node are unlimited.** Some branches of the tree will be thickly populated with subarcs, others sparsely. Some branches will end early, others will go very deep.

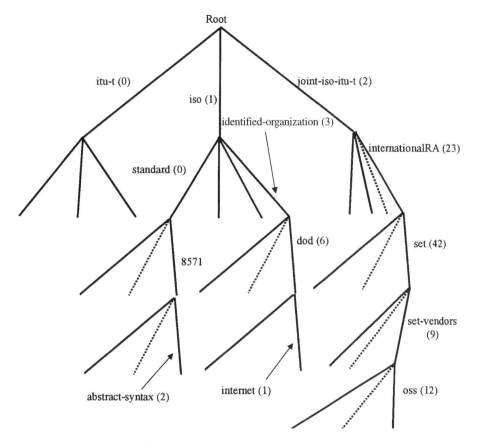

Figure 8.1 A small part of the object identifier tree.

Every node is administered by some authority. That authority allocates arcs beneath that node, leading to a subordinate node, and determining

- The authority to which delegated responsibility for further allocation (beneath the subordinate node) has been passed, or an **information object** which is associated with that (leaf) node. (The "information object" concept is discussed further below.)

- A number (unambiguous within all arcs from the current node) to identify the subordinate node from the current node (zero upwards, not necessarily consecutive).

- **Optionally** a name to be associated with the arc for use by human beings, and again providing identification within the arcs from the current node.

The name in the third bullet is required to conform to the ASN.1 rules for a value-reference-name, that is, it must begin with a lowercase letter, and continue with letters (of any case) and digits and hyphens (but with no two consecutive hyphens).

When "ccitt" became "itu-t", the ASN.1 standardizers tacitly accepted synonyms for names on arcs.

Perhaps because of this, many users of ASN.1 now feel that arc names are relatively unimportant (certainly they do not affect the bits-on-the-line), and that once you have obtained a (numerical) object identifier allocation, you can use value notation for that object identifier with any names you choose when you wish to identify yourself, or to publish allocations beneath your node. Some would even assert the right to vary the names used in higher-level nodes.

As at mid-1999, this area is in a state of flux. Earlier views would have said that names were allocated by the superior of an arc, and were immutable, otherwise there is much scope for human confusion. However, the text in the specification does not entirely support this view, although I know it was the original intent!

The contrary view (that in published OIDs any name can be used) is supported on two grounds:

- There are issues of copyright or trademark of names, which superior nodes are often unwilling to get involved in, so they make no name allocation to their subordinate arcs, only a number.

- Lower arcs can sometimes be sensitive about appearing to be subordinate to (or part of) organizations whose names identify arcs between themselves and the root. In many cases such an association is at best a loose one, and some organizations will give out object identifier space to anyone who asks for it.

It is likely that the standard will be clarified to assert not only that names are optional in the value notation for an object identifier, but also that all such names are arbitrarily chosen by those who include object identifier values in publications. **However, it would be irresponsible to use misleading names on arcs, and it is probably best either to omit the name or to use the generally recognized one from any arcs above that which points to your node.**

8.3 Information Objects

The term **information object** used in this context emphasizes the fact that object identifiers are usually used to identify relatively abstract objects, such as ASN.1

modules, the definition of some operation that a computer can perform, attributes of some system that can be manipulated by a management protocol, and so on. In other words, they usually identify some piece of specification (not necessarily written using ASN.1). In fact, an organization can be seen as just another type of information object, and in general a node can both be associated with an information object (of any sort) and **also** have further subordinate nodes.

If an organization has been allocated a node, we say they have been "hung" from the tree. It is also possible to "hang" inanimate objects (such as ASN.1 modules) from the tree, once you are the proud owner of a node!

It is very easy to learn the top bits of the tree, and then to "cheat"; to "steal" an arc from some node, publishing allocations beneath that. **Do not do it!** It is not hard to get "legal" object identifier name-space. But see Figure 999; there are those who advocate a top-level arc where arcs below that are only unambiguous within a very closed community—anyone can use any number, and caveat emptor! What this is really saying is that there is a

> Distributed registration authorities provide space enough for all. Have you got hung on the object identifier tree yet? Get a piece of the action!

suggestion that some object identifier values should be **context-specific,** all such values being identified by a special top-level arc. However, this proposal is merely that, a proposal. Such a top-level arc does not yet (mid-1999) exist, although the RELATIVE-OID type discussed in Section IV performs a similar role.

To identify an organization or object, we use an object identifier value. At the abstract level, this is simply a path from the root to the organization or object being identified. This path can be specified by giving the number of each arc in turn, together with the names (which may be empty/nonexistent) associated with each of these arcs. The encoding rules use only the numbers of the arcs, so nonexistent names are not a problem. The value notation has various forms (see following text) that allow both the names and numbers to be specified. Figure 8.1 shows one small part of the tree, with two branches taken to a depth of 4 and 5 arcs.

N O T E

The term "information object" was used in OBJECT IDENTIFIER text long before the introduction of the "Information Object Class" concepts and (perhaps confusingly) refers to a more general concept than the same words used in connection with Information Object Classes.

8.4 Value Notation

Note that in all the examples that follow, it would be legal to replace any number by a value-reference name of type INTEGER. If this value reference name had been assigned the value given in the examples that follow, then the resulting object identifier value is unchanged. It is, however, not common practice to do this.

The value notation consists of a series of components, one for each arc leading to an identified object. In Figure 8.1 we can identify the objects at the bottom of the figure by

```
{iso standard 8571 abstract-syntax (2)}
```

and

```
{iso identified-organization dod (6) internet (1) }
```

and

```
{joint-iso-itu-t  internationalRA (23) set (42) set-vendors (9) oss (12) }
```

or equivalently, but less readably, by

```
{1   0   8571   2}
```

and

```
{1   3   6   1}
```

and

```
{2   23   42   9   12}
```

The first value names an information object in the ISO Standard 8571, the second gives object identifier space to the IETF, and subarcs of this are heavily populated in the Internet specification for the Simple Network Management Protocol (SNMP). The third value gives object identifier name-space to Open Systems Solutions, a vendor associated with the Secure Electronic Transactions (SET) consortium.

It is always permissible to use only numbers (but not common). In one case "8571" an arc has a number but no name, so the number appears alone, **not** in brackets. In most other cases, the name is given followed by the number in brackets. (The number is **required** to be in brackets if both are given). It is only for the top arcs (iso, standard, joint-iso-itu-t) that the numbers can be omitted, as these are "well-known" arcs, with their numerical values listed in the ASN.1 specification pre-1988 (they are now listed in X.660/ISO 9834-1). Although seeing specifications with these top-level numbers omitted is quite common, it is becoming increasingly the practice, particularly as ASN.1 is now being used by organizations only loosely associated with ITU-T or ISO (or not associated at all), to list the numbers in parenthesis for all arcs.

Notice that this value notation does not contain commas between components. This is unusual for ASN.1 value notation, and was done to promote easy human readability, particularly of the early components with the numbers omitted.

There is one other facility available when specifying object identifier values. We have already met it in Figure 3.8, where we chose to define an object identifier value "wineco-OID" with five components, and then use that name immediately after the curly bracket in our IMPORTS statement. (It is only allowed immediately after the curly bracket.) This is something that is quite commonly done, but note that it is **not** allowed for the module identifier, as the scope of reference names in the module has not yet been entered. Some specifications will define a large number of object identifier values, particularly in association with the definition of information objects, and a very common style is to assign these values in a single module to a series of value-reference-names, exporting those names. They will then be imported and used as necessary in other modules.

8.5 Uses of the Object Identifier Type

It is a common occurrence for a protocol to be written where there is a need to carry identification of "things". These "things" may be

- what it is:
  - operating on,
  - ordering,
  - reporting on,
- information that it is carrying;
- identification of specific actions to be undertaken on receipt of a message;
- components of some more complex structure, such as Directory (X.500) names; and others.

Some existing uses are listed in the "Summary" at the start of this chapter.

We use the term "information objects" for "things", because at the end of the day a physical "thing" is identified by some piece of text or specification—a piece of information, and sometimes the "thing" is not a physical object but is a rather abstract "thing" such as an organization, but the "thing" is still identified by some specification—a piece of information. What is really being identified by an object identifier value is that more elaborate and precise specification of the thing—an "information object", rather than the "thing" itself, but the two are in 1-1 correspondence, so there is really no distinction.

Where there is a need for the identification of an information object,

- which must be world-wide unambiguous; and

- where allocations of identification to such information objects need to be widely available to almost anyone; then

use of ASN.1 object identifier values is a good way to go.

In general, almost all users of ASN.1 have found the need for a naming scheme to identify information objects relevant to their application, and have chosen to use object identifier values for this purpose, and to include in their protocol fields that are OBJECT IDENTIFIER types to carry such values. The OBJECT IDENTIFIER type and its associated naming structure are important and very much used.

The Character String Types

(Or: Overcoming Genesis, Chapter 11!)

Summary

This chapter discusses the complete set of character string types that include

- NumericString

- PrintableString

- VisibleString (ISO646String)

- IA5String

- TeletexString (T61String)

- VideotexString

- GraphicString

- GeneralString

- UniversalString

- BMPString

- UTF8String

It describes their value notations, and gives recommendations on their use.

Discussion of the character string "hole" type—CHARACTER STRING—is deferred until Chapter 14.

9.1 Introduction

Here we will describe all the available (up to 1988) character string types apart from "CHARACTER STRING", which is described later under "Hole Types". For a full understanding of these types, the reader must be aware of the various approaches that have been taken to character encoding schemes for computers generally over the years. A full discussion of this, and of the historical development of support for character string types in ASN.1, is given in Section IV. Sufficient information is given here for the writing and understanding of ASN.1 specifications.

> And God was displeased with the people of Babel for building their tower unto heaven, and sent a thunderbolt and scattered the peoples to the corners of the world giving them different languages.

If you want to skip some of this material, just flip to 9.13, "Recommended character string types" on page 171, and look at the paragraphs here about the ones mentioned there. That is probably all you need!

Character string types are considered by some to be unnecessary (can a good old OCTET STRING do the job?). (See Figure 999!). Yes, an OCTET STRING could be used. But you would then need to spell out clearly the precise encoding to be used, and to make clear to implementors the range of characters that were to be supported. Moreover, that specification would be in normal human-readable text or in ASN.1 comment, could not be understood by any tool assisting an implementation, and (as it is new text) would be a potential source of ambiguity and interworking problems.

The types provided in ASN.1 cover the spectrum from the simplest requirements to the most ambitious. In general, if your character set requirements for a particular string are restricted, use the more restricted character set types to make this clear, even if the encoding is the same as for a type with a wider character repertoire.

Note also that some of the latest character string types can only be supported **easily** by a programming language (such as Java) that uses 16 bits per character, supporting the *Unicode* encoding scheme. (This scheme is fully described in Section IV.) Increasingly, however, (late 1990s) programming languages and operating systems and browsers and word processors, etc. are all providing Unicode support, either for the 16-bits-per-character repertoire, or in some cases for a 32-bits-per-character repertoire.

This does not mean that if the application designer has specified a field as (for example) UTF8String or UniversalString, you cannot implement that protocol in a language (or operating system) that does not have Unicode support; it just means that it may be harder work!

9.2 NumericString

Values of the type are strings of characters containing the digits zero to nine and space. The BER encoding is ASCII (8 bits per character), and the PER encoding is

4 bits per character unless the character repertoire has been further restricted by a "permitted alphabet constraint" (see Chapter 10), when it could be less.

9.3 PrintableString

Values of the type are strings of characters containing an ad hoc list of characters defined in a table in the ASN.1 specification, and copied here as Figure 9.1.

This is basically the old *telex* character set, plus the lowercase letters. You would probably tend not to use it today unless you had an application likely to be associated with devices with limited character input or display capabilities.

9.4 VisibleString (ISO646String)

The name "ISO646String" is a deprecated synonym for VisibleString (deprecated because the name contains a Standard number, which is not in fact used in its

Name	Graphic
Capital letters	A, B, ... Z
Small letters	a, b, ... z
Digits	0, 1, ... 9
Space	(space)
Apostrophe	'
Left Parenthesis	(
Right Parenthesis	)
Plus sign	+
Comma	,
Hyphen	-
Full stop	.
Solidus	/
Colon	:
Equal sign	=
Question mark	?

Figure 9.1 Characters in PrintableString.

definition, post-1986!), but you may encounter it. The character repertoire is described in the very old ISO Standard ISO 646, which laid the foundation for the better-known ASCII. While this character repertoire was originally strictly **not** ASCII, but rather "the International Reference Version of ISO 646", it was widely interpreted by all ASN.1 users and implementors as simple plain ASCII, but **printing characters plus space only.** The original definition was by reference to the ISO 646 Standard, but post-1986 the definition was formally "Register Entry 2 (plus space) of the International Register of Coded Character Sets to be used with Escape Sequences". (See Section IV for more detail.) This was changed in 1994 to reference "Register Entry 6", which **is** strict ASCII, recognizing the normal interpretation by ASN.1 users. The coding in BER is 8 bits per character, and it is the same in PER if there is no subtyping applied to the type to restrict the range of characters (if there is, it could be less).

9.5 IA5String

"International Alphabet 5" is specified in a very old ITU-T Recommendation, which again was the original reference for this type. Again, this was close to ASCII (ASCII was a "national variant" of International Alphabet 5, but the type is widely assumed to mean simply "the whole of ASCII, including control characters, space, and del". The precise reference today is "Register Entries 1 and 6 (plus space and delete) of the International Register of Coded Character Sets to be used with Escape Sequences", which is strict ASCII. The encoding is again 8 bits per character (possibly less in PER).

9.6 TeletexString (T61String)

Again, the synonym is deprecated. Originally CCITT Recommendation T.61 specified the character repertoire for Teletex, and was referenced by the ASN.1 specification. (Today the corresponding specifications are in the ITU-T T.50 series.) The precise definition of this type has changed over time to reflect the increasing range of languages supported by the ITU-T Teletex Recommendations. Today it includes Urdu, Korean, Greek, ... Formally, it is Register Entries 6, 87, 102, 103, 106, 107, 126, 144, 150, 153, 156, 164, 165, 168, plus SPACE and DELETE! The encoding of each register entry is 8 bits per character, but there are defined escape codes (the ASCII "ESC" encoding followed by some defined octet values) to switch between the different register entries. It is quite hard to implement full support for this character string type, but it is extensively used in X.400 and X.500 work. The character repertoires referenced have increased with each new version of ASN.1, and may continue to do so, under pressure to maintain alignment with the ITU-T Teletex Recommendations, which themselves are under pressure to support more and more of the world's character sets. This makes this type effectively an open-ended set of character repertoires, and would make any claims of "conformance" hard to define or sustain. Today, it is best avoided, but it was popular in the mid-1980s, and you will often encounter it.

9.7 VideotexString

A little-used character string type that gives access to the "characters" used to build crude pictures on videotext systems. Typically a "character" is a 3×2 array, with each cell containing either a foreground color or a background color (determined by transmission of one of about five control characters), giving 64 different printing "characters" that can be used to build the picture. Formally, it is again a list of 17 register entries, partially overlapping those specified for TeletexString.

9.8 GraphicString

This was a popular string type in the main OSI (Open Systems Interconnection) standards produced during the 1980s, and allowed **any** of the Register Entries in the International Register for printing characters (but not the control character entries). In its heyday the International Register had a new entry added about every month or so, and eventually covered most of the languages of the world. If this text is used in an academic course, an interesting student exercise would be to discuss the implementation implications of using such a wide (and ever expanding!) type definition. Since the development of ISO 10646/Unicode, additions to the International Register have become much less common, and coding schemes based on this Register can be regarded as obsolescent.

9.9 GeneralString

This is similar to GraphicString, except that the register entries for control characters (of which there are many) can also be used.

9.10 UniversalString

This is a string type that was introduced into ASN.1 in 1994, following the completion of the ISO Standard 10646 and the publication of the Unicode specification (see Section IV for more information on ISO 10646 and Unicode). The ISO 10646 standard (and the ASN.1 encoding in BER) envisages a 32 bits per character encoding scheme, sufficient to cover all the languages of the world without using "combining characters", with a fair bit left over for the languages of Mars and most of the rest of the undiscovered Universe! It is only this type and UTF8String (see 9.12) that can cover all the characters for which computer encodings have been defined (not quite true—there are

> UNICODE is supported by UniversalString and BMPString and by UTF8String.

some weird glyphs in the International Register that have not yet been put into ISO 10646). This type has not, however, proved popular among ASN.1 users.

9.11 BMPString

The name comes from the Basic Multilingual Plane (BMP) of ISO 10646, which contains all characters with any commercial importance (all living languages), and can be encoded (and is in BER) with a fixed 16-bits per character. While the formal ASN.1 definition references ISO 10646, the character set is the same as that defined in and more commonly known as the *Unicode Standard* produced by the Unicode Consortium. (Search the Web if you want to know more about Unicode, or see Section IV). The fixed-size representation of 16 bits per character, holding Unicode characters, is becoming common in revisions of programming languages and operating systems, and is rapidly replacing ASCII as the default encoding for manipulating character data. This ASN.1 type was widely used during the mid-1990s by those application specifications upgrading to the 1994 ASN.1 specification. (It was not present in ASN.1 pre-1994.)

9.12 UTF8String

> *UTF8String is the recommended character string type for full internationalization without unnecessary verbosity.*

This encoding scheme was developed in the mid-1990s and the type was added to ASN.1 in 1998. The acronym stands for "Universal Transformation Format, 8 bit", but that does not matter much. Formally, the character repertoire is exactly the same as UniversalString—all defined characters can be represented.

UTF8 is, however, a **variable length** encoding for each character, with the rather interesting property that (7 bit) ASCII characters encode as ASCII—in a single octet with the top bit set to zero, and none of the octets in the representation of a non-ASCII character have the top bit set to zero. ASCII is paramount! Most European language characters (like c-cedilla or u-umlaut) will encode in two octets, and the whole of the

Basic Multilingual Plane, together with all characters identified so far, encode in at most three octets per character. If we ever do populate the whole of the ISO 10646 32-bit space, then UTF8 would use a maximum of six octets per character.

While use of a fixed 16 bits per character is becoming the norm for operating system interfaces and programming languages, use of UTF8 for storage and transmission of character data is the way everyone is going (as of mid-1999). As an implementor of an ASN.1-based application, you can expect that if you use an ASN.1 tool with a language that supports Unicode, the UTF8 transformations will be applied by the tool, invisibly to you, as part of the ASN.1 encode/decode process, giving you a simple 16 bits (or 32 bits) per character to work with in memory, but with an efficient transfer syntax.

9.13 Recommended Character String Types

So having read right to the end, you can now make an informed judgment on which character string types to use! Here it is assumed you are writing a new specification and will conform to the post-1994 ASN.1, and hence can use all the facilities in the latest ASN.1. (A fuller discussion of the pre-1994/post-1994 issues appears in Section IV.)

If, for the expected implementation of your application, the input/output devices involved are likely to be able to handle the full Unicode character set, and you want to be as general as possible, then UTF8String is for you! The earlier UniversalString and BMPString offer few if any advantages, and should be ignored. If, however, input or output is likely to be done on more limited devices, then you may wish to consider a more restricted character string type.

> For full internationalization, use UTF8String. Otherwise use the most restrictive character string type available for your needs. If input/output devices restrict your application, consider NumericString or PrintableString or VisibleString or IA5String.

GeneralString and GraphicString, based on the International Register, are obsolete, and there is no case for using them in new specifications, although they were important in the 1980s.

The same remark applies to TeletexString (T61String) and VideotexString—you are unlikely to want to use these unless you have strong links to the associated ITU-T Recommendations.

If your application does require use of input/output devices that may only be able to support a limited range of characters, then you must seriously consider using only NumericString, PrintableString, VisibleString (ISO646String), or IA5String. NumericString is **very** limited, and is not fully international, but is better from the internationalization point of view than the other three (arabic numbers are accepted over more of the world than the full range of ASCII characters). PrintableString has the slight merit that it is hardwired into ASN.1, so there can be no misunderstandings about what characters are included, but it is essentially a cutdown ASCII with few advantages over ASCII. If you want full ASCII, then you need VisibleString (no control characters) or IA5String (includes control characters). This will be fine for English-speaking communities, and is livable with for a number of other European languages, but is generally deprecated in any sort of international specification.

Ultimately, the choice has to be yours as the application designer; ASN.1 merely provides the notational tools, but you probably want to restrict your choice to NumericString, PrintableString, VisibleString, IA5String, and UTF8String. You should use UTF8String if input/output devices are not likely to play a strong determining role in implementations of your application (for example, if all associated input/output will be using general purpose computer software for keyboard input and display).

9.14 Value Notation for Character String Types

This book gives full coverage of the ASN.1 notation, but there are a number of parts of that notation that you will rarely need or encounter. Value notation for character strings is in that category, and value notation for control characters or characters appearing in several languages is even less commonly needed. Just scan this section and return to it later if you find you need it!

The only value notation for character string types pre-1994 was to list the characters in quotation marks. This was fine for simple repertoires like PrintableString, but did not enable

> Names exist for all UNICODE characters, and can be used in ASN.1 to give precision to the specification of character string values without concern about ambiguity of glyphs or the character set available on your publication medium. Cell references can also be used.

control characters to be specified for a type such as IA5String, and gives ambiguity problems in printed specifications with strings such as

"HOPE"

if the repertoire includes Cyrillic and Greek as well as ASCII! (Each of these four glyphs appears as a character in more than one of these alphabets). There are also potential problems in printed specifications in determining what white space in character string values is intended to represent (how many spaces, "thin" spaces, etc.).

Post-1994, two additional mechanisms became available for defining a character string precisely, both of them based on listing the characters individually.

The notation is illustrated by the following:

```
my-string1 UTF8String ::= {cyrillicCapitalLetterEn,
                           greekCapitalLetterOmicron,
                           latinCapitalLetterP,
                           cyrillicCapitalLetterIe}
my-string2 IA5String ::= {nul, soh, etx, "ABC", del}
my-string3 UTF8String ::= { {0, 0, 4, 29},
                            {0, 0, 3, 159},
                            {0, 0, 0, 80},
                            {0, 0, 4, 21} }
my-string4 IA5String ::= { {0, 0},
                           {0, 1},
                           {0, 3},
                           "ABC",
                           {7, 15} }
```

As you will guess, my-string3 is the same as my-string1 (and could be printed as "HOPE"!), and my-string4 is the same as my-string2. The last two notations reference the cells (giving group, plane, row, cell) of ISO 10646 or of ASCII (formally, of Register Entry 6 of the International Register) (giving table column as 0 to 7 and table row as 0 to 15).

The last two notations can be used freely, but the character names used in the first two notations are only available if they have been imported into your module from a module that is defined (algorithmically) in the ASN.1 specification by reference to character names assigned in ISO 10646 (and Unicode).

To make these value notations valid, you need the following IMPORTS statement in your module:

```
IMPORTS cyrillicCapitalLetterEn, greekCapitalLetterOmicron,
        latinCapitalLetterP, cyrillicCapitalLetterIe,
        nul, soh, etx, del FROM
        ASN1-CHARACTER-MODULE
{joint-iso-itu-t asn1(1) specification(0) modules(0) iso10646(0)};
```

You will also note that you can mix the different notations—character names, quoted strings, cell references—within a single value definition.

This approach works, but if your "HOPE" was actually intended to be the ASCII characters, there is now a less verbose method available (post-1998). You can simply write:

```
my-string5 UTF8String(BasicLatin)::= "HOPE"
```

where "BasicLatin" is imported from the ASN.1 module. You can then, in a SEQUENCE say, have an element:

```
string-element UTF8String DEFAULT my-string5
```

What we are doing here is fairly obvious—we are "qualifying" the UTF8String type to say that we are only using the BasicLatin (ASCII) part, so the "HOPE" is now unambiguously the ASCII characters. Note that in the SEQUENCE, we use the full UTF8String type. This rather simple notation rests on two powerful and general concepts, those of subtyping and of value mappings. Subtyping is the definition of a new type that contains only a subset of the values of the so-called *parent type*. In this case the parent type is "UTF8String", and we are using a subtype of that (defined in the ASN.1 module) called "BasicLatin" to subtype it here. The preceding example could actually have been written

```
my-string5 BasicLatin ::= "HOPE"
```

which perhaps makes it clearer that "my-string5" is Latin characters, but makes it less clear that it can be used as a DEFAULT value for UTF8String (although it still can). Subtyping is discussed in more detail in the next chapter. Whichever way "my-string5" is defined, its use as a default value for UTF8String is dependent on a general concept in ASN.1 that if something is a value-reference-name of a subtype of some type, it can also be used as a value-reference-name for a value of the parent type, and in some cases of other "similar" types. This is the *value mapping* concept in the ASN.1 semantic model (introduced briefly in Section I and discussed more fully in Section IV), and in this case allows "my-string5" to be used not just as a value for UTF8String, but also, should you wish it, as a value for PrintableString and VisibleString.

9.15 The ASN.1-CHARACTER-MODULE

This module has already been mentioned. It provides value-reference-names for all the ASCII control characters (explicitly listed), and for all the characters in Unicode/ISO 10646. The character names listed in the ISO 10646 Standard (and Unicode) are given in all uppercase with spaces between words. To convert to an ASN.1 name you keep the uppercase letter for the first letter of every word except for the first name, change all other letters to lowercase, then remove the spaces! This produces the names we used above, and also the rather long name

```
cjkUnifiedIdeograph-4e2a
```

for the Chinese/Japanese/Korean (CJK) character that looks (to a Western eye!) like a vertical bar with a caret over it, and is named in ISO 10646 as "CJK Unified Ideograph-4e2a".

ISO 10646 also defines 84 *collections*—useful sets of characters. These names are mapped into ASN.1 names for subtypes of UTF8String by the same algorithm, except that as they are types (sets of string values, not single character values), they keep their initial uppercase letter. Here are a few examples of the names that are available for import:

```
BasicLatin

Latin-1Supplement

LatinExtended-A

IpaExtensions

BasicGreek

SuperscriptsAndSubscripts

MathematicalOperators

BoxDrawing

etc
```

9.16 Conclusion

The ASN.1 character string types have evolved over time as the character set standards themselves have changed, and as input/output devices and packages have become more capable of handling a wider and wider range of characters.

Partly to provide a mechanism that would accommodate **any** character repertoire and encoding scheme, the CHARACTER STRING hole type was introduced. This is described in a later chapter.

Mechanisms were also added over time to provide for a more precise tailoring of character repertoires to users' needs, and to provide a precise and unambiguous value notation for character strings that does not depend on (the perhaps restricted set of) glyphs available for any printed ASN.1 specification, or on the character repertoire (such as perhaps only ASCII) available for any machine-readable ASN.1 specification.

The end result is a perhaps confusing, but wide-ranging and up-to-date set of types for character string fields.

Subtyping

(Or: Tighten Up Your Data Types!)

Summary

This chapter describes the ASN.1 subtype notation that allows the precise definition of the set (subset) of values that you wish to allow for a type. You can, for example, specify

- the range of an integer;

- minimum and/or maximum length of a string;

- the precise characters wanted from a character set; and

- minimum and/or maximum number of iterations in a SEQUENCE OF or SET OF.

The full notation has considerable power and flexibility, but these examples are the ones most commonly met.

10.1 Introduction

The ASN.1 "subtype notation" is very powerful, and it would be nice to say that it is one of the things that makes ASN.1 great! However, while the simpler instances of its use (length limits on strings, limits on iterations of SEQUENCE OF, ranges on integers) are common, and it is impor-tant that you use them where you can, some of the other features of this notation are seen less often, and are perhaps less important.

Note also (before reading on—or skipping!) that flexibility in subtype notation was considerably enhanced in 1994, so some of the examples to be given here were not legal pre-1994. Check the actual ASN.1 specification!

> Customize your types to just the precise values you need—it can often reduce the number of bits-on-the-line by more than a fac-tor of two (if PER is in use), and gives clear guidance to imple-mentors for memory allocation decisions, such as the size of integer to use.

We have very briefly met subtyping in Figure 2.1, where (omitting the distinguished values) we had a sequence element of

```
no-of-days-reported-on INTEGER (1..56)
```

restricting the range of the integer field to the values 1 to 56.

In the pre-1994 ASN.1, this notation in round brackets was regarded as producing a new type consisting of a subset (hence **sub**typing) of the values in the original or **parent** type. Post-1994, the viewpoint tends to be more that we are **constraining** the integer to be in the range 1–56. Why the difference? Well, post-1994 a number of other constraint mechanisms were introduced (also within a pair of round brackets following the type being constrained), but more importantly, focusing on the notation as a **constraint** raises the question "And what if I get incoming material that violates the constraint?" The general issue of constraints (and associated exception handling) is left to Chapter 14 of this section, but here we will fully discuss the simple subtype notation, first introduced into ASN.1 in 1986.

When subtyping was introduced into ASN.1, the Basic Encoding Rules were not changed. They were TLV-based, and using subtype information to, for example, eliminate the "L" part, would have destroyed the structure of the encoding. So up to 1994, application of subtyping merely helped the writer of application-code, it did not affect encoding, or the number of bits-on-the-line. With the introduction of the Packed Encoding Rules (PER), encoding is affected by subtyping (particularly of integers). To gain maximum benefit from PER, application designers should include range information (and length constraints on strings, and iteration constraints on SET OF and SEQUENCE OF) whenever they reasonably can.

In PER there is the concept of "PER-visible constraints"—things that affect the encoding. Not all subtyping constructs are PER-visible (and in particular inner subtyping—see 10.8—is never PER-visible for good reasons). It is tempting to suggest (see Figure 999 again!) that you can ignore—do not learn about, do not use—any subtyping notation that is not PER-visible, but this would be bad advice, as a new super-PER could at some stage be defined that would take account of the more complex constraints. The right advice is: "If you intend your applications to use only a subset of the values of some type, then try to express that formally using the ASN.1 subtype notation, not just as comment."

10.2 Basic Concepts and Set Arithmetic

Before looking at the different forms of subtype notation, it is important to recognize that subtype notation (like tagging—see the next chapter) is formally producing a new type. So wherever ASN.1 requires/allows type-notation, you can instead write:

```
type-notation subtype-notation
```

although the "subtype-notation" has to be one of the allowed notations for the parent type given by "type-notation". The "subtype-notation" construction always begins and ends with round brackets.

This idea can be recursively applied. So you can, for example, write

```
My-string1 ::= PrintableString (SIZE (1..10)) (FROM ("A" .. "Z"))
```

This first defines a type that is PrintableString restricted to strings between 1 and 10 characters, then further restricts this to strings that contain only the characters "A" to "Z".

There is another subtype notation that can, in one fell swoop, do the same job using set arithmetic. We can write:

```
My-string2 ::= PrintableString
                ( SIZE (1..10) INTERSECTION FROM ("A" .. "Z") )
```

In this notation, the "SIZE (1..10)" selects the set of all values of PrintableString that have lengths between 1 and 10 inclusive. The "FROM ("A" .. "Z")" selects all values of PrintableString that contain only the characters "A" to "Z". The mathematical intersection of these sets gives exactly the same set of PrintableString values as was specified by My-String1 here.

> The subtype notation is applied to a type (the parent type) and produces a new type that contains a subset of the set of abstract values in the parent type.

In general, the construction in round brackets contains a number of terms separated by the words "INTERSECTION", "UNION", "EXCEPT", with the "normal" precedence (INTERSECTION binds tightest, EXCEPT binds least tightly). Each term formally identifies a set of values of the parent type (PrintableString in the preceding example), and normal set arithmetic is applied to determine which values are in the resulting new type.

(As an aside, it is illegal ASN.1 if the set-arithmetic results in a type being defined that has no values!)

Note also that, to avoid confusion for the reader on precedence

```
INTEGER ( A EXCEPT B EXCEPT C )
```

is disallowed, and has to be written as

```
INTEGER ( ( A EXCEPT B ) EXCEPT C )
```

or

```
INTEGER ( A EXCEPT ( B EXCEPT C ) )
```

whichever was intended. There is no equivalent restriction for UNION and INTERSECTION, because if both the "EXCEPT"s here are replaced by "UNION" (or by "INTERSECTION"), the two different bracket patterns produce identical resulting sets.

It is also possible to write

```
INTEGER ( ALL EXCEPT (1..20) )
```

with the obvious meaning. ("ALL" can only be followed by "EXCEPT".)

A more complex example (exercise for the reader—find a real-world example where this sort of construction would be useful!) would be

```
My-string3 ::= PrintableString
          ( SIZE (1..10) INTERSECTION FROM ("A" .. "Z")
            UNION
            ("yes" UNION "no" UNION maybe)
            EXCEPT
            "A" UNION B)
```

I think you can work out what that means, but if not, come back to it when you have read what follows! Note that the absence of quotation marks around "maybe" and "B" above was **not** a typo! Here "maybe" is assumed to be a value-reference-name for a value of type PrintableString (assigned elsewhere in this module), and B is assumed to be a type-reference-name for a subtype of PrintableString (also assigned elsewhere in this module)! Remember that wherever explicit value-notation for a value is allowed, a value-reference-name is also allowed (provided it refers to a value of the parent type), and (less obviously perhaps) wherever a subset is needed for set arithmetic, a type-reference-name can be used (provided it refers to a subtype of the parent type).

The alert-alert-reader(!) may be beginning to ask what the exact rules are about the way a value-reference-name or type-reference-name has to be defined in order to be legal in some set-arithmetic with a particular governor (parent type). This is covered in the description of the ASN.1 Semantic Model in Chapter 19.15, but it is sufficient to note for now that if it would make sense to a human reader it is almost certainly legal!

Note that value-notation for a type defined using subtype-notation is not affected by that notation—it remains the normal value notation for the parent type.

One final global comment: the word "INTERSECTION" can be replaced by the "caret" symbol: "^", and the word "UNION" by the "vertical-bar" symbol: "|", but you are recommended not to mix and match in any one application specification! For me, ASN.1 specifications tend to be quite verbose anyway—longish names are common—so I prefer the words!

What then are the basic terms that we can use—either as standalone subtype constraints in round brackets, or as part of a possibly complex set-arithmetic expression, and what set of values do they identify?

We treat each possibility in 10.3 to 10.7. Note that in some cases the text has "subtyping" or "subtype" in its heading, and in other cases the word "constraint" is used. This reflects the terms used in the ASN.1 specification itself, and reinforces the point that for most purposes the two words are interchangeable.

10.3 Single Value Subtyping

This can be applied to any parent type. (Remember that there is value notation for any type we can define in ASN.1.) We just list the permitted value! Normally this would be accompanied by use of either vertical bar or UNION. So,

```
Yes ::= PrintableString ("Yes")
```

and

```
Yes-No ::= PrintableString ("Yes" | "No")
```

are examples that use single value subtyping. The set of values identified by each use of single value subtyping is just that single value identified by the value notation.

10.4 Value Range Subtyping

This can only be applied directly to integer and real types, but the same construction following the word "FROM" is used to restrict the set of characters that are permitted in some character string types (see "permitted alphabet" in 10.5).

Value range subtyping is frequently applied to specify the range of integer values.

The end-points of a range of values are given, and the set of values identified by the notation are precisely those from one end-point to the other (including the end-points). This is the notation we encountered earlier, and which is often seen to constrain integer values,

```
Days-reported-on ::= INTEGER (1..56)
```

As usual, intersections and unions of these constraints are possible, but are rarely seen.

10.5 Permitted Alphabet Constraints

Some encoding rules (unaligned PER) will use the minimum number of bits per character, depending on how many different characters you allow in a string, so imposing alphabet constraints can save bits on the line.

This is a constraint that can only be applied to the character string types (not including the type "CHARACTER STRING").

In its simplest form this constraint is the word "FROM" followed by a character string containing a set of permitted characters. Thus:

```
String-of-vowels1 ::= PrintableString ( FROM ("AEIOU") )
```

or

```
String-of-vowels2 ::= PrintableString ( FROM ("AEIOU")

                                         UNION

                                         FROM ("aeiou") )
```

would be possible examples. The opening bracket following "FROM" may appear unnecessary and looks cumbersome, but the syntax definition allows a fully general constraint following FROM, so

```
String-of-vowels3 ::= PrintableString ( FROM ("AEIOU"

                                         UNION

                                         "aeiou") )
```

is also permitted.

The constraint following "FROM" is required to be one that could be directly applied to the parent type to produce a set of string values (call this **the defining set of string values** (a term used only in this book). The effect of "FROM" is to allow (in the subset of string values selected by "FROM") all strings of the parent type that contain (only) any of the characters in any of the string values in the defining set.

An exercise: Read this definition carefully, then answer the question "Are String-of-vowels2 and String-of-vowels3 equivalent definitions?" Read on when you have your answer!

We reason it through. With "String-of-Vowels2", we first define two sets of PrintableString values. One is all strings made up of uppercase vowels only and the other is all strings made up of lowercase vowels only, and we take the union of these two sets. Thus the end result allows strings containing only vowels, but each string must be entirely uppercase or entirely lowercase. With "String-of-Vowels3", we first produce a set with just two string values, each of five characters: "AEIOU" and "aeiou". We then apply "FROM" to this set, allowing as the end result strings made up of arbitrary combinations of upper- and lowercase vowels, so "String-of-Vowels2" and "String-of-Vowels3" are **not** the same.

The preceding example used only single value subtype notation in the constraint following FROM, but any subtype notation that can be applied to the parent type can be used. In particular, value range subtyping is explicitly permitted for application to certain character string types when it is used in the constraint following FROM, and is restricted to strings containing only a single character.

Thus we can write:

```
Hex-digit-String ::= PrintableString (FROM ("0".."9" UNION "A".."Z"
                                            UNION "a".."z" ))
```

which first forms the set of all single character strings using digits and letters (62 string values), and then applies FROM to this set to generate the set of all PrintableString values containing only these 62 characters.

The value range constraint can be used in this way for those character string types for which an ordering of the characters is well-defined (BMPString, IA5String, NumericString, PrintableString, VisibleString, UniversalString, UTF8String), but not for character string types based on the International Register of Coded Character Sets (GeneralString, GraphicString, TeletexString, or VideotexString), where ordering is not easy to define.

10.6 Size Constraints

A size constraint has a similar structure to a permitted alphabet constraint. It consists of the word "SIZE" followed by any constraint specification (in parentheses) that can be applied to a nonnegative integer. It can (only) be applied to a bit string, an octet string, a character string (including the type "CHARACTER STRING" introduced in a later chapter) or to a "SEQUENCE OF" or "SET OF" construction. Its effect is to select those values of the parent type

> Size constraints use value ranges to specify the permitted lengths of strings and iteration counts. Their use can again save bits on the line.

that contain a number of characters or iterations equal to one of the integer values in the set selected (from nonnegative integers) by the constraint following the word "SIZE".

In the case of "SEQUENCE OF Xyz" and "SET OF Xyz", the constraint can appear after the type definition, or immediately before the "OF". This is necessary to allow constraints to be applied to both the iteration counts and to the type being iterated, in cases such as

```
SEQUENCE OF SEQUENCE OF PrintableString (SIZE (10))
```

This syntax would restrict the PrintableString to exactly ten characters, and cannot be used to constrain the iteration counts. To constrain these, you would use

```
SEQUENCE (SIZE (10)) OF SEQUENCE OF PrintableString
```

or

```
SEQUENCE OF SEQUENCE (SIZE (10)) OF PrintableString
```

Once again, ASN.1 is fully general in this area—the constraint notation appearing before the OF is a general constraint that can contain unions and intersections etc., although the pre-1994 specifications were more restrictive.

In practice, the constraint following the word "SIZE" is almost always a single value constraint or a value range constraint, such as:

```
SEQUENCE ( SIZE (1..100) ) OF SEQUENCE ( SIZE (20) ) OF
                      PrintableString ( SIZE (0..15) )
```

which could represent a table of 1 to 100 rows with 20 columns, each cell containing a PrintableString that is either empty or up to 15 characters long.

Going back to our Wineco-protocol, and referring to Figure 4 in Section I, we originally defined "sales-data" as an unlimited number of "Report-item". It is generally quite hard for an implementor to support unlimited numbers of things, although with increasing memory sizes now easily available and large capacity disks, implementation of "effectively unlimited" (which is what we mean here) is possible. Both the BER and PER encodings will support the transfer of effectively unlimited numbers (and sizes) of things, but with PER the encoding will be more efficient if it is possible to limit counts and integer values, for example to values that can be held in two or four octets.

It would be common practice to replace the "sales-data" line with:

```
sales-data SEQUENCE (SIZE (1..sales-ub)) OF Report-Item
```

The value reference "sales-ub" is required to be an integer value reference, and might be assigned in a module that collects together all such bounds, using EXPORTS/IMPORTS to make it available in the context of Figure 4.1. A typical assignment might be:

```
sales-ub INTEGER ::= 10000
```

Consider a final example using both FROM and SIZE:

```
PrintableString ( SIZE (1..10) INTERSECTION FROM ("A".."Z"))
```

Take a moment to work out what this means before reading on.

We first select the (finite) set of all strings with 1 to 10 characters in them, and we intersect that with the (infinite set) of all strings made up solely of the characters "A" to "Z". The end result is the set of strings of 1 to 10 characters that contain only the letters "A" to "Z". Note that exactly the same result is obtained by any of

```
PrintableString (SIZE (1..10)) (FROM ("A".."Z"))
```

or

```
PrintableString (FROM ("A".."Z")) (SIZE (1..10))
```

or

```
First (FROM ("A".."Z"))
```

or

```
        Second (SIZE (1..10))
```

or

```
        PrintableString ( First INTERSECTION Second )
```

or

```
        PrintableString (First) (Second)
```

where

```
        First ::= PrintableString (SIZE (1..10))
```

and

```
        Second ::= PrintableString (FROM ("A".."Z"))
```

10.7 Contained Subtype Constraints

We have met this notation informally on a couple of preceding occasions. This form of constraint is where we provide a type reference name (for a subtype of the parent type) to identify the set of values to be included. This would not normally be useful unless it was within a more complex constraint using intersections, or with repeated application of constraints, as in the cases

```
        PrintableString ( First INTERSECTION Second )
```

and

```
        PrintableString (First) (Second)
```

of 10.6.

Note that pre-1994, use of a type reference name in this way in a constraint required the name to be preceded by the word "INCLUDES", and it is still permissible to write (e.g.),

```
        PrintableString (INCLUDES First INTERSECTION INCLUDES Second)
```

or

```
        PrintableString (INCLUDES First EXCEPT INCLUDES Second)
```

but these do not read very well, and it is best to omit the word "INCLUDES".

10.8 Inner Subtyping

10.8.1 Introduction

Inner subtyping is an important and underused tool. It is often the case that application designers have invented a new meta-notation of their own (not supported by ASN.1 tools) to produce specifications that could more sensibly have been written using inner subtyping (which is supported by the OSS tool). Not only does this require the reader to get used to the ad hoc notation, but it can also make the implementor's work unnecessarily hard, with some sort of ad hoc preprocessing of the specification needed before use of ASN.1 tools.

> Inner subtyping is an important mechanism that can help to give precision to the specification of subsets or conformance classes of a protocol.

It is likely, perhaps probable, that this occurs through ignorance. Inner subtyping has an overall importance that is not brought out by its positioning as "just another subtyping notation" in the ASN.1 specification.

The subtype notations described so far provide a very powerful tool for application designers to specify clearly the range of permitted values in their protocols for the basic types, but there is another requirement: Some designers have a requirement to define a number of different subsets of a protocol to suit different purposes, different so-called "conformance classes".

In the simplest case, we have a "Full Class" protocol in which each message is some defined ASN.1 type such as the "Wineco-Protocol" in Figure 3.8 of Section 1, but we also wish to define a "Basic Class" protocol in which some of the optional elements of sequences are required to be omitted, others are required to be always included, some of the choices are restricted, and some of the iterations and/or integer values have restricted values.

If you consider the set of abstract values of the "Wineco-Protocol" type, you will recognize that all the restrictions described earlier (including requiring some optional elements to be present and others to be absent) are simply the selection of a particular subset of the "Wineco-Protocol" values—in other words, subtyping!

There are, however, two additional requirements:

- First, it needs to be possible to define both of the conformance classes without duplication of text (and hence scope for error).

- Secondly (for some but not all applications) the encoding of those values that are present in both the "Basic Class" protocol and the "Full Class" protocol should be the same in both protocols.

The latter requirement enables easy interworking between "Full Class" and "Basic Class" implementations.

There is a relationship between this area and the "extensibility" issues to be described later, but there are differences. "Extensibility" refers to differences in specifications over time (different versions) where the maximal functionality is not known when the first systems are deployed, whereas here we are concerned with differences in implementations where maximal functionality is known from the start, permitting a somewhat simpler approach.

In order to define all conformance classes without duplication of text, it is necessary to:

- (first) define the "Wineco-Protocol" type with maximal functionality, providing it with a type reference name; then

- to use this type reference name and apply to it the constraints that generate the "Basic-Ordering-Class" and "Basic-Sales-Data-Class" (or other conformance classes). The latter is achieved by placing subtype constraint notation, in parentheses, following the type reference name. So we have,

```
Basic-Ordering-Class ::= Wineco-Protocol (.......)
```

The (.......) is the inner subtyping constraint, where we constrain the inner components of "Wineco-Protocol".

It is important to note that in both BER and PER, the application of these constraints does **not** affect the encoding of the values that are in the selected subset— they are encoded exactly as in the "Full-Class" protocol. By contrast, if constraints (such as removal of some choices, or making optional fields mandatorily present or absent) were specified by an ad hoc meta-language that modified the ASN.1 text (or by explicitly writing out the Basic Class protocols), the encoding of values in the Basic Class would be different from that of the corresponding values in the Full Class, and care would also need to be taken that rules on unambiguous tags (see 11.4) were not violated with any of the variants that were produced.

This is another reason why use of inner subtyping should be preferred to an ad hoc "preprocessor" notation—it ensures that encodings and taggings are the same in all classes.

```
Wineco-Protocol   ::=   CHOICE
                {ordering [APPLICATION 1] Order-for-Stock,
                 sales    [APPLICATION 2] Return-of-sales-data,
                 ... ! PrintableString : "See clause 45.7",
                 e-cash-return -- Added in version 2 --
                         [APPLICATION 3] Cash-upload}

                Basic-Ordering-Class ::= Wineco-Protocol
                (WITH COMPONENTS
                  {ordering (Basic-Order)  PRESENT,
                   sales                   ABSENT } )
                Basic-Sales-Class ::= Wineco-Protocol
                (WITH COMPONENTS
                  {ordering                ABSENT ,
                   sales (Basic-Return)    PRESENT } )
```

Figure 10.1   Constraining in version 2.

10.8.2 Subsetting Wineco-Protocol

Once again, let us proceed with an illustration first. Consider Figure 10.1. This repeats the top-level definition of Figure 3.8, but now we have moved to version 2 (produced in AD 2002!), and have an additional top-level choice available to enable us to upload the contents of the electronic cash in our till. (The fact that this follows an extension marker makes no difference to the inner subtyping notation, and for the moment the presence of the extension marker line should be completely ignored.) Refer also to Appendix 2, which contains the full definition of Wineco-Protocol.

Here we have restricted the outer-level choice by making precisely one of the version 1 alternatives always present and the other always absent. We are further applying *contained subtype constraints* (see 10.7) "Basic-Order" and "Basic-Return" to the alternative that is present, restricting it further. We will shortly define the types "Basic-Order" and "Basic-Return".

Notice that here we have listed every alternative present in version 1, giving PRESENT or ABSENT. This is called a "full specification". Despite being called a "full specification", it is not actually necessary to list every alternative. ABSENT is implied for any not listed, so the definition of "Basic-Sales-Class" is equivalent to:

```
                Basic-Sales-Class ::= Wineco-Protocol
                (WITH COMPONENTS
                  {ordering                ABSENT ,
                   sales (Basic-Return)    PRESENT,
                   e-cash-return           ABSENT } )
```

and to

```
Basic-Sales-Class ::= Wineco-Protocol

(WITH COMPONENTS

  {sales (Basic-Return)     PRESENT} )
```

(Note that there must be at least one alternative listed, and that there must be exactly one listed as PRESENT in the "full specification".)

There is also a "partial specification" notation in which the constraint starts with "... ",. This is shown in Figure 10.2, where we wish the Basic-Sales-Class2 protocol to include both "sales" and "e-cash-return" messages. "Partial specification" differs from the "full specification" only in that any alternatives not listed remain as possible unconstrained choices, and any listed are neither required to be ABSENT nor PRESENT if neither of these words is present (but may be constrained in other ways). Thus in Figure 10.2, either the "sales" (constrained by "Basic-Return") or the "e-cash-return" message (unconstrained) are available and have to be implemented, but the "ordering" messages should never be sent or received and need not be implemented.

Let us go on to specify what is a "Basic-Return". This is shown in Figure 10.3 as a constrained "Return-of-sales". Note that as usual in ASN.1, we could have put the constraint "in-line" in Figure 10.3 and made no use of the type reference name "Basic-Report-Item". This is just a matter of style. Figure 10.4 shows the same definition but with the constraint "in-line" (we have not repeated the comments in Figure 10.4). While more compact, it is arguable that the lack of a name to associate with the inner constraint on "Report-item" in Figure 10.4 makes that style less readable than the slightly more verbose style of Figure 10.3. Both notations do, however, express exactly the same semantics.

Figure 10.3 needs a little explanation of "sales-data". Here we are further constraining the number of "Report-item"'s, and also restricting each "Report-item" to the subset "Basic-report-item". Notice that when we apply inner subtyping to a SEQUENCE or SET, we start the constraint with "WITH COMPONENTS", and then

```
Basic-Sales-Class2 ::= Wineco-Protocol
                ( WITH COMPONENTS
                  {... ,
                   ordering ABSENT,
                   sales (Basic-Return) } )
```

Figure 10.2   Constraining only the sales alternative.

```
Basic-Return ::= Return-of-sales
  ( WITH COMPONENTS
    {... ,
      no-of-days-reported-on (7)
      -- reports must be weekly --,
      reason-for-delay  ABSENT,
      additional-information  ABSENT,
      sales-data (SIZE (1..basic-sales-ub)
                    INTERSECTION
                    (WITH COMPONENT
                       (Basic-report-item) } )
  Basic-report-item ::= Report-item
    ( WITH COMPONENTS
      {...,
        item-description ABSENT
          --  ersion 2 of Report-item allows omission
          -- of item-description even for newly-stocked
          -- items --} )
```

Figure 10.3   Constraining "Return-of-Sales"

```
Basic-Return ::= Return-of-sales
  ( WITH COMPONENTS
    {... ,
      no-of-days-reported-on (7),
      reason-for-delay  ABSENT,
      additional-information  ABSENT,
      sales-data (SIZE (1..basic-sales-ub)
                    INTERSECTION
                    (WITH COMPONENT
                      ( WITH COMPONENTS
                          {...,
                            item-description ABSENT } )
                                                    } )
```

Figure 10.4   Applying the constraint "in-line".

have paired curly brackets with the constraints (if any) on each component listed within the brackets following the name of the component. (You can see this with the constraint on "Report-item" (which is a SEQUENCE) in Figure 10.3). Now suppose that one of the components of the outer SEQUENCE is a SEQUENCE OF or SET OF, then we can apply a constraint to the number of iterations of the SEQUENCE OF or SET OF by directly listing it following the component name, but if we wish to constrain the type being iterated, we have to apply a further inner subtyping constraint, but this time beginning with the words "WITH COMPONENT" (instead of "WITH COMPONENTS"), followed directly by the constraint to be applied to the type being iterated.

10.8.3 Inner Subtyping of an Array

As a final example, let us return to our two-dimensional array of PrintableString introduced earlier. We will first define:

```
Generic-array ::= SEQUENCE OF SEQUENCE OF PrintableString
```

and we will then produce a "Special-array" by inner subtyping that will be (almost—see the following text) equivalent to our original definition of

```
SEQUENCE ( SIZE (1..100) ) OF SEQUENCE ( SIZE (20) ) OF
                    PrintableString ( SIZE (0..15) )
```

This is what we need:

```
Special-array ::= Generic-array
        ( SIZE (1..100) INTERSECTION
            WITH COMPONENT
              (SIZE (20) INTERSECTION
                  WITH COMPONENT (SIZE (0..15) )
              )
        )
```

Why only **almost** equivalent? It is important to remember that a PER encoding of a Generic-array with inner subtyping is always the general encoding (inner subtype constraints are not PER visible), so an implementation of "Special-array" with its constraints will produce bits on the line identical with the corresponding values of "Generic-array", while putting in the constraints explicitly will produce a different (more compact) encoding. Where the constraints apply to all classes of implementation, or where interworking between different classes is not required, it is clearly better to embed the constraints explicitly. Where, however, interworking is required between a full implementation and a constrained implementation, it is generally better to use inner subtyping to express the constraint.

10.9 Conclusion

"Simple subtyping" can indeed be simple—as when a range is specified for an INTEGER type, but requires care in writing (and a good understanding of the syntax when reading) if the very powerful set arithmetic and inner subtyping features are used.

Because in the old Basic Encoding Rules (BER), subtyping never affected the bits on the line, there was a tendency for writers of ASN.1 protocols not to bother to think about subtyping, and there are many specifications that, if taken at face value, would require implementations to support indefinite length integers, even though everyone knows that was never the intention.

Both to give precision to the requirements on implementation, and also because the more recent Packed Encoding Rules **will** reduce the bits on the line if subtyping is applied, it is now strongly recommended that in producing new or revised protocols, subtyping is applied wherever possible and sensible. This is particularly important for ranges of integers and iterations of SEQUENCE OFs or SET OFs.

> The simplest forms of range and size constraint are very simple to apply, and should be used whenever possible. The more complex forms using set arithmetic or inner subtyping are very powerful, but are for more specialized use.

## CHAPTER 11

Tagging

(Or: Control It or Forget It!)

Summary

Tagging was an important (and difficult!) part of the ASN.1 notation pre-1994. Its importance (and the need to understand it) is much less now, due to three factors:

- the ability to set an AUTOMATIC TAGS environment in the module header as described in Chapter 3;

- the provision for extensibility without relying on tags to achieve this; and

- the introduction of PER, which does not encode tags.

There are four tag classes

- UNIVERSAL

- APPLICATION

- PRIVATE

- context-specific

and a tag value is a class and a number (zero upwards, unbounded).

This chapter describes the requirements on use of tags in a legal piece of ASN.1, and gives stylistic advice on the choice of tag class.

11.1 Review of Earlier Discussions

We have already discussed the idea of including tags, and have introduced the concepts of *implicit tagging* and *explicit tagging*, describing these in terms of their effect on a BER encoding: changing the "T" in the TLV for the type (implicit tagging), or adding a new TLV wrapper (explicit tagging).

This is clearly not an academically satisfactory way of discussing tagging (but might satisfy many readers!), given that the notation is supposed to be independent of the encoding rules, and that there are now other ASN.1 encoding rules that do not use the "TLV" concept. We will therefore introduce below an encoding-rule-independent, and slightly more abstract (sorry!), description of tags.

In earlier text we have implied (wrongly!)—but never stated—that the name-space for tag values is a simple integer. Indeed, we did use a tag "[APPLICATION 1]" in Figure 3.8, which might imply a more complex name-space. We describe in the following text the complete set of available values for tags, and the way these are normally used.

> Tags were originally closely related to the "T" in the "TLV" of the Basic Encoding Rules (BER), and gave users control over the "T" values used for different elements and choices. This was important if interworking between version 1 and version 2 was to be easy in a BER environment with no explicit extensibility marker.

Finally, we have already briefly mentioned that there are rules about when tags are required to be distinct (broadly, wherever the "T" of a TLV needs to be distinct from that of some other TLV to ensure unambiguity in BER encodings). We give in 10.4 the actual rules.

But as a last important reminder: post-1994 you can establish an automatic tagging environment in which you need know nothing about tags, and need never include them in your type definitions. This is the recommended style to adopt for new specifications, and is absolutely the right approach for anyone who gets confused with the text that follows.

Let us look at the global level for a moment. Wherever ASN.1 requires or allows type-notation, it is permissible to write:

```
tag-notation type-notation
```

In other words, tagging formally defines a new type from an old type, **and tag notation can be repeatedly applied to the same type notation.** So the following is legal:

```
My-type ::= [APPLICATION 1] [3] INTEGER
```

but would be rather pointless in an environment of implicit tagging, as the "[3]" is immediately overridden! You will rarely see this sort of construction—tag-notation is normally applied to a type-reference or to untagged type-notation.

Finally, if a type is defined using tag-notation, the tag-notation is ignored for the purposes of value-notation. Value notation for My-type above is still simply "6" (for example).

11.2 The Tag Name-Space

Tags

- [UNIVERSAL 29]: do not use UNIVERSAL class tags.
- [APPLICATION 10]: use for commonly used types or top-level messages. Do not reuse.
- [PRIVATE 0]: Rarely seen. Use to extend a standard with private additions (if you really must!).
- [3]: Use and reuse in a different context. The most common form of tagging.

Staying with BER encodings for the moment: a tag encodes in 7 bits of the "T" part of a BER TLV.

The remaining bit is nothing to do with tagging, and is set to one if the "V" part is itself a series of TLVs (a *constructed* encoding such as that used for "SEQUENCE" or "SET"), and to zero if the "V" part is not composed of further TLVs (a *primitive* encoding such as that used for "INTEGER" or "BOOLEAN" or "NULL").

A tag is specified by giving a *class* and a *tag-value* (the latter is indeed a simple positive integer—zero upwards, unbounded). But the class is one of four possibilities:

```
UNIVERSAL class
APPLICATION class
PRIVATE class
context-specific class
```

In the tag notation, a number alone in square brackets denotes the tag-value of a context-specific class tag. For the other classes, the name (all uppercase) of the class appears after the opening square bracket.

For example:

UNIVERSAL 0	Reserved for use by the encoding rules
UNIVERSAL 1	Boolean type
UNIVERSAL 2	Integer type
UNIVERSAL 3	Bit-string type
UNIVERSAL 4	Octet-string type
UNIVERSAL 5	Null type
UNIVERSAL 6	Object identifier type
UNIVERSAL 7	Object descriptor type
UNIVERSAL 8	External type and Instance-of type
UNIVERSAL 9	Real type
UNIVERSAL 10	Enumerated type
UNIVERSAL 11	Embedded-pdv type
UNIVERSAL 12	UTF8String type
UNIVERSAL 13–15	Reserved for future editions of this Recommendation ǀ International Standard
UNIVERSAL 16	Sequence and Sequence-of types
UNIVERSAL 17	Set and Set-of types
UNIVERSAL 18–22	Character string types
UNIVERSAL 23–24	Time types
UNIVERSAL 35–30	More character string types
UNIVERSAL 31–...	Reserved for addenda to this Recommendation ǀ International Standard

Figure 11.1   Assignment of UNIVERSAL class tags.

```
[UNIVERSAL 29]      tag-value 29,  "universal" class
[APPLICATION 10]    tag-value 10,  "application" class
[PRIVATE 0]         tag-value 0,   "private" class
[3]                 tag-value 3,   "context-specific" class
```

I like to think of the four classes of tag as just different "colors" of tag (red, green, blue, yellow). The actual names do not matter. For most purposes, the "color" of the tag does not matter either. All that matters is that tags be distinct where so required, and they can differ either in their "color" (class) or in their tag-value. The color you choose to use is mainly a matter of **style.**

There is only one hard prohibition: users are not allowed to tag types with a UNIVERSAL class tag. This class is (always) used for the "default tag" on a type, and values of such tags can **only** be assigned within the ASN.1 specification itself.

Figure 11.1 is a copy of a table from X.680/ISO 8824-1 (including all amendments up to September 1998), and gives the UNIVERSAL class tag assigned as the default tag (used unless overridden by implicit tagging) for each of the type notations and constructor mechanisms defined in ASN.1.

The main reason for forbidding use of UNIVERSAL class tags by users is to avoid problems when future extensions to ASN.1 occur. It is, however, important to note that this is no real hardship, as every tag has equal status with every other tag, no matter what its "color" (class).

There have been specifications that conformed to pre-1994 ASN.1, but wanted to use UTF8String (added 1998), and decided to copy the text of the post-1994 definition into their own application specification. This is probably harmless, but is strictly in violation of the specification. As well as being illegal, it is also **unnecessary** to copy the text and to assign a UNIVERSAL class tag in the copied text; an APPLICATION class tag can be used in the definition of the type, and provided the type is implicitly tagged wherever it is used, the end-result is indistinguishable from an initial assignment with a UNIVERSAL class tag, as later implicit tagging will override either.

So what about the other three classes of tag? Which one should be used when? To repeat: They are all equivalent. Use PRIVATE class tags absolutely everywhere if you wish! But as a matter of **style,** most people use **context-specific class** tags most of the time (they are the easiest to write—just a number in square brackets!). The name "context-specific" implies that they are only unambiguous within some specific context (typically within a single SEQUENCE, SET, or CHOICE), and it is normal to use (and to reuse) these tags (from zero upwards) whenever you need to tag the alternatives of a CHOICE or the elements of a SEQUENCE or SET to conform to the rules requiring distinct tags in particular places (see 11.4).

It is also common practice (but by no means universal nor required) to use APPLICATION class tags in the following way:

- An application class tag is used only **once** in the entire application specification; it is never applied twice.

- If the outermost type for the application is a CHOICE (it usually is), then each of the alternatives of that choice is tagged (implicitly if possible) with APPLICATION class tags (usually [APPLICATION 0], [APPLICATION 1], [APPLICATION 2], etc.). We saw this approach in Section I, Figure 3.8.

- If there are some complex types that are defined once and then used in many parts of the application specification, then when they are defined they are given an application class tag (and this tag is never given to anything else), so they can be safely used in a choice (for example) with no danger of a violation of any rules requiring distinct tags (unless the identical type appears again in the CHOICE—presumably with different semantics).

An example of this might be the types "OutletType" and "Address" in Figures 2.1 and 3.1 of Section I. So in Figure 3.1 we might write instead:

```
OutletType ::= [APPLICATION 10] SEQUENCE
        { ....
          ....
          ....}
Address ::= [APPLICATION 11] SEQUENCE
        { ....
          ....
          ....}
```

taking the decision to use application class tags 0 to 9 for top-level messages, and 10 onwards for commonly used types.

There is no limit to the magnitude of a tag-value, but when we examine BER in Section III, we will see that a "T" will encode in a single octet provided the tag-value to be encoded is less than or equal to 30; so most application designers usually try to use tag-values below 31 for all their tags (but there are specifications with tag values in the low hundreds).

PRIVATE class tags are never used in standardized specifications. They have been used by some multinationals that have extended an international standard by adding extra elements at the end of some sequences or sets. The assumption here (as with most jiggery-pokery with tags) is that BER is being used, and the (reasonable) hope is that by adding new elements with PRIVATE class tags, these will not clash with any extension of the base standard in the future.

11.3 An Abstract Model of Tagging

Please note that this material is not present in the ASN.1 specification. It is considered by this author to be a useful model to provide an encoding-rule-independent description of the meaning of tagging at the notational level, and a means of specifying the behavior of encoding rules. Most ASN.1 "experts" would probably accept the model, but might argue that it is not needed, and is only one of several possible ways of modeling what the ASN.1 notation is specifying, in order to link it cleanly to encoding rules. (See Figure 999 again!)

> We can model tagging as affecting a tag-list associated with every ASN.1 abstract value. Some encoding rules use some or all of the tags in the tag-list as part of the encoding.

In order to provide a means of describing the effects of tagging we introduce a model of ASN.1 abstract values (the "things" that are in ASN.1 types), which involves some structure to these values. This is shown in Figure 11.2.

In Figure 11.2 we see that each ASN.1 abstract value is made up of a basic-value (like "integer 1", "boolean true", etc.), together with an ordered tag-list consisting of one or more tags (an innermost, closest to the basic-value, and an outermost, furthest away). Each tag consists of, as described earlier, a class and a tag-value.

When a type is defined using ASN.1 type-notation such as "BOOLEAN" or "INTEGER", or as the result of using notation such as SEQUENCE or SET, all its values

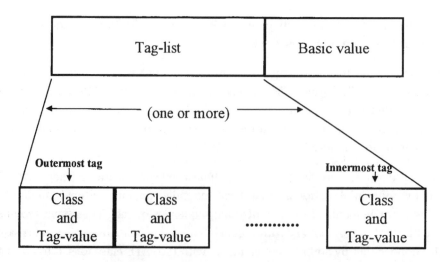

Figure 11.2   Model of ASN.1 abstract values.

are given the same tag-list—a single tag (which is both innermost and outermost) of the UNIVERSAL class. The tag-value for each type notation is specified in the ASN.1 specification, and repeated in Figure 11.1. (We have referred to this as the "default tag" for the type in earlier text.)

There are only two operations that are possible on a tag-list. If a type is **implicitly tagged,** then the outermost tag is replaced by the new tag specified in the tagging construction. If a type is **explicitly tagged,** then a new outermost tag is **added** to the tag list. Note that all ASN.1 abstract values always have at least one tag. They acquire additional tags by explicit tagging, and can never have the number of tags reduced.

With this model of tagging, we can now define our Basic Encoding Rules as encoding a "TLV" for each tag in the tag-list, from the outermost to the innermost tag, where the tag forms the "T", the "L" identifies the length of the remainder of the encoding of the ASN.1 abstract value, and each "V" apart from the last contains (only) the next TLV. The last "V" contains an encoding identifying the basic value.

The reader will recognize that this gives exactly the same encoding as was obtained when we described explicit tagging as "adding an extra layer of TLV", but the use of the abstract model makes it unnecessary to describe the meaning of the notation in encoding rule terms. We use the concept of a tag-list as a sort of indirection between the notation and the encoding rules. The tag-list represents information which an ASN.1 tool will normally need to retain between syntax analysis and other functions.

Finally, but very importantly, note that for most types, all the values in the type have exactly the same tag-list. If we apply further tagging to the type, we will change the tag-list (add a new tag or replace the outer-level tag) for each and every value in that type.

Moreover, for many purposes (in particular what tag values are permitted) all that matters is the outermost tag. It is thus meaningful to talk about "the tag of the type", because every abstract value of that type has the same tag-list (and hence the same outer-level tag). There is, however, one exception to this simple situation.

The CHOICE constructor is modeled as forming a new type whose values are the union of the set of values in each of the alternatives, **with each value retaining its original tag-list.** Thus for the choice types, it is **not** meaningful to talk about "the tag of the type", as different abstract values in the type have different tag-lists. (It is important to remember this if you see text in canonical encoding rules saying "the elements are sorted into tag-order"—look for some qualifying text to cover the case of a choice type!)

Suppose, however, that a choice type is explicitly tagged (the only form of tagging allowed for choice types). Then while the tag-list on different abstract values may (will) still differ, the **outermost tag** is the same for all abstract values in the type, and the explicitly tagged choice is just like any ordinary type—every abstract value has the same outer-level tag and we can talk about this as "the tag of the type".

So we can now recognize that most types have a single associated tag (the common outer-level tag for all abstract values of that type), that we can call "the tag of the type", but that an untagged choice type has many tags associated with it (all the outer-level tags of any of its values). If none of the alternatives of this choice are themselves choices, then the number of outer-level tags (all distinct) associated with this choice type will be equal to the number of its alternatives. If, however, some alternatives are themselves choice types, they will each bring to the table multiple (distinct) outer-level tags, and the outer-level choice type will have more (distinct) tags associated with it than it has alternatives.

For example, if

```
My-choice ::= CHOICE
    {alt1    CHOICE
                {alt1-1  [0]  INTEGER,
                 alt1-2  [1]  INTEGER},
     alt2    [2] EXPLICIT My-choice2}
```

then the tags associated with "My-choice" are context-specific 0, 1, and 2. Any tags in "My-choice2" are hidden by the explicit tagging.

With this concept of "the tag of the type", or rather "the tags associated with the type" (which are always distinct), we can go on to discuss the rules for when distinct tags are required.

| When do we need distinct tags? |

11.4 The Rules for When Tags Are Required to Be Distinct

The rule is that distinct tags are required:

- for the alternatives of a CHOICE;

- for the elements of a SET; and

- for consecutive DEFAULT or OPTIONAL elements and any following mandatory element in a SEQUENCE.

There—it is simple really. (Skip the rest!)

The rules given in what follows (and in the ASN.1 specification) are expressed in terms of tag uniqueness, but are most easily remembered if you know that they are the **minimum necessary rules** to enable a TLV-style of encoding to be unambiguous! Alternatively, just remember the rules and forget the rationale!

Within a CHOICE constructor, the collection of tags brought to the table by each alternative have to be distinct. (Remember, each alternative brings just one tag to the table—the common outer-level tag of the tag-list of its abstract values, unless it is an untagged choice type, when it brings to the table at least one tag for each alternative of the choice type, but these are all distinct.)

Similarly, within a SET constructor, the tags of all the elements have to be distinct, with any elements that are choice types again potentially contributing several distinct tags to the matching process.

Within a SEQUENCE constructor, the rules are a little more complicated. In the absence of DEFAULT or OPTIONAL, there are **no** requirements for distinct tags on the elements of a sequence type. However, in the presence of DEFAULT or OPTIONAL, the situation changes slightly: For any block of successive elements marked DEFAULT or OPTIONAL, **together with the next mandatory element, if any,** the tags of all elements in that block are required to be distinct.

You will want to think about that for a moment. Clearly the block of DEFAULT or OPTIONAL elements must all have distinct tags, or (in BER) the receiver will not know which are present and which missing, but equally, if one of those tags matched the next mandatory element there could again be confusion. By requiring that the following mandatory element has a tag distinct from any element of the preceding block, then the appearance of that tag in an encoding gives complete knowledge that the block of OPTIONAL or DEFAULT elements is complete, and processing of the remainder of the sequence elements can proceed in a normal manner.

There is only one small additional complication if you are trying to control your tags without using automatic tagging. That is an interaction between the extensibility marker and the rules for distinct tags, in circumstances where there are multiple extension markers within a sequence (for example, one on a choice element in the sequence and one at the end of the sequence). The purpose of the rules here is to ensure that if a version 2 specification adds elements, a version 1 system receiving those elements will be in no doubt (with BER—there is never a problem with PER!) on whether the version 2 specification (of which, of course, it has no knowledge!) had extended the choice element or added further elements to the sequence. (This can matter if different exception handling had been specified in version 1 in the two cases.) For details of these additional requirements see the discussion in the next chapter (Chapter 12) on extensibility.

For those of a philosophical bent, you may wish to ponder how much simpler these rules could have been if (in BER, which really dictated the rules) all CHOICE constructions had automatically produced a TLV wrapper with a default tag (say UNIVERSAL 15), in the same way as SEQUENCE! Anyone using this book as an academic text might want to set that question as an exercise for the better students! Please note that while PER does **not** have a TLV philosophy, it nonetheless does have explicit encoding associated with CHOICE, which BER does not. One day someone will invent the **perfect** encoding rule philosophy.

11.5 Automatic Tagging

This material is solely for implementors.

What tags are applied in an "automatic tagging" environment? First, if any piece of SET, SEQUENCE or CHOICE notation contains a textually present tag on any of its outer-level elements or alternatives, automatic tagging is disabled for the outer-level of that notation. Otherwise, tags [0], [1], [2], etc. are successively applied to each element or alternative in an environment of implicit tagging. (So elements/alternatives that are CHOICE types get explicitly tagged and all other elements get implicitly tagged.)

11.6 Conclusion

Tagging appears complex, but once understood it is a relatively simple matter. In early specifications it became common, as a matter of style, to simply tag all elements of SEQUENCEs and SETs and alternatives of CHOICEs with context-specific (implicit) tags from zero upwards (avoiding the word "IMPLICIT" if the type being tagged was itself a CHOICE).

With the introduction of an "implicit tagging" environment, this became somewhat easier, but if this is desired, it is essentially what automatic tagging provides.

There are few specifications where the minimum necessary tagging is used. Writers of ASN.1 protocols tend to be more "symmetric" (or lazy?) than a minimalist approach would require.

It is the firm recommendation of this author that all new modules be produced with automatic tagging, and for tags to be forgotten.

## CHAPTER 12

Extensibility, Exceptions, and Version Brackets

(Or: There Is Always More To Learn!)

Summary

This chapter

- describes the "extensibility" concept of interworking between version 1 systems and later version 2 systems;

- explains the need for an "extension marker" to indicate where version 2 additions might occur;

- describes all the places where an extension marker is permitted;

- explains the need for defined exception handling when an extension marker is used;

- describes the notation for "version brackets" to group together elements added in later versions; and

- describes the interaction between extensibility and the requirements for distinct tags.

Presence in appropriate places of the extension marker is key to use of the Packed Encoding Rules (PER) which generate encodings approximately 50% the size of those produced by the Basic Encoding Rules (BER).

Writers of ASN.1-based protocols are very strongly encouraged to include extension markers (with defined exception handling) in their version 1 specifications in order to minimize problems in the future.

12.1 The Extensibility Concept

What is "extensibility"? "Extensibility" refers to a combination of notational support, constraints on encoding rules, and implementation rules. This support enables a protocol specified (and implemented) as version 1 to be upgraded some years later to version 2 in specifically permitted ways. Provided the version 2 extensions are within the permitted set of extensions (and provided the version 1 protocol was marked as "extensible"), then there will be a good interworking capability between the new version 2 systems and the already deployed and unmodified version 1 systems.

> You wrote your specification three years ago, there are many fielded implementations—success! But you want to make additions. How do you migrate? What will version 1 systems do with your additions? ASN.1 extensibility gives you control.

The keys to extensibility are

- To ensure that version 2 additions or extensions are "wrapped up" with length counts in encodings, and can be clearly identified by version 1 systems as "foreign material".

- To provide a clear specification that version 1 systems should process the parts of the encoding that are not "foreign material" in the normal version 1 way, and should take defined and predictable actions with the "foreign material".

- To avoid unnecessary (and verbose) wrappers and identifications in encodings by using notational "flags" where version 2 additions or extensions may need to be made.

For the extensibility concept to be successful, all three of these components must be present.

A detailed discussion of possible exception handling actions is given in Section I, Chapter 7.

With the BER encoding rules, all fields have a tag and a length associated with them, covering the first of points, but producing the verbosity we want to avoid

NOTE

In this chapter, the acronyms BER (Basic Encoding Rules) and PER (Packed Encoding Rules) are used without further explanation.

in the third point. BER itself says nothing about point 2. Some forward-thinking application designers did include text such as: "Within a SEQUENCE or SET, implementations should ignore any TLV with a tag that is not what is expected in their version", but this was by no means universal, and it was in general not possible to specify different action on "foreign material" in different parts of the protocol. With the PER encoding rules, length wrappers are often missing, and tags are always missing. PER has to be told where to insert length wrappers and to encode presence or absence of version 2 material if extensibility is to be achieved without undue cost. This is the primary purpose of the "extension marker".

12.2 The Extension Marker

What does the extension marker look like? We have already encountered it in Section I, Figures 3.8 and 4.1. It is the ellipsis (three dots) following the "sales" alternative in line 26 of Figure 3.8, and following the "sales-data" element in Figure 4.1.

If the reader now refers to Figure 10.1, we see another element being added after the extension marker in the "Wineco-protocol" CHOICE of Figure 3.8. This is our version 2 addition.

> Look out for the three little dots. Put them in as often as you like, they cost you little on the line. (Zero in BER, one bit in PER).

(Note that an ellipsis is also used following "WITH COMPONENTS {". This is a separate use of three dots, predating the extensibility work, and should not be confused with extensibility.)

12.3 The Exception Specification

It is strongly recommended that all uses of extensibility be accompanied by an exception specification, unless the same exception handling is specified for the entire application.

> Unless you intend uniform exception handling throughout your application, add an exception specification to your extension marker.

The exception specification makes clear what implementors of version 1 systems are supposed to do with "foreign material" in this position in the message (as in Figures 3.8 and 4.1), but this recommendation is not universally followed at this time.

The syntax of the exception specification (which can appear immediately after any ellipsis that indicates extensibility) is either an integer value, or the name of any ASN.1 type followed by a colon followed by a value of that type. Typical examples would be:

```
!3
!10
!PrintableString:"Incorrect error code for operation"
!My-Type:{field1 returnError, field2 "Code26"}
```

The first two might be used where there are a list of numbered exception handling procedures, and would identify which to apply in each position of added material. The third might be used where exceptions always give error reports, and the value is just the text for the error report. The final example might be used where "My-Type" has been defined as a SEQUENCE with the first element an enumeration of possible actions (for example, "abort", "returnError", "ignore", "treatAsMaximum" and the second (optional) element as a character string qualifying those actions. Note that "treatAsMaximum" might be an appropriate exception handling procedure for an ellipsis that was within a constraint, while "Ignore" is clearly only applicable to added material in a SEQUENCE or SET. For an unexpected CHOICE alternative, "returnError" might be desired. ASN.1 provides the notational tools, but only the application designer can decide how to use them appropriately. (For more discussion, see Chapter 7.)

12.4 Where Can the Ellipsis Be Placed?

In the first ASN.1 extensibility specification, ellipses could be placed (and extensions added serially after them) as follows (illustrations in Figure 12.1 give the version 1 text followed by the version 2 text):

- At the end of any SEQUENCE or SET or CHOICE (see Figures 3.8 and 10.1).

- Wherever there is a constraint (see Figure 12.1).

- At the end of the list of enumerations in an ENUMERATED type (see Figure 12.1).

```
INTEGER (0..255, ... )              or  INTEGER (0..255, ... !1)
INTEGER (0..255, ..., 0..65535)         INTEGER (0..255, ... !1, 0..65535)
ENUMERATED {red, blue, green, ... }
ENUMERATED {red, blue, green, ..., purple }
```

Figure 12.1　Illustrations of extensibility marker use.

```
SEQUENCE
     {field1  TypeA,
      field2  TypeB,
      ... ! PrintableString : "See clause 50",
      -- Version 2 material goes here.
      ... ,
      field3  TypeC}
```

Figure 12.2   An insertion point between elements 2 and 3.

An early addendum to the ASN.1 extensibility specification allowed the insertion point for new material in a SEQUENCE, SET, or CHOICE (but nowhere else) to be not just at the end, but in the middle. This was flagged by the use of two ellipsis elements as shown in Figure 12.2. Again we have included the exception specification to remind implementors that the handling of foreign material at this position is specified in clause 50 of the application specification.

12.5 Version Brackets

The same addendum introduced **version brackets,** with an opening bracket of a pair of "[[" and a closing bracket of "]]". These were introduced to reduce the number of length wrappers needed at any given insertion point to the minimum necessary—one wrapper for each new version, and also because application designers felt they would like to be able to identify for historical purposes what was in version 1, version 2, version 3, etc. With extensions for versions 2 and 3, Figure 12.2 could look like Figure 12.3.

It should be noted that extensibility can be identified independently for

> Version brackets not only save bits on the line but provide an historical record of the additions that have been made to the protocol.

each SEQUENCE, SET, and CHOICE, even if these constructs are nested within other extensible constructs. However, within any one such construct there can be at most one insertion point at the outer level of that construct, with material being successively added at the insertion point after any already inserted material.

To provide a clear documentation of the revision history, version brackets should normally be employed even if there is only one element added.

Note also that version brackets can only be inserted in SEQUENCE, SET, and CHOICE constructs, not in ENUMERATED or constraints.

At the time of writing this book (mid-1999), there are a number of published specifications that have inserted extension markers, and some that contain added material and version brackets.

```
SEQUENCE
    {field1   TypeA,
     field2   TypeB,
     ... ! PrintableString : "See clause 59",
     -- The following is handled by old systems
     -- as specified in clause 59.
     [[ v2-field1   Type2A,
        v2-field2   Type2B ]],
     [[ v3-field1   Type3A,
        v3-field2   Type3B ]],
     ... ,
     -- The following is version 1 material.
     field3   TypeC}
```

Figure 12.3   An insertion point with two version additions.

12.6 The {...} Notation

You will encounter what appears to be an extensible empty "table constraint" (see later) in a number of specifications. This relates to the use of Information Object Classes, and discussion of it is deferred until Chapter 14.

12.7 Interaction Between Extensibility and Tagging

When tagging was discussed in the previous chapter, it was noted that extensibility gave rise to some further requirements on the distinctness of tags.

These requirements arise because if there are several extension markers in an ASN.1 type, they may have different exception specifications associated with them, and it is therefore important for version 1 systems to be able to unambiguously associate "foreign" material with a specific insertion point and hence exception specification.

It is fortunate (as PER does not encode tags) that there are no problems in this area with a PER encoding. However, with BER, constructions like the following give real problems:

NOTE

Explanations given in this text may be hard to understand without a clear understanding of the BER encoding rules. Readers who are progressing sequentially through this book should either just accept that there are further rules on tagging that are ad hoc and curious, or else read the text on BER and return to this section. Sorry! I can do no better!

```
Example1 ::= SEQUENCE
        {field1  CHOICE
                    {alt1  INTEGER,
                    ...!1 } OPTIONAL,
        ...!2 }
```

or

```
Example2 ::= CHOICE
                {alt2  CHOICE
                        {alt3 INTEGER,
                        ...!3 },
                ...!4}
```

Now suppose that in version 2 additions are made at the insertion points with exception handling !1 or !2. If "field1" had not been optional it would have been easy—presence of foreign material before the presence of "alt1" is clearly a !1 case, and after it a !2 case. But with field1 optional, there is no way for version1 systems to determine whether we have new material at !1, or !1 is missing and there is new material at !2. A similar problem arises with new material at !3 or !4.

Note that the problem is not with the tag on any added material, but that it is fundamental to the use of extensibility in these constructs.

Unless BER were to be changed (shrieks of horror—BER long precedes extensibility!) it is necessary to make the Example 1 and Example 2 (and other similar) constructs illegal. How to do that?

The ASN.1 Specification adopts a slightly curious approach. It says that wherever there is an extension marker, you should add (at the end of any existing extensions) a "conceptual element" whose tag matches that of no other element except other "conceptual element"s. Then you apply rules about when distinct tags are required, and if they are satisfied, you are legal (and there will be no problems for a version 1 system to unambiguously assign foreign material to a single insertion point).

In Example 1, addition of the conceptual element in the !1 position means that "field1" brings to the table both the INTEGER tag **and** the tag of the conceptual element. The latter clashes with the tag of the following (mandatory) conceptual element in the !2 position, so the construction is illegal.

In Example 2, "alt2" brings to the table the tag of the conceptual element (as well as the INTEGER tag), which again clashes with the tag of the conceptual element in the extension !4. So again we have illegality.

(Please refer to Figure 999 again!) It is important to note here that this is a distinct complexity with extensibility. Having given earlier advice that you should use AUTOMATIC TAGS, and then forget about tagging, I am now saying (and the ASN.1 Specification is saying) that in order to determine whether some extensibility constructions are legal or not requires that you have a fairly sophisticated understanding of tagging. Of course, if you use a tool such as that provided by OSS to check your ASN.1, it will instantly tell you that you have broken the rules, although whether you will understand the error message in these cases is more questionable!

So we need some simple advice:

- If a CHOICE is OPTIONAL in some SEQUENCE, make sure it is not the last element before an extension marker, or make sure it is not itself extensible. (And do not follow it by another extensible CHOICE!)

- If a CHOICE is in a SET, make sure that only **one** of the CHOICE and the SET are extensible.

- Never put an extensible CHOICE in another extensible CHOICE.

In summary, treat extensible CHOICEs like radioactive material—keep them well apart and clearly separated from other extension markers! If you do that, there will never be any problems.

These rules really are ad hoc, but they are simple to apply, and will eliminate the problems described earlier.

Of course, if you break these rules, you are writing *de jure* illegal ASN.1, and a **good** tool will tell you so, and probably refuse to encode it! But if you encode it yourself, ..., well, problems only arise in practice if you have different exception handling on the various extensions. Just keep the earlier discussion in mind, and you should be OK.

12.8 Conclusion

We have described the extension marker and its association with the exception specification, and the complications arising from BER, which give rise to the need to produce some complex rules on when apparently innocuous extension markers are illegal.

Finally, it is important to note that the interworking that extensibility provides between version 1 and version 2 systems is dependent on the extension marker being present in version 1, and in changes being made to the protocol only as permitted by the extensibility provisions (addition of elements, alternatives, enumerations, at the insertion point, and relaxation of constraints).

If changes are made to a specification that are not covered by the extensibility provisions (such as random insertion of new elements), then the encodings of that new version are likely to produce unpredictable effects if sent to a version 1 system. Similarly, insertion of an extensibility marker in version 2 that was not present in version 1 means that encodings of the version 2 material will produce unpredictable effects if sent to version 1 systems.

The unpredictability described here may be simply between "Will they abort in some way or will they ignore the apparent error?", but could be "With encodings of some version 2 values version 1 systems will think they are correct encodings of totally unrelated version 1 values" and will act accordingly, which could be **very** dangerous. So it is generally important to **prevent** encodings of version 2 types that do not obey the extensibility rules from being sent to version 1 systems. This can, of course, be done in many ways, the most common of which is some form of version negotiation when a connection is first established.

Extensibility and exception handling are powerful tools, and enable highly optimized encoding rules to be used. They are safe if the rules governing their use are obeyed.

It is, however, very important to insert extension markers fairly liberally into version 1 specifications (or to use the EXTENSIBILITY IMPLIED notation).

## CHAPTER 13

Information Object Classes, Constraints, and Parameterization

(Or: Completing the Incomplete—with Precision)

Summary

This chapter

- provides a brief description of the concept of "holes" in protocols;

- describes briefly the Remote Operations Service Element (ROSE) protocol in order to provide a specific example of the need to define types with "holes" in them, and the need for notation to support clear specifications in the presence of "holes"; and

- provides a clear statement of the Information Object, Information Object Class, and Information Object Set concepts, and the use of those Object Sets to complete a partial protocol specification by constraining "holes" (and the consistency relationships for filling in multiple holes) left in a carrier protocol.

It goes on to describe

- the syntax for defining an Information Object Class, Information Objects, and Information Object Sets, using a development of the Wineco protocol as examples;

- the means by which defined Information Object Sets can be related to the "holes" that they are intended to constrain, using a simplified version of the ROSE protocol as an example; and

- the need for parameterization, and the parameterization syntax of ASN.1 specifications.

It is supposed to be bad practice to tell a student that "what I am about to say is difficult"! But the information object concepts are among the more conceptually difficult parts of ASN.1, and we will introduce these concepts gently in this chapter and fill in the final details in the next chapter. Just skim this chapter if it is all too easy!

13.1 The Need for "Holes" and Notational Support for Them

13.1.1 OSI Layering

This is probably the first time in this book that Open Systems Interconnection (OSI) has been seriously discussed, although it was within the OSI stable that ASN.1 was first standardized.

OSI was perhaps the first protocol suite specification to take seriously the question of documenting its **architecture,** with the production of

> A diversion into human psychology: Never write anything that is complete—it limits its use!

the OSI 7-layer model. Many vendor-specific protocols had some concept of layering, and the TCP/IP work had split off IP from TCP in the late 1970s, but the OSI model was the most complete attempt at describing the concept of layering.

The 7-layer model was (in 1984) just the latest attempt to try to produce a simplification of the (quite difficult) task of specifying how computers would communicate, by dividing the task into a number of separate pieces of specification with well-defined links between those pieces of specification.

Although this "architecture" aimed primarily at making it possible for several groups to work on different parts of the specification simultaneously, an important offshoot was to provide **reusability** of pieces of specification. This included reusability of network specifications to carry many different applications over the same network, or reusability of application specifications to run over many different network technologies, some of which may not have been invented when the application specification was first written.

The reader should contrast this with the early so-called "link" protocols (mainly deployed in the military arena, but also in telephony), where a single monolithic specification (document) completely and absolutely defined everything from application semantics to electrical signaling.

In the International Standards Organization (ISO) 7-layer model, each layer provided a partial specification of messages that were being transmitted, each message having a "hole" in it (called **user-data**) that carried the bit-patterns of the messages defined by the next higher layer. However, there was a "fan-out" and "fan-in" situation: Many possible lower layers (for example, transport or network protocols) could be used to carry any given higher-layer messages, and any given transport (or network) could carry many different higher-layer messages. It was a very flexible many-to-many situation.

> OSI was full of holes! Every layer of specification defined a small part of the total message, then left a massive hole that was to be filled in by bits specified in the next higher layer of specification.

But the basic concept in the original ISO/OSI model was that every application layer specification would fill in the final hole—each application layer standard would produce a complete specification for some application.

It was the CCITT 7-layer model (eventually adopted by ISO) that brought to the table the concept of partial specifications of "useful tools" in the application layer, recognizing a potentially infinite set of layers, each filling in a "hole" in the layer beneath, but itself leaving "holes" for other groups to fill in due course.

As ASN.1 increasingly became the notation of choice for defining application specifications, there clearly became a need for support in ASN.1 for "holes".

13.1.2 Hole Support in ASN.1

> Holes did not stop at the application layer: people wanted to write "generic" specifications with "holes" left in. And people filling in those holes still wanted to leave a few further holes!

Forget about theoretical models for now. It rapidly became clear that people writing application specifications using ASN.1 in 1984 wanted to be able to write a "generic" or "carrier" specification, with "holes" left in their datatypes, with other groups (multiple, independent, groups) providing specifications for what filled the holes.

At this point it is important to recognize that "leaving some things left undefined, for others to define", can (most obviously) be an undefined part of the format of messages (the user-data in OSI layering), or one of the elements in an ASN.1 sequence, but can also be an undefined part of the **procedures** for conducting a computer exchange. Both types of "holes" have occurred in real specifications, and notation is needed to identify clearly the presence and nature of any "holes" in a specification, together with notation for "user" specifiers to fill in the "holes".

There is one other important point: If several different (user) groups provide specifications for applications that fit in the holes of some carrier or generic protocol, it often happens that implementations wish to support several of these user specifications, and need to be able to determine at communication-time precisely which specification has been used to fill in the hole in a given instance of communication. This is rather like the "protocol id" concept in a layered architecture. We recognize the need for holes to carry not just some encoding of information for the user specification, but also an identification of that specification.

The earliest ASN.1 support for "holes" was with the notation "ANY", which (subject to a lot of controversy!) was withdrawn in 1994, along with the "macro notation", which was an early and largely unsuccessful attempt to relate material defining the contents of a hole (for a particular application) to a specific hole occurrence (in a carrier specification).

In 1994, the ASN.1 "Information Object Class" and related concepts matured as the preferred way of handling "holes". In this chapter we next introduce the concepts of ROSE (Remote Operations Service Element), showing how ROSE had the need for notation to let its users complete the holes left in the ROSE protocol. We then briefly describe the nature of the information that has to be supplied when a user of the ROSE specification produces a complete application specification. We then proceed to the concepts associated with ASN.1 "Information Object Classes".

13.2 The ROSE Invocation Model

13.2.1 Introduction

One of the earliest users of the ASN.1 notation was the Remote Operations Service Element (ROSE) specification—originally just called Remote Operations Service (ROS). This still provides one of the easiest to understand examples of the use of the Information Object Class concept, and a little time is taken here to introduce ROSE.

The reader should, however, note that this treatment of ROSE is NOT complete, and that when tables of information are introduced, the latest version of ROSE has many more columns than are described in the following text. There have been a number of specifications that have written their own version of ROSE, with some simplifications and/or with some extensions, so if you see text using "OPERATION" or "ERROR", check where these names are being imported from. They may be imported from the actual ROSE specification, or they may be a ROSE "look-alike". The definitions in this text are a ROSE "look-alike"—they are a simplification of the actual ROSE definitions.

> INVOKE an operation (invocation id, operation id, argument values), get back an operation-independent REJECT (predefined error codes) or a RESULT (invocation id, result values) or an ERROR (invocation id, error code, parameters associated with the error).

A common approach to the specification of protocols by a number of standardization groups (of which the latest is CORBA) is to introduce the concept of one system invoking an operation (or method, or activating an interface) on a remote system. This requires some form of message (defined in ASN.1 in the case of ROSE) to carry details for the operation being invoked, where the three most important elements are:

- some identification of this invocation, so that any returned results or errors can be associated with the invocation;

- some identification of the operation to be performed; and

- the value of some ASN.1 type (specific to that operation), which will carry all the arguments or input parameters for the operation.

This is called the ROSE INVOKE message (defined as an ASN.1 type called "Invoke"). ROSE introduced the concept of the "invocation identification" because it recognized that multiple instances of (perhaps the same) operation might be launched before the results of earlier ones had come back, and indeed that results might not come back in the same order as the order operations were launched in.

It is important here to note that the ROSE specification will define the concepts, and the form of the invocation message, but that lots of other groups will independently assign values to identify operations, define the ASN.1 type to carry the arguments or input parameters, and specify the associated semantics. They need a notation to do this, and to be able to link such definitions clearly to the holes left in the ASN.1 definition of the ROSE INVOKE message.

Used in this context, ASN.1 is being used as what is sometimes called an "Interface Definition Language" (IDL), but it is important to remember that ASN.1 is not restricted to such use and can be applied to protocol definition where there is no concept of remote invocations and return of results.

The INVOKE message itself is not a complete ASN.1 type definition. It has a "hole" that can carry whatever ASN.1 type is eventually used to carry values of the arguments of an operation. This "hole", and the value of the operation code field in the INVOKE message, clearly have to be filled in in a consistent manner—that is, the op-code and the type must match.

13.2.2 Responding to the INVOKE Message

The ROSE concept says that an INVOKE message may be responded to by a REJECT message, carrying operation-independent error indications, such as "operation not imple-

> ROSE messages are full of holes—except for REJECT, which is complete!

mented" (strictly, "invoke-unrecognizedOperation"), "system busy" (strictly, "resourceLimitation"), etc.). ROSE has about 40 different error or problem cases that can be notified with a REJECT message.

If, however, there is no such message, then the operation is successfully invoked and will result in an "intended result" (the RESULT message) or an operation-dependent "error response" (the ERROR message).

The ROSE invocation is illustrated in Figure 13.1.

This separation of "intended result" and "error response" is not strictly necessary, but simplifies the ASN.1 definition. The assumption here is that any one group will be defining a number of closely related operations, each of which will have an identification and precisely one ASN.1 type to carry the input arguments in the INVOKE message hole, and precisely one ASN.1 type to carry the output arguments in the RESULT message hole. However, for this complete set of operations, there are likely to be a set of possible error returns, such that any given operation can give rise to a specified subset of these errors. For each error we need an error code, and an ASN.1 type to carry additional information (which ROSE calls parameters) about the error, and of course we need to be able to specify which errors can arise from which operations.

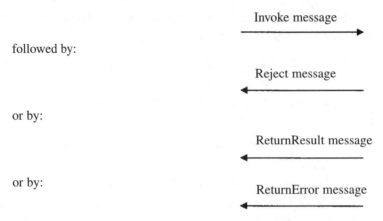

followed by:

or by:

or by:

Figure 13.1   Rose message exchanges.

13.3 The Use of Tables to Complete the User Specification

We return here to our Wineco protocol, and will first use an informal tabular format to show how we use the ROSE (incomplete) protocol to support our Wineco exchanges. We have already specified two main messages using ASN.1, namely

```
        Order-for-stock
and     Return-of-sales
```

We will add, without defining the ASN.1 types themselves, two further Wineco messages we might wish to pass with a ROSE INVOKE, namely

```
        Query-availability
and     Request-order-state
```

The first of these messages queries the availability of items for immediate delivery, and the second asks for an update on the state of an earlier order.

Expressing Wineco exchanges as a set of remote operations— you don't have to, but it might be simple and convenient.

We will make all four of these messages a ROSE operation, which will either produce a response or an error return. The response to an "Order-for-stock" will be an "Order-confirmed" message. Successful processing of a "Return-of-sales" will result in an ASN.1 NULL being returned. The response to

"Query-availability" will be an "Availability-response" and the response to a "Request-order-state" will be an "Order-status" response.

We envisage that some or all of these requests (operations) can produce the following errors (in each case with some additional data giving more details of the failure):

- Security check failure;

- Unknown branch;

- Order number unknown; or

- Items unavailable.

Note that there are other operation-independent errors carried in the ROSE Reject message that are provided for us by ROSE, but we do not need to consider those. Here we are only interested in errors specific to our own operations.

13.3.1 Specifying the Tables

We need to say all this rather more formally, but we start by doing it in an informal tabular form as shown in Figures 13.2 and 13.3.

In the figures, names such as "asn-val-....." are ASN.1 value reference names of a type defined by ROSE (actually, a CHOICE of INTEGER or OBJECT IDENTIFIER) used to identify operations or errors, and names such as "ASN-type-...." are ASN.1 types that carry more details about each of our possible errors. Note that in the case of the error "Order number unknown", we decide to return no further information, and we have left the corresponding cell of the table empty. We could have decided to return the ASN.1 type NULL in this case, but the element in the ROSE "ReturnError" SEQUENCE type that carries the parameter is OPTIONAL, and by leaving the cell of our table blank, we indicate that that element of the "ReturnError" SEQUENCE is to be omitted in this case. We will see later how we know whether we are allowed to leave a cell of the table empty or not.

```
        Error Code                    Parameter Type
        ==========                    ==============
asn-val-security-failure      ASN-type-sec-failure-details
asn-val-unknown-branch        ASN-type-branch-fail-details
asn-val-unknown-order
asn-val-unavailable           ASN-type-unavailable-details
```

Figure 13.2 The Wineco ERROR table.

```
Op Code           Argument Type        Result Type            Errors
======            =============        ===========            ======
asn-val-order     Order-for-stock      Order-confirmed        security-failure
                                                              unknown-branch

asn-val-sales     Return-of-sales      NULL                   security-failure
                                                              unknown-branch

asn-val-query     Query-availability   Availability-Response  security-failure
                                                              unknown-branch
                                                              unavailable

asn-val-state     Request-order-state  Order-status           security-failure
                                                              unknown-branch
                                                              unknown-order
```

Figure 13.3   The Wineco OPERATION table.

The Figure 13.2 table has one row for each possible error, and has just two columns:

- the error codes assigned (as values of the type determined in the ROSE specification); and

- the corresponding ASN.1 type (defined in our module) to carry parameters of the error.

We might normally expect a small number of rows for this table for any given application that uses ROSE to define its protocol (in our case we have four rows), and it may be that for some errors there is no additional parameter information to return, and hence no ASN.1 type needed for parameters of that error, as in the case of "asn-val-unknown-order".

The table in Figure 13.3 is the other information needed to complete the ROSE protocol for our Wineco application. It lists an operation code, which is again a value of the type—as specified by ROSE:

```
CHOICE {local INTEGER,
        global OBJECT IDENTIFIER}
```

together with the ASN.1 type that carries the input arguments for the operation, the ASN.1 type that carries the result values, and a list of the errors that the operation can generate.

In the real ROSE specification, there are additional columns to assign a priority value for operations and for error returns, to identify so-called "linked operations", and to determine whether results are always returned, values of error parameters needed, and so on. Discussion of these details of ROSE would go beyond the scope or the needs of this text, and we have not included these features in the illustration.

Given then the ROSE concept of messages (ASN.1 datatypes) with "holes" in them, we see

- The need for a syntax for ROSE to specify the information its users need to supply to complete the ROSE data-types by the specification of a number of operations and errors (definition of the number and form of the tables in Figures 13.2 and 13.3).

- The need for a strict ASN.1 syntax (machine-readable) for ROSE users to specify the information shown informally in Figures 13.2 and 13.3.

- The need for notation in ASN.1 to identify "holes" in ASN.1 types, and to link the information shown in Figures 13.2 and 13.3 clearly with the "hole" it is intended to complete.

13.3.2 From Specific to General

In the general case, there may be many different tables needed to complete any given "generic" protocol, and each table will have a number of columns determined by that "generic" protocol. The nature of the information needed for each column of the table (and the column headings to provide a "handle" for each piece of information) will all vary depending on the "generic" protocol in question.

Thus the specifier of a "generic" protocol needs a notation that will provide a clear statement of the form of the tables (the information needed to complete the "generic" protocol). We call the specification of this the **specification of Information Object Classes**. When a **user** of the

> ROSE is just one example of incomplete (generic) protocols. There are many other examples where specifiers leave it to others to complete the specification, and need to be able to (formally) say what additional information is needed. This is an Information Object Class specification.

"generic" protocol provides information for a row of a table we say that they are **specifying an Information Object** of the class associated with that table. The total set of rows of a given table defined to support any one user specification is called **an Information Object Set**.

Notation is thus needed in ASN.1 for:

- The definition of a named Information Object Class (the form of a table).

- The definition of named Information Objects of a given class (completing the information for one row of the table).

- Collecting together all the Information Objects (of any given class) defined in a specification into a named Information Object Set (a completed table).

- Linking a named information object set to the "holes" in the carrier protocol that it is designed to complete.

13.4 From Tables to Information Object Classes

The table metaphor is a very useful one in introducing the Information Object Class concepts, but the term "table" is not used in the ASN.1 Standard itself (except in the term "table constraint", discussed later).

> Tables are fine for human-to-human communication. For computer processing we use ASN.1 notation to define the form of tables and the contents of those tables.

We say that each Information Object has a series of **fields**, each with a **field name**. Defining an Information Object Class involves listing all the fields for objects of that class, giving the field-name for each field, and some properties of that field. The most important property is the nature of the information needed when defining that field. This is most commonly the specification of some ASN.1 type (with the semantics associated with that type), or the specification of an ASN.1 value of some fixed ASN.1 type. However, we will see later that there are a number of other sorts of fields that can be defined.

In the case of ROSE, we have two Information Object Classes defined by ROSE: the OPERATION class and the ERROR class. (Names of Information Object Classes are required to be all uppercase).

All objects of class OPERATION will have four fields containing

- A value of type

```
CHOICE {local   INTEGER,
        global  OBJECT IDENTIFIER}
```

to identify the operation.

- An ASN.1 type capable of carrying input values for the operation.

- An ASN.1 type capable of carrying the result values on successful completion of the operation.

- A list of information objects of class ERROR, each of which is an error that this particular operation can produce.

All objects of class ERROR will have two fields containing:

- A value of type

```
CHOICE {local   INTEGER,
           global OBJECT IDENTIFIER}
```

to identify the error.

- An ASN.1 type capable of carrying the values of the parameters of the error.

To summarize: An Information Object Class definition defines the amount and form of information that is needed to specify an object of that class. An Information Object definition provides that information. The nature of the information needed can be very varied, and we talk about the form of the fields of the Information Object Class according to the information needed for that field when defining an Information Object.

In the earlier discussion, we have introduced:

- *Type fields*: Fields that need an ASN.1 type definition to complete them.

- *Fixed type value fields*: Fields that need the value of a single (specified) ASN.1 type to complete them.

- *Object set fields*: Fields that need a set of information objects of a single (specified) Information Object Class (in this case the ERROR class) to complete them.

There are a number of other forms of field that can be specified when defining an Information Object Class, and we shall see more of these later.

If you see names in all uppercase, you can be reasonably sure that you are dealing with Information Object Classes, but another certain way to tell is the presence of names beginning with the & (ampersand) character. In order to avoid confusion with other pieces of ASN.1 notation, the names of fields of Information Object

Classes are **required** to begin with an &. Thus the field of the OPERATION class that contains the object identifier value for some particular operation is called:

```
OPERATION.&operationCode
```

The field that has to be supplied with a type definition for the arguments of the INVOKE message is called:

```
OPERATION.&ArgumentType
```

Note that the &operationCode field contains a single ASN.1 value, and after the & we have a lowercase letter (this is a requirement), while the &ArgumentType field contains an ASN.1 type, and after the & we have an uppercase letter (again a requirement). Where a field contains a single value (usually—but not always—of some fixed type) or a single information object (of some fixed class) the field-name after the & starts with a lowercase letter. Where a field contains multiple values or multiple information objects (as with the list of errors for an operation), the field-name after the & starts with an uppercase letter. It is important to remember these rules when trying to interpret the meaning of an ASN.1 Information Object Class definition.

We have already seen that names of Information Object Classes are required to be all uppercase. Names given to individual Information Objects are required to start with a lowercase letter (similar to value references), and names given to Information Object Sets (collections of Information Objects of a given class) are required to start with an uppercase letter.

There is in general a strong similarity between the concepts of types, values, and sets of values (subtypes), and the concepts of Information Object Classes, Information Objects, and Information Object Sets, and naming conventions in relation to the initial letter of names follow the same rules.

There is, however, an important difference between types and information object classes. All ASN.1 types start life populated with a set of values, and new types can be produced as subsets of these values. Information Object Classes have **no** predefined objects, they merely determine the notation for defining objects of that class, which can later be collected together into information object sets, which are really the equivalent of types.

When you define a class you provide it with a reference name; this is also the case for Information Objects and Information Object Sets. These reference names can then be used in other parts of the ASN.1 notation to reference those classes, objects, and sets, just like type reference and value reference names are assigned to type and value definitions and then used elsewhere. Reference names for classes, objects, and object sets are imported and exported between modules in the IMPORTS and EXPORTS statements just like type and value reference names.

13.5 The ROSE OPERATION and ERROR Object Class Definitions

Figure 13.4 shows a simplified form of the definition of the OPERATION and ERROR classes of ROSE, and is the first introduction of the actual ASN.1 syntax for defining Information Object Classes.

Remember, this syntax essentially defines the table headings and the information content of the informal tables shown in Figures 13.2 and 13.3, but it is doing it with a syntax that is similar to ASN.1 type and value definition syntax, and which is fully machine-processable.

> At last! We get to see an example of a real Information Object Class definition. Two in fact! The OPERATION class and the ERROR class from ROSE.

In Figure 13.4, we see the definition of four fields for OPERATION and two for ERROR, as expected. Compare that figure with the table headings of Figures 13.2 and 13.3, and let us go through the fields in detail. (Remember, each class definition corresponds to the definition of the form of a table, and each field corresponds to the definition of the form of a column of that table.)

For the OPERATION class, we have the "&operationCode" field, which is required to be completed with a value of the specified type. (It is called a **fixed type value**

```
OPERATION ::= CLASS
  {&operationCode   CHOICE {local INTEGER,
                            global OBJECT IDENTIFIER}
                  UNIQUE,
    &ArgumentType,
    &ResultType,
    &Errors    ERROR OPTIONAL }


ERROR ::= CLASS
   {&errorCode    CHOICE {local INTEGER,
                          global OBJECT IDENTIFIER}
                 UNIQUE,
     &ParameterType    OPTIONAL }
```

Figure 13.4   The OPERATION and ERROR class definitions.

field). This field is also flagged as "UNIQUE". When defining an object of this class, any value (of the specified type) can be inserted in this field, but if a set of such objects is placed together to form an Information Object Set (using notation we will see later), there is a requirement (because of the "UNIQUE") that all values in this field are different for each object in the set. If you regard the object set as representing a completely filled-in table, then in database terminology, fields marked "UNIQUE" provide a key or index into the table. More than one field can be marked "UNIQUE" (but this is uncommon), but there is no mechanism in the notation to require that the **combination** of two fields has to be unique within an information object set. If you needed to specify that, you would have to use comment within the class definition.

The next two fields, "&ArgumentType" and "&ResultType" have names that begin with a capital letter, and no type definition after them. This means that they have to be completed by the specification of an ASN.1 type (usually, but not necessarily, by giving a type reference rather than an explicit definition of a type).

The fourth and last field is more interesting. "&Errors" begins with a capital letter, so you complete it with a set of things. But the name following is not an ASN.1 type reference, it is a class reference. So this field has to be completed with a set of Information Objects of that (the ERROR) class, defined next. This field is also flagged as "OPTIONAL". This means that in the definition of objects of this class, it is not a requirement to define information for this field—it can be left blank. This would imply that the corresponding operation never produced a "ReturnError" response.

It is left to the reader to examine the definition of the error class, which should now be understandable.

13.6 Defining the Information Objects

The Information Object Class definition tells you what information you need to provide in order to define an OPERATION or an ERROR object. Now we see the syntax you use to define such objects.

Let us now use the notation for defining objects of a defined class (in this case OPERATION and ERROR). We take the informal definition of operations and errors given in Figures 13.2 and 13.3 and express them in the ASN.1 notation for defining objects. This is shown in Figures 13.5 (the ERROR objects) and 13.6 (the OPERATION objects).

```
sec-fail ERROR ::=
{&errorCode         asn-val-security-failure,
 &ParameterType    ASN-type-sec-failure-details}

unknown-branch ERROR ::=
{&errorCode         asn-val-unknown-branch,
 &ParameterType    ASN-type-branch-fail-details}

unknown-order ERROR ::=
{&errorCode         asn-val-unknown-order}

unavailable ERROR ::=
{&errorCode         asn-val-unavailable,
 &ParameterType    ASN-type-unavailable-details}
```

Figure 13.5   Definition of the Wineco ERROR Information Objects.

These figures should be fairly understandable, and a line-by-line commentary will not be given, but there are some points to which the reader's attention is drawn.

Note that the left of the "::=" looks rather like the definition of a value reference—compare:

```
my-int-val INTEGER ::= 3
```

which is read as "my-int-val of type INTEGER has the value 3". In a similar way, we read Figures 13.5 and 13.6 as (for example) "sec-fail of class ERROR has the fields ....". Following the "::=" we list (in curly brackets) each of the fields in the class definition, in order, and separated by commas, giving in each case the name of the field and the definition of that field for this particular object.

Note also that the "unknown-order" ERROR object has no definition for the &ParameterType field—this is permissible only because that field was marked OPTIONAL in the class definition of Figure 13.4.

Turning to the "&Errors" field, note that when we want to define a set of errors, we use a list of reference names separated by a vertical bar and enclosed in curly brackets. This may seem less intuitive than if a comma had been used as the list separator, but it is in fact a special case of a much more powerful mechanism for grouping objects into sets using **set arithmetic** (see 13.7). The vertical bar is used for set UNION, so we are producing a set for the "&Error" field of "order", which is the union of "security-failure" and "unknown-branch".

Finally, note that the names used in the definition of the "&Error" fields are themselves defined as errors in Figure 13.5. Those definitions would be in the same module as the Figure 13.6 definitions, or would be imported into that module.

```
order OPERATION ::=
   {&operationCode    asn-val-order,
    &ArgumentType     Order-for-stock,
    &ResultType       Order-confirmed,
    &Errors           {security-failure |
                       unknown-branch }}

sales OPERATION ::=
   {&operationCode    asn-val-sales,
    &ArgumentType     Return-of-sales,
    &ResultType       NULL,
    &Errors           {security-failure |
                       unknown-branch }}

query OPERATION ::=
   {&operationCode    asn-val-query,
    &ArgumentType     Query-availability,
    &ResultType       Availability-Response,
    &Errors           {security-failure |
                       unknown-branch |
                       unavailable }}

status OPERATION ::=
   {&operationCode    asn-val-state,
    &ArgumentType     Request-order-state,
    &ResultType       Order-status,
    &Errors           {security-failure |
                       unknown-branch |
                       unknown-order }}
```

Figure 13.6   Definition of the Wineco OPERATION Information Objects.

Figure 13.5 and 13.6 definitions may appear more verbose (they are!) than the informal tabular notation used in Figures 13.2 and 13.3; however, they are very explicit, but more importantly, they are machine-readable, and ASN.1 tools can process them and use these definitions in checking and decoding the content of "holes" in incoming messages.

13.7 Defining an Information Object Set

Why do we need to combine the definition of individual Information Objects into an Information Object Set? Well, we saw a use of this in defining the "&Errors" field of the OPERATION class above, but there is a more important reason. The whole purpose of defining Information Object Classes and Information Objects is to provide an ASN.1 definition of the complete (informal) table we saw earlier that determines what can fill in the holes in a carrier or generic protocol, and to link that ASN.1 definition to the "holes" in the generic or carrier protocol.

So we need a notation to allow us to define Information Object Sets (collections of Information Objects of a given class), with a name assigned to that set which can be used elsewhere in our specification.

Information Object Sets are collections of Information Objects, much as types

> The next step on the way. Someone has defined some Information Object Classes. We define some Information Objects. Now we pull them together into a named Information Object Set.

can be seen as collections or sets of values. So it is not surprising that the names for Information Object Sets are required to start with an uppercase letter. If we want a name for the collection of operations we have defined in Figure 13.6, we can write:

```
My-ops OPERATION ::= {order  |
                       sales  |
                       query  |
                       status }
```

Read this as "My-ops of class OPERATION is the set consisting of the union of the objects order, sales, query, and status".

This is the most common form, but general set arithmetic is available if needed. Suppose that A1, A2, A3, and A4 have been defined as Information Object Sets of class OPERATION. We can write expressions such as:

```
New-Set OPERATION ::= {(A1 INTERSECTION A2)
                       UNION (A3 EXCEPT A4) }
```

but as a colleague of mine frequently says: "No one ever does!"

If you leave the brackets out, the most binding is EXCEPT, the next INTERSECTION, and the weakest UNION. Although all the round brackets in the example could be omitted without change of meaning, it is usually best to include them to avoid confusing a reader. (Some people seem to find it intuitive that "EXCEPT" should be the least binding, so clarifying brackets when "EXCEPT" is used are always a good idea.)

I will not bore you with a long-winded example of the result for various sets A1 to A4—invent your own and work it out—or ask your teenage daughter to help you!

The caret character "^" is a synonym for "INTERSECTION", and the vertical bar character "|" is a synonym for "UNION". There is no single character that is a synonym for EXCEPT—you must write that out in full.

We have already noted the similarity between Information Objects and values, and Information Object Sets and types or subtypes (collections of values). Where do classes fit into this pattern? This is less clearcut. Information Object Classes are in some ways like types, but unlike types, they start off with no Information Objects in them, merely with a mechanism for the ASN.1 user to define objects of that class. By contrast, built-in types come with a ready-made collection of values and value notation, from which you can produce subsets using constraints.

Nonetheless, because of the similarity of objects and values, when ASN.1 was extended to introduce the information-object-related concepts, it was decided to allow the same syntax as was introduced for defining sets of objects to be used for defining sets of values (subsets of some type). Because of this, the so-called **value set assignment** was introduced into the ASN.1 syntax. This allows you to write (should you so wish!):

```
First-set INTEGER ::= {0..5}
Second-set INTEGER ::= {10..15 UNION 20}
Third-set INTEGER ::=
   {First-set UNION Second-set EXCEPT 13}
Fourth-set INTEGER ::= {0..5 | 10..12 | 14 | 15 | 20}
```

"Fourth-set" is, of course, exactly the same subset of INTEGER as is "Third-set".

It is testing time! Or put it another way, time for some fun! With the preceding definitions, can you write

```
selected-int Fourth-set ::= 14
```

and as an element of a SEQUENCE

```
Third-set DEFAULT selected-int
```

Yes you can! This question of *exactly* what is legal ASN.1 in such cases has vexed the Standards group for several years, but is now largely resolved. It is, however, best to rely on a good tool to give you the answer, rather than to pore over the Standard text itself! Or maybe better still to keep your ASN.1 simple and straight-forward!

Before we leave this discussion, let us look at "My-ops" again. It is likely that in a future version of the Wineco protocol we will want to add some additional operations, and hence to extend "My-ops". This has implications for version 1 systems, which will need to have some defined error-handling if they are requested to perform an operation that they know nothing about. We will see in a moment the way the error handling is specified, but first we need to indicate that "My-ops" may be extended in the future. We do this by rewriting it as:

```
My-ops OPERATION ::= {order   |
                      sales   |
                      query   |
                      status , ... }
```

with a possible version 2, with an added operation "payment", being written:

```
My-ops OPERATION ::= {order   |
                      sales   |
                      query   |
                      status , ..., payment }
```

13.8 Using the Information to Complete the ROSE Protocol

Let's get back to our main theme. Designers of "generic" protocols want to have elements of SEQUENCES and SETS that they do not define. They want other groups to define the types to fill these positions. Frequently the other groups will want to carry many different types in these elements at different times. The Information Object concepts enable the definition of the types that will fill these elements. But how are these "holes" identified in an ASN.1 type definition? And how are the Information Object (Set) definitions linked to the "holes"?

Largely for historical reasons, ASN.1 takes a three-stage approach to this problem. The first step is to allow reference to a field of an Information Object Class to be used wherever an ASN.1 type (or in some cases an

> No point in defining classes, objects, and object sets unless they are going somewhere. After all, you can't encode them and send them down the line. So what good are they? Answer: to fill in holes.

ASN.1 value) is required. The second stage is to allow an Information Object Set to be used as a **constraint** on such types, requiring that that element be a type (or a value) from the corresponding field of that Information Object Set. This is called a table constraint. The third step is to allow (additionally) two or more elements of a

SET or SEQUENCE (that are defined as fields of the same Information Object Class) to be linked using a pointer between them (the "@" symbol is used to provide the link). Use of this linking mechanism says that the linked fields have to be filled consistently in accordance with some Information Object of the constraining Information Object Set. In other words, the linked fields have to correspond to cells from a single row of the defining table. Constraints expressing a linkage between elements are called **relational constraints**.

Figure 13.7 shows a (simplified) ROSE "Invoke" data-type, illustrating these features. It uses the Information Object Set "My-ops" (of class OPERATION), defined in 13.7, and relational constraints on the elements of "Invoke".

Figure 13.7 is quite complex so take it a step at a time. The "opcode" element of the sequence says that it is a value from the "&operationCode" field of the class "OPERATION". In itself, this is just a synonym for

```
CHOICE
   {local INTEGER,
    global OBJECT IDENTIFIER}
```

because this is a fixed-type value field of this type. Or to put it another way, all values of this field are of this type.

However, by referencing the type through the field of the Information Object Class, we are then allowed to constrain it with an Information Object Set ("My-ops") of that class. (Such a constraint would not be allowed if we had simply written the element as "CHOICE ... etc.".)

The curly brackets around "My-ops" are a stupidity (sorry—there are a few!) in the ASN.1 syntax. The requirement here is for the syntactic construct "ObjectSet". A **reference name** for an object set (which is what "My-ops" would be) is not allowed. However, we can generate an "ObjectSet" from "My-ops" by

```
Invoke ::= SEQUENCE
   { invokeId    INTEGER,
     opcode      OPERATION.&operationCode
                    ({My-ops} ! invoke-unrecognisedOperation),
     argument    OPERATION.&ArgumentType
                    ({My-ops}
                     {@opcode} ! invoke-mistypedArgument) OPTIONAL
}
```

Figure 13.7 The ROSE Invoke data-type.

importing "My-ops" into an object set definition, that is to say, by enclosing it in curly brackets.

Put simply, there is no good reason for it, but you have to put the curly brackets in!

The effect of the "My-ops" constraint is to say that the only values permitted for this element are those assigned to the "&operationCode" field one of the Information Objects of "My-ops". In other words, the field must contain an op-code for one of the four (in version 1) operations defined for Wineco. This is all fully machine-readable, and encoders/decoders can use this specification to help with error checking.

The "!" introduces an exception specification, and says that if this constraint is not satisfied (a different op-code value appears), the error handling is to return a REJECT with the integer value "invoke-unrecognizedOperation". The designers of the Wineco protocol need not concern themselves with specifying such error handling. This is all done within the ROSE specification. Note that this is precisely the error situation that will arise if a version 1 implementation is hit with a request to perform the "payment" operation.

Now we move onto the "argument" element. This is the true "hole". In its unconstrained form, it simply says that this element can be "any ASN.1 type" (because any ASN.1 type can be used for this field of an Information Object of the OPERATION class). Such notation is described in ASN.1 as "Open Type" notation, and is handled rather specially by encoding rules.

In particular, it is important that encodings enable a decoder to find the end of an open type encoding before they know in detail what type is encoded within it (the "opcode" element of the SEQUENCE could have been written after the "argument" element—there is no restriction).

In BER, there is no problem—the end of an encoding can always be determined using the "L" field of the "TLV", for all ASN.1 BER encodings of types. In PER, however, this is not the case. Unless a decoder knows what the type being encoded is, it cannot find the end of the encoding of a value of the type. So in PER, an extra "length" wrapper is always added to an open type.

As an aside, you will sometimes find people deliberately defining an element as an open type (typically using a class with just one field, a type field), and then constraining that element to be a single fully defined ASN.1 type. The sole purpose of this is to produce the additional length wrapper, and relates to implementation architecture. Such constructs are used to encapsulate security-related data, where the implementation architecture is likely to be to pass an encapsulated set of octets to a security kernel, with the insecure part of the application having no detailed knowledge of the security-related data. (Government Health Warning —Figure 999—again, you must judge for yourself whether such provision is sensible or not. It happens. At worst it just means an unnecessary length field!)

Finally, we address the "@" part of "argument". This turns the constraint into a relational constraint, linking the "argument" and "opcode" fields, and requiring them to be consistent with some row of the constraining table. (Whoops! To be consistent with some object in the constraining Information Object Set—we should use the correct terminology!).

The "@" construction could equally well, and with the same effect, have been placed on the "opcode" field (as well, or instead of). All that is being formally said is that the two (and there could be more) linked fields have to be consistent with an object in the set. We know, of course, that "OPERATION.&operationCode" was defined as "UNIQUE" in the class definition, so there will be at most one object in the Information Object Set that matches a value in the "opcode" field of the "Invoke" message. In the general case, this is not necessarily true, and the only requirement is that the values and/or types of linked fields are consistent with at least one of the information objects in the constraining object set (consistent with at least one row of the constraining table).

Finally, note the "invoke-mistypedArgument" error return. In BER, there is a great deal of redundancy in an encoding, and it can usually be easily detected if an encoding does not represent a value of the type we think it should (or might) be. In PER, this is not so often the case, as there is much less redundant encoding. In PER, the main detection of "invoke-mistypedArgument" occurs if the encoding of the open type (as determined by the added length field) does not have the right length for some value of the type we are trying to match it with (the one identified by the "opcode" value).

There is always an argument among protocol designers on the extent to which one should specify the actions of an implementation on receipt of erroneous material (presumably from a bust sending implementation, or due to the very, very rare occurrence of undetected errors in lower layers), or whether such actions should be left as implementation-dependent. ASN.1 provides notation to go in either direction. ROSE chose to be very prescriptive on error handling, and made full use of ASN.1 exception handling to specify the required behavior on receipt of "bad" material. If you are a protocol designer, this is a decision you will make. ASN.1 gives you the tools to be prescriptive, but there is no requirement to use those tools, and many specifiers choose not to.

Note that there is a certain difference between the "!" on the opcode element and that on the "argument" element. In the first case we know it can get activated if a version 2 system tries to invoke "payment" on a version 1 system. In the second case it should never get activated if systems are conforming and lower layer communications are reliable.

13.9 The Need for Parameterization

I wonder how many readers noticed that the approach described in 13.8, while looking attractively precise and implementable, has a major problem associated with it?

If we were to rewrite the whole of ROSE in our Wineco specification, the approach described in 13.8 would work fine. We might have a series of modules defining our main types, as illustrated in earlier chapters (call these MAIN modules) and another

> But unfortunately it just doesn't work! Many people are defining their own "My-op" object sets, but there is just one ROSE specification of "Invoke"!

module defining the OPERATION and ERROR classes, and the "Invoke", "Reject", "ReturnResult", and "ReturnError" (call this the ROSE module). Then we have a final module (call this the INFORMATION OBJECTS module) that defines our information objects and the "My-op" set.

From MAIN we export all top-level Wineco types. From the ROSE module we export our Information Object Class definitions. In the INFORMATION OBJECTS module we import the Information Object Class definitions, and export "My-op". Finally, in the ROSE module, as well as exporting the class definitions, we import "My-op" for use in the "Invoke" etc. messages as already described, and define our top-level PDU, which now defines our Wineco abstract syntax as:

```
wineco-PDU ::= CHOICE
    {invoke    Invoke,
     reject    Reject,
     result    ReturnResult,
     error     ReturnError }
```

Now we have a complete and working protocol.

However, this approach does not work if we want the ROSE specifications to be published totally separately from the Wineco specification, with many different applications (of which Wineco would be just one) that want to produce a ROSE-based specification. Copying the ROSE text for each application would not be a good idea! (That said, there are specifications that define their own ROSE-equivalent classes and PDUs, usually in a simplified form, simply because they wish to be complete in their own right and to have control so that the ROSE part cannot change under their feet. This "copying with simplification" occurs with other popular specifications, not just with ROSE.)

If the ROSE specification is to be independent of the Wineco application, then clearly it cannot import the "My-op" type. How then can it supply a constraint to say how the hole is to be filled in?

Here we introduce a new and very powerful ASN.1 concept, that of **parameterization**.

All programmers are fully familiar with the concept of functions or subroutines or methods having a set of dummy parameters that are referred to in the body of the function or subroutine or method specification. When those functions or subroutines are called, the calling code supplies a set of actual parameters that are used instead of the dummy parameters for that call.

ASN.1 has a very similar concept. When we define a type, such as the ROSE "Invoke" type, we can list after the type name a dummy parameter list. These dummy parameters can then be used on the right-hand side of the type definition as if they were normal reference names. We call such a type a **parameterized type**, and we can export parameterized types (for example from the generic ROSE specification, with import into one or more application specifications such as Wineco). In the importing specification (or anywhere else the parameterized type is used) we supply an actual parameter specific to that use. Figure 13.8 shows the ROSE module, and Figure 13.9 the Wineco module. Note that now all exporting is **from** ROSE—ROSE does no imports at all.

There are a few things to notice in Figure 13.8. We could have exported separately the Invoke, Reject, ReturnResult, and ReturnError messages, but we chose to bundle these together as a "Rose-PDU" CHOICE type and to export that. This meant that "Rose-PDU" had to be parameterized with the "User-ops" dummy parameter, with that dummy parameter supplied as the actual parameter to the use of Invoke and ReturnResult and ReturnError within that CHOICE. Invoke, ReturnResult, and ReturnError are slightly confusingly use the same name for **their** dummy parameter, which is then used for the table and relational constraint. This situation where a dummy parameter is passed down through a chain of nested type definitions is quite common, and it is also quite common for the same name to be used each time. But please note that formally these are distinct names—as you would expect, the

```
 ROSE-module
{joint-iso-itu-t remote-operations(4) generic-ROS-PDUs(6)}
DEFINITIONS
AUTOMATIC TAGS
BEGIN
EXPORTS OPERATION, ERROR, Rose-PDU{};

Rose-PDU {OPERATION:User-ops} ::=
          CHOICE
        {invoke    Invoke {User-ops},
         reject    Reject,
         result    ReturnResult {User-ops},
         error     ReturnError {User-ops} }

Invoke {OPERATION:User-ops} ::= SEQUENCE
  { invokeId    INTEGER,
    opcode      OPERATION.&operationCode
                ({User-ops} ! invoke-unrecognisedOperation),
    argument    OPERATION.&ArgumentType
                ({User-ops}
                 {@opcode} ! invoke-mistypedArgument) OPTIONAL }

Reject ::=  etc
ReturnResult {OPERATION:User-ops} ::= etc
ReturnError {OPERATION:User-ops} ::= etc
END
```

Figure 13.8   Defining and exporting a parameterized type.

scope of a dummy parameter name is limited to the right-hand side of the parameterized type.

Note also the occurrence of "{}" after Rose-PDU in the EXPORTS list (and later in the IMPORTS list of Figure 13.9). This is not a requirement, but helps to clarify for a human reader that this is a parameterized type.

The dummy parameter list in this case has just one dummy parameter (if there were more it would be a comma-separated list), and here we see the syntax for a dummy parameter that is an Information Object Set. It is the class name ("OPERATION"), a ":" (colon), then the dummy parameter name, **which must start with a capital letter because it is an Information Object Set**. We will see in the next chapter that dummy parameters can be many other things as well, and that things other than types can be parameterized, but this will suffice for now.

Figure 13.9 shows the import into Wineco-main, and the definition of the new ROSE-based abstract syntax with the supply of the Wineco-specific "My-ops" as the actual parameter to the Rose-PDU parameterized type.

```
Wineco-main
{ joint-iso-itu-t internationalRA(23) set(42)
     set-vendors(9) wineco(43) modules(2) main(5)}
DEFINITIONS
AUTOMATIC TAGS
BEGIN
IMPORTS
Rose-PDU{} FROM Rose-module
{joint-iso-itu-t remote-operations(4) generic-ROS-PDUs(6)}
My-Ops FROM Wineco-operations
{ joint-iso-itu-t internationalRA(23) set(42)
       set-vendors(9) wineco(43)  modules(2) ops(4)};

wineco-abstract-syntax ABSTRACT-SYNTAX ::=
    { Rose-PDU{My-ops} IDENTIFIED BY
{ joint-iso-itu-t internationalRA(23) set(42)
       set-vendors(9) wineco(43) abstract-syntax(2)}
                        HAS PROPERTY
                        {handles-invalid-encodings}
                        -- See the Rose specification -- }
END
```

Figure 13.9   Using the ROSE-PDU to define the Wineco abstract syntax.

13.10 What Has Not Been Said Yet?

This chapter has given the reader a good understanding of the concepts related to Information Objects, and the principle of parameterization of ASN.1 constructs, but it has not told the full story.

In the next chapter, we will provide more detail on the full possibilities for the sorts of fields you can define when you specify an Information Object Class.

There is also an important facility called **variable syntax,** which enables a more user-friendly (and sometimes less verbose) notation to be used for defining objects of a given class (replacing the notation of Figure 13.6).

> Why is there always more to say?

On the question of constraints, we saw in earlier chapters the simple subtype constraints, and in this chapter table and relational constraints have been introduced. The next chapter will explore some further examples of constraints, and will also introduce the remaining type of constraint, the so-called **user-defined constraint**.

On parameterization, a little more discussion is necessary, including mention of so-called **parameters of the abstract syntax** and the **extensible empty set**.

Finally, we will mention the remaining ASN.1 constructs that provide alternative means of leaving holes in specifications. Readers will be pleased to know that at the end of that chapter, they can be certified as "ASN.1 Complete" as far as the notation is concerned, and if that is their only interest in reading this book, they can stop there!

## CHAPTER 14

More on Classes, Constraints, and Parameterization

(Or: More Than You Ever Wanted To Know!)

Summary

This chapter

- describes all the different sorts of Information Object Class Field that are available for use in a class definition;

- describes the "variable syntax" for defining Information Objects (this is arguably the most important area covered in this chapter—read this material if you read nothing else);

- completes the discussion of both constraints and parameterization;

- describes the TYPE-IDENTIFIER built-in class; and

- completes the discussion of ASN.1 notational support for "holes".

14.1 Information Object Class Fields

There are many different sorts of information that generic protocol specifiers have found they wanted to collect from their users to complete their protocol, and ASN.1 allows the specification of a variety of different sorts of Information Object Class Field. Here we briefly look at each in turn. Figure 14.1 gives an artificial example of an Information Object Class in which all the different sorts of field appear.

> There are many sorts of fields for Information Object Classes. Some are frequently used, some are rarely encountered. This text lists all of them!

There are examples of all these different sorts of fields in current protocol specifications, but some are much more common than others.

```
ILLUSTRATION ::= CLASS
                {&Type-field,
                 &fixed-type-value-field    INTEGER,
                 &variable-type-value-field &Type-field,
                 &Fixed-type-value-set-field  My-enumeration,
                 &Variable-type-value-set-field  &Type-field,
                 &object-field            OPERATION,
                 &Object-set-field        ERROR }
```

Figure 14.1 An illustration of the different sorts of field.

References to these fields such as

```
ILLUSTRATION.&fixed-type-value-field
```

are possible in ASN.1 notation (constrained by an actual object set or uncon-strained). Use of this notation is called **information from object class**.

It is also in general possible to have references to fields of defined Information Objects and defined Information Object Sets using notation such as

```
illustration-object.&Type-field
Illustration-object-set.&fixed-type-value-field
```

Use of this notation is called **information from object** and **information from object set**.

In some cases, such notation is forbidden (see the Standard for a simple table of what is legal and what is not, and the text that follows for a general description). A good guide, however, is **if it makes some sort of sense, then it is legal**. We dis-cuss in what follows the meaning and usefulness of these notations for each sort of field, and the circumstances in which you might want to use them.

14.1.1 Type Fields

We have already encountered the **type field.** The field-name has to start with a cap-ital letter, and may be followed immediately by a comma, or we can write, for example:

```
&Type-field-optional OPTIONAL,
&Type-field-defaulted DEFAULT NULL,
```

In the case of OPTIONAL, then that field may be left undefined when an Information Object of that class is defined. That field is then **empty**, and "empty" is distinct from any value that could be put into the field. The rules for applying an Information Object Set as a constraint dictate that a match occurs with an empty field only if the corresponding element in the SEQUENCE is missing. Thus it only makes sense to write OPTIONAL in the class definition if OPTIONAL also appears on the corresponding element (the "hole") in the type definition of the protocol. By contrast, DEFAULT places no requirements on the protocol; it merely provides the type to be used if none is specified in the definition of a particular information object. In the example we have specified NULL. It could, of course, be any ASN.1 type, built-in or user-defined, but use of NULL with DEFAULT is the most common.

> Type fields are common and important. They fill in the holes in protocols, and the need for them drove the development of the Information Object Class concept.

If we use the "information from object class" notation unconstrained, we have what is called an "open type". This means an incomplete specification with no indication of who will provide, and where, the completion of the specification. Such use is not forbidden, but it should have been! Do not do it! Use with a simple table constraint is not much better, as the decoder has no way of knowing which of a set of types has been encoded, and without such knowledge encodings can be ambiguous. There is a special constraint that can be supplied to an "open type" called a **type constraint**. This was mentioned briefly in 13.8. Here we might write

```
ILLUSTRATION.&Type-field(My-type)
```

In terms of the semantics it carries, it is exactly equivalent to writing just "My-type", but it gets an extra length wrapper in PER, and is generally handled by tools as a pointer to a separate piece of memory rather than being embedded in the containing data-structure. It is useful if there are a number of places in the protocol that have some meta-semantics associated with them (such as types carrying security data), so that by writing as an element of a SEQUENCE or SET

```
SECURITY-DATA.&Type-field (Data-type-1)
```

you identify the element as the ASN.1 type "Data-type-1", but clearly flag it as a "SECURITY-DATA" type.

Use of "information from object set" for a type field is illegal. This would in general produce a set of ASN.1 types (one from each of the objects in the object set), and there is nowhere in ASN.1 where you can use a set of types.

Use of "information from object" for a type field produces a single type, and an alternative to the previous SEQUENCE or SET element using "Data-type-1" could in suitable circumstances be

```
object1.&Type-field
```

with

```
object1   SECURITY-DATA ::=
              {&Type-field   Data-type-1,
              etc }
```

Note that this latter construction flags Data-type-1 as a SECURITY-DATA type, but it does not produce the encapsulation that the earlier construct produced. Use of "object1.&Type-field" produces **exactly** the same encoding as use of "Data-type-1" would produce.

14.1.2 Fixed Type Value Fields

The names of these fields are required to begin with a lowercase letter, and the name is required to be followed by an ASN.1 type, which specifies the type of the value that has to be supplied for that field. It is again permissible to include OPTIONAL and DEFAULT in this specification, and also UNIQUE (as described in the last chapter).

> Closely linked to type fields, these are again frequently encountered.

The most common types for these fields are INTEGER or OBJECT IDENTIFIER, or a choice of the two, but BOOLEAN or an ENUMERATED type are also quite common. The latter two are used when the information being collected is not designed to be carried in a protocol message, but rather completes a "hole" in the procedures.

For example, to take our ROSE example again, suppose that we allow the possibility that for some operations "ReturnResult" carries no information. This could be handled by putting OPTIONAL in the class definition of OPERATION.&ResultType, and also on the "hole" element of the "ReturnResult" SEQUENCE. However, we may want to go further than that. In cases where there is no result type, we may want to specify that, for some noncritical operations, the "ReturnResult" is never sent (a "Reject" or "ReturnError" will indicate failure); for others it must always be sent as a confirmation of completion of the operation, and for still others it is an option of the remote system to send it or not. In this case the fixed type value field might read:

```
&returnResult ENUMERATED {always, never, optional}
                  DEFAULT always,
```

and the ROSE user would specify a value of "never" or "optional" for operations where this was the required behavior.

The use of the "information from object class" construct in this case produces simply the type of the fixed type value field. So use of

```
ILLUSTRATION.&fixed-type-value-field
```

is (almost) exactly equivalent to writing

```
INTEGER
```

The difference is that you cannot apply a table constraint with an object set of class ILLUSTRATION to the type INTEGER. You can apply it (and frequently do) to the "information from object class" construct.

Both "information from object" producing (in this illustration) a single integer value and "information from object set" producing a set of integer values (a subset of type integer) are allowed in this case. Thus with an object set "Illustration-object-set" of class ILLUSTRATION, we could write

```
Illustration-object-set.&fixed-type-value-field
```

instead of

```
ILLUSTRATION.&fixed-type-value-field (Illustration-object)
```

What is the difference? Not much. In the latter case, you could use "@" with a relational constraint (on a type field of class ILLUSTRATION) to point to this element. In the former case you could not. The latter is what you will normally see.

14.1.3 Variable Type Value Fields

This is probably the second least common sort of field. Its main use is to provide a default value for a type that is provided in a type field.

The field name is followed by the name of some type field (&T-F say) **defined in this class definition**. The value supplied for the variable type value field in the definition of an information object of this class is required to be a value of the type that was supplied for the &T-F field.

> Much less common. An interesting example of a theoretically useful concept!

This field can be marked OPTIONAL or DEFAULT, but there are then rules that link the use of OPTIONAL and DEFAULT between this field and the field &T-F. Roughly, if it makes sense it is allowed, if it does not it is disallowed. Check the Standard (or use a tool to check your ASN.1) if you are unsure what is allowed and what is not. Roughly, both this field and &T-F must have, or not have, the same use of OPTIONAL or DEFAULT, and in the latter case, the default value for this field must be a value of the default type for the &T-F field.

As you would expect for a field that holds a single value, the field-name has a lowercase letter following the "&".

The use of "Illustration-object-set.&variable-type-value-field" is forbidden (not legal ASN.1). The use of "illustration-object.&variable-type-field" produces the value assigned to that field.

14.1.4 Fixed Type Value Set Fields

These are fields that hold a set of values of a fixed type, and hence the field-name starts with an uppercase letter after the ampersand.

The information required here is a set of values of the type following the field-name (the governor type), or in other words, a subset of that type. These values can be supplied either by a type-reference to a type that is the governor type with a simple subtype constraint applied to it, or can be supplied using the value-set notation described in the last chapter.

> Quite frequently used, mainly where we need to fill in holes in the procedures of a protocol, and have a list (an enumeration) of possible actions, some of which need to be selected and others forbidden.

The most common occurrence of this field is where there are a number of possibilities, and the definer of an Information Object is required to select those that are to be allowed for this Information Object.

Thus, in a class definition:

```
&Fixed-type-value-set-field
    ENUMERATED   {confirm-by-post, confirm-by-fax,
                  confirm-registered, confirm-by-e-mail
                  confirm-by-phone},
```

might be used to let the user specify that, for some particular information object, some subset of the enumeration possibilities can be used. It is left to the reader's imagination to flesh out this definition into a real fictitious scenario!

Extraction of information from both objects and object sets using this field both produce a (sub)set of values of the type used in the class definition, containing just those values that appear in any of the objects concerned.

14.1.5 Variable Type Value Set Fields

> In this box I can say "this has never been used!" In the body of the text I am more cautious!

I am not at all sure that this sort of field actually **does** occur in practice. It was added largely because it seemed to be needed to "complete the set" of available sorts of field! Find a good use for it!

It begins with an uppercase letter, and the field-name is followed by the name of some type field (&T-F) in the same class definition. The field is completed by giving a set of values (a subset) of the type that is put into &T-F.

Extraction of information from an object gives the value assigned to that field, but notation to extract information from an object set is illegal for this field type.

14.1.6 Object Fields

Perhaps surprisingly, this is less common than the object set field to be described in 14.1.7, but it is used.

The object field carries the identification (an information object reference name) of some object of the class that follows the field name.

This is the object-and-class equivalent of the fixed type value field.

Its main use is to help in the structuring of information object definitions. If every object of one class (MAIN-CLASS say) is going to require certain additional information to be specified that would add a number of fields to MAIN-CLASS (and if the same additional information is likely to be specified frequently for different objects of MAIN-CLASS), then it makes sense to define a separate class (ADDI-TIONAL-INFO-CLASS say). Objects of ADDITIONAL-INFO-CLASS carry just the additional information, and references to them are included in an object field of MAIN-CLASS.

Information from an object and from an object set produces a single object or a set of objects, respectively. Use of these constructions is useful

> The main use of this is to let the user easily reference defini-tions of a set of fields (which are given the same definition for several objects) without hav-ing to repeat the definitions of these fields for each object.

mainly if we have two classes defined that are closely related (the Directory OPER-ATION-X and CHAINED-OPERATION-X are examples), with one having the fields of the other as a subset of its fields. In this case it can avoid "finger-trouble" in the definition (and provide a clearer specification) if objects defined for CHAINED-OPERATION-X have the fields that correspond to OPERATION-X defined by extracting information from the corresponding OPERATION-X object, rather than repeating the definition over again. (This point actually applies to the use of infor-mation from object for all the different sorts of field.)

14.1.7 Object Set Fields

We have already seen this in use to list the errors associated with an opera-tion. As expected for something that is a **set** of objects, the & is followed by an uppercase letter.

> This is another well-used sort of field. It is best known for its use as the &Errors field of the ROSE OPERATION class.

Information from object and from object set is again permitted, with the obvious results.

14.1.8 Extended Field Names

When you are referencing fields of a class, object, or object set, you may end up with something that is itself a CLASS or object or object set (for example, OPERA-TION.&Errors delivers the ERROR class). When this happens, you are able to add a further "." (dot) followed by a field-name of the class you obtained.

> You will never see these used except in the examples in the Standard! Skip this text!

Thus

```
OPERATION.&Errors.&ParameterType
```

and

```
OPERATION.&Errors.&errorCode
```

are valid notations, and are equivalent to:

```
ERROR.&ParameterType
```

and

```
ERROR.&errorCode
```

Similar constructions using an information object set of class OPERATION are more interesting.

Here

```
My-ops.&Errors.&errorCode
```

delivers the set of values that are error codes for any of the operations in "My-ops", and

```
my-look-up-operation.&Errors.&errorCode
```

delivers that set of values that identify the possible errors of "my-look-up-operation".

Of course, this can proceed to any length, so if we have an object set field of class OPERATION that is itself a set of objects of class OPERATION (this actually occurs in ROSE—the field is called "&Linked" and records so-called "linked operations"), we can write things like:

```
my-op.&Linked.&Linked.&Linked.&Linked.&Errors.&errorCode
```

Although this is utterly fascinating, the reader is challenged to find a real use for it! (To be fair to ASN.1, these sorts of notation come out naturally if one wants consistency and generality in the notation, and cost little to provide. It is better that they are allowed than that what are fairly obvious notations be disallowed.)

14.2 Variable Syntax for Information Object Definition

Historically, before the concept of Information Object Classes was fully developed, an earlier feature of ASN.1 (now withdrawn), the so-called **macro notation**, was used by ROSE (and others) to provide users with a notation for defining the information needed to fill in the holes in their protocols. The notation that ROSE (and others) provided was quite user friendly. It certainly did not contain the "&" character, and often did not contain any commas. It frequently read like an English sentence, with conjunctions such as "WITH" being included in the notation, or as a series of keyword-value pairs.

> A few techies define information object classes, but a lot of users define objects of those classes, and even more (non-techie) people read those definitions. We need a user friendly notation to define objects of a given class. "Variable syntax" is important and much used.

For example, to define a ROSE operation, you would write:

```
my-op OPERATION
        ARGUMENT Type-for-my-op-arg
        RESULT Type-for-my-op-result
        ERRORS {error1, error4}
    ::= local 1
```

(In the following text, we call this the **ad hoc-notation**.)

This was ad hoc-notation defined by ROSE. (Other groups would define similar but unrelated syntax—in particular, some used commas to separate lists of things, others used a vertical bar).

It is important to note here that when this syntax was provided (in advance of the Information Object Class concept) there was little semantics associated with it. The ad hoc-notation **formally** (to an ASN.1 tool) was nothing more than a convoluted syntax for saying:

```
my-op CHOICE {local INTEGER, global OBJECT IDENTIFIER}
        ::= local:1
```

and typically the value reference "my-ops" was never used anywhere. A lot of information was apparently being collected, but was then "thrown on the ground" (in terms of any formal model of what the text meant).

As an aside, the inclusion of the ":" (colon) after "local" is not fundamental to this discussion—it resulted from the fact that a choice value was expressed in early work as (e.g.) "local 1" and post-1994 as "local:1".

This notation was, however, designed really to serve the same purpose that you achieve today with the object definition:

```
my-op OPERATION ::=
            {&operationCode      local:1,
            &ArgumentType        Type-for-my-op-arg,
            &ResultType          Type-for-my-op-result,
            &Errors              {error1 | error4} }
```

(In what follows we call this the **object-definition-notation**.)

We can observe a number of things. First, the ad hoc-notation is probably easier for a human to read than the object-definition-notation, although the lack of a clear semantic underpinning would confuse more intelligent readers! Second, because the notation **was** ad hoc, it was very difficult to produce any tool support for it. Third, because the notation was ad hoc, a tool had no means of knowing when this ad hoc-notation terminated and we returned to normal ASN.1 (there were no brackets around the ad hoc-notation). Finally, there was no formal link (such as we get by using an Information Object Set as a constraint) between use of this notation and holes in the ROSE protocol.

Nonetheless, when the Information Object Class material was introduced into ASN.1 (and the use of macro notation withdrawn) in 1994, it was felt important to allow a more human friendly (but still fully machine friendly, and with full semantics) notation for the definition of objects of a given class.

The aim was to allow definers of a class to be able to specify the notation for defining objects of that class, which would let them get as close as possible (without sacrificing machine processability) to the notation that had hitherto been provided as ad hoc-notation. The "variable syntax" of ASN.1 supports (fulfills) this aim.

Variable syntax requires that a class definition be followed immediately by the keywords "WITH SYNTAX" followed by a definition of the syntax for defining objects of that class. If those keywords are not present following the class definition, then the only available syntax for defining objects is the object-definition-notation. (The latter can still be used by users defining objects even if there **is** a "WITH SYNTAX" clause.)

Figure 14.2 adds WITH SYNTAX to the OPERATION class definition. (Again we must emphasize that the real ROSE specification is a little more complex than this—we are not producing a full tutorial on ROSE!)

```
OPERATION ::= CLASS
    {&operationCode CHOICE {local INTEGER,
                            global OBJECT IDENTIFER}
                    UNIQUE,
    &ArgumentType,
    &ResultType,
    &Errors ERROR OPTIONAL }
WITH SYNTAX
    { ARGUMENT &ArgumentType
      RESULT    &ResultType
      [ERRORS &Errors]
      CODE   &operationCode }
```

Figure 14.2   Inclusion of WITH SYNTAX in the definition of OPERATION.

What is this saying/doing? It allows an object of class operation to be defined with the syntax:

```
my-op OPERATION ::=
    { ARGUMENT   Type-for-my-op-arg
      RESULT Type-for-my-op-result
      ERRORS {error1 | error4}
      CODE local:1   }
```

The reader will notice the disappearance of the unsightly "&", the strong similarity between this and the ad hoc-notation, but also the presence of curly brackets around the definition, which is needed to maintain machine processability.

What can you write following "WITH SYNTAX"? Roughly you have the power normally used in defining command-line syntax—a series of words, interspersed with references to fields of the class. In defining an object, the definer must repeat these words, in order, and give the necessary syntax to define any field that is referenced. Where a sequence of words and/or field references are enclosed in square brackets (as with "[ERRORS &Errors]" in Figure 14.2), then that part of the syntax can be omitted. (Of course, the inclusion of the square brackets was only legal in the definition of the "WITH SYNTAX" clause because "&Errors" was flagged as "OPTIONAL" in the main class definition.)

A "word" for the purpose of the WITH SYNTAX clause is defined as a sequence of uppercase (not lowercase) letters (no digits allowed), possibly with (single) hyphens in the middle.

It is also possible to include a comma (but no other punctuation) in the WITH SYN-TAX clause, in which case the comma has to appear at the corresponding point in the definition of an object of that class.

```
OPERATION ::= CLASS
   {&operationCode CHOICE {local INTEGER,
                             global OBJECT IDENTIFER}
                    UNIQUE,
      &ArgumentType,
      &ResultType,
      &Errors ERROR OPTIONAL }
WITH SYNTAX
   { ARGUMENT &ArgumentType
     RESULT   &ResultType [REQUIRED]
     [ERRORS &Errors]
     CODE   &operationCode }
```

Figure 14.3   Illegal specification of WITH SYNTAX.

Square brackets can be nested to produce optional sections within optional sections. However, there are some quite severe restrictions on the use of "WITH SYNTAX", which are designed both to prevent the apparent acquisition of information with no effect on the actual object definition, and also to ensure easy machine processability. Writers of a WITH SYNTAX clause should read the Standard carefully. Figure 14.3 would, for example, be illegal.

This is because it allows the definer of an object to provide information by inclusion or not of the word "REQUIRED", which is nowhere recorded in a field of the object. If it is desired to let the definer of an object specify whether the return of a result is required or not, the definition of Figure 14.4 could be used, allowing:

```
my-op OPERATION ::=
   { ARGUMENT  Type-for-my-op-arg
     RESULT Type-for-my-op-result
        does-not RETURN-RESULT
     ERRORS {error1 | error4}
     CODE local:1  }
```

Finally, we try to provide a tabular notation for the compact definition of an object of class OPERATION similar to the table defined originally in Figure 13.3. This is shown in Figure 14.5.

```
           OPERATION ::= CLASS
               {&operationCode CHOICE {local INTEGER,
                                       global OBJECT IDENTIFER}
                               UNIQUE,
               &ArgumentType,
               &ResultType,
               &ReturnsResult   ENUMERATED
                     {does, does-not},
               &Errors ERROR OPTIONAL }
           WITH SYNTAX
              { ARGUMENT &ArgumentType
                RESULT     &ResultType
                &ReturnsResult RETURN-RESULT
                [ERRORS &Errors]
                CODE   &operationCode }
```

Figure 14.4   Collecting information on requirements to return a result.

With the definition in Figure 14.4 we would be allowed to write (compare Figures 13.3 and 13.6):

```
My-ops OPERATION ::=
  { {asn-val-order Order-for-stock      Order-confirmed
                                                {security-failure
                                                | unknown-branch} }
  | {asn-val-sales Return-of-sales      NULL    {security-failure
                                                | unknown-branch} }
  | {asn-val-query Query-availability  Availability-response
                                                {security-failure
                                                | unknown-branch
                                                | unavailable   } }
  | {asn-val-state Request-order-state Order-state {security-failure
                                                | unknown-branch
                                                | unknown-order } } }
```

We have now come full circle. The informal tabular presentation we used in Figure 13.3 was replaced with the formal but more verbose definition of Figure 13.6, which (using WITH SYNTAX) can be replaced with syntax very like that of Figure 13.3.

It should by now be clear to the reader that WITH SYNTAX clauses should be carefully considered. Not only must the rules of what is legal be understood, but a good compromise between verbosity and intelligibility in the final notation has to be determined. As with all human interface matters, there is no one right decision, but a little thought will avoid bad decisions.

```
OPERATION ::= CLASS
    {&operationCode CHOICE {local INTEGER,
                            global OBJECT IDENTIFER}
                    UNIQUE,
    &ArgumentType,
    &ResultType,
    &Errors ERROR OPTIONAL }
WITH SYNTAX
    { &operationCode
      &ArgumentType
      &ResultType
      [&Errors]
      }
```

Figure 14.5   WITH SYNTAX allowing a tabular definition of objects.

14.3 Constraints Revisited—the User-Defined Constraint

There is not a lot to add on constraints. We have covered earlier all the simple sub-type constraints, and in the last chapter the table and relational constraints. There is just one other form of constraint to discuss, the so-called **user-defined constraint**.

> User-defined constraints—little more than a comment! Why bother?

We have already discussed the earlier availability of a notation (the macro notation) that allowed people to define new ad hoc-notation (with no real semantics) for inclusion in an ASN.1 module. When this "facility" was removed in 1994, it turned out that the Information Object concept did not **quite** cover all the requirements that had been met by use of this macro notation, and the user-defined constraint concept was introduced to meet the remaining requirements. This form of constraint would probably not have been introduced otherwise, as it is little more than a comment, and tools can make little use of it. It is almost always used in connection with a parameterized type, introduced in Chapter 13.9.

One piece of ad hoc-notation that was defined using the macro notation was the ability to write:

```
ENCRYPTED My-type
```

as an element of a SET or SEQUENCE.

Although not implied by the ASN.1 formal text, this actually meant that the element was a BITSTRING, whose contents were an encryption (according to an encryption algorithm specified in English text) of the encoding of the type My-type.

We can get slightly more clarity if we define a parameterized type "ENCRYPTED" as :

```
ENCRYPTED {Type-to-be-encrypted} ::= BITSTRING
```

and then use

```
ENCRYPTED {My-type}
```

as the SEQUENCE or SET element.

(Note that we violate convention, but not the **rules** of ASN.1, by using all capitals for the ENCRYPTED type. This is for historical compatibility with the original ad hoc-notation "ENCRYPTED My-type". Note also that the new formal notation includes a new pair of curly brackets, as we saw—for a slightly different reason—with the move from ad hoc-notation to object-definition-notation.)

We have avoided the use of an ad hoc-notation, but it is curious for the dummy parameter of "ENCRYPTED" not to be used at all on the right-hand side of the assignment. It is clear that the actual value of the BITSTRING will depend on the "Type-to-be-encrypted" type (and also on the encryption algorithm and keys, which we cannot define using ASN.1).

So we introduce the **user-defined constraint**. In its basic form, we would write:

```
ENCRYPTED {Type-to-be-encrypted} ::= BITSTRING
             (CONSTRAINED BY {Type-to-be-encrypted} )
```

which shows that the dummy parameter is used to constrain the value of BIT-STRING. (If there were multiple parameters used in the constraint, these would be in a comma-separated list within the curly braces after CONSTRAINED BY.)

The constraint is called a "user-defined" constraint because the precise nature of the constraint is not specified with formal ASN.1 notation. This construction almost invariably contains comment that details the precise nature of the constraint. So we would more commonly write:

```
ENCRYPTED {Type-to-be-encrypted} ::= BITSTRING
       (CONSTRAINED BY {Type-to-be-encrypted}
       -- The BITSTRING is the results of
       -- encrypting Type-to-be-encrypted
       -- using the algorithm specified
       -- in the field security-algorithm,
       -- and with the encryption parameters
       -- specified in Security-data — )
```

The reader should know enough by now (assuming earlier text has been read and not skipped!) to realize that "security-algorithm" will turn out to be a (UNIQUE) fixed type value field (probably of type object identifier) of some SECURITY-INFORMATION class, with "Security-data" being a corresponding type field of this class that, for any given object of SECURITY-INFORMATION, is defined with an ASN.1 type that can carry all necessary parameters for the algorithm defined by that object. There might be other fields of SECURITY-INFORMATION that statically define choices of procedures in the application of the algorithm, filling in procedural "holes" in this process.

14.4 The Full Story on Parameterization

> It is obvious, powerful, and simple! How unusual for ASN.1!

There is not a lot more to add on parameterization, and it is all pretty obvious stuff. But here it is.

14.4.1 What Can Be Parameterized and Be a Parameter?

> Answer: Anything and everything!

The box says it all. Any form of reference name—a type reference, a value reference, a class reference, an object reference, an object set reference, can all be parameterized by adding a dummy parameter list after the reference name and before the "::=" when the "thing" the name references is being defined.

Here is an example of a reference name with a complete range of parameters:

```
Example-reference {INTEGER:intval,
              My-type,
              THIS-CLASS,
              OPERATION:My-ops,
              ILLUSTRATION:illustration-object} ::=
```

As we would expect, the initial letter of dummy parameters is uppercase for types, classes, and object sets, and lowercase for objects and values. Note that for values, object sets, and objects, the dummy parameter list includes the type or class of these parameters followed by a ":" (colon). The only one of the these examples that I have not seen in an actual specification is a dummy parameter that is a class (THIS-CLASS in the example).

Normally, the dummy parameter is used somewhere on the right-hand side of the assignment, but it can also be used within the parameter list itself (before or after its own appearance). So we could, for example, write:

```
Example1 {My-type:default-value, My-type} ::=
```

This notation is extremely general and powerful, and has many applications. We have seen the ROSE examples where an Information Object Set is declared as a dummy parameter. This is probably the most common thing that is used as a dummy parameter, but next to that is a value of type INTEGER that is used on the right-hand side as the upper-bound of INTEGER values, or as an upper-bound on the length of strings.

There is also an important use in the Manufacturing Messaging Formats (MMF) specification. Here the bulk of the protocol specification occurs in a "generic" module, and is common to all cells on a production line. However, specific cells on the production line require some additional information to be passed to them. In the generic module we use a dummy parameter (a type) and include it in our protocol specification as an element of our SEQUENCE and export this parameterized type. Modules for specific cells define a type containing the additional information for that cell, import the generic type, and declare the protocol to be used for that type of cell as the generic type, supplied with the type containing the additional information as the actual parameter. This is similar to the ROSE example, but uses a type rather than an information object set.

Let us explore the question of bounds a little further. Few protocols "hardwire" upper-bounds into the specification, but it is always a good idea to specify such bounds, as designers rarely intend to require implementors to handle arbitrarily large integers, iterations of sequences, or arbitrarily long strings. Where such bounds are fixed for the entire protocol, then it is common practice to assign the various bounds that are needed to an integer reference name in some module, then to use EXPORTS and IMPORTS to get those names into the modules where they are used as bounds.

Where, however, there are generic types (such as a CHOICE of a number of different character string types) that are used in many places but with different bounds for each use, then using an INTEGER dummy parameter for the bounds is a very effective and common practice.

It is actually quite rare to see long dummy parameter lists. This is because any collection of information (apart from a class) can easily be turned into an Information Object Set. So with the earlier example (taking MY-CLASS out) of:

```
Example-reference {INTEGER:intval,

                   My-type,

                   OPERATION:My-ops,

                   ILLUSTRATION:illustration-object} ::=
```

we could instead define:

```
PARAMETERS-CLASS ::= CLASS

      {&intval   INTEGER,

       &My-type,

       &My-ops   OPERATION,

       &illustration-object ILLUSTRATION}
```

and then our parameter list becomes just:

```
Example-reference {PARAMETERS-CLASS:parameters} ::=
```

and on the right-hand side we use (for example) "parameters.&My-type" instead of "My-type". This may seem more cumbersome than using several dummy parameters, but if the same parameter list is appearing in several places, particularly if dummy parameters are being passed down as actual parameters through several levels of type definition, it can be useful to bundle up the dummy parameters in this way.

A particular example of this is when a protocol designer has identified twelve situations (iterations of sequences, lengths of strings, sizes of integers) where bounds are appropriate, with potentially twelve different integer values for each of these situations, probably with each of the twelve values being used in several places in the protocol. This is again a good case for "bundling". We can define a class:

```
BOUNDS ::= CLASS
            {&short-strings    INTEGER,
             &long-strings     INTEGER,
             &normal-ints      INTEGER,
             &very-long-ints   INTEGER,
             &number-of-orders INTEGER}
        WITH SYNTAX
        {STRG &short-strings, LONG-STRG &long-strings,
         INT &normal-ints, LONG-INT &very-long-ints,
         ORDERS &number-of-orders}
```

and routinely and simply make an object set of this class a dummy parameter of every type that we define, passing it down as an actual parameter of any types in SEQUENCE, SET, or CHOICE constructions. We can then use whichever of the fields we need in the various places in our protocol. In some type definitions, we might use none of them, and the dummy parameter for that type would be redundant (but still legal), or we might use one or two of the fields, or (probably rarely) all of them.

At the point where we define our top-level type (usually a CHOICE type, as we discussed in the early parts of this book), we can set our bounds and supply them as an actual parameter. So if "Wineco-protocol" is our top-level type, we could have:

```
bounds BOUNDS ::= {STRG  32, LONG-STRG 128,
                        etc }
Wineco-protocol {BOUNDS:bounds} ::= CHOICE
        {ordering [APPLICATION 1] Order-for-stock
                                  {BOUNDS:bounds},
          sales [APPLICATION 2] Return-of-sales
                                  {BOUNDS:bounds}
        etc.  }
```

No doubt there are some readers who will be asking "What is the point of passing this stuff down as parameters, when (provided "bounds" is exported and imported everywhere), it can be directly used?" The answer in this case is "Not much!" If, for any given type, any set of bounds is always going to be fixed, then there is no point in making it a parameter; a global reference name can be used instead, with a simpler and more obvious specification. But read on to the next section!

14.4.2 Parameters of the Abstract Syntax

Protocol designers are often hesitant about fixing bounds in the body of a protocol definition, even if they are defined in just one place and passed around either by simple import/export or by additionally using dummy parameters. The reason for the hesitation is that bounds can very much "date" a protocol for two reasons: First, what seems adequate initially (for example, for the number of iterations of the "details" SEQUENCE in our "Order-for-stock" type in Figure 2.1) can well prove inadequate 10 years later when the business has expanded and mergers have occurred! Second, bounds are usually applied to ease the implementation effort when implementing on machines with limited memory capacity, or without support for calculations with very long integer values. Such technological limitations do, however, have a habit of disappearing over time. So, while 15 years ago, many designers felt that it was unreasonable to have messages that exceeded 64K octets, today implementors on most machines would have no problem handling messages that are a megabyte long. (An exception here would be specifications of data formats for smart cards, where memory is still very limited. This is an area where ASN.1 has been used.)

> So you want to leave some things implementation-dependent? Coward! But at least make them explicit (and define exception-handling to help interworking between different implementations). Parameters of the abstract syntax let you do that, but they are a rarely used feature.

So, ..., if we do not want to put our bounds into the main specification, what do we do? Just leave them out? This will undoubtedly cause interworking problems, with some systems not being able to handle things of the size that some other systems generate, and we are not even flagging this as a potential problem in our ASN.1 specification.

Providing a "bounds" parameter, but never setting values for it, can help with this problem. We have already seen in Figure 3.8 that we can specify our top-level type using the "ABSTRACT- SYNTAX" notation. Let us repeat that, with our parameterized Wineco-protocol developed in 14.4.1.

```
wineco-abstract-syntax {BOUNDS:bounds} ABSTRACT-SYNTAX ::=
                {Wineco-protocol {BOUNDS:bounds} IDENTIFIED BY etc}
```

We are now defining our abstract syntax with a parameter list. We have parameters of the abstract syntax. ASN.1 permits this, provided such parameters are used only in constraints. These constraints are then called **variable constraints**, because the actual bound is implementation-dependent. The important gain that we have now made, however, is that this implementation-dependence has been made very clear and specific. Where we have a variable constraint, we would normally provide an exception marker to indicate the intended error handling if material is received that exceeds the local bounds.

In the OSI work, there is the concept of International Standardized Profiles (ISPs) and of Protocol Implementation Conformance Statements (PICS). The purpose of ISPs is to provide a profile of options and parameter values to tailor a protocol to the needs of specific communities, or to define different classes (small, medium, large, say) of implementation. The purpose of the PICS is to provide a format for implementors to specify the choices they have made in implementation-dependent parts of the protocol. Clearly, the use of parameters of the abstract syntax aids in both these tasks, with values for those parameters either being specified in some profile (which an implementation would then claim conformance to) or directly in the PICS for an implementation.

> Providing extensibility is all very well, but make sure that your requirements on implementations are clearly specified. Do they have to implement everything but can add more? Implement the bits they choose but NOT add more? Or a combination of both? In many cases you can express these requirements formally.

Parameters of the abstract syntax (with exception markers on all variable parameters) provide a very powerful tool for identifying areas of potential interworking problems, but it is (for this author at least) sad that, to date, these features are not yet widely used.

14.4.3 Making Your Requirements Explicit

14.4.3.1 The TYPE-IDENTIFIER Class

A very common Information Object Class is one that has just two fields, one holding an object identifier to identify an object of the class, and the other holding a type associated

> One of only two built-in classes (the other is ABSTRACT-SYNTAX) in ASN.1, and quite well used.

with that object. This class is in fact predefined (built-in) in ASN.1 as the TYPE-IDENTIFIER class. It is defined as:

```
TYPE-IDENTIFIER ::= CLASS

    {&id   OBJECT IDENTIFIER UNIQUE,
     &Type }

    WITH SYNTAX {&Type IDENTIFIED BY &id}
```

There are many protocols that make use of this class. It is the foundation stone for a very flexible approach to extensibility of protocols.

14.4.3.2 An Example—X.400 Headers

(As with ROSE, the following is not an exact copy of X.400.)

In X.400 (an e-mail standard), there is the concept of "headers" for a message. A wide range of headers are defined. In the earliest version of X.400, these were hard-wired as types within a SEQUENCE, but it rapidly became clear that new headers would be added in subsequent versions. Of course, the SEQUENCE could just have had the extensibility ellipsis added, with defined exception handling on the ellipsis, ensuring interworking between versions 1 and 2, but an alternative approach is to define the headers as:

```
HEADER-CLASS ::= TYPE-IDENTIFIER
```

and the actual headers as:

```
Headers-type {HEADER-CLASS:Supported-headers} ::=
                SEQUENCE OF SEQUENCE
    {id       HEADER-CLASS.&id ( {Supported-headers} !100 ),
     info     HEADER-CLASS.&Type ( {Supported-headers}{@id}!101 ) }
```

Exception handling 100 and 101 will be specified in the text of the protocol definition. Handling of 100 is likely to be "silently ignore" and of 101 (a bad type) "send an error return and otherwise ignore".

The question is, when we eventually supply an actual parameter for Header-type, what do we provide? Let us examine some options.

There will certainly be some headers defined in this version of the protocol, and we will undoubtedly expect to add more in subsequent versions, so we would first define an extensible information object set something like:

```
Defined-Headers HEADER-CLASS ::=
            {header1 | header2 | header3 , ..., header4 }
```

where header4 was added in version 2.

But what do we supply as the actual parameter for our protocol? Let us take the most general case first. We consider providing two parameters of the abstract syntax, both object sets of class HEADER-CLASS. One is called "Not-implemented" and the other "Additional-headers". We might want to provide one or both of these or neither, depending on the decisions made in response to the options presented in 14.4.3.3 to 14.4.3.6. I think you are probably getting the idea!

Let us now look at various possible views we might take on the requirements of implementations to support headers.

14.4.3.3 Use of a Simple SEQUENCE

We decide we want to define a fixed set of headers, all to be implemented, no additions, and we will never make later changes. Some headers will be required, others optional.

> We got it right first time!

This case is easy, and we do not need Information Object Sets; we simply use:

```
Headers ::= SEQUENCE
    {header1  Header1-type --must be included--,
     header2  Header2-type OPTIONAL,
          etc }
```

This is simple and forward, but very inflexible. Where the decisions on what headers to provide (as in the case of e-mail headers) are rather ad hoc and likely to need to be changed in the future, this is NOT a good way to go!

Note that in this case the identification of what header is being encoded in a group of OPTIONAL headers is essentially done (in BER) using the tag value. (In PER it is slightly different—a bit-map identifies which header has been encoded in a particular position).

14.4.3.4 Use of an Extensible SEQUENCE

In the case of e-mail headers, it is highly likely that we will want to add more types of header later, so making the SEQUENCE extensible would be a better approach. And we should specify exception handling so that we know how version 1 systems will behave when they are sent headers from a version 2 system (and how version 2 systems should behave if headers

> We are in control. You do what we say. We won't remove anything, but we might add more later.

that are mandatory in version 2 are missing because a version 1 system is generating the headers).

| Giving ourselves more options, but still keeping control. |

14.4.3.5 Moving to an Information Object Set Definition

Now we make quite a big jump in apparent complexity, and use the "Headers" type we have already introduced, that is:

```
Headers-type {HEADER-CLASS:Headers} ::= SEQUENCE OF SEQUENCE
   {identifier   HEADER-CLASS.&id({Headers} !100),
    data         HEADER-CLASS.&Type({Headers}{@identifier} !101) }
```

We have now moved to use of an object identifier to identify the type of any particular header, and potentially we now allow any given header type to be supplied multiple times with different values. But we have lost the ability to say whether a header is optional or not, and we have no easy way of saying which headers can appear multiple times.

We can address these problems by adding fields to our HEADER-CLASS. So instead of defining it as TYPE-IDENTIFIER, we can define it as:

```
HEADER-CLASS ::= CLASS
   {&id  OBJECT IDENTIFIER UNIQUE,
    &Type,
    &Required   BOOLEAN DEFAULT TRUE,
    &Multiples  BOOLEAN DEFAULT TRUE}
   WITH SYNTAX {&Type IDENTIFIED BY &id,
                [REQUIRED IS &Required],
                [MULTIPLES ALLOWED IS &Multiples]}
```

We can now specify (when each header object is defined) whether it is optional or not, and whether multiple occurrences of it are permitted or not. Of course, when we used a SEQUENCE, we could flag optionality, and we could have indicated that multiples were allowed by putting SEQUENCE OF around certain elements. But the approach using information objects is probably simpler if we want all of that, and paves the way for more options.

Of course, when we define the information object set "Defined-Headers", we will make it extensible, indicating the possibility of additions in version 2, and will put an exception specification on the ellipsis to tell version 1 systems what to do if they get headers they do not understand.

We could actually go further than this, as X.500 does in a similar circumstance: We could put another field into HEADER-CLASS defining the "criticality" of a header, and we could provide a field in "Headers-type" to carry that value. Our exception specification could then define different exception handling for unknown headers, depending on the value of the "criticality" field associated with it in the message.

We have advanced some way from the rather restricted functionality we had with SEQUENCE.

14.4.3.6 The Object Set "Headers"

An extensible "Defined-Headers" merely gives us control over what version 1 does when we add new material in version 2. It in no way says

> Now we give flexibility to the implementors. We use the parameters of the abstract syntax.

that implementations (probably on some user-group or vendor-specific basis) can agree and add new headers. It also says that to conform to version x, you must support all the headers listed in the "Defined- Headers" for version x.

But, suppose we define:

```
Supported-Headers

        {HEADER-CLASS:Additional-Headers,

        HEADER-CLASS:Excluded-Headers} HEADER-CLASS::=

    { (Defined-Headers | Additional-Headers)

            EXCEPT Excluded-Headers) }
```

where "Additional-Headers" and "Excluded-Headers" are parameters of the abstract syntax, as described, and where "Supported-Headers" is supplied as the actual parameter for our dummy parameter "Headers" in an instantiation of "Header-type" when we define our top-level PDU (and then "Supported-Headers" is passed down for eventual use in the constraints on "Header-type").

As usual, we could, if we wish, bundle the two object sets together as an object set of a new object class, making just one parameter of the abstract syntax covering both specifications.

With this definition, we are clearly saying that we have some defined headers, implementors may support others, and indeed may choose not to support some of the defined headers. Total freedom! Possibly total anarchy! But most implementations will probably choose to implement most of the defined headers, and the exception handling should cope with interworking problems with those that decide to omit a few headers from their implementation (for whatever reason).

It is left as a (simple!) exercise for the reader to write an appropriate definition of Supported-Headers where we

a) decide to allow additional headers, but require support for all defined headers; or

b) decide to allow some defined headers not to be supported, but disallow implementation-dependent or vendor-specific additions.

Of course, at the end of the day, you can never ENFORCE a requirement to implement everything, nor can you prevent people from extending a standardized protocol. But you CAN make it very clear that they are then not conforming to the Standard; ASN.1 provides the tools for doing this.

14.4.4 The (Empty) Extensible Information Object Set

It makes little sense in most protocols to have an information object set with no members, even if it is extensible:

        { . . . }

It has become a fairly common practice (now supported by text in the Standard) to use this notation as a shorthand for "a parameter of the abstract syntax". When this is used as a constraint, it quite simply says that the specification is incomplete, and that you must look elsewhere for the specification of what is or is not supported.

> You must go back to Figure 999 (Government Health Warning) when reading this. This is probably the most controversial text in this book!

This is called a "dynamically extensible object set", the idea being that implementations will determine in an instance of communication what objects they deem it to contain, and may indeed (depending on whether it is raining or not!) accept or reject some objects at different times.

If you get the impression that this author disapproves of the use of this construct, you will not be incorrect!

It provides no functionality beyond that provided (far more clearly) by parameters of the abstract syntax. It does, however, have one advantage. Parameters of the abstract syntax appear at the top-level, and need to be passed down as parameters to succeeding nested types until they reach the point at which they are to be used. This adds to the size of a specification, and can sometimes make it less easily readable. (Work was once proposed to add the concept of "global parameters" to ASN.1. This would effectively have enabled a top-level parameter to become a normal reference name, usable anywhere, without being passed from type to type as a sequence of actual dummy parameters. However, this work was never progressed.)

The use of the "{...}" notation in a constraint provides a direct statement at the bottom level that this constraint is implementation-dependent. But on the opposite side again—you cannot tell by looking at the top-level definition that there are (effectively) parameters of the abstract syntax, that is, that the specification is incomplete. You have to look through perhaps a hundred pages of ASN.1 definitions to spot occurrences of "{...}.

The advice of this author is DO NOT USE THIS CONSTRUCT. But you do need to know what it is supposed to mean if you encounter it, and there are many specifications that use it (more than use parameters of the abstract syntax).

There is an informative annex (not part of the Standard) in X.681 that says that ANY object set that is made extensible implies that random additions and removals of objects can be made when considering constraints imposed by that object set. It is not often that this author criticizes the ASN.1 Standards—I wrote a lot of the text. But this annex gives bad advice, and is not really supported by normative text in the body of the Standard.

So ... how do you decide what a particular specification means when it uses an extensible nonempty set? Read the specification carefully, and it will usually be clear. If it uses {...} it is probably saying that all extensible object sets can have implementation-dependent additions or exceptions (but then has no way of countering that in specific cases except by comment). If (like X.400), it has explicit parameters of the abstract syntax, it surely will NOT be implying that, and you should use the interpretation given in 14.4.3.6 for "Headers".

> You and me both—we must be getting tired! There is not much more to say. We'll try to keep it brief. This is not difficult stuff, but it IS used, and IS important.

14.5 Other Provision for "Holes"

There are some other mechanisms, mainly predating the information object concept, that support holes in ASN.1 specifications. We need to have a brief discussion of these.

14.5.1 ANY

This has two important claims to fame. First, it was the only support for black holes in the original 1984 ASN.1 Specifications! And second, it was withdrawn in 1994, causing a fairly major uproar among some ASN.1 users.

> A (bad?) first attempt? 'Twas the best we could do in 1984. Holes were not really understood then.

If you wrote type "ANY" in a SEQUENCE or SET, it literally meant that **any** ASN.1 type could be slotted in there to replace the ANY. It was frequently accompanied in early CCITT specifications with the comment:

```
-- For further study --
```

This comment clearly indicated that it was merely a place-holder in an incomplete specification. Usually in such cases, the SEQUENCE element read:

```
ANY OPTIONAL
```

so you basically knew that that element was not implementable—YET!

Used in this way it did no harm, but was probably not really useful. It provided part of the functionality we get today by using the extensibility ellipsis. It said "there is more to come in a later version, but we don't really know what yet."

There were, however, other uses. One was in X.500 until recent times, where an element of a SEQUENCE read:

```
bi-lateral-information ANY OPTIONAL
```

The intent here was to allow implementation-dependent additional information to be passed, where the ASN.1 type for this information would be determined elsewhere (community of interest, or vendor-specific). If several vendors or communities produced different specifications for the type to fill this field, then you would typically look at the calling address to determine what the field was saying. (Yet another—nonstandard—way of providing an identifier for the content of a hole!)

In practice, this field was never implemented by X.500 implementors.

Another option for determining the type (and its semantics) that filled the field would be to see if it was raining or not, but I do not think anyone ever used this particular mechanism for "hole-identification"!

14.5.2 ANY DEFINED BY

This was an attempt in 1986/88 to shore up the ANY. There was by now a recognition that a black hole absolutely had to have somewhere close to it in the protocol some value that would point to the definition of the actual type (and, more importantly, the semantics associated with that type) that was filling the hole. Suddenly the hole became a bit less black!

(The light in the "coal cellar" really got switched on when information objects appeared in the 1994 specification. I am grateful to Bancroft Scott for the analogy between the introduction of information object concept and switching on a light in a coal cellar. When he first made the remark,

> Dawn breaks (but just a bit!). It was recognized that any hole really MUST have associated with it a mechanism for determining what (and with what semantics) fills the hole.

someone (I've forgotten who) replied "That sounds rather dramatic. Things that dramatic can cause tidal waves". The reply was a good one! Information objects did not replace ANY and ANY DEFINED BY easily. Eventually they did, but it took close to seven years before the waves subsided!)

With ANY DEFINED BY a typical SEQUENCE might now contain:

```
identifier   OBJECT IDENTIFIER,
hole         ANY DEFINED BY identifier
```

The reader will recognize that this provides the same sort of link between the two fields that is now provided by use of a relational constraint (the @ notation) between "information from object class" constructs, but that it lacks any information object set reference to define the precise linkage, the types that can fill the "ANY" field, and the semantics associated with those types..

There were also (too severe) restrictions on the linkages that could be specified using the ANY DEFINED BY notation, which made it impossible for some existing specifications to move from ANY to ANY DEFINED BY, even though they DID have a field (somewhere) in their protocol that defined the content of the ANY hole.

14.5.3 EXTERNAL

EXTERNAL was introduced in 1986/88, and is still with us. The name is in recognition of the fact that people want to embed material that is **external** to ASN.1, that is, material that is not defined using ASN.1 (for example, a GIF image). It was, however, also intended as a better version of ANY and ANY DEFINED BY, because it encapsulated identification of what was in the hole with the hole itself.

> But you want to include material that is not defined using ASN.1. And you want to identify the type of material and the encoding of it. Roll your own using OCTET STRING or BIT STRING and a separate identifier field. That would work. But EXTERNAL tried to provide a ready-made solution.

EXTERNAL was defined when ASN.1 was very much part of the OSI family, and recognized (among other possibilities) identification of the hole contents using a "presentation context" negotiated using the Presentation Layer facilities of OSI. This mechanism was probably never used by any actual implementation.

EXTERNAL can also make a claim to fame: its definition is almost certainly the only place in any ASN.1 specification where the type "ObjectDescriptor" is used! (But it is OPTIONAL—and I will wager that no implementation has ever transmitted an "ObjectDescriptor" value within an EXTERNAL.)

Finally, EXTERNAL was born in the early days of understanding about abstract and transfer syntaxes, and (if you exclude the option of using the OSI Presentation Layer) used only a single object identifier value to identify the combination of abstract and transfer syntax for the material that filled the hole. Today, we generally believe that it is appropriate to identify the set of abstract values in the hole (for example, that it is a still picture) with one object identifier, and the encoding of those values (the encoding of the picture) with a separate object identifier. So while EXTERNAL remains (unchanged from its original introduction in 1986/88) in the 1998 specification, it has serious flaws, and new specifications should instead use "EMBEDDED PDV" (described in 14.5.4) if they wish to carry non-ASN.1-defined material.

14.5.4 EMBEDDED PDV

EMBEDDED PDV was introduced in 1994. It was, quite simply, an attempt to "improve" EXTERNAL. It has all the functionality of EXTERNAL that anyone cares about. It got rid of the Object Descriptor that no one ever used, and it allowed (but did not require) separate object identifiers for the identification of the abstract syntax and the transfer syntax (encoding) of the material that filled the hole.

Why is it so difficult to get it right the first time? EMBEDDED PDV is really just mending the deficiencies of EXTERNAL. EXTERNAL looked pretty good in 1986/88, but by 1994, it needed a refit.

Perhaps more importantly, it included the ability for a protocol designer to specify (statically) either or both of the abstract and transfer syntaxes for the "hole" (using constraint notation).

One important use for this is in security work, where EMBEDDED PDV is used to carry the encryption of a type, the type (abstract syntax of hole contents) being statically specified, and the encryption mechanism (transfer syntax) being transferred at communication time.

In appropriate circumstances, a designer can specify statically both the abstract (type of material) and transfer syntax (encoding) of what fills the hole. If this is done, then EMBEDDED PDV produces no overheads other than a length wrapper around the embedded material.

A brief word about the name. (Figure 999 again). It is certainly a bad name for the type. "EMBEDDED" is fine. It represents a hole that can take embedded material. But "PDV"? Most readers will never have met the term "PDV". It actually stands for "Presentation Data Value", and is the term used by the OSI Presentation Layer Standard to describe the unit of information passed between the Application Layer and the Presentation Layer, or (in terms more related to the description given here of ASN.1) an abstract value from some abstract syntax (not necessarily defined using ASN.1).

Don't worry about the name! For embedded material defined as an ASN.1 type you probably want to use the information object-related concepts to handle your holes. But if the material you want to embed is not defined using ASN.1, use EMBEDDED PDV.

14.5.5 CHARACTER STRING

CHARACTER STRING is actually just a special case of EMBEDDED PDV, and there is a lot of shared text in the specification of these types in the ASN.1 Standard.

CHARACTER STRING was an (unsuccessful) attempt to produce a character string type that would satisfy all possible needs FOREVER. It was intended to make it possible for the maintainers of the ASN.1 Standard to say (as new character sets and encodings emerged in the world), "We do not need to change ASN.1, use CHARACTER STRING".

> Another (rather special) form of hole. Designed to hold character strings from any repertoire using any encoding, with announcement of the repertoire and encoding contained in the hole. A great idea, but it never really took off. But still . . . you might want to use it.

The CHARACTER STRING type extends the concept of abstract and transfer syntax. It introduces the term "character abstract syntax" (an abstract syntax all of whose values are strings of characters from some defined character set), and "character transfer syntax" (a transfer syntax that provides encodings for all possible strings in a given character abstract syntax).

Put in slightly less technical terms, a character abstract syntax object identifier identifies a character repertoire, and a character transfer syntax OBJECT IDENTIFIER identifies an encoding for strings of those characters.

Unconstrained, an encoding of the CHARACTER STRING type includes the two object identifiers that identify its character abstract syntax (repertoire) and its character transfer syntax (encoding) with each string that is transmitted. This is an unfortunate(!) overhead, as constructs like

```
SEQUENCE OF CHARACTER STRING
```

(where the repertoire and encoding are the same for each element of the SEQUENCE OF) are quite common. As with EMBEDDED PDV, however, it is possible statically to constrain the CHARACTER STRING type so that only the actual encodings of characters are transmitted.

Object identifier values have been assigned for many character repertoires and subrepertoires, and for many encoding schemes, but unfortunately not for all. UTF8String was added to ASN.1 after CHARACTER STRING. It could have been defined as a constrained CHARACTER STRING, but in fact it was "hardwired" into ASN.1 as a new type defined using English text, just like PrintableString and

IA5String etc. That is why "unsuccessful!" appeared in the second paragraph of 14.5.5.

14.5.6 OCTET STRING and BIT STRING

Of course, the ultimate blackest of black holes is to use OCTET STRING or BIT STRING to carry embedded material. It happens. You are really "rolling your own". ASN.1 will provide the delimitation (the length wrapper), but you must sort out the problems of identifying to a receiver the semantics of what fills the octet string or bit string hole.

Those who believe in using a very cut-down ASN.1 use these types for their holes. I guess one can not complain. They make it work. But there are more powerful specification tools available in the ASN.1 armory, and I hope that anyone who has read this far in this text will not be tempted to use OCTET STRING or BIT STRING when they need to introduce a hole!

14.6 Remarks to Conclude Section II

I wonder if there is a single reader (even my reviewers!) who can say they read from the start through to here? E-mail me at j.larmouth@salford.ac.uk if you did. (But don't bother if you just jumped around and got here from the index!)

This text has tried to cover the whole of the ASN.1 concepts, mechanisms,

> And now it's goodnight, farewell, good-to-know-you!

notation. It is believed to be complete ("ASN.1 Complete" is the title!). There are further sections concerned with encoding rules and history and applications, but the description of the notation itself is now complete.

Or complete, as of 1999! If you are reading this book in 2010, there might be a later version available, which you should get, because by that point there will probably be much that is not included in the current text. But I can not provide you a reference to a later version—try a Web search, and in particular try the URL given in Appendix 5 (which might or might not still work in 2010!).

At the time of writing, there were many suggestions bubbling up in the ASN.1 standardization group that could give rise to additions to the ASN.1 notation. Recent (post-1994) history, however, has been that of only introducing changes to clarify existing text or add very minor (from a technical viewpoint) and simple new functionality (such as UTF8String), not of earth-shaking additions. Indeed, possibly earth-shaking additions that have been proposed in the last decade have a history of being abandoned—examples include light-weight encoding rules, global parameters, and dynamic constraints.

Good luck in reading, writing, or implementing ASN.1 specifications!

THE END.

Well ... of this section!

Encodings

## CHAPTER 15

Introduction to Encoding Rules

(Or: What No One Needs to Know!)

Summary

This first chapter of Section III

- discusses the concept of encoding rules;

- describes the TLV principle underlying the Basic Encoding Rules (BER);

- discusses the question of "extensibility", or "future proofing";

- describes the principles underlying the more recent Packed Encoding Rules (PER);

- discusses the need for "canonical" encoding rules; and

- briefly mentions the existence of other encoding rules.

The discussion of encoding rules in earlier chapters can provide a useful introduction to this concept, but this section has been designed to be complete and to be readable without reference to other sections.

The next two chapters of Section III describe in detail the Basic Encoding Rules and the Packed Encoding Rules, but assume an understanding of the principles and concepts given here.

15.1 What Are Encoding Rules, and Why the Chapter Subtitle?

"What no one needs to know!" At the end-of-the-day, computer communication is all about "bits-on-the-line"—what has in the past been called "concrete transfer syntax", but today is just called "transfer syntax". (But if you think about it, a "bit" or "binary digit" is itself a pretty abstract concept—what is "concrete" is the electrical or optical signals used to represent the bits.)

ASN.1 has taken onboard some concepts that originated with the so-called "Presentation Layer" of the ISO/ITU-T specifications for Open Systems

Interconnection (OSI). (Note that the term "Presentation Layer" is a bad and misleading one—"Representation Layer" might be better.)

The concepts are of a set of "abstract values" that are sent over a communications line, and which have associated with them bit patterns that represent these abstract values in an instance of communication.

The set of abstract values to be used, and their associated semantics, is at the heart of any application specification. The "encoding rules" are concerns of the (Re)Presentation Layer, and define the bit patterns used to represent the abstract values. The rules are a complete specification in their own right (actually, there are a number of variants of two main sets of rules—these are described later). The encoding rules say how to represent with a bit-pattern the abstract values in each basic ASN.1 type, and those in any possible constructed type that can be defined using the ASN.1 notation.

> You don't know or care about the electrical or optical signals used to represent bits, so why care about the bit patterns used to represent your abstract values?

ASN.1 provides its users with notation for defining the "abstract values" that carry user semantics and that are to be conveyed over a communications line. (This was fully described in Sections I and II). Just as a user does not care (and frequently does not know) what electrical or optical signal is used to represent zero and one bits, so in ASN.1, the user should not care (or bother to learn about) what bit patterns are used to represent his abstract values.

So details of the ASN.1 "encoding rules", which define the precise bit-patterns to be used to represent ASN.1 values, while frightfully important, are "What no one needs to know".

It is the case today that there are good ASN.1 tools (called "ASN.1 compilers") available that will map an ASN.1 type definition into a type definition in (for example), the C, C++, or Java programming languages (see Chapter 6), and will provide run-time support to encode values of these data structures in accordance with the ASN.1 Encoding Rules. Similarly, an incoming bit-stream is decoded by these tools into values of the programming language data-structure. This means that application programmers using such tools need have no knowledge of, or even interest in, the encoded bit-patterns. All they need to worry about is providing the right application semantics for values of the programming language data structures. The reader will find some further discussion of these issues in the Introduction to this book, and in Chapter 1. A detailed discussion of ASN.1 compilers is provided in Chapter 6.

There are, however, a few groups of people who will want to know all about the ASN.1 Encoding Rules. These are

- The intellectually curious!

- Students being examined on them!

- Standards writers who wish to be reassured about the quality of the ASN.1 Encoding Rules.

- Implementors who, for whatever reason, are unable to use an ASN.1 compiler (perhaps they are working with an obscure programming language or hardware platform, or perhaps they have no funding to purchase tools), and have to "hand-code" values for transmission and "hand-decode" incoming bit-patterns.

- Testers and troubleshooters who need to determine whether the actual bit-patterns being transmitted by some implementation are in accordance with the ASN.1 Encoding Rules specification.

If you fall into any of these categories, read on! Otherwise this section of the book is not for you!

15.2 What Are the Advantages of the Encoding Rules Approach?

Chapter 1 discussed a number of approaches to specifying protocols. The ASN.1 approach (borrowed from the Presentation Layer of OSI) of completely separating off and "hiding" the details of the bit-patterns used to represent values has a number of advantages, which will be discussed in the next few paragraphs.

> The encoding rules approach enables a degree of information hiding (and flexibility in making future changes to encodings) that is hard to match with other approaches to specifying encodings.

The first point to note is that a clear separation of the concept of transmitting abstract values from the bit-patterns representing those values enables a variety of different encodings to be used to suit the needs of particular environments. One often-quoted example (but I am not sure you will find it in the real world!) is of a communication over a high-bandwidth leased line with hardware encryption devices at each end. The main concern here is to have representations of values that impose the least CPU-cycle cost at the two ends. But a bulldozer goes through the leased line! And the back-up provision is a modem on a telephone line with no security device. The concern is now with maximum compression, and some selective field encryption. The same abstract values have to be communicated, but what is the "best" representation of these values has now changed.

The second example is similar. There are some protocols where a large bulk of information has to be transferred from the disk of one computer system to the disk of another computer system. If those systems are different, then some work will be needed by one or both systems to map the local representations of the information into an agreed (standard) representation for transfer of the values over a communication line. But if, in some instance of communication, the two systems are the **same** type of system, CPU-cycles can probably be saved by using a representation that is close to that used for their common local representation of the information.

Both of these examples are used to justify the OSI concept of **negotiating** in an instance of communication the representation (encoding) to be used from a set of possible representations. However, today ASN.1 is more commonly used in non-OSI applications, where the encoding is fixed in advance, and is not negotiable at communications time (there is no OSI Presentation Layer present).

There are, however, a few other advantages of this clear separation of encodings from abstract values that **are** important in the real world of today for the users of ASN.1.

We have seen over the last 20 years considerable progress in human knowledge about how to produce "good" encodings for abstract values. This is reflected in the difference between the ASN.1 Basic Encoding Rules developed in the early 1980s and the Packed Encoding Rules developed in the early 1990s. But application specifications defined using ASN.1 in the 1980s require little or no change to the specification to take advantage of the new encoding rules—the application specification is unaffected, and will continue to be unaffected if even better encoding rules are devised in the next century.

There is a similar but perhaps more far-reaching issue concerned with tools. The separation of encoding issues from the application specification of abstract values and semantics is fundamental to the ability to provide ASN.1 compilers, relieving application implementors from the task of writing (and more importantly, debugging) code to map between the values of their programming language data-structures and "bits-on-the-line". Moreover, where such tools are in use, changing to a new set of encoding rules, such as PER, requires nothing more than the installation of a new version of the ASN.1 compiler, and perhaps the changing of a flag in a run-time call to invoke the code for the new encoding rules rather than the old.

15.3 Defining Encodings—the TLV Approach

Chapter 1 discussed briefly the approach of using character strings to represent values, giving rise to a variety of mechanisms for precisely specifying the strings to be used, and to "parsing" tools to recognize the patterns in incoming strings of characters. These approaches tend to produce quite verbose protocols, and generally do not give rise to as complete tool support as is possible with ASN.1. They are not discussed further, and we concentrate here on approaches that more directly specify the bit-patterns to be employed in communication.

> Type, Length, Value for encoding basic items, nest a series of TLVs as a V within an outer Type and Length, repeat to any depth, and you have a powerful recipe for transferring structured information in a very robust (but perhaps verbose) fashion.

As the complexity of application specifications developed over the years, one important and early technique to introduce some "order" to the task of defining representations was the so-called "TLV" approach.

With this approach, information to be sent in a message was regarded as a set of "parameter values". Each parameter value was encoded with a parameter identification (usually of fixed length, commonly a single octet, but perhaps overflowing to further octets), followed by some encoding that gave the length (octet count) of the parameter value (again as a single octet with occasionally the need for two or more octets of length encoding), and then an encoding for the value itself as a sequence of octets.

The parameter id was often said to identify the **type** of the parameter, so we have a **T**ype field, a **L**ength field, and a **V**alue field, or a **TLV** encoding.

In these approaches, all fields were an integral number of octets, with all length counts counting octets, although some of the earliest approaches (not followed by ASN.1) had 16-bit words as the fundamental unit, not octets.

Once the way of encoding types and lengths is determined, the rest of the specification merely needs to determine what parameters are to appear on each message, what their exact id is, and how the values are to be encoded.

This structure has a number of important advantages:

- It makes it possible to give freedom to a sender to transmit the parameters in any order, perhaps making for simpler (sender) implementation. (Note that this is today seen as actually a **bad** thing to allow, not a good one!)

- It makes it possible to declare that some parameters are optional—to be included only when needed in a message.

- It handles items of variable length.

- It enables a basic "parsing" into a set of parameter values without needing any knowledge about the actual parameters themselves.

- And importantly—it enables a version 1 system to identify, to find the end of, and to ignore (if that is the desired behavior), or perhaps to relay onwards, parameters that were added in a version 2 of the protocol.

The reader should recognize the relationship of these features to ASN.1—the existence of "SET" (elements transmitted in any order), the "OPTIONAL" notation that can be applied to elements of a SET or SEQUENCE, and the variable length nature of many ASN.1 basic types. The version 1/version 2 issue is what is usually called "extensibility" in ASN.1.

The major extension beyond this "parameter" concept developed in the late 1970s with the idea of "parameter groups", used to keep close together related parameters. Here we encode a "group identifier", a group length encoding, then a series of TLV encodings for the parameters within the group. As before, the groups can appear in any order, and a complete group may be optional or mandatory, with parameters within that group in any order and either optional or mandatory for that group. Thus we have effectively two levels of TLV—the group level and the parameter level.

It is a natural extension to allow arbitrarily many levels of TLV, with the V part of all except the innermost TLVs being a series of embedded TLVs. This clearly maps well to the ASN.1 concept of being able to define a new type as a SEQUENCE or SET of basic types, then to use that new type as if it were a basic type in further SEQUENCEs or SETs, and so on to any depth.

Thus this nested TLV approach emerged as the natural one to take for the ASN.1 Basic Encoding Rules, and reigned supreme for over a decade.

To completely understand the Basic Encoding Rules we need

- To understand the encoding of the "T" part, and how the identifier in the "T" part is allocated.

- To understand the encoding of the "L" part, for both short "V" parts and for long "V" parts.

- To understand for each basic type, such as INTEGER, BOOLEAN, and BIT STRING, how the "V" is encoded to represent the abstract values of that type.

- To understand for each construction mechanism, such as SEQUENCE or SET, how the encodings of types defined with that mechanism map to nested TLV structures.

This is the agenda for the next chapter.

15.4 Extensibility or "Future Proofing"

The TLV approach is very powerful at enabling the specification of a version 1 system to require specified action on TLV elements where the "T" part is not recognized. This allows new elements (with a distinct "T" part) to be added in version 2 of a specification, with a known pattern of behavior from version 1 systems that receive such material.

This interworking between version 1 and version 2 systems without the need for version 2 implementations to implement both the version 1 and the version 2 protocol is a powerful and important feature of ASN.1.

It is a natural outcome of the TLV approach to encoding in the Basic Encoding Rules, but if one seeks encodings where there is a minimal transfer of information down the line, it is important to investigate how to get some degree of "future-proofing" to allow interworking of version 1 and version 2 systems without the verbosity of the TLV approach.

Early discussions in this area seemed to indicate that future-proofing was only possible if a TLV style of encoding was used, but later work showed that provided the places in the protocol where version 2 additions might be needed were identified by a new notational construct (the ASN.1 "extensibility" ellipsis—three dots), then future-proofing becomes possible with very little overhead even in an encoding structure that is not in any way a TLV type of structure.

It was this recognition that enabled the so-called **Packed Encoding Rules** (PER) to be developed.

15.5 First Attempts at PER—Start with BER and Remove Redundant Octets

This was a blind alley!

The first approach to producing more compact (packed) encodings for ASN.1 was based on a BER TLV-style encoding, but with recognition that in a BER encoding there were frequently octets sent down the line where this was the only possible octet value allowed in this position (at least in this version of the specification). This applied particularly to the "T" values, but also frequently to the length field if the value part of the item (such as a BOOLEAN value) was of fixed length.

> If at first you don't succeed, try, try, again!

By allowing the Packed Encoding Rules to take account of constraints (on, for example, the length of strings or the sizes of INTEGERs), we can find many more cases where explicit transmission of length fields is not needed, because both ends know the value of the "L" field.

A final "improvement" is to consider the "L" field for a SEQUENCE type. Here each element of the SEQUENCE is encoded as a TLV, and there is an outer level "TL" "wrapper" for the SEQUENCE as a whole. If we modify BER so that the "L" part of this wrapper is a count not of octets, but of the number of TLVs in the value part of the SEQUENCE, this count is again fixed (unless the SEQUENCE has OPTIONAL elements), and therefore often need not be transmitted, even if there are inner elements whose length might vary.

Consider the ASN.1 type shown in Figure 15.1. The BER encoding (modified to count TLVs rather than octets for non-inner length fields) is shown in Figure 15.2.

You will see from Figure 15.2 that there are a total of 23 octets sent down the line, but a receiver can predict in advance the value of all but 11 of them—those marked

N O T E

Those with no knowledge of BER may wish to at least skim the next chapter before returning to the following text, as some examples show BER encodings.

```
Example ::= SEQUENCE
   {first    INTEGER (0..127),
    second   SEQUENCE
             {string  OCTET STRING (SIZE(2)),
              name    PrintableString (SIZE(1..8)) },
    third    BIT STRING (SIZE (8)) }
```

Figure 15.1   An example for encoding

as {????} (and knows precisely where these 11 occur). Thus we need not transmit the remaining 12 octets, giving a 50% reduction in communications traffic. Attractive!

The approach, then, was to take a BER encoding as the starting point, determine rules for what octets need not be transmitted, and delete those octets from the BER encoding before transmission, reinserting them (from knowledge of the type definition) on reception before performing a standard BER decode.

Work was done on this approach over a period of some three years, but it fell apart. A document was produced, getting gradually more and more complex as additional (pretty ad hoc) rules were added concerning what could and could not be deleted from a BER encoding, and went for international ballot. An editing meeting was convened just outside New York (around 1990), and the comments from National Bodies were faxed to participants only at the start of the meeting.

Imagine the consternation when the dozen or so participants realized that EVERY National Body had voted "NO", and, moreover, with NO constructive comments! The approach was seen as too complex, too ad hoc, and (because it still left everything requiring an integral number of octets) insufficient to produce efficient encodings of things like "SEQUENCE OF BOOLEAN". It was quite clearly dead in the water.

Many people had prebooked flights that could not be changed without considerable expense, but it was clear that what had been planned as a week-long meeting was over. The meeting broke early at about 11 am for lunch (and eventually reconvened late at about 4 pm). Over the lunch-break much beer was consumed, and the proverbial back-of-a-cigarette-pack recorded the discussions (actually, I think it was a paper napkin—long since lost!). PER as we know it today was born! The rest of the week put some flesh on the bones, and the next two years produced the final text for what was eventually accepted as the PER specification. Implementations of tools supporting it came a year or so later.

```
{U 16}               -- Universal class 16 ("T" value for SEQUENCE)
{    3}               -- 3 items ("L" value for SEQUENCE)
  {U  2}             -- Universal class 2 ("T" value for "first")
  {    1}            -- 1 octet ("L" value for "first")
  {????}             --  alue of "first"
  {U 16}             -- Universal class 16 ("T" value for "second")
  {    2}            -- 2 items ("L" value for "second")
    {U  3}           -- Universal class 3 ("T" value for "string")
    {    2}          -- 2 octets ("L" value for "string")
    {????}{????}     --  alue of "string"
    {U 24}           -- Universal class 24 ("T" value for "name")
    {????}           -- 1 to 8 ("L" value for "name" - 5 say)
    {????}{????}{????}{????}{????}  — alue of "name"
{U  4}}              -- Universal class 4 "T" value for "third"
{    3}              -- 3 octets ("L" value for "third")
{    0}              -- 0 unused bits in last octet of "third" " "
{????}{????}         --  alue of "third"
```

Figure 15.2 Modified BER encoding of Figure 15.1.

15.6 Some of the Principles of PER

15.6.1 Breaking Out of the BER Straightjacket

Probably the most important decisions in that initial lunch-time design of PER were:

> Initial "Principles"
>
> · Forget about TLV.
>
> · Forget about octets—use bits.
>
> · Recognize constraints (sub-types).
>
> · Produce "intelligent" encodings.
>
> · Forget "extensibility" (initially).

- To start with a clean piece of paper (or rather napkin!) and ignore BER and any concept of TLV. This was quite radical at the time, and the beer probably helped people to think the unthinkable!

- Not to be constrained to using an integral number of octets—another quite radical idea.

- To take as full account of constraints (subtyping) in the type definition as could sensibly be done. (BER ignored constraints, perhaps largely because it was produced before the constraint/subtype notation was introduced into ASN.1, and was not modified when that notation came in around 1986.)

- To produce the sort of encoding that a (by now slightly drunk!) intelligent human being would produce—this was quite a challenge!

- Not to consider "extensibility" issues. This was a pragmatic decision that made the whole thing possible over a (long) lunch-time discussion, but of course provision for "future-proofing" had to be (and was) added later.

So how would you the reader encode things? Whatever you think is the obvious way is **probably** what PER does! In all the following cases, the "obvious" solution is what PER does.

What about the encoding of BOOLEAN? Clearly a single bit set to zero or one is the "obvious" solution.

What about

```
INTEGER (0..7)
```

and

```
INTEGER (8..11)
```

Clearly a 3-bit encoding is appropriate for the former and a 2-bit encoding for the latter.

An INTEGER value restricted to a 16-bit range could go into two octets with no length field.

But what about an unconstrained INTEGER? (Meaning, in theory, integer values up to infinity, and with BER capable of encoding integer values that take millions of years to transmit (even over super-fast lines)? Clearly an "L" will be needed here to encode the length of the integer value (and here you probably want to go for a length count in octets).

If you have read about the details of BER encodings of "L", you will know that for length counts of up to 127 octets, "L" is encoded in a single octet, but that BER requires **three** octets for "L" once the count is more than 255. In PER, the count is a count of bits, items, or octets, but only goes beyond two octets for counts of 64K or more—a 50% reduction on the size of "L" in many cases compared with BER.

For virtually all values of an unconstrained INTEGER, we will get a one octet "L" field, followed by the minimum number of octets needed to hold the actual value being sent. This is the same as BER.

15.6.2 How to Cope with Other Problems that a "T" Solves?

So far, no mention has been made of a "T" field for PER. Do we ever need one? There are three main areas in BER where the "T" field is rather important. These are:

- To identify which actual alternative has been encoded as the value of a CHOICE type (remember that all alternatives of a CHOICE are required to have distinct tags, and hence have distinct "T" values).

> · Use a "choice-index".
>
> · SET in a fixed order.
>
> · Bit-map for OPTIONAL elements.

- To identify the presence or absence of OPTIONAL elements in a SEQUENCE (or SET).

- To identify which element of a SET has been encoded where (remember that elements of a SET can be encoded and sent in any order chosen by the sender).

How are these things done without a "T" encoding for each element?

To cope with alternatives in a CHOICE, PER encodes a "choice-index" **in the minimum bits necessary**: up to two alternatives, one bit; three or four alternatives, two bits; five to seven alternatives, three bits; etc.

> The important field-length principle or rule: Encode into fields of an arbitrary number of bits, but the length of fields must be statically determinable from the type definition, for all values.

At this point we can observe one important discipline in the design of PER. **The field width (in bits) for any particular part of the encoding** (in this case the field width of the choice-index) **does not (must not) depend on the abstract value being transmitted, but can be statically determined by examining the type definition**. Hence it is known unambiguously by both ends of the communication—assuming they are using the same type definition. But there is the rub! If one is using a version 1 type definition and the other a version 2 type definition ... but we agreed not to consider this just yet!

What about OPTIONAL elements in a SET or SEQUENCE? Again, the idea is pretty obvious. We use one bit to identify whether an OPTIONAL element is present or absent in the value of the SET or SEQUENCE. In fact, these bits are all collected together and encoded at the start of the SET or SEQUENCE encoding rather than in the position of the optional element, for reasons to do with "alignment" (discussed in 16.4).

And so to the third item that might require a "T". What about the encoding of SET—surely we need the "T" encodings here? Start of a big debate about the importance of SET (where elements are transmitted in an order determined by the sender) over

SEQUENCE (where the order of encodings is the order of elements in the type definition), and of the problems that SET causes. In addition to the verbosity of introducing some form of "T" encoding, we can also observe that:

> Allowing sender's options produces a combinatoric explosion in any form of exhaustive test sequence (and hence in the cost of conformance checking) to check that (receiving) implementations behave correctly in all cases.

The existence of multiple ways of sending the same information produces what in the security world is called a "side-channel"—a means of transmitting additional information from a Trojan horse by systematically varying the sender's options. For example, if there are eight elements in a SET, then 256 bits of additional information can be transmitted with each value of that SET by systematically varying the order of elements.

This discussion led to the development of a further principle for PER: there shall be NO sender's options in

> The sender's options principle/rule: Don't have any!

the encoding unless there is an excellent reason for introducing them. PER effectively has no sender's options. A canonical order is needed for transmitting elements of a SET, and after much discussion, this was taken to be the tag order of the elements (see the next chapter for more detail), rather than the textually printed order. (In allocating choice-index values to alternatives of a choice, the same tag-order rather than textual order, is also used, for consistency.)

It should, however, be noted that the term "PER" strictly refers to a family of four closely related encoding rules. The most important is "BASIC-PER" (with an ALIGNED and an UNALIGNED variant discussed later). Although BASIC-PER has no sender's options, it is not regarded as truly a canonical encoding rule because values of the elements of a SET OF are not required to be sorted into a fixed order, and no restrictions are placed on the way escape sequences are used in encodings of GeneralString. (If neither of these two types is used in an application specification, then BASIC-PER is almost canonical; there are some other unimportant complex cases that never arise in practice where it is not fully canonical.) There is a separate CANONICAL-PER (also with an ALIGNED and an UNALIGNED version) that is truly canonical even when these types are present.

15.6.3 Do We Still Need T and L for SEQUENCE and SET Headers?

Clearly we do not! We need **no** header encodings for these types, provided we can identify the presence or absence of optional elements (which is done by the bit-map that was described earlier).

"Wrappers" are no longer needed. (Well—that is sort of true—but see the discussion of extensibility that follows, and which reintroduces wrappers for elements added in version 2!)

15.6.4 Aligned and Unaligned PER

But here we look at another feature of PER. Basically, PER produces encodings into fields that are a certain number of bits long and which are simply concatenated end-to-end for transmission. But there was recognition from the start that for some ASN.1 types (for example, a sequence of 2-byte integers), it is silly to start every component value at, say, bit 6. Insertion of two **padding bits** at the start of the SEQUENCE OF value would probably be a good compromise between CPU costs and line costs.

> You add padding bits for CPU-cycle efficiency, but then you are asked to take them out for really low-bandwidth lines! Result: ALIGNED and UNALIGNED variants of BASIC-PER and of CANONICAL-PER.

This led to the concept of encoding items into **bit-fields** (which were simply added to the end of the bits in earlier parts of the encoding) or into **octet-aligned-bit-fields** where padding bits were introduced to ensure that the octet-aligned-bit-fields started on an octet boundary.

The intellgent reader (aren't you all?) will note that while the length of fields is (has to be) statically determined from the type, the number of padding bits to be inserted before an octet-aligned-bit-field is **not** fixed. The number of bits in the earlier part of the encoding can depend on whether optional elements of SET and SEQUENCE are present or not, and on the actual alternative chosen in a CHOICE. But of course, the encoding always contains information about this, and hence a receiving implementation can always determine the number of padding bits that are present and that have to be ignored. Notice that whether a field is a bit-field or an octet-aligned-bit-field again has to be (and is) statically determined from the type definition—it must not depend on the actual value being transmitted, or PER would be a bust!

The concept of "octet-aligned-bit-fields" and "padding bits" was in the original design, but later people in air traffic control wanted the padding bits removed, and we now have two variants of PER. Both formally encode into a sequence of "bit-fields" and "octet-aligned-bit-fields", depending on the type definition, but for "unaligned PER", there is no difference in the two—padding bits are never inserted at the start of "octet-aligned-bit-fields". With aligned PER, they are.

There are actually a couple of other differences between aligned and unaligned PER, but these are left to Chapter 17 for details.

As a final comment, if you want to try to keep octet alignment for as long as possible after insertion of padding bits, then using a single bit to denote the presence or absence of an OPTIONAL element in a SEQUENCE or SET is probably not a good idea—better to collect all such bits together as a "bit-map" at the start of the encoding of the SEQUENCE or SET. This was part of the original back-of-cigarette-pack design and was briefly referred to earlier. That feature is present in PER.

15.7 Extensibility—You Have to Have It!

Third attempt!

One bit says it all—it is a version 1 value, or it contains wrapped-up version 2 material.

When the second approach to better encodings (described in 15.6) was balloted internationally, it almost failed again.

It is clear from the preceding discussion that unless both ends have exactly the same type definition for their implementation, all hell will break loose. They will have different views on the fields and the field lengths that are present, and will produce almost random abstract values from the encodings.

> If at first you don't succeed, try, try again!

But do we really want to throw in the towel and admit that a very verbose TLV style of encoding is all that is possible if we are to be "future-proof"? NO!

How to allow version 2 to add things? How about notation to indicate the end of the "root" (version 1) specification, and the start of added version 2 (or 3 etc.) material? Will this help?

The most common case for requiring "extensibility" is the ability to add elements to the end of SETs and SEQUENCEs in version 2.

Later, people argued—successfully—for the need to add elements in the **middle** of SETs and SEQUENCEs, and we got the "insertion point" concept described in an earlier section.

But let's stick to adding at the end for now. Suppose we have added elements (most of which are probably going to be OPTIONAL) at the end of a SEQUENCE, or added alternatives in a CHOICE, or added enumerations in an ENUMERATED, or relaxed constraints on an INTEGER (that list will do for now!).

How to handle that? We first require that a type be marked "extensible" if we want "future-proofing" (this is the ellipsis that can appear in many ASN.1 types). This warns the version 1 implementation that it may be hit with abstract values going beyond the version 1 type, but more importantly, it introduces one "extended" bit at the head of the version 1 encodings of all values of that type.

The concept is that any of these "extensible" types has a "root" set of abstract values—version 1 abstract values. If the abstract value being sent (by a version 1, version 2, or version 3, etc. implementation) is within the root, the "extended" bit is set to zero, and the encoding is purely the encoding of the version 1 type. But if it is set to 1, then abstract values introduced in version 2 or later are present, and version 1 systems have a number of options, but importantly, extra length (and sometimes identification) fields are included to "wrap-up" parts or all of these new abstract values to enable good interworking with version 1 systems. The "exception marker" enables specifiers to say how early version systems are to deal with material that was added in later versions, and (in the views of this author) should always be included if the extensibility marker is introduced.

The exact form of encodings for "extensible" types is discussed in more detail in Chapter 17.

15.8 What More Do You Need to Know About PER?

It is interesting to note that although PER is now defined without any reference to BER (except for encoding the value part of things like object identifiers and generalizedtime and real types), a PER encoding of a value of the type shown in Figure 15.1 actually produces exactly the same 11 octets (shown in Figure 15.2) that would have been produced in the earlier (abandoned) approach!

This chapter has introduced most of the concepts of PER, but there are rather more things to learn about PER than about BER. These are all covered in the next chapter—but—one.

You need to know (well, you probably do not, unless you are writing an ASN.1 compiler tool! See the first part of this chapter!):

- What constraints (subtyping) affect the PER encoding of various types (these are called "PER-visible constraints").

- What the general structure of the encoding ("bit-fields" and "octet-aligned-bit-fields") is and how a "complete encoding" is produced.

- When length fields are included, and when "lengths of lengths" are needed, and how they are encoded.

- How PER encodes SEQUENCEs, SETs, and CHOICEs. (You already have a good idea from the earlier text).

- How PER encodes all the other ASN.1 types. (Actually, it references the BER "V" part encoding much of the time.)

- How the presence of the "extensibility marker" affects PER encodings. (Again, earlier text has given some outline of the effect—a one-bit overhead if the abstract value is in the root, and generally an additional length field if it is not.)

These are all issues that have been touched on above, but are treated more fully later.

15.9 Experience with PER

There is now a lot of experience with PER applied to existing protocol specifications, and there is a growing willingness among specifiers to produce PER-friendly specifications (that is, specifications where constraints are consistently applied to integer fields and lengths of strings where appropriate).

There were some surprises when PER implementations first became available.

First of all, it became possible to apply general-purpose compression algorithms to both the BER and the PER encodings of existing protocols, and it turned out that such compression algorithms produced about a 50% reduction in BER encodings (known for a long time), but also produced a

- Bandwidth reductions (even with added general-purpose compression—surprise?).

- CPU-cycle reductions (real surprise).

- Complexity—only at analysis time!

- Relation to use of tools— increases the advantages of tools.

50% reduction in PER encodings, which (uncompressed) turned out to be about a 50% reduction of the uncompressed BER encodings. Interesting!

If you apply Shannon's information theory, it is perhaps not quite so surprising. A BER encoding more or less transmits complete details of the ASN.1 type as well as the value of that type. PER transmits information about only the value, assuming that full details of the type are already known at both ends. So an uncompressed

PER encoding carries less information, and can be expected to be smaller than an uncompressed BER encoding but the same statement applies to compressed versions of these encodings. This is borne out in practice.

Secondly, and this WAS a surprise to most ASN.1 workers, the number of CPU cycles needed to produce an ASN.1 PER decoding proved to be significantly fewer than those required to produce an ASN.1 BER encoding (and similarly for decoding). Why? Surely PER is more complex?

It is true that determining the encoding to produce (what constraints apply, the field-widths to use, whether a length field is needed or not) is much more complex for PER than for BER. But that determination is **static**. It is part of generating (by hand or by an ASN.1 "compiler") the code to do an encoding.

At encode time, it is far fewer orders to take an integer from memory, mask off the bottom three bits, and add them to the encoding buffer (that is what PER needs to do to encode a value of "INTEGER (0..7)") than to generate (and add to the encoding buffer) a BER "T" value, a BER "L" value (which for most old BER implementations means testing the actual size of the integer value, as most old BER implementations ignored constraints), and then an octet or two of actual value encoding. This is also true for decoding.

There is a further CPU-cycle gain in the code handling the lower layers of the protocol stack, simply from the reduced volume of the material to be handled when PER is in use.

So PER seems to produce good gains in both bandwidth and CPU cycles, even for "old" protocols. Where a specification tries to introduce bounds on integers and lengths, where they are sensible for the application, the gains can be much greater. And protocols that have many boolean "flags" benefit heavily. Figure 15.3 shows a (slightly artificial!) SEQUENCE type for which the BER encoding is 19 octets and the PER encoding is a single octet!

```
SEQUENCE
    { firstfield          INTEGER (0..7),
      secondfield         BOOLEAN,
      thirdfield          INTEGER (8..11),
      fourthfield         SEQUENCE
          {fourA     BOOLEAN,
           fourB     BOOLEAN } }
```

Figure 15.3 Another example for encoding.

There is a view in the implementor community that use of PER requires the use of a tool to analyze the type definition, determine what constraints affect the encoding (and follow possibly long chains of parameterization of these constraints if necessary), in order to generate correct code for use in an instance of communication to encode/decode values.

There is no doubt that it is easier to make mistakes in PER encoding/decoding by hand than with BER. The PER specification **is** more complex, and is probably more difficult to understand. (In my honest opinion, it is actually less well written than the BER specification! Mea culpa!)

All these points increase the importance of using a well-debugged tool to generate encodings rather than trying to do it by hand. But hand-encodings of PER do exist, and are perfectly possible—but be prepared to put a wet towel over your head and drink lots of coffee! And, more importantly to test the encodings/decodings produced using a tool. These points also apply to hand-encoding of BER, but to a much lesser extent.

15.10 Distinguished and Canonical Encoding Rules

We observed earlier that encoding rules in which there are no options for the encoder are a *good thing*.

Encodings produced by such encoding rules are usually called "distinguished" or "canonical" encodings. At this level (no capitals!) the two terms are synonymous!

However, if options are introduced (such as the indefinite and definite length encodings in BER—see Chapter 16) because you cannot agree, how do you agree on encoding rules with all options removed? The answer is two Standards! The Basic Encoding Rules come in three variants:

> Your job is to produce Standards. If you can't agree, make it optional, or better still another Standard. After all, if one Standard is good, many Standards must be better!

- BER—which allow options for the encoder.

- DER (Distinguished Encoding Rules)—which resolve all options in a particular direction.

- CER (Canonical Encoding Rules)—which resolve all options in the other direction!

It is arguably the case that CER is technically superior, but there is no doubt that DER has become the de facto distinguished/canonical encoding for BER.

When we come to PER, the term "distinguished" is not used, but there is defined a BASIC-PER and a CANONICAL-PER with both aligned and unaligned versions as described previously.

We mentioned earlier the problem with encodings of the "SET OF xyz" type. (There are also problems with the encoding of GraphicString and GeneralString that are discussed in chapters to follow). In a formal sense, the order of the series of "xyz" encodings that are being sent has no significance at the abstract level (it is a SET, not a SEQUENCE), so the order of encodings is clearly a sender's option. To determine a single "canonical" encoding for the values of this type requires that the series of "xyz" encodings be SORTED (based on the binary value of each of these encodings) into some defined order. As this can put a very significant load on both CPU cycles and "disk-churning", it is not something to be undertaken lightly.

So "normal PER" is not strictly speaking canonical if a specification contains uses of "SET OF" (although there are those who would argue that we get into "How many angels can dance on the head of a pin"? issues here).

"Canonical PER" specifies sorting of the "xyz" encodings to produce a truly **one-to-one** mapping of an (unordered) set of values into bit strings, each bit string representing one possible set of (unordered) values of the type "xyz".

Author's opinion: I know of no applications where this degree of formality or precision matters. CANONICAL-PER is basically not a good idea, but neither is the use of "SET OF" in specifications! Try to avoid both. (Others may not agree!)

15.11 Conclusion

This chapter has provided an introduction to the ASN.1 Basic Encoding Rules and the ASN.1 Packed Encoding Rules, showing their approach to encodings and their relative advantages and disadvantages.

It has also discussed issues of extensibility or "future-proofing", and mentioned canonical/distinguished encoding rules.

The chapter has formed a basic introduction to the detailed, factual (and dry!) description of BER and PER in the next two chapters.

Readers may also have heard of ASN.1 Encoding Rules with names such as "Minimum Bit Encoding Rules" (MBER), "Lightweight Encoding Rules" (LWER), "Clear text encoding rules", "BACNet Encoding Rules", "Session Layer Encoding Rules", and perhaps others. These represented attempts (sometimes outside the standards community, sometimes within it) to develop other Encoding Rules for ASN.1 that might be superior to both BER and PER in some circumstances (or which were partial early attempts to move toward PER). None of these is regarded as important today for general use with ASN.1, but they are discussed a little more in Chapter 18.

## CHAPTER 16

The Basic Encoding Rules

(Or: Encodings for the 1980s—Simple, Robust, But Inefficient!)

Summary

This chapter provides details of the Basic Encoding Rules. It describes

- The form of the T part of a TLV encoding (the identifier octets), including the primitive/constructed bit.

- The short, definite, and indefinite forms of encoding for the L part of the TLV (the length octets).

- The V part of the TLV encoding (the contents octets) for each of the primitive types, taken roughly in order of increasing complexity.

- The encoding of the constructed types (such as SET and SEQUENCE).

- The encoding of remaining types, such as the character string and time types and types that represent "holes" of various sorts.

16.1 Introduction

The TLV principles underlying BER encodings have been extensively introduced in earlier chapters, and the reader should have little difficulty in going to the actual Standard/Recommendation for authoritative details.

> You have already learned the principles of BER encodings, now for the details.

For completeness, however, this chapter provides examples of all the encodings, and gives some further explanation in a few cases.

16.2 General issues

16.2.1 Notation for Bit Numbers and Diagrams

One of the problems with encoding specifications in the late-1970s was that the bits of an octet were sometimes numbered from left to right in diagrams, sometimes the other way, and sometimes the most significant bit was shown at the right, and sometimes at the left. The order of octet

> If the specs are not clear on what order the bits in an octet are sent, there will be problems! There were in the late 1970s—largely OK now, but be careful!

transmission from diagrams could also be right to left in some specifications and left to right in others. Naturally there was often confusion.

In the case of ASN.1 (and this book), we show the first transmitted octet to the left (or above) later transmitted octets, and we show each octet with the most significant bit on the left, with bit numbers running from 8 (most significant) to 1 (least significant) as shown in Figure 16.1.

Whether within an octet the most or least significant bit is transmitted first (or the bits are transmitted in parallel) is not prescribed in ASN.1. This is determined by the carrier protocols. On a serial line, most significant first is the most common. It is the terms "most significant bit" and "least significant bit" that link the ASN.1 specifications to the lower layer carrier specifications for the determination of the order of **bits** on the line.

The order of **octets** on the line is entirely determined by ASN.1. When encoding a multioctet integer value, ASN.1 specifies that the most significant octet of the value is transmitted first, and hence is shown in diagrams in the standard (and in this

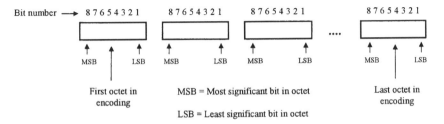

Figure 16.1 Bit numbering and order of octets.

book) as the leftmost octet of the value (see the encoding of the integer type later in this chapter).

16.2.2 The identifier Octets

First the T part, encoding the tag value.

Every ASN.1 type has a tag of one of four classes, with a number for the tag, as discussed earlier. In the simplest case these values are encoded in a single octet as shown in Figure 16.2.

We see that the first two bits encode the class as follows:

```
Class              Bit 8    Bit 7
Universal            0        0
Application          0        1

Context-specific     1        0
Private              1        1
```

The next bit (bit 6) is called the primitive/constructed (P/C) bit, and we will return to that in a moment.

The last five bits (bits 5 to 1) encode the number of the tag. Clearly this will only cope with numbers that are less than 32. In fact, the value 31 is used as an escape marker, so only tag numbers up to 30 encode in a single octet.

For larger tag values, the first octet has all ones in bits 5 to 1, and the tag value is then encoded in as many following octets as are needed, using only the least significant seven bits of each octet, and using the minimum number of octets for the encoding. The most significant bit (the "more" bit) is set to 1 in the first following octet, and to 0 in the last. This is illustrated in Figure 16.3.

Thus tag numbers between 31 and 127 (inclusive) will produce two identifier octets, tag numbers between 128 and 16383 will produce three identifier octets. Most ASN.1 specifications keep tag numbers below 128, so either one identifier

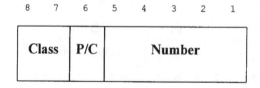

Figure 16.2 Encoding of the identifier octet (number less than 31).

octet—most common—or two identifier octets is what you will normally see, but I have seen a tag number of 999!

What about the primitive/constructed bit? This is required to be set to 1 (constructed) if the V part of the encoding is itself a series of TLV encodings, and is required to be set to 0 (primitive) otherwise. Thus for the encoding of an integer type or boolean type (provided any tagging was implicit), it is always set to 0. For the encoding of a SET or SET OF etc., it is always set to 1. In these cases it is clearly redundant, provided the decoder has the type definition available.

But having this bit present permits a style of decoding architecture in which the incoming octet-stream is first parsed into a tree-structure of TLV encodings (with no knowledge of the type definition), so that the leaves of the tree are all primitive encodings. The tree is then passed to code that **does** know about the type definition, for further processing.

There is, however, a rather more important role for this bit. As we will see later, when transmitting a very long octet string value (and the same applies to bit string and character string values), ASN.1 permits the encoder to **either** transmit as the entire V part the octets of the octet string value (preceded by a length count), **or** to fragment the octet string into a series of fragments that are each turned into TLV encodings, which then go into the V part of the main outer-level encoding of the octet string value. Clearly a decoder needs to know which option was taken, and the primitive/constructed bit tells it precisely that.

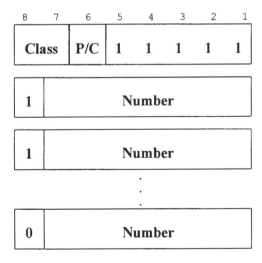

Figure 16.3 Encoding of the identifier octets (numbers greater than 30).

Why is fragmentation in this way useful? This will become clearer in 16.2.3, when we consider the form of the "L" encoding; but the problem is roughly as follows.

If our V part is primitive, clearly all possible octet values can appear within it, and the only mechanism that ASN.1 provides for determining its length is to have an explicit count of octets in the "L" part. For extremely long octet values, this could mean a lot of disk churning to determine the exact length (and transmit it) before any of the actual octets can be sent. If however, the V part is made up of a series of TLVs, we can find ways of terminating that series of TLVs without an upfront count, so we can transmit octets from the value as they become available, without having to count them all first.

> Now the L part—three forms are available in general, sometimes only two, and occasionally only one. The encoder chooses the one to use.

16.2.3 The Length Octets

There are three forms of length encoding used in BER, called the short form, the long form, and the indefinite form. It is not always possible to use all three forms, but where it is, it is an encoder's option which to use. This is one of the main sources of optionality in BER, and the main area that canonical/distinguished encoding rules have to address.

> Very obvious—one octet with the top bit zero and the remaining bits encoding the length as an octet count.

16.2.3.1 The Short Form

This is illustrated in Figure 16.4.

The short form can be used if the number of octets in the V part is less than or equal to 127, and can be used whether the V part is primitive or constructed. This form is identified by encoding bit 8 as 0, with the length count in bits 7 to 1 (as usual, with bit 7 the most significant bit of the length).

16.2.3.2 The Long Form

If bit 8 of the first length octet is set to 1, then we have the long form of length. This form can be used for **all** types of V part, no matter how long or short, no matter

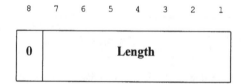

Figure 16.4 The short form encoding of a length (lengths up to 127).

whether primitive or constructed. In this long form, the first octet encodes in its remaining seven bits a value N, which is the length of a series of octets that themselves encode the length of the V part. This is shown in Figure 16.5.

There is no requirement that the minimum number of octets be used to encode the actual length, so all the length encodings shown in Figure 16.6 are permitted if the actual length of the V part is 5.

This was actually introduced into ASN.1 in the early 1980s just before the first specification was finalized (early drafts required length encodings to be as small as possible). It was

> For longer lengths—a length of the length field, then the length itself. Commonly a total of three octets, the first being set to 2.

introduced because there were a number of implementors that wanted N to have a fixed value (typically 2), then the N (2) octets that would hold the actual length value, then the V part. There are probably still BER implementations around today that always have three length octets (using the long form encoding), even where one octet (using the short form encoding) would do.

There is a restriction on the first length octet in the long form. N is not allowed to have the value 127. This is "reserved for future extensions", but such extensions are now highly unlikely. If you consider how long the V part can be when N has the maximum value of 126, and how large an integer value such a V part can hold, you will find that the number is greater than the number of stars in our galaxy. It was

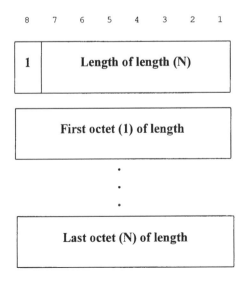

Figure 16.5   The long form encoding of a length (all lengths).

```
 87654321
┌─────────┐
│00000101│
└─────────┘
```

```
 87654321    87654321    87654321
┌─────────┐ ┌─────────┐ ┌─────────┐
│10000010│ │00000000│ │00000101│
└─────────┘ └─────────┘ └─────────┘
```

```
 87654321    87654321    87654321    87654321
┌─────────┐ ┌─────────┐ ┌─────────┐ ┌─────────┐
│10000011│ │00000000│ │00000000│ │00000101│
└─────────┘ └─────────┘ └─────────┘ └─────────┘
```

etc

Figure 16.6 Options for encoding a length of 5.

also calculated that if you transmit down a line running at one tera-bit per second the longest possible V part, it would take one hundred million years to transmit all the octets! So there is no practical limit imposed by BER on the size of the V part, or on the value of integers.

16.2.3.3 The Indefinite Form

The indefinite form of length can **only** be used (but does not have to be) if the V part is constructed, that is to say, consists of a series of TLVs. (The length octets of each of these TLVs in this contained series can independently be chosen as short, definite, or indefinite where such choices are available—the form used at the outer level does not affect the inner encoding.)

> With this form you do not need to count your octets before you start to send them—just ship a series of fragments and terminate with 0000.

In the indefinite form of length the first bit of the first octet is set to 1, as for the long form, but the value N is set to zero. Clearly a value of zero for N would not be useful in the long form, so this serves as a flag that the indefinite form is in use. Following this single octet, we get the series of TLVs forming the V part, followed by a special delimiter that is **a pair of zero octets**.

This is shown in Figure 16.7.

How does this work? The most important thing to note is that a decoder is processing the series of TLVs, and when it hits the pair of zero octets it will interpret them as the start of another TLV. So let us do just that. The zero T looks like a primitive encoding (bit 6 is 0) with a tag of UNIVERSAL class ZERO, and a definite form length encoding of zero length (zero octets in the V part).

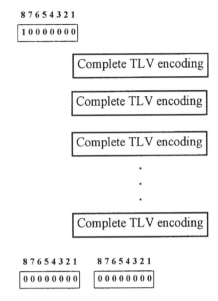

Figure 16.7 An indefinite length encoding.

If you now refer back to the assignment of UNIVERSAL class tags given in Figure 16.4, you will see that UNIVERSAL class zero is "Reserved for use by Encoding Rules" (and remember that users are not allowed to assign UNIVERSAL class tags). A pair of zero octets can never appear as a TLV in any real encoding, and this "special" TLV can safely be defined by BER as the delimiter for the series of TLVs in the V part of an indefinite form encoding.

We stated earlier that, within an indefinite form TLV we may have inner TLVs that themselves are constructed and have an indefinite form of length. There is no confusion: A pair of zero octets (when a TLV is expected) terminates the innermost "open" indefinite form.

16.2.3.4 Discussion of Length Variants

Why do we need so many different variants of length? Clearly they all have some advantages and disadvantages. The short form is the briefest when it can be used, the long form is the only one that can handle very large primitive encodings, and seems to many to be intuitively simpler than the indefinite form. The indefinite is the only one that allows very large OCTET STRING values or SEQUENCE OF values to be transmitted without counting the number of octets in the value before starting.

The disadvantage of having three options is the extra implementation complexity in decoders, and the presence of encoding options creating side-channels and extra debugging effort. If we want to remove these options, then we have to say either "use indefinite length form whenever possible" (and make statements about the size of fragment to use when dividing an octet string), or "use short form where possible, otherwise use long form with the minimum value of N needed for the count". Both of these approaches are standardized! The distinguished/canonical encoding rules that take the former approach are called the Canonical Encoding Rules (CER), and those that take the latter approach are called the Distinguished Encoding Rules (DER). Applications with requirements for canonical/distinguished encoding rules will mandate use of one of these in the application specification.

16.3 Encodings of the V Part of the Main Types

In the examples for this clause we use the ASN.1 value notation to specify a value of a type, and then show the complete encoding of that value using hexadecimal notation for the value of each octet.

> Encoding the V part is specific to each type. In many cases it is obvious, but the majority of types present problems that produce a little complexity in the encoding.

The primary focus here is to illustrate the encoding of the V part for each type, but it must be remembered that there will be other permissible length encodings in addition to the one illustrated (as discussed earlier), and that if implicit tagging were to be applied, the T part would differ.

The encoding of each of the following types is always primitive unless stated otherwise. The types are taken roughly in ascending order of complexity.

> Utterly simple!

16.3.1 Encoding a NULL Value

The value of

```
null NULL ::= NULL
```

(the only value of the NULL type) is encoded as

```
             T         L         V
null:        05        00        empty
```

Note that while we have described our structure as TLV, it is (as in this case) possible for there to be zero octets in the V part if the length is zero. This can arise in cases other than NULL. So for example, a SEQUENCE OF value with an iteration count of zero would encode with an L of zero. Similarly a SEQUENCE, all of whose elements were optional, and which in an instance of communication were all missing, would again encode with an L of zero.

16.3.2 Encoding a BOOLEAN Value

The values of

```
boolean1 BOOLEAN ::= TRUE
boolean2 BOOLEAN ::= FALSE
```

are encoded as

	T	L	V
boolean1:	01	01	FF
boolean2:	01	01	00

> Still pretty obvious, but we now have encoder options!

For the value TRUE, an encoding of hex FF is shown. This is the only permissible encoding in DER and CER, but in BER any nonzero value for the V part is permitted.

16.3.3 Encoding an INTEGER Value

A two's complement encoding of the integer values **into the smallest possible V part** is specified. When two's complement is used "smallest possible" means that the first (most significant) **nine** bits of the V part cannot be all zeros or all ones, but there **will** be values that will encode with the first **eight** bits all zeros or ones.

Note that it would in theory have been possible to use an L value of zero and no V part to represent the integer value zero, but this is expressly forbidden by BER—there is always at least one octet in the V part.

> Top nine bits must not be the same—nine? Yes NINE.

Thus the values of

```
integer1 INTEGER ::= 72
integer2 INTEGER ::= 127
integer3 INTEGER ::= -128
integer4 INTEGER ::= 128
```

are encoded as

	T	L	V
integer1	02	01	48
integer2	02	01	7F
integer3	02	01	80
integer4	02	02	0080

If the integer type was defined with a distinguished value list, this does not in any way affect the encoding.

16.3.4 Encoding an ENUMERATED Value

The definition of an enumerated type may include integer values to be used to represent each enumeration during transfer, or (post-1994) may allow those values to be automatically assigned in order from zero. In the latter case all such values will be positive, but in the general case a user is allowed to assign **negative** values for enumerations (no one ever does). BER takes no account of the (common) case where all associated values are positive: the encoding of an enumerated value is exactly the same as the (two's complement) encoding of the associated integer value (except that the tag value is different of course).

> You might expect only positive values for enumerations—not so! Encode as a general integer.

In practice, this only makes an efficiency difference if there are more than 127 enumerations, which is rare.

16.3.5 Encoding a REAL Value

The encoding of a real value is quite complex. First of all, recall that the type is formally defined as the set of all values that can be expressed base 10, together with the set of all possible values that can be expressed base 2, even if these are the same numerical value. This means that different encodings are applied to these two sets of values, and the application may apply different semantics. (There is one exception to this—the value zero has just **one** encoding, zero octets in the V part.) For base 10 values, the encoding is character-based, for base 2 values, it is binary floating point.

> Forget about floating point format standards. What matters is how easily you can encode/decode with real hardware.

There are also two further values of type REAL–PLUS-INFINITY and MINUS-INFINITY, with their own special encodings.

Note that it is possible to subtype type REAL to contain only base 10 or base 2 values, effectively giving the application designer control over whether the character-based encoding or the binary-based encoding of values of the type is to be used.

16.3.5.1 Encoding Base 10 Values

If the (nonzero) value is base 10, then the contents octets (the V part) start with one octet whose first two bits are 00 (other values are used for the base 2 values and the special values PLUS-INFINITY and MINUS-INFINITY). Octets after this initial octet are a series of ASCII characters (eight bits per character) representing digits 0 to 9, space, plus sign, minus sign, comma or full-stop (for "decimal mark"), and capital E and small e (for exponents), in a format

> A character encoding base 10 is available. (But not much used!)

defined in the ISO Standard 6093. This standard has a lot of options, and in particular defines "Numerical Representation 1" (NR1), NR2, and NR3. Which of these is used is coded as values 1, 2, or 3, respectively into the bottom six bits of the first contents octet. Even within these representations, there are many options. In particular, arbitrary many leading spaces can be included, plus signs are optional, and so on.

When used with DER and CER (and all versions of PER), options are restricted to NR3, spaces and leading zeros are in general forbidden, the full-stop has to be used for any "decimal mark", and the plus sign is required for positive values. The mantissa is required to be normalized so that there are no digits after the "decimal mark". In each case that follows, the second column shows the way the same real value would be encoded in DER/CER/PER.

We will not attempt here a detailed description of ISO 6093, but give some examples of the resulting strings. Note that while there may be leading spaces, there are never trailing spaces. There may also be leading zeros and trailing zeros.

NR1 encodes only simple whole numbers (no decimal point, no exponent). Here are some examples of NR1 encodings, where # is used to denote the space character:

```
4902                4902.E+0

#4902               4902.E+0

###0004902          4902.E+0

###+4902            4902.E+0

-004902             -4902.E+0
```

NR2 requires the presence of a "decimal mark" (full-stop or comma as an encoder option). Here are some examples of NR2 encodings:

```
4902.00                     4902.E+0
###4902,00                  4902.E+0
000.4                       4.E-1
#.4                         4.E-1
4.                          4.E+0
```

NR3 extends NR2 by the use of a base 10 exponent represented by an uppercase E or lowercase e. Examples of NR3 are:

```
         +0.56E+4                   56.E2
         +5.6e+03                   56.E2
         #0.3E-04                   3.E-5
         -2.8E+000000               -28.E-1
####000004.50000E123456789         45.E123456788
```

16.3.5.2 Encoding Base 2 Values

Base 2 values are encoded in a form that is similar to the floating point formats used when a computer system dumps the contents of a floating point unit into main memory. We talk about the mantissa (M), the base (B), and the exponent (E) of the number.

> A more "traditional" floating point format is also available. This is where effort was expended to make encoding/ decoding easy.

However, in real floating point units, the base may be either 2, 8, or 16 (but is fixed for that hardware). In an ASN.1 encoding, the value of B has to be sent. This is done in the first contents octet. We then need the value of the exponent for this numerical value, and of the mantissa.

Let us look at the first contents octet in the case of base 2 values (recall that the first contents octet for base 10 values started 00 and then encoded NR1, NR2, or NR3). This first content octet is illustrated in Figure 16.8.

NOTE

For a full understanding of this material the reader will need some familiarity with the form of computer floating point units—something assembler language programmers of the 1960s were very familiar with, but something today's programmers can usually forget about! You may want to skim this material very quickly, or even totally ignore it.

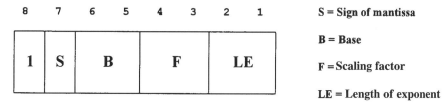

Figure 16.8   Encoding of the first contents octet of a base 2 real value.

The first bit (bit 8, most significant) is set to 1 to identify this as a base 2 value. The next bit (S) is the sign of the number, with the mantissa represented (later) as a positive integer value. The next two bits (B) encode the base (2, 8, or 16, with the fourth value reserved for future use). The next two bits encode a "scaling factor" value called F, restricted to values 0 to 3, and the final two bits encode the length (LE) of the exponent encoding (the exponent is encoded as a two's complement integer value immediately following this initial octet). The four values of LE allow for a 1-octet, 2-octet, or 3-octet exponent, with the fourth value indicating that the exponent field starts with a 1-octet length field, then the exponent value. Following the encoding of the exponent field we get the mantissa (M) as a positive integer encoding, terminated by the end of the contents octets (V part) in the usual way.

The actual value of the real number encoded in this way is:

```
S x M x (2 ** F) x (B ** E)
```

where ****** denotes exponentiation and x denotes multiplication.

This is a fairly familiar way to represent floating point numbers, apart from the presence of F. We also need to discuss a little more the use of sign and magnitude instead of a 2's complement (or even 1's complement) mantissa.

In the early 1980s, there was very considerable variation in the form of floating point units, even within a single computer manufacturer, and although there are now *de jure* standards for floating point representation, there is in practice still a wide de facto variation.

What has to be achieved (and was achieved) in the ASN.1 encoding of real is a representation that makes it (fairly) easy and quick for **any** floating point architecture to encode or decode values.

Consider the choice between sign and magnitude or two's complement for the mantissa. If your actual hardware is two's complement, you can easily test the number and set the S bit, then negate the number, and you have a sign and magnitude format. If, however, your hardware was sign and magnitude and you are asked to generate a two's complement representation for transfer, the task is much more difficult. It is clear then that sign and magnitude is right for transfer, no matter which type of machine is most common.

The scaling factor F is included for a similar reason. All mantissas have an implied decimal point position when the floating point value is dumped into main memory, but this is frequently **not** at the end of the mantissa field, that is, the mantissa is not naturally considered as an integer value. However, it is an integer value we wish to transfer in the ASN.1 encoding, and rather than try to encode the position of the implied decimal point, instead we recognize that the implied point can be moved one place to the right if we subtract one off the exponent value (for base 2). If the base is 8, one off the exponent value moves the implied decimal point three places right, and base 16 four places. Thus with a fixed (for this hardware) decrement to the exponent, we can get the implied decimal point close to the end of the mantissa: in particular, to within three positions of the end for a base 16 machine. By encoding an F value (which again is fixed for any given hardware), we can move the implied decimal point the remaining zero to three bits to get it exactly at the end. Of course a decoder has to multiply the resulting number by 2 to the power F, but this is quick and easy to do in a floating point unit.

When this encoding was developed in the mid-1980s, there was a lot of discussion of these issues, and there was agreement over a range of vendors that the format provided a very good "neutral" format that they could all encode into and decode out of from a range of actual floating point hardware. Recommendation X.690/ISO 8825 Part 1 has a substantial tutorial annex about both the rationale for including F and also describing in some detail the algorithm needed to statically determine the encodings for a given floating point unit, and for encoding and decoding values. The interested reader is referred to this tutorial for further detail.

Once again, in producing a canonical/distinguished encoding, we have to look at what options are being permitted, and eliminate them. We also have to concern ourselves with "normalization" of the representation. (This was illustrated in the character case already presented here, where we required 4.E-1 rather than 0.4. A similar concern arises with the binary encoding.) For DER/CER/PER (all forms) we require that B be 2, that the mantissa be odd, that F be zero, and that the exponent and mantissa be encoded in the minimum number of octets possible. This is sufficient to remove all options.

16.3.5.3 Encoding the Special Real Values

There were early discussions about allowing special encodings for real values of the form "underflow" and "overflow", and for pi and other "interesting" values, but the only special values standardized so far (and there are unlikely to be any others now) are PLUS-INFINITY and MINUS-INFINITY.

> And finally there are "special" real values that cannot easily be represented by normal character or floating point formats.

Recall that for a base 2 encoding the first (most significant) bit of the first contents octet is 1, and that for a base 10 encoding, the first **two** bits are zero. A special value encoding has the first two bits set to zero and one, with the remaining six bits of the first (and only) content octet identifying the value (two encodings only used).

16.3.6 Encoding an OCTET STRING Value

> Pretty simple again—except that if you have a very long octet string you may want to fragment it to avoid counting it before transmission. Again, an encoder's option.

As was pointed out, there are two ways of encoding an octet string— either as a primitive encoding, or as a series of TLV encodings, which we illustrate using the indefinite form for the outer-level TLV.

Thus:

```
octetstring OCTET STRING ::=
    '00112233445566778899AABBCCDDEEFF'H
```

encodes as either

```
                T       L       V
octetstring:    04      10      00112233445566778899AABBCCDDEEFF
```

or as

```
octetstring:    24      80
                        T       L       V
                        04      08      0011223344556677
                        04      08      8899AABBCCDDEEFF
                0000
```

There are a number of points to note here. Of course fragmentation makes little sense for such a short string, but it illustrates the form. We chose here to fragment into two equal halves, but in general we can fragment at any point. We chose not to further divide our fragments, but we are actually permitted to do so! In DER fragmentation is forbidden. In CER the fragment size is fixed at 1000 octets (no fragmentation if 1000 octets or under), and additional division of fragments is forbidden.

Finally, note that if the OCTET STRING had been implicitly tagged, the outermost T value (24—universal class 4, constructed), would reflect the replacement tag, but the tag on each fragment would remain 04 (universal class 4, primitive).

16.3.7 Encoding a BIT STRING Value

For a BIT STRING value, we talk about the leading bit of the BIT STRING and the trailing bit, with the leading bit numbered as bit zero if we list named bits. The leading bit goes into the most significant bit of the first octet of the contents octets. Thus using the diagram conventions detailed earlier, the bits are transmitted with the leftmost on the paper as the leading bit, proceeding to the rightmost. When specifying a BIT STRING value, the value notation declares the leftmost bit in the notation as the leading bit, so there is general consistency, except that the numbering of bits in a BIT STRING type goes in the opposite direction to the numbering of bits in an octet.

> BER length counts are always in octets. So how to determine the exact length of a bit string encoding? And what bit-value to pad with to reach an octet boundary? (Answer to the latter—encoder's option!)

As with an OCTET STRING value, BIT STRING value encodings can be primitive or broken into fragments. There is only one additional complication—the length count in BER is always a count of octets, so we need some way of determining how many unused bits there are in the last octet. This is handled by adding an extra contents octet at the **start** of the contents octets saying how many unused bits there are in the last octet. (In CER/DER these unused bits are required to be set to zero. BER has their values as a sender's option.)

If fragmentation of the BIT STRING into separate TLVs is performed, the fragments are required to be on an octet boundary, and the extra octet already described is placed (only) at the start of the **last** fragment in the fragmented encoding.

Thus:

```
bitstring BIT STRING ::=
    '1111000011110000111101'B
```

encodes as either

```
                 T       L
bitstring:       03      0F      02F0F0F4
```

or as

```
bitstring:       23      80
                         T       L
                         03      02      F0F0
                         03      02      02F4
                 0000
```

Again, fragmentation makes little sense for such a short string, and again in DER fragmentation is forbidden. In CER the fragment size is again fixed at 1000 octets (no fragmentation if 1000 octets or under), and additional division of fragments is forbidden.

Apart from the extra octet detailing the number of unused bits, the situation is in all respects the same as for OCTET STRING.

16.3.8 Encoding Values of Tagged Types

If an implicit tag is applied (either by use of the word IMPLICIT, or because we are in an environment of automatic or implicit tagging), then as described in Section II, the class and number of the new tag replaces that of the old tag in all the preceding encodings.

If however, an explicit tag is applied, we get the original encoding with the old tag, placed as a (single) TLV as

> The final discussion of tagging! If it is not clear by the end of the material here, throw the book in the river!

the contents octets of a constructed encoding whose T part encodes the new (explicit) tag.

For example:

```
integer1 INTEGER ::= 72
integer2 [1] IMPLICIT INTEGER ::= 72
integer3 [APPLICATION 27] EXPLICIT INTEGER ::= 72
```

are encoded as

	T	L				
integer1	02	01	48			
integer2	C1	01	48			
integer3	7B	03				
			T	L		
			02	01	48	

where the 7B is made up, in binary, as follows:

Class	P/C	Number
APPLICATION	Constructed	27
01	1	11011 → 01111011 = 7B

16.3.9 Encoding Values of CHOICE Types

> This is either obvious or curious! There is no TLV associated with the CHOICE construct itself— you just encode the TLV for a value of the chosen alternative.

In all variants of BER, there are no additional TL wrappers for choices. The encoding is just that of the chosen item. The decoder knows which was encoded, because the tags of all alternatives in a choice are required to be distinct.

So (compare with the encodings for the INTEGER and BOOLEAN types given previously, with)

```
value1 CHOICE
        { flag  BOOLEAN,
          value INTEGER} ::= flag:TRUE
```

and

```
value2 CHOICE
        {flag  BOOLEAN,
          value INTEGER} ::= value:72
```

we get the encodings:

```
                     T      L
value1               01     01      FF
`value2              02     01      48
```

16.3.10 Encoding SEQUENCE OF Values

This is quite straightforward—an outer (constructed) TL as the wrapper, with a TLV for each element (if any) in the SEQUENCE OF value.

> You should know this already from the general discussion of the TLV approach. Nothing new here.

Thus

```
temperature-each-day SEQUENCE SIZE (7) OF INTEGER
          ::= {21, 15, 5, -2, 5, 10, 5}
```

could be encoded as:

```
temperature-each-day:   T      L
                        30     80
                                      T      L
                                      02     01      15
                                      02     01      0F
                                      02     01      05
                                      02     01      FE
                                      02     01      05
                                      02     01      10
                                      02     01      05
                        0000
```

Of course, we could have employed definite length encoding at the outer level, which in this case would have saved two octets if the short form had been employed.

16.3.11 Encoding SET OF Values

The encoding of SET OF is just the same as for SEQUENCE OF except that the outer T field is 31. If, however, this were a CER or DER encoding then the seven TLVs would be sorted into ascending order and we would get:

> What is the actual set of abstract values? Is {3, 2} the same value as {2, 3}? It should be! So we must have just one encoding in distinguished/ canonical encoding rules for this single value. This produces a significant cost at encode time. Best not to use SET OF if you want to have distinguished/canonical encodings.

```
        unordered-weeks-temps SET SIZE (7) OF INTEGER
             ::= {21, 15, 5, -2, 5, 10, 5}
weekstemperatures:      T         L
                        31        80
                                          T         L
                                          02        01        FE
                                          02        01        15
                                          02        01        10
                                          02        01        0F
                                          02        01        05
                                          02        01        05
                                          02        01        05
                        0000
```

Notice that the sort is on the final encodings of each element, so the temperature −2 sorts ahead of the temperature 21.

16.3.12 Encoding SEQUENCE and SET Values

These are exactly similar, except that now the inner TLVs (one for each element of the sequence or set) will be of varying size and have varying tags. In some cases these elements may themselves be sequences or sets, so we may get deeper nesting of TLVs (to any depth).

> Back to simplicity again. Nested TLVs, to any depth.

If there are optional elements, and the abstract value of the sequence or set does not contain a value for these elements, then the corresponding TLV is simply omitted.

In the case of SET, BER allows the nested TLVs to appear in any order chosen by the encoder. In DER, the elements are sorted by the tag of each element (which again are required to be distinct). However, if we have

```
My-type ::= SET OF
         {field1  INTEGER,
          field2  CHOICE
             { flag  BOOLEAN,
               dummy NULL} }
```

then each SET OF value contains an integer value plus **either** a boolean or a null value. But in the sort into ascending order of tag, a boolean value would come before an integer value but a null value after it. Thus depending on which value of field2 is chosen, it may appear before or after the value of field1! In CER, a slightly more complicated algorithm applies, which says that the maximum tag that appears in any value of field2 is the NULL tag, and that it determines the position of field 2 no matter what value is actually being sent. This is marginally more difficult to explain and perhaps understand, but avoids having to do a sort at encode time.

16.3.13 Handling of OPTIONAL and DEFAULT Elements in SEQUENCE and SET

There are no problems caused by OPTIONAL (the use of tags makes it unambiguous what has been included and what has not). However, in the case of DEFAULT, BER leaves it as a sender's option whether to omit a default value (implying possibly complex checking that it **is** the default value), or whether to encode it anyway!

Again, this gives DER and CER problems to remove this encoder's option. In this case they both require that an element whose value equals the default value be **omitted**, no matter how complicated the check might be. (However, in practice, DEFAULT is normally applied only to elements that are very simple types, rarely to elements that are complex structured sequences and sets.)

> The TLV approach was designed to make handling of OPTIONAL easy. No surprises here. The handling of DEFAULT again raises issues of encoder's options and problems in distinguished/canonical encoding rules.

When we discuss PER more fully in the next chapter, however, we find that PER specifies mandatory omission for "simple types" (which it lists) and a sender's option otherwise, avoiding verbosity and options in common cases, but avoiding implementation complexity in the other cases.

16.3.14 Encoding OBJECT IDENTIFIER Values

The value is basically a sequence of integers, but we need a more compact encoding than using "SEQUENCE OF INTEGER". The "more bit" concept comes in again here, but with a curious (and nasty) optimization for the top two arcs.

Figure 16.9 is a repeat of Figure 15.1, and shows a part of the object identifier tree.

Object identifier values are paths down this tree from the root to a leaf, and one such path is defined by

```
{iso(1) standard(0) 8571 abstract-syntax(2)}
```

but the only information that is encoded is a value of

```
{1 0 8571 2}
```

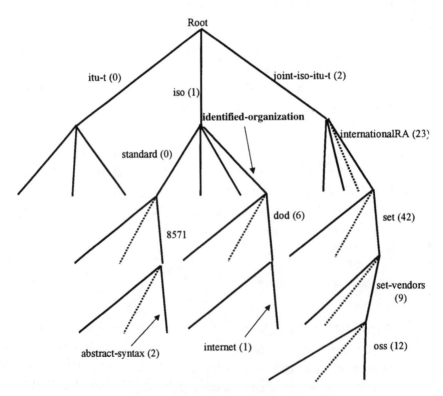

Figure 16.9   A small part of the object identifier tree.

This could in theory be carried by an encoding of "SEQUENCE OF INTEGER", but the presence of T and L fields for each integer value makes this rather verbose, and a different (ad hoc) encoding is specified.

The "more bit" concept (also used in the encoding of tags—see Figure 16.3) is used. For each object identifier component (the values 1, 0, 8571 and 2), we encode it as a positive integer value into the minimum necessary number of bits (the standard requires that the minimum multiple of seven bits is used), then place those bits into octets using only the least significant seven bits of each octet (most significant octet first). Bit 8 (most significant) of the last octet is set to 0, earlier bit 8 values (the "more" bit) are set to 1.

The result of encoding

```
ftam-oid OBJECT IDENTIFER ::= {1 0 8571 2}
```

would be (in hex):

```
                 T        L
ftam-oid:        06       05        01   00   C27B   02
```

However, the actual encoding of this object identifier value is

```
                 T        L
                 06       04        28 C27B 02
```

How come?

A dirty trick was played—and like most dirty tricks, it caused problems later.

The octets encoding the first two arcs were (in 1986) thought to be unlikely ever to have large values, and that using two octets for these two arcs was "a bad thing". So an "optimization" (mandatory) was introduced.

We can take the top two arcs of Figure 16.9 and "overlay" them with the dotted arcs shown in Figure 16.10, producing a single (pseudo-) arc from the root to each second level node. How to number these pseudo-arcs?

There are three top-level arcs, and we can accommodate encodings for up to 128 arcs (0 to 127) in a single octet with the "more bit" concept as already described. And 128 divided by 3 is about 40! We will assume the first two top-level arcs will never have more than 40 subarcs, and allocate the first 40 pseudo-arcs to top-level arc 0, the next 40 to top-level arc 1, and the remainder to top-level arc 2.

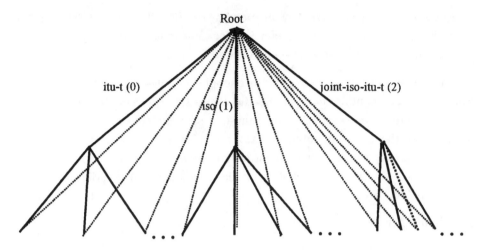

Figure 16.10   Making the top two arcs into a single arc.

The assumption here is that there will never be more than 40 arcs beneath top-level 0 (ccitt—as it was in 1986) and 1 (iso), but that there could be more beneath top-level 2 (joint-iso-ccitt), in which case a multi-octet representation for the pseudo-arc would be needed.

Then for any second level arc beneath top-level arc 0 we use the second level arc number as the number for the pseudo-arc. For any second-level arc beneath top-level arc 1 we use the second level arc number plus 40 as the number for the pseudo-arc; for any second-level arc beneath top-level arc 2 we use the second level arc number plus 80 as the number for the pseudo-arc.

We then obtain the encoding of {1 0 8571 2} as

```
        T        L
        06       04       28 C27B 02
```

as described earlier.

As was pointed out, where you are "hung" on the object identifier tree is unimportant, except that your object identifiers will be longer the lower down you are. In mid-1995 this surfaced as an issue, with other major international players wanting top-level arcs. This "fudge" with the top two arcs makes it difficult (not impossible, but difficult) to add new top-level arcs, and to alleviate this problem the RELATIVE-OID constructor was proposed for addition to ASN.1.

If an organization has the need to allocate object identifiers beneath a root such as:

```
{joint-iso-itu-t(2)  internationalRA(2) set(42)}
```

and has a protocol that is specifically designed to carry (always or commonly) object identifier values beneath this root, then it can define

```
SET-OIDs ::= RELATI E OID
                -- Relative to{2  2  42}
```

and use that type in its protocol, either alone or as a CHOICE of that and a normal OBJECT IDENTIFIER.

A relative object identifier type is only capable of carrying object identifier values that hang below a known node (in this case {2 2 42}), but the encoding of the value encodes only the object identifier components **after** {2 2 42}, saving in this case two octets.

The saving can be more significant in PER, where encodings are generally smaller anyway. In the case of Secure Electronic Transactions (SET), getting ASN.1 encodings of certificates down to a size that will fit easily on a smart card posed some challenges, and the use of PER and the relative object identifier technique was important.

At the time of going to press, the RELATIVE-OID work was not finalized, so do check details with the latest standard. (And/or look for errata sheets for this book on the Web site listed in Appendix 5).

16.3.15 Encoding Character String Values

The character string types (as with the time types described in 16.3.16) are encoded by reference to other standards. A more detailed description of these character set standards is included in Section IV, but the basic characteristics of each encoding are described here.

> Here's where you have to go out and buy additional specifications—almost all the character string encodings are by reference to other specifications.

There is probably more text in this book than in the ASN.1 Standard itself!

Starting with the simplest character string types—NumericString, PrintableString, VisibleString, and GraphicString—the contents octets of these are just the ASCII encoding of the characters.

The next group is TeletexString, VideotexString, GraphicString and GeneralString. These have encodings whose structure is specified in ISO 2022, using "escape sequences" specified for each Register Entry in the International Register to "designate and invoke" that register entry. After the appropriate escape sequence, subsequent 8-bit encodings reference characters from that register entry until the next escape sequence occurs. It is important to note that there are many characters that appear in multiple register entries, so there are frequently many encodings for a given character string. It is also theoretically possible to have a succession of escape sequences, each one overriding the last, with no intervening character encoding. In the distinguished/canonical encoding rules, all these options are eliminated.

The next two character set types to consider are UniversalString and BMPString. UniversalString supports all the characters of ISO 10646 (the most recent character code standard, using 32 bits per character in the encoding. BMPString supports only those characters in the "Basic Multilingual Plane" (sufficient for all normal earthly activity!), which also corresponds to the "Unicode" character set, using 16 bits per character.

Finally, UTF8String uses a variable number of octets per character (from one for the ASCII characters to a maximum of six octets). None of the octets in a UTF8String encoding have the top bit set to zero unless they are the (single octet) encoding of an ASCII character. The encoding of octets that form a single character always start with "10" unless they are the first octet of the encoding of a character, so even if you start at a random point in the middle of an encoding, you can easily identify the start of the next character encoding.

A UTF8 encoding of a character has an "initial octet" that either starts with a "0" bit (in which case we have a single octet ASCII encoding), or starts with two to six one bits followed by a zero bit. Remaining bits in this first octet are available to identify the character. The number of one bits gives the number of octets being used to encode the character. Each subsequent octet has the top two bits set to "10", and the remaining six bits are available to identify the character. The character is identified by its number in the ISO 10646 32-bit coding scheme, which is encoded into the available bits (right justified), using the minimum number of octets necessary. Thus characters with values less than two to the power 11 (which is all "European" characters) will encode into two octets, and characters with values less than two to the power 16 will encode into three characters, and so on.

Some examples of UTF8 encodings of characters are given in Figure 16.11 as hex representations.

```
Name of character        Unicode/10646 number    Encoding in binary
LATIN CAPITAL LETTER H                    72      01001000
LATIN DIGIT ZERO                          48      00110000
LATIN CAPITAL LETTER C WITH CEDILLA      199      11000011 10000111
GREEK CAPITAL LETTER BETA                914      11001110 10010010
CYRILLIC CAPITAL LETTER EN              1053      11010000 10011101
ARABIC LETTER BEHEH                     1664      11011010 10000000
KATAKANA LETTER KA                     12459      11100001 10100001 10101011
```

Figure 16.11   Some examples of UTF8 encodings.

16.3.16 Encoding Values of the Time Types

The time types are specified as strings of characters, and their encoding is simply the ASCII encoding of those characters.

There were problems with the precision of GeneralizedTime. The actual referenced standard is ISO 3307, which from its first edition in 1975 permitted seconds to have any number of decimal places. But somehow some parts of the ASN.1 implementor community operated under the impression that the precision was limited to milliseconds, and would not accept values to a greater precision.

> Simply an ASCII encoding of the characters. But watch out for issues of precision in the distinguished/canonical rules.

There are also issues with what is the precise set of abstract values. The ASN.1 specification states that GeneralizedTime allows the representation of times to a variety of precisions. So, for example, is a time of:

> "199205201221.00Z"

the same abstract value as

> "199205201221.0Z"

If so, then the canonical and distinguished encoding rules should forbid one or the other encoding (or even both!). But if it is regarded that different precisions are different abstract values (and may carry different semantics), then all such encodings need to be allowed in the canonical and distinguished encoding rules.

The eventual ruling was that the implied precision by the inclusion of trailing zeros was not a primary part of the abstract value, and that in the distinguished and canonical encoding rules trailing zeros should be **forbidden**—a time to an implied precision of 1/100 s is the same time (abstract value) as one to an implied precision of 1/10 s, and should not carry different semantics, and should have the same encoding in the distinguished and canonical encoding rules.

> Most of the more complex types are defined as ASN.1 SEQUENCE types, and their values encode by encoding values of those sequence types.

16.4 Encodings for More Complex Constructions

16.4.1 Open Types

ASN.1 has had the concept of "holes" from its inception, originally described as a type called "ANY", and later as a so-called "open type" specified with syntax looking like:

```
OPERATOR.&Type
```

and which states that the type that will fill this field is the value of some ASN.1 type that is assigned to the &Type field of an information object of the OPERATOR class (see Chapter 13).

BER handles open types very simply: What eventually fills this field has to be an ASN.1 type, and the encoding of the field is simply the encoding of a value of that type.

Remember that in BER there is a strict TLV structure, so it is always possible to find the end of a BER TLV encoding without any knowledge of the actual type being encoded. In the case of an open type, the identification of that type may appear later in the encoding than the occurrence of the encoding of a value of the type. That gives no problem in BER, because the TLV structure is independent of the type.

16.4.2 The EMBEDDED PDV Type and the EXTERNAL Type

As described in Section II, these are slightly obscure names for ASN.1 types, but the "embedded" means that here we have foreign (non-ASN.1-defined) material embedded in an ASN.1 type, and the "external" means more or less the same thing—material external to ASN.1 is being embedded.

Historically, EXTERNAL came first, and EMBEDDED PDV was added in 1994 with slightly greater functionality (new specifications should always use EMBEDDED PDV, not EXTERNAL).

Both these types have "associated types", which are sequence types, and which have fields capable of carrying all the semantics of the type. Broadly, this is the encoding of some material (carried as a bit string in the most general case) and identification (using one object identifier in the case of EXTERNAL and zero to two in the case of EMBEDDED PDV) of the abstract and transfer syntax for the encoding in the bit string. (There is some slight additional complexity as a result of the inclusion of options that apply when the encodings are transferred over an OSI Presentation Layer protocol, but this does not affect the encoding in the non-OSI case.) The BER encoding is simply defined as the encoding of these "associated types".

16.4.3 The INSTANCE OF Type

The INSTANCE OF type provides a very simplified version of EXTERNAL or EMBEDDED PDV, designed specifically for the case where what we want to put into our "hole" is a (single) object identifier to identify the (ASN.1) type whose value is encoded into the "hole", followed by a value of that ASN.1 type. This type relates to the built-in very simple information object class TYPE-IDENTIFIER described in Section II.

It is encoded as a SEQUENCE type with just two fields—an object identifier and the value of an ASN.1 type (as an open type).

16.4.4 The CHARACTER STRING Type

The CHARACTER STRING type was introduced in 1994, and is almost identical to EMBEDDED PDV in its encoding. The idea here is that we have the value of a character string (from some repertoire identified by a character abstract syntax object identifier) encoded according to a character transfer syntax object identifier. Thus we have essentially an encoding of a sequence comprising zero to two object identifiers (as with EMBEDDED PDV, there are options where either or both object identifiers take fixed values determined by the protocol specification and which, therefore, do not need to be encoded), followed by the encoding of the actual characters in the string.

16.5 Conclusion

The ASN.1 specification of BER is just 17 pages long—fewer pages than this chapter! (Ignoring the Annexes and details of DER and CER.) The inter-

> Now you know all there is to know about BER—just go and read the specification and see!

ested reader should now have no problems in understanding the specification. Go away and read it!

## CHAPTER 17

The Packed Encoding Rules

(Or: Encodings for the New Millennium—as Good as You Will Get—for Now!)

Summary

This chapter provides details of the Packed Encoding Rules. It has two main parts. In the first part further details are given of some of the global features of PER and the terminology employed in the actual specification. In this first part we cover

- the overall structure of a PER encoding and the terminology used (preamble, length determinant, contents), with discussion of the four variants of PER,

- the general nature of encodings for extensible types,

- PER-visible constraints,

- effective size and alphabet constraints,

- canonical order of tags, and the use of this ordering,

- the form of a general length field, when needed, and

- the OPTIONAL bit-map and the CHOICE index (for extensible and nonextensible choices).

The second part gives details of the encodings of each ASN.1 type in much the same way as was done for BER in the previous chapter. The order is again chosen in a way that moves from the simpler to the slightly more complex encodings. We cover the encodings of

- NULL and BOOLEAN values,

- INTEGER values,

- ENUMERATED values,

- length determinants of strings,

- character string values,

- encoding of SEQUENCE and SET,

- encoding of SEQUENCE OF and SET OF,

- encoding of REAL and OBJECT IDENTIFIER, and

- encoding of the remaining types (GeneralizedTime, UTCTime, ObjectDescriptor, and types defined using the "ValueSet" notation).

Most of these later topics are covered by simply giving examples, as they follow the general approaches that are fully covered in the first part of this chapter.

17.1 Introduction

The principles underlying PER encodings (no encoding of tags, use of a bit-map for OPTIONAL, use of a CHOICE index, and the sorting of SET elements and CHOICE alternatives into tag order have already been introduced in Chapter 15 of this section. In this chapter we complete the detail.

The latter part of this chapter provides examples of all the encodings, and gives some further explanation where needed.

> You have already learned the principles of PER encodings, now for the details.

This chapter is not totally free-standing. It is assumed that the reader will have read the relevant parts of Chapter 15 before starting on this chapter, but there are also a number of cases where PER codings are the same as BER (or more usually CER/DER) encodings, and in such cases reference is made to Chapter 16.

The bit-numbering and diagram convention (first octet of the encoding shown on the left, bits numbered with 8 as the most significant and shown on the left) that was used for BER is used here also.

However, with PER there are sometimes padding bits inserted to produce octet alignment at the start of some field. Where padding bits may have to be inserted (depending on the current bit position within an octet, there may be anything from zero to seven padding bits), a capital "P" is used at the start of the field in the examples given in this chapter.

17.2 Structure of a PER Encoding

17.2.1 General Form

You will already know that PER does not necessarily encode into fields that are a multiple of eight bits, but the BER concept of encodings of (for example) SEQUENCE, being some up-front header followed by the complete encodings of each element also applies to PER.

> It sounds a bit like BER—preamble, length determinant, contents. But don't be misled. Much of the time all we have are contents!

In the case of PER, the "header" is called the **preamble**, but is present for SEQUENCE only if there are optional elements; otherwise it is null and we have simply the encoding of each element.

There is also a difference in the "L" part of an encoding from BER. Once again, it can frequently be missing (whenever the length is known in advance in fact), but also the terminology changes to "length determinant". This change was made because while the length octets of BER are always a count of octets (apart from the indefinite form), in PER the length determinant encodes a value that may be

- a count of octets (as in BER), or

- a count of bits (used for the length of an unconstrained BIT STRING value), or

- a count of **iterations** (used to determine the length of a SEQUENCE OF or SET OF value).

It is also the case that in PER the length determinant is not necessarily an integral multiple of eight bits.

The precise form and encoding of a length determinant is described later.

Each of the three pieces of encoding encode into what is called a **bit-field**. The length of this bit-field is either statically determinable from the type definition, or that part of the encoding will be preceded by a length-determinant encoding. The term "bit-field" is used to imply that the field is not necessarily an integral multiple of eight bits, nor, in general, is the field required to start on an octet boundary.

As we proceed through the encoding of a value of a large and complex structured type, we generate a succession of bit-fields. At the end of the encoding, these are simply placed end-to-end (in order), ignoring octet boundaries, to produce the complete encoding of the value.

17.2.2 Partial Octet Alignment and PER Variants

There are a couple of further wrinkles on the overall structure, of which this is the first!

There are some fields where the designers of PER felt that it would be more sensible to ensure that the field started on an octet boundary (for simplicity of implementation and minimization of CPU cycles). Fields to which this applies can be identified from the type definition (and do not depend on the particular value being transmitted). Such cases are said to encode into **octet-aligned-bit-fields**. In the final concatenation of bit-fields, **padding bits** are inserted as necessary before any octet-aligned bit-fields to ensure that they start at a multiple of eight bits from the start of the entire encoding of the outer-level type—the message, or "protocol data unit" (PDU).

> Horses for courses! The ALIGNED variant of PER makes pragmatic judgments on when to pad to an octet boundary for fields. The UNALIGNED version is for those who say "bandwidth is all that matters!"

There are some applications (air traffic control is one) where the padding bits are not wanted—minimizing bandwidth is considered the primary need. There are therefore formally two **variants** of PER. They are

- the ALIGNED variant (with padding bits), and

- the UNALIGNED variant (with no padding bits, and with some other bandwidth-reduction features that will be described later).

17.2.3 Canonical Encodings

This is another area that gives rise to further encoding rules within the general PER family.

Notice that while BER has many encoder options, leading to the production of specifications for CER and DER, PER avoids options in the basic encoding, and looks at first sight to be canonical. (It is certainly far more canonical than BER!)

However, to produce truly canonical encodings (as with BER) requires a sort of SET OF elements, and adds complexity to encoding character string types like GeneralString and GraphicString. So-called BASIC-PER (with both ALIGNED and UNALIGNED variants) does not do this, and produces canonical encodings ONLY if these types are not involved. CANONICAL-PER (with an ALIGNED and an UNALIGNED variant) is fully canonical, and introduces sorting of SET OF and special rules for GeneralString, etc. The actual rules are exactly the same (and are specified by reference) as those used to turn BER into CER.

> BASIC-PER is largely canonical, but there are some types (SET OF, some character string types, time types, and some occurrences of DEFAULT) where being 100% canonical is "expensive". So BASIC-PER (being pragmatic!) has noncanonical encodings for these types. CANONICAL-PER is fully canonical.

17.2.4 The Outer-Level Complete Encoding

Another slight complication arises at the outer level of a complete encoding (the total message being sent down the line). (This is a pretty detailed point, and unless you are heavily involved in producing encodings you can skip to 17.3.)

There are a few theoretical cases where a message may encode into **zero** bits with PER. This would occur, for example, with an outer-level type of NULL, or of a SET OF constrained to have zero iterations (both are highly unlikely to occur in practice, but ...!).

> Unless you are a hand-encoder, skip this. Suffice to say that all PER encodings of "outer-level" types—complete messages—are a multiple of eight bits, and at least one octet long.

The problem here is that if the way a carrier protocol is used allows multiple values of that type to be placed into the carrier, a multiple of zero bits is still zero bits, and the receiver would not know how many values had been sent, even with complete knowledge of the type definition!

So PER requires that if the complete encoding of the outer-level type is zero bits (which would mean that the outer-level type contains only one abstract value), then a single one-bit is used for that encoding instead.

Finally, recognizing that carrier protocols often provide "buckets" that are only able to contain multiples of eight bits, PER specifies that the complete encoding should always be padded at the end with zero bits to produce an integral multiple of eight bits. (Again, this is to ensure that there is no doubt at the decoding end about the number of values that have been encoded into the octet bucket that the carrier uses to convey the PER encoding from encoder to decoder.)

Thus the minimum size of a complete outer-level PER encoding is one octet, and it is always a multiple of eight bits, but individual component parts are generally not a multiple of eight bits, and may be zero bits.

17.3 Encoding Values of Extensible Types

PER has a uniform approach to extensibility. Refer in what follows to Figure 17.1 for an illustration of the encoding of extensible INTEGER and string values, to Figure 17.2 for an illustration of the encoding of extensible SET and SEQUENCE values, to Figure 17.3 for an illustration of the encoding of extensible CHOICE val-

> PER is consistent: An extensible type has one bit up front indicating whether the value being encoded is in the root. If so, it encodes "normally". Otherwise, there is a special encoding.

ues, and to Figure 17.4 for an illustration of the encoding of extensible ENUMERATED values.

Any type (a constrained INTEGER, a constrained string, a SEQUENCE, a SET, a CHOICE, or an ENUMERATED) that has an extensibility marker (the ellipsis) in its type definition or in a PER-visible constraint has a value of that type encoded as follows:

- there is a one-bit-long bit-field encoded up front—the **extensions bit,**

```
Either:
                  0
followed by:
                  An encoding of a value of the type, which
                  is the same as that for the type without
                  an extensibility marker or extensions.
Or:
                  1
followed by:
                  An encoding for a value of the extensible type
                  which is outside the root, which is the same as
                  that for values of the unconstrained type.
```

Figure 17.1 Extensible constrained INTEGER or string encodings.

Either:

    0

followed by:

An encoding of a value of the type, which
is the same as that for the type without
an extensibility marker or extensions.

Or:

    1

followed by:

An encoding as for 0, but with a special
encoding for the extensions, inserted at
the insertion point.

Figure 17.2   Extensible SET or SEQUENCE type encodings.

- the extensions bit is set to zero if the value being encoded is in the root (one of the original INTEGER or ENUMERATED values, or a SET or SEQUENCE value in which all extension additions—if any—are absent),

- the extensions bit is set to one otherwise (values outside the root), and

- if the "extensions bit" is set to zero, what follows is **exactly** the same encoding (for **all** types that can be marked extensible) as if the extension marker (and all extensions) was absent.

If the "extensions bit" is set to one, the following encoding is sometimes the same as for the unconstrained type, but sometimes different, as follows:

- if the "extensions bit" is set to one when encoding an extensible INTEGER or extensible string, what follows is an encoding that is the same as for a value of the unconstrained type;

- if the "extensions bit" is set to one when encoding a SEQUENCE or SET value, what follows is the encoding of the elements that are in the root, with a special encoding (see 17.15.2) inserted at the insertion point to carry the values of elements outside the root (and to identify their presence);

- if the "extensions bit" is set to one when encoding a CHOICE value, what follows is a special encoding of the choice index (recognizing that although theoretically unbounded, the value will usually be small), followed by an

NOTE

Only implementations of versions greater than 1 will set the extensions bit to one, but all implementations may encode a root value, and hence set the extensions bit to zero.

g Φ ctsell

.ng of the choice index (identifying
ative which is present in the
ich is the same as that for the
but an extensibility marker.

.ng of a value of the chosen
e within the root.

: encoding for the choice index,
g an alternative outside the root).

g of a value of the chosen
that is outside the root.

Figure 17.3   Extensible CHOICE encodings.

encoding of the chosen alternative. (See 17.8.2 for the encoding of a "normally small whole number".)

- if the "extensions bit" is set to one when encoding an ENUMERATED value, the same encoding is used as for the choice index, because again the value is theoretically unbounded, but in practice it will usually be small.

It will be seen from the preceding that the only cost in version 1 of including an extensibility marker is 1 bit (possibly causing the insertion of up to seven padding bits after it). We will see later that if the type actually has extensions, and values outside the root are encoded, we generally get an additional overhead of a length field for such values.

The encoding for values of extensible types that lie outside the root is described in the following text after the description of the encoding for types that were not defined to be extensible (and for values of extensible types that are within the root).

It will be clear from the preceding description that encoders and decoders must agree on whether or not a type is extensible, and if so, on precisely which abstract values are in the root. Where a type has an ellipsis as a direct part of the type definition—SET, SEQUENCE, CHOICE, ENUMERATED, there is little problem. But where a type such as integer or a character string is constrained with a constraint that contains an ellipsis, the situation is (perhaps surprisingly!) not so clear cut, and the

Either:

        0

followed by:

        An encoding of a value of the type, which
        is the same as that for the type without
        an extensibility marker or extensions.

Or:

        1

followed by:

        An encoding for a value of the extensible
        type which is outside the root.

Figure 17.4   Extensible ENUMERATED type encodings.

type may well be declared to be **not** extensible for PER encodings, despite the clear presence of an ellipsis! This area is discussed at the end of the discussion on PER-visible constraints.

17.4 PER-Visible Constraints

17.4.1 The Concept

PER-visible constraints are constraints that PER uses to produce less verbose encodings—for example—INTEGER (0..7) encodes into just three bits because the (0..7) constraint is PER-visible. BER ignores all constraints, and hence always needs a length field. PER takes a pragmatic view and uses constraints that are "easily" used and produce important bandwidth gains, but ignores other more complex constraints.

Crucial to understanding PER-encodings is the concept of **PER-visible constraints**. These are (subtype) constraints, which, if present, affect the encoding of the parent type.

The most important PER-visible constraints are those placed on the INTEGER type and on the lengths of strings (or on iteration counts for SET OF and SEQUENCE OF). There are also constraints on the alphabet of some character string types that are PER-visible (see 17.6), and can reduce the number of bits per character for these character strings.

Constraints that are PER-visible in the preceding cases are quite widely defined. They may be applied "a bit at a time", through repeated use of type references, or they may be applied through the use of parameterization. Or they may be extremely complicated subtype specifications involving included subtype constraints, intersections, and unions.

There are two comments to make on this: first, most specifications are pretty simple, so hand-coders do not have to do too much work to calculate the actual constraint in the real world; second, an ASN.1 compiler has no problems in resolving such expressions of arbitrary generality down to a precise record of the permitted values for the integer type, the length of the string, etc.

17.4.2 The Effect of Variable Parameters

One major exception to PER-visibility is if, in trying to determine the actual constraint, a **variable parameter** (a parameter that still does not have a value when the abstract syntax is defined) is **textually** referenced in the resolution of the actual constraint, then the constraint ceases to be PER-visible, and would encode as if that constraint were not present.

> Presence of a variable parameter in a constraint means that PER totally ignores that entire constraint.

This is the first of several cases where a type that is formally extensible encodes as if it was not extensible. In this case, it contains an ellipsis in a constraint that is not PER-visible, so (assuming no other constraints have been applied) it will encode as not extensible and not constrained.

Variable parameters are still not heavily used, so this is not too big an issue, but the term **textually** in the preceding text refers to the possibility of constructing union and intersection expressions that appear to use the value of such a parameter, but where the actual result of the expression evaluation proves to be the same no matter what the value the variable parameter might have. Even if the parameter does not affect the result, its textual presence kicks the constraint out of court. This was done to ease implementation efforts for compilers, and to avoid possible errors in hand-encoding.

17.4.3 Character Strings with Variable Length Encodings

Another major exception to PER-visibility that should be noted is that a constraint on the length of a character string applies to the number of (abstract) characters that can appear in the string. If the encoding is something like UTF8 (or GeneralString), where the number of octets needed to

> Keeping it simple again—PER ignores length constraints unless each character encodes into the same number of bits.

encode each character is different for different characters (and in the case of

GeneralString can depend on encoder options), the length constraint is not much help at the encoding level—a length field is still needed in order to find the end of the encoding.

(The preceding statement is not strictly true. If the itty-gritty details of an encoding scheme such as UTF8 are fully understood, then knowledge of the number of abstract characters being encoded is in fact sufficient to find the end of the encoding, but PER wants a decoder to be able to find the end of the encoding without resorting to such detailed analysis.)

Character set types that have a fixed number of octets for each abstract character are called **known multiplier types,** and length constraints on such types are PER-visible (and will give rise to reduced or eliminated length encodings). For character string types that are not "known multiplier types", the constraints are not PER-visible (do not affect the encoding of values of the type), and any extension markers in these constraints are ignored for the purpose of PER encodings.

> Real specifications are rarely complicated in the constraints that they apply, but specifications of encoding rules have to consider all permitted syntax. This section really IS only for the intellectually curious!

17.4.4 Now Let Us Get Complicated!

This book is called "ASN.1 Complete", so we had better explore PER-visibility and extensibility a bit more.

First, we note that there are a number of different sorts of subtype constraint that may be used alone, but which in the general case combine together using EXCEPT, INTERSECTION, and UNION. We call the basic building blocks **component constraints,** and the complete constraint the **outer-level constraint.** Both component constraints and outer-level constraints may contain an ellipsis!

Whether a component constraint is PER-visible will depend in general on the sort of component constraint it is, and on the type being constrained. Figure 17.5 gives a list.

Two important points to note from Figure 17.5 are that a single-value constraint is only visible if applied to INTEGER, and a contained subtype constraint is always visible. This can give rise to some distinctly nonobvious effects in relation to known-multiplier character string types such as IA5String! Suppose we have

Variable constraint   Never visible.

Single value constraint   Visible for INTEGER only.

Contained subtype constraint Always visible.

Value range   Visible for INTEGER only
              and in an alphabet constraint
              on a known-multiplier character
              string type.

Size constraint   Visible for OCTET STRING, SET and
              SEQUENCE OF, and known-multiplier
              character string types.

Permitted alphabet   Visible for known-multiplier.
              character string types.

Inner subtyping   Never visible.

Figure 17.5 PER-visibility of constraints.

```
Subtype ::= IA5String ("abcd" UNION "abc" UNION SIZE(2))

MyString ::= IA5String (Subtype INTERSECTION SIZE(3))
```

In MyString, all the component constraints are PER-visible, and we expect to be able to work out the outer-level constraint. In Subtype, the first two component constraints are not PER-visible but the third is PER-visible. What is the effect on Subtype and on MyString? This question, and a number of related ones produced some lengthy discussion within the ASN.1 group

> An outer-level constraint is only PER-visible if all of its component constraints are PER-visible.

with "keep it simple" colliding to some extent with "keep it general and intuitive".

The first important rule is that if **any** component constraint is not PER-visible, then the entire outer-level constraint is declared to be not PER-visible, and will not affect the encoding. Notice here that if there is an ellipsis in either a component or in the outer-level constraint, because we are ignoring the entire constraint, the type is NOT encoded as an extensible type. So Subtype in the preceding example is treated by PER as **unconstrained,** and contributes all abstract values of an unconstrained IA5String in the set arithmetic for MyString.

For MyString, all component constraints are PER-visible, so the SIZE(3) applies, and values of the string encode as if it contained all possible abstract values of length 3.

There is one additional rule related to the use of the ellipsis. When performing set arithmetic to determine whether a PER-encoding is extensible and what values are in the root, all ellipsis marks (and any actual additions) in a component constraint (or any of the component constraints of that component—such as Subtype in the preceding example) are **ignored.** A constrained type is extensible for PER-encodings if and only if an ellipsis appears at the outer level of a constraint, all of whose component constraints are PER-visible. This is simple, but perhaps not quite what you might have expected.

> A constrained type is only extensible for PER-encoding if the ellipsis appears at the outer level of the constraint.

Now consider a version 2 specification, where the constraint in version 1 was PER-visible, but in version 2 things (such as a single-value constraint) are added that would normally wreck PER-visibility. This does not (and can not be allowed to) affect PER-visibility of the original version-1 constraint, otherwise interworking would be prejudiced. So it is only those parts of a constraint that appear in the root that affect PER-visibility (and that affect the way a value is encoded).

But as someone once said, "Such contorted constraint specifications only ever appear in discussions within the ASN.1 group, never in real user specifications." And he (it *was* a he) is correct!

17.5 Encoding INTEGERs—Preparatory Discussion

> It's the largest and smallest values that matter. Gaps in between do not affect the encoding.

What matters for a PER-encoding of the INTEGER type (and of the lengths of known-multiplier character strings) is not the actual values, but the **range** of values permitted by PER-visible constraints. It is the largest and smallest value that matter. An integer constrained to have only the two values 0 and 7 will still encode in **three** bits, not two. What matters is the range, **not** the number of values.

Figure 17.6 illustrates some simple constraints that are PER-visible, and the values that PER assumes need encoding.

For any integer that has a lower bound (and similarly for the lengths of strings), what is encoded in the PER-encoding is the offset from the lower bound. Thus the encoding of values of SET3 in Figure 17.6 would use only 2 bits.

```
Type definition                              Values assumed to need encoding
    INTEGER (0..7)                                      0 to  7
    INTEGER (0 UNION 7)                                 0 to  7
    SET1 ::= INTEGER (15..31)                          15 to 31
    SET2 ::= INTEGER (0..18)                            0 to 18
    SET3 ::= INTEGER (SET1 INTERSECTION SET2)          15 to 18
    SET (SIZE (0..3)) OF INTEGER   Iteration count      0 to  3
    INTEGER (1 UNION 3 UNION 5 UNION 7)                 1 to  7
```

Figure 17.6   Values assumed to need encoding.

When we look at the encoding of integers (and of the lengths of strings) we will see that there are three distinct cases:

- we have a finite upper and lower bound (called a **constrained value**);

- we have a finite lower bound, but no upper bound (called a **semiconstrained value**);

- we do not have a lower bound (this can not occur for the length of strings, as zero is always a lower bound); this is called an unconstrained value (even if there is a defined upper bound!—the upper bound is ignored in this case).

We describe in what follows the encoding of constrained, semiconstrained, and unconstrained integers, and of constrained and semiconstrained lengths of strings in subsequent text, also addressing any special encodings that arise in the case of an extensible type. In the case of a constrained integer (or length), there are several different encodings depending on the range permitted by the constraint. (Remember that the absolute values permitted do not matter.)

The reader may wonder whether it is worth bothering with using "range" (and off-set from the lower bound), rather than just determining the coding based on whether or not negative values are allowed or not, and then using enough bits to handle the largest value permitted by the constraint. Certainly INTEGER (10..13) and INTEGER (-3..0) are not likely to occur in the real world! But INTEGER (1..4) may be more common, and will use just two bits with the "offset-from-lower-bound" rule, rather than three if we encoded the actual values.

Working with "offset from lower bound" may appear to be an additional complexity, but this is actually simpler than a specification saying "First see if all allowed values are positive or not, then etc. etc.", and amounts to just a couple of orders in a couple of places in actual implementations.

17.6 Effective Size and Alphabet Constraints

17.6.1 Statement of the Problem

We have already mentioned (but did not emphasize) that constraints such as

```
MyString ::= PrintableString (FROM ( ("0" .."9")

                                      UNION ("#")

                                      UNION ("*") ) )
```

are PER-visible, and would result in just four bits per character for the encoding of values of "MyString" (which consists of all strings that contain only zero to nine and hash and star—twelve characters).

This is described more fully in the discussion of the encoding of character string values in 17.14, but note here that for alphabet constraints, what matters is the actual **number** of characters permitted, not the **range** of characters. This is different from the treatment of constrained integers, as the need to define a character string type with an almost random selection of characters being permitted is far more likely to arise than the need to define an integer type with a random selection of integer values.

There is, however, a slightly difficult interaction between alphabet constraints such as that in the preceding example and length (size) constraints that can also be applied.

For example, consider

```
MyString1 ::= IA5String (FROM ("01") INTERSECTION SIZE (4) )

MyString2 ::= IA5String (FROM ("TF") INTERSECTION SIZE (6) )

MyString3 ::= IA5String (Mystring1 UNION Mystring2)
```

All constraints are PER-visible, and it is clear that MyString1 has a fixed length of 4 characters and thus should encode without a length field, and it contains only two characters "0" and "1", and should encode with just one bit per character. Similarly, MyString2 has an alphabet constraint restricting its character set to "T" and "F" (again giving one bit per character), and a size constraint of 6.

But what is the alphabet and size constraint on MyString3? Does it have them? This is where the concept of an **effective size constraint** and an **effective alphabet constraint** enters.

17.6.2 Effective Size Constraint

An "effective size constraint" is defined to be a single size constraint such that a length is permitted by that size constraint if and only if there is at least one abstract value in the constrained type that has that length.

So in the earlier example, MyString3 has abstract values of length 4 and 6 only. But what matters is the range of a size constraint, which is 4 to 6. This is equivalent to 0 to 2 when we remove the lower bound, so the length field of MyString3 would encode with 2 bits.

17.6.3 Effective Alphabet Constraint

In an exactly equivalent fashion, an "effective alphabet constraint" is defined to be a single permitted alphabet constraint such that a character is permitted by that alphabet constraint if and only if there is at least one abstract value in the constrained type that contains somewhere within it that character.

In the earlier example, all the characters "0", "1", "T" and "F" are used by at least one abstract value, and the effective alphabet constraint allows these (and only these) characters; so two bits will be used per character.

It is normally a simple matter for both a human and a computer to work out the effective alphabet and effective size constraints in every case, provided the rules on what is PER-visible are understood and applied.

This is particularly true for a human because constraints are in practice quite simple. For a computer (which in an ASN.1 tool needs to be programmed to handle all possible constraints, no matter how complex or extreme), a program can be written that can take any arbitrarily complex set arithmetic expression (using only size and alphabet constraints) and resolve it down to an effective alphabet and an effective size constraint. It does this using equalities such as

        A EXCEPT B   equals   A INTERSECTION (NOT B)

and

        NOT (A UNION B) equals (NOT A) INTERSECTION (NOT B)

etc.

If single-value constraints had been allowed on character string types, this would have been a much more difficult task.

17.7 Canonical Order of Tags

The reader will recall that PER requires a choice index, which means numbering the alternatives in a CHOICE in some order. Similarly, it avoids the need to encode a tag with elements of a SET by determining a fixed order for transmission of values of those elements.

> We define an ordering of tags that lets us place any collection of types with distinct outer-level tags into an order known by both encoder and decoder, and use that order for encoding choices and sets.

It would have been possible to have used the textual order of the alternatives and elements for this purpose, but this was felt to be inappropriate, as any change in the textual order (perhaps in going from version 1 to version 2, for purely editorial reasons) would change the encoding on the line. Essentially, such a change of order would have to be forbidden, which was felt to be counterintuitive.

As all alternatives in a CHOICE and all elements in a SET are already required to have distinct (outer-level) tags, there is an obvious alternative available to that of using textual order: define an order for tag values, and then effectively reorder CHOICE and SET into tag order before determining the choice index or the order of transmission for SET elements. This is what is done.

The so-called **canonical tag order** is defined to be

```
Universal Class (first)
Application Class
Context-specific Class
Private Class (last)
```

with lower tag numbers coming before higher ones within each class.

There is only one small complication—there always is! Recall that most types have the same outer-level tag for all their abstract values, and we can validly talk about the "tag of the type". The only case where this is not true is for an untagged choice type. In this case different abstract values may have different outer-level tags, and we can not talk about "the tag of the type" so easily. (But remember that **all** these tags are required to be distinct from any of the tags of any other type in a SET or CHOICE). PER defines the tag of an untagged choice type as the smallest tag of any of its values, for the purpose of putting types into a canonical order, and the problem is solved.

17.8 Encoding an Unbounded Count

If constraints are placed on lengths, iteration counts, or sizes of integers, PER will often omit the length field completely, or will use a highly optimized encoding for the length

> At last we are done with the concepts, and can look at actual encodings!

(described later); otherwise it will use length encodings similar to (but different from) those of BER. It is these encodings that are described here.

17.8.1 The Three Forms of Length Encoding

PER has an equivalent of the BER short and long definite length and indefinite length forms, but there are a number of important differences, and apart from the short definite form the encodings are not the same as BER.

Here, the form used for length determinants is described for cases where a count is needed that is potentially

> Quite similar to the BER approach, but different and a bit less verbose.

unbounded. This is generally the case only when there are no PER-visible constraints on the length of strings, iteration counts of SEQUENCE OF and SET OF, or on the size of integers.

Where there are such constraints, PER will have a much more optimized length field (described later), or no length field at all.

The first important difference from BER is in what PER counts. (BER always counts the number of octets in the contents). PER counts the number of bits in a BIT STRING value, abstract characters in a known-multiplier character string values, the iteration count in a SEQUENCE OF or SET OF, and octets in all other cases. We speak here of the **count** in the **length determinant.**

Figures 17.7 to 17.9 illustrate the three forms of encoding for the length determinant.

In the first form (corresponding to the BER short form, although PER does not use this term), we have the same encoding as BER, with the encoding placed in an octet-aligned-bit-field (in other words, there will be padding bits in the ALIGNED variants). The top bit of the octet is set to zero, and the remainder of the octet encodes count values from zero to 127.

In the second form (corresponding roughly to the BER long definite form), there are always exactly two octets of length determinant. The first octet has the first bit

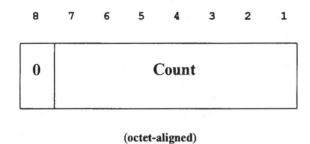

8 7 6 5 4 3 2 1

| 0 | Count |

(octet-aligned)

Figure 17.7 The single octet encoding of a count (counts up to 127).

set to one and the second bit set to zero, and the remaining 14 bits of those two octets encode count values from 128 to 16K-1.

The third form (corresponding roughly to the BER indefinite form, but with a very different mechanism) has an initial octet with both the top two bits set to one. The remaining six bits encode (right justified) the values 1 to 4—call this value "m". This octet states two things, namely,

- that "m" times 16K bits, iterations, abstract characters, or octets of the contents follow, and

- that after this fragment of the contents, there will be a further length field (of either of the three forms) for the rest of the contents, or for another fragment.

PER requires that each fragment should be as large as possible, so there are no encoder options in the choice of "m". Notice that in principle the largest permitted "m" could have been made much greater (there are six bits available to encode it), but the designers of PER chose to enforce fragmentation into fragments of at most 64K (4 times 16K) items for long octet strings, etc.

Figure 17.10 illustrates the encoding (in binary) for count values (for example for a SEQUENCE OF) of 5, 130, 16000, 32768, and 99000. The insertion of one or more padding bits is shown with a "P", the length determinant is prefixed with "L:", and fragments of content with "C:" (a convention used throughout this chapter).

Note that where we have fragmentation in Figure 17.10, although the fragments will be encoding multiples of 16K values of the same type, the encodings for each value are not necessarily the same length if the type being iterated has extensions, so padding bits may again be required before the length determinant after a fragment, as all these length determinants are specified as octet-aligned.

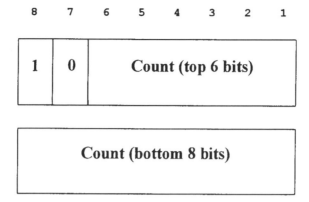

Figure 17.8   The two-octet encoding of a count (counts up to 16K-1).

17.8.2 Encoding "Normally Small" Values

PER has one further encoding for counts that are potentially unbounded. This encoding is used in cases where, although there is no upper-bound on the values that may need to be encoded, the values are expected to be "normally small" (and are all zero or positive). This is described as "encoding a normally small nonnegative whole number".

This case is applied to encode a choice index for a choice alternative that is not in the root—there could be millions of additional choices in version 2, and a version-1 system has no idea how many, but actually it is unlikely to be more than a few.

A second application is to encode values of an enumerated type that are outside the root, where again the possible values are unbounded but are usually going to be small.

> Unbounded, yes, but usually small—PER optimizes.

In both these cases, encoding the value as an unbounded integer value (which would require an octet-aligned length field—usually set to 1—and an integer encoding of one octet) is not optimal. The specified encoding in this case is to use instead just seven bits (not octet-aligned), with the top bit set to zero and the other six encoding values up to 63. Thus we avoid the octet alignment, and use only seven bits, not sixteen. Why use seven bits and not eight? Remember that this encoding will frequently appear following an extensions bit, so the two together give us exactly eight bits and if we had alignment at the start, we still have it.

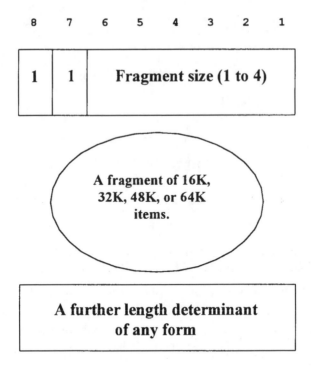

Figure 17.9 The encoding for large counts.

Of course, there is a penalty in optimizing for small values! If the normally small nonnegative whole number actually turns out to be more than 63, then we add a one-bit bit-field set to one, followed by a positive integer encoding into minimum octets preceded by a general length field as described in 17.8.1.

Figure 17.11 illustrates the encoding of a count as a normally small nonnegative whole number for values of 5, 60, 254, and 99000. (There is no way the latter will occur in any real specification, and a tool that failed to provide code for this case—simply saying "not supported"—would be very unlikely to be unmasked! The specification is, however, complete, and will encode any value no matter how large.) Note the absence of padding bits in the first two cases.

17.8.3 Comments on Encodings of Unbounded Counts

The fragmentation mechanism in PER is not reliant on nested TLV structures, and can be applied to any contents encoding, and in particular to encodings of unbounded integers. Because the number of 64K fragments is unlimited, PER can truly encode indefinitely large integers, but we have already seen that the actual

```
      5:      L:P00000101 C:(5 items of content)
    130:      L:P10000000 10000010 C:(130 items of content)
  16000:      L:P10111110 10000000 C:(16000 items of content)
  32768:      L:P11000010
              C:(32K items of content)
              L:P00000000
  99000:      L:P11000100
              C:(64K items of content)
              L:P11000010
              C:(32K items of content)
              L:P10000010 10111000
              C:(696 items of content)
```

Figure 17.10   Encoding various iteration counts.

limit BER imposes is for all practical purposes irrelevant. The fragmentation mechanism of PER, particularly the lack of encoder options, however, is probably simpler than that of BER.

The main advantage of the PER encoding over BER is that length fields will generally be two octets, and counts of less than 128 are

> Does it all matter? Is BER simpler (or just more familiar)? You must judge!

required to be done using the short form. With BER, length fields of three octets (long definite form) are permitted (and some implementations use them always), even for a contents length of, say, five octets. This is a big verbosity overhead for such implementations.

The main advantage of the encoding of normally small nonnegative whole numbers is that they (usually) encode into a bit-field without padding bits. If the value becomes too big (unlikely to occur in practice), there is still only an additional penalty of one bit over a general length encoding.

17.9 Encoding the OPTIONAL Bit-Map and the CHOICE Index

17.9.1 The OPTIONAL Bit-Map

We already know that when encoding a sequence or set value PER encodes a preamble into a bit-field with one bit for each OPTIONAL or DEFAULT element (zero bits if there are no OPTIONAL or DEFAULT elements). The bit is set to one if a value of the element is present in the encoding, otherwise it is set to zero. The encoding of each element then follows.

```
      5       L:0000101 C:(5 items of content)
     60       L:0111100 C:(60 items of content)
    254       L:1 P00000001 11111110 C:(254 items of content)
  99000:       L:1 P11000100
              C:(64K items of content)
              L:P11000010
              C:(32K items of content)
              L:P10000010 10111000
              C:(696 items of content)
```

Figure 17.11 Encoding normally small nonnegative whole numbers.

This applies to elements in the root. A similar bit-map is used at the insertion point for elements that are extension additions, but this is described later.

> These are the last of our "generic" encodings. After this we deal with the complete encoding of specific types.

Under normal circumstances, there is no length determinant for this bit-map (as both sender and receiver know its length from the type definition), but if (and it will never occur, so a "not supported" response from a tool would be OK!) the length of the bit-map (the number of optional or default elements) exceeds 64K, then a length determinant is included and the bit-map breaks into 64K fragments.

17.9.2 The CHOICE Index

For a CHOICE value, there is again a preamble. If the type is not extensible, or the value is in the root, we have an upper-bound on this choice index (and a lower bound of zero—the choice index starts at zero with the alternative that has the lowest tag value, as described earlier). This value is encoded as a constrained integer value—one that has both an upper- and a lower-bound. We will see in 17.11.3 that integer values that are constrained to a range of, say, 0 to 15 (up to 16 alternatives in the CHOICE type) encode into a bit-field of four bits.

If the chosen alternative is outside of the root, then the "extensions bit" is set to one in a bit-field (as described earlier), followed (usually) by seven bits in a bit-field encoding the normally small nonnegative whole number that is the index of the alternative within the extension additions (taking the first addition alternative as value zero). Note that while version brackets are allowed in a CHOICE, their presence makes no difference to the encoding; it is only for SEQUENCE and SET that the encoding is affected.

Notice that if we started on an octet boundary, we have added exactly eight bits and will remain on an octet boundary, and we have not forced any octet alignment in these encodings. Illustrations of these encodings are given in 17.16 describing the complete encoding of choice values.

17.10 Encoding NULL and BOOLEAN Values

These are easy. No PER-visible constraints can apply, and optionality is sorted by the bit-map.

Zero bits for NULL. That is all you need. One bit for BOOLEAN—set to 1 for TRUE and set to zero for FALSE.

> At last! How do we actually encode something?

And of course there are no padding bits in the ALIGNED version.

17.11 Encoding INTEGER Values

Remember—when we talk about constraints in what follows, we are concerned only with PER-visible constraints as discussed earlier.

> The only interesting parts of this discussion concern encoding constrained integers when "minimum bits" tend to be used. For unconstrained integers, we get the standard length determinant and an encoding in the minimum octets. There are, however, differences between the ALIGNED and UNALIGNED variants (apart from adding or not adding padding bits).

17.11.1 Unconstrained Integer Types

It is most important with the encoding of INTEGER types to determine whether or not a lower bound exists on the value. If it does not, we encode into the minimum octets as a signed number, with a general length deter-

> If there is no lower- bound, we get a 2's-complement encoding into minimum octets with a general length determinant (all variants).

minant (as described earlier) containing a count of the number of octets. So,

```
integer1 INTEGER ::= 4096
integer2 INTEGER (MIN .. 65535) ::= 127
integer3 INTEGER (MIN .. 65535) ::= -128
integer4 INTEGER (MIN .. 65535) ::= 128
```

are all described as "unconstrained" and encode as (with "L:" preceding the length determinant—if any—and "C:" preceding the contents encoding—if any):

```
integer1:        L:P00000010   C:00010000 00000000
integer2:        L:P00000001   C:01111111
integer3:        L:P00000001   C:10000000
integer4:        L:P00000010   C:00000000 10000000
```

This is the same as BER (for values up to 127 octets), but without the identifier octets. Remember that in the UNALIGNED variant P bits are never inserted.

17.11.2 Semiconstrained Integer Types

Once we have a lower-bound (which will typically be zero or one, but could be anything), then we only need to encode a positive value, using the offset from the base as the value to be encoded.

> Encode the (positive) offset from the lower-bound.

As for unconstrained integer types, the encoding is into the minimum necessary multiple of eight bits preceded by a length determinant counting the number of octets. So,

```
integer5 INTEGER (-1.. MAX) ::= 4096
integer6 INTEGER (1 .. MAX) ::= 127
integer7 INTEGER (0 .. MAX) ::= 128
```

encode as

```
Integer5:        L:P00000010   C:00010000 00000001
Integer6:        L:P00000001   C:01111110
Integer7:        L:P00000001   C:10000000
```

(Compare the encoding of integer7 with that of integer4.)

17.11.3 Constrained Integer Types

It is in the encoding of integers with both a lower- and an upper-bound that PER tries hardest to "do the sensible thing". However, "the sensible thing" as determined by the proponents of the UNALIGNED variant turned out to be different from "the sensible thing" as determined by the proponents of the ALIGNED version, so the approaches are not quite the same. Which is the most sensible **you** must judge!

The standard talks about the "range" of the values, defining the "range" as the upper-bound minus the lower-bound plus one. Thus a constraint of (0..3) has a "range" of four. Thus "range" is essentially defined as the total number of values between (and including) the upper- and lower-bounds.

> Differences between the UNALIGNED variants (minimum bits for the range) and the ALIGNED version—several different encodings depending on the range.

If the "range" is one, then only one value is possible. This is not likely to occur in practice, but the encoding follows naturally from the treatment of larger ranges and is similar to the handling of NULL: there are **no** bits in the encoding!

We first describe all the cases that can arise, then we give examples.

For larger ranges, the UNALIGNED case is the easiest to describe. It encodes the offset from the lower-bound into the minimum number of bits needed to support all values in the range. Thus a constraint of (1..3)—or (6..8) or (11..13) or (–2..0)—has a range of three, and values will encode into a bit-field of 2 bits (as would a range of 4). A constraint of (0..65535) will produce encodings of **all** values into exactly 16 bits, and so on. Remember that with the UNALIGNED variants, there are never any padding bits, so in this last case successive integers in the encoding of SEQUENCE OF INTEGER (0..65535) will all be 16 bits long, but may all be starting at bit 3, say, of an octet.

The ALIGNED case is a bit more varied!

If the range is less than or equal to 255 (**note:** 255, not 256), then the encoding is into a bit-field that is the minimum necessary to encode the range, and there will be no padding bits. If, however, the range is 256, for example, the constraint might be (0..255) or (1..256), then the value encodes into eight bits, but they go into an octet-aligned field—we get padding bits if necessary.

If the range is greater than 256 but no greater than 64K, we get two octets (octet-aligned).

If we need to exceed two octets (the range is more than 64K), we encode each value (as a positive integer offset from the lower-bound) into the minimum number of octets necessary (except that zero always encodes into an octet of all zeros, not into zero bits, so we always have a minimum of one octet), and prefix a length determinant giving the number of octets used. In this case, however, the general length determinant described earlier is **not** used! Instead, we look at the range of values that this octet count can take (lower-bound one, remember, because zero encodes into one octet), and encode the value of the length in the minimum number of bits needed to encode a positive number with that range, offset from one.

Let's have some examples. What follows is **not** correct value notation—for compactness of the examples, we give a value, then a comma, then another value, etc., and use commas to separate the encodings in the same way.

```
integer8   INTEGER (3..6)  ::= 3, 4, 5, 6
integer9   INTEGER (4000..4254) ::= 4002, 4006
integer10  INTEGER (4000..4255) ::= 4002, 4006
integer11  INTEGER (0..32000) ::= 0, 31000
integer12  INTEGER (1..65538) ::= 1, 257, 65538
```

will encode as follows:

```
integer8        C:00, C:01,  C:10, C:11
integer9        C:00000010,  C:00000110
integer10       C:P00000010, C:P00000110
integer11       C:P00000000 00000000, C:P01111001 00011000
integer12  (UNALIGNED)  C:0 00000000 00000000,
                        C:0 00000001 00000000,
                        C:1 00000000 00000001
           (ALIGNED)    L:00 C:P00000000,
                        L:01 C:P00000001 00000000,
                        L:10 C:P00000001 00000000 00000001
```

You will see that where there is no length determinant, the field is the same size for all values of the type, and can be deduced from the type notation. (If this were not true, PER would be a bust specification!) Where the field size varies, a length determinant is encoded so that the decoder knows the size of the field, with the length of the length determinant the same for all values, and again derivable from the type definition. As stated earlier, these are necessary conditions for an encoder and decoder to be able to interwork. Study these examples!

There is one further (and final) case for encoding the ALIGNED variant of a constrained integer: If the **number of octets** needed to encode the range of the integer value exceeds 64K .... Need I go on? This will never **ever** arise in practice! But if it did, then a general length encoding is used, and the fragmentation procedures discussed earlier come into play.

17.11.4 And if the Constraint on the Integer Is Extensible?

There is nothing new or unexpected here. The principles of encoding extensible types have been discussed already.

> It's just the usual one bit upfront, a constrained encoding if in the root, and an unconstrained encoding otherwise.

But let's have some examples:

```
integer13  INTEGER (MIN .. 65535, ..., 65536 .. 4294967296) ::= 127, 65536

integer14  INTEGER (-1..MAX, ..., -20..0 ) ::= 4096, -8

integer15  INTEGER (3..6, ..., 7, 8) ::= 3, 4, 5, 6, 7, 8

integer16  INTEGER (1..65538, ..., 65539) ::= 1, 257, 65538, 65539
```

will encode as (the "extensions bit" has "E:" placed before it for clarity):

```
    integer13:          E:0  L:P00000001 C:01111111,
                        E:1  L:P00000011 C:00000001 00000000 00000000
    integer14:          E:0  L:P00000010 C:00010000 00000001,
                        E:1  L:P00000001 C:11111000
    integer15:          E:0  C:00, E:0  C:01, E:0  C:10, E:0  C:11,
                        E:1  L:P00000001 C:00000101,
                        E:1  L:P00000001 C:00001000
 integer16: (UNALIGNED)    E:0  0 00000000 00000000,
                           E:0  0 00000001 00000001,
                           E:0  1 00000000 00000001,
                           E:1  L:00000011 C:00000001 00000000 00000010
            (ALIGNED)      E:0  L:00 C:P00000000,
                           E:0  L:01 C:P00000001 00000000,
                           E:0  L:10 C:P00000001 00000000 00000001,
                           E:1  L:00000011 C:00000001 00000000 00000011
```

OK—Now you know it all! It is not difficult, but there are many cases to remember. Come back BER! All the other types are much more straightforward! No doubt you will want to write notes on this lot, and hope that your examination is an open book one! But by now (if you really read this far!) you should certainly have a very good understanding of the principles involved in the PER encodings.

17.12 Encoding ENUMERATED Values

First, we consider the encoding of an enumerated type that is not marked extensible (and remember, the encoding of an extensible type for a value that is in the root is just the same except that it is preceded by an extensions bit set to zero). Encoding of enumerations outside of the root are covered later.

> In BER, enumerated values encode like integers, using the associated numerical value given in the type definition, but in PER they are known to be constrained, and normally have small associated numerical values, so the encoding is different—and essentially simpler!

The numerical value associated with an enumeration is always bounded above and below. Moreover, it is possible to order the enumerations into ascending order (even if some have negative associated values), and then to renumber each enumeration from zero upward.

This gives us a compact set of integer values (called the enumeration index) with a lower- and an upper-bound. Any value of the enumerated type now encodes like the corresponding constrained integer.

In principle, all possible constrained integer encodings are possible, but, in practice, definitions of enumerated types never have more than a few tens of enumerations—usually much less, so we are essentially encoding the enumeration index into a bit-field of size equal to the minimum necessary to cope with the range of the index.

If the enumeration is extensible, then enumerations outside the root are again sorted by their associated numerical value, and are given their own enumeration index starting at zero again. (Remember, the extensions bit identifies whether or not an encoded value is a root one, so there is no ambiguity, and starting again at zero keeps the index values as small as possible.) For a value outside the root, the encoding is the encoding of the enumeration index as a "normally small nonnegative whole number" described earlier.

No doubt you want some examples! Here we give a few (with a way-out example first!)—and again we use commas to separate lists of values and of encodings, for brevity:

```
enum1 ENUMERATED {red(-6), blue(20), green(-8)}
        ::=  red, blue, green
```

```
enum2 ENUMERATED {red, blue, green, ..., yellow, purple}
       ::= red, yellow, purple
```

These encode as:

```
enum1:  C:01, C:10, C:00
enum2:  E:0 C:00,
        E:1 C:0000000,     (These are the "normally small"
        E:1 C:0000001       encodings of zero and one.
                            Note the absence of a "P".)
```

If we had more than 63 extension additions ... No! I am not going to give an example for that. It won't happen! Produce your own example! (You have been told enough to be able do it.)

17.13 Encoding Length Determinants of Strings, etc.

The "etc." in the heading refers to iteration counts in SEQUENCE OF and SET OF.

Remember that for iteration counts, the length determinant encodes the number of iterations, for the length of bitstrings it encodes the number of bits, for the length of known-multiplier character strings it encodes the number of abstract characters, and for everything else it encodes the number of octets.

> A length determinant that is constrained by an effective size constraint encodes in exactly the same way that an integer with an equivalent constraint would encode (well, almost—read the following details if you wish!).

A length determinant can, however, have values that are constrained by an effective size constraint, and in many ways we can view this as similar to the situation when an integer value (a count) is constrained by a direct constraint on the integer.

Note that we are talking here only about lengths of strings or iteration counts—the form of the length determinant for integer values has been fully dealt with (and illustrated) earlier. We have also discussed earlier the general case of a length determinant where there are no PER-visible size constraints. So here we are discussing only the case where there is an effective size constraint, and as earlier, we consider first the case of a constraint without an extension marker (which also applies to encoding counts within the root if there is an extension marker).

The discussion of length encodings for strings, etc. has been deliberately delayed until after the description of integer encodings was given, and the reader may like to review that description before proceeding.

A length or iteration count is basically an integer value, except that it is **always** bounded below (by zero if no other lower-bound is specified). So if we need to encode the lengths of strings, we can draw on the concepts (and the text!) used to describe the encoding of values of the integer type. For a semiconstrained count (no upper-bound), it would be pointless to encode a semiconstrained integer value (with its "length of length" encoding), and instead a general length determinant as described in 17.8 is encoded.

For a constrained count, where the count is restricted to a single value (a fixed-length string, for example, or a fixed number of iterations in a SEQUENCE OF), then there is **no** length determinant—we simply encode the contents. Otherwise, we need a length determinant.

For a constrained count, the count is encoded (in both the ALIGNED and UNALIGNED versions) **exactly** like the encoding of a corresponding constrained integer, **except where the maximum allowed count exceeds 64K.** In this latter case the constraint is ignored for purposes of encoding, and a general length determinant is used, with fragmentation into 64K hunks (as described in 17.8) if the actual value has more than 64K bits, octets, iterations, or abstract characters.

Finally, we need to consider an extensible constraint. If the effective size constraint makes the type extensible, then the general provisions for encoding extensible types discussed earlier apply to the type as a whole—we do not encode an extensible integer for the length determinant. So we get the extensions bit up-front saying whether the count (and any other aspect of the value, such as the alphabet used) is in the root, and if so we encode the count according to the size constraint on the root. If not, then the extensions bit is set to one and a general length determinant is used.

To summarize:

- with no PER-visible size constraint, or a constraint that allows counts in excess of 64K, we encode a general length determinant;

- for abstract values outside the root, a general length determinant is again used;

- with a size constraint that gives a fixed value for the count, there is no length determinant encoding;

- otherwise, we encode the count exactly like an integer with the equivalent constraint.

We illustrate this with some IA5String examples, but remember that the same length determinant encodings also apply to iteration counts, etc. In the examples you will see "P" for padding bits in the contents. These are a consequence of the main type being IA5String with more than two characters, and would not be present if we had used BIT STRING for the examples (or if we had an IA5String whose length was restricted to at most two characters—discussed later). Where padding bits are shown in the length determinant, these would be present for all types. We give the E: and L: fields in binary, but the C: fields in hexadecimal, for brevity.

If the reader wants some exercise, then try writing down the encodings of each value before reading the answers that follow! (For very long strings, we indicate the contents with the count in characters in brackets, and do the same when giving the encoding.)

With the following value definitions:

```
string1 IA5String (SIZE (6)) ::= "012345"

string2 IA5String (SIZE (5..20)) ::= "0123456"

string3 IA5String (SIZE (MIN..7)) ::= "abc"

string4 IA5String ::= "ABCDEFGH"

string5 IA5String (SIZE (0..7, ..., 8)) ::= "abc", "abcdefgh"

string6 IA5String (SIZE (65534..65535)) ::= "(65534 chars)"

string7 IA5String (SIZE (65537)) ::= "(65537 chars)"
```

we get the following encodings (using hex or binary as appropriate):

```
string1:   C:P303132333435

string2:   L:0001  C:P30313233343536

string3:   L:011   C:P616263

string4:   L:P00001000  C:4142434445464748

string5:   L:011   C:P616263,

           L:P00001000  C:6162636465666768

string6:   L:0  C:(65534 octets)

string7:   L:P11000100  C:(65536 octets)  L:P00000001  C:(1 octet)
```

17.14 Encoding Character String Values

17.14.1 Bits per Character

We have discussed in 17.13 the encoding of the lengths of strings. To recap, the length determinant gives the count of the number of abstract characters for the "known multiplier" character string types, and of octets for the other character string types.

In the case of the known multiplier character string types, the number of bits used in the encoding of the UNALIGNED variants of PER is the minimum needed to represent each character unambiguously. For the ALIGNED versions, the number of bits for each character is rounded up to a power of two (one, two, four, eight, sixteen, etc.), to ensure that octet alignment is not lost between characters.

> Encoding of known multiplier character strings uses the minimum number of bits for each character, except that in the ALIGNED variants this number is rounded up to a power of two, to avoid losing alignment.

The known multiplier types, with the number of characters that the unconstrained type is defined to contain (and the number you need to exclude to improve the encoding in the UNALIGNED variants) are as follows.

Type name	Number of chars	Number of reductions needed for better encoding
IA5String	128 characters	64
PrintableString	74 characters	10
isibleString	95 characters	31
NumericString	11 characters	3
UniversalString	2**32 characters	2**31
BMPString	2**16 characters	2**15

For all other character string types, the length determinant gives the count in octets, because the number of octets used to represent each character can vary for different characters. In this latter case, constraints are not PER-visible, and the encoding of each character is that specified by the base specification, is outside the scope of this chapter, and is the same as for BER.

All that remains is to discuss the encoding of each character in the known multiplier character string types, as the encoding of these characters is affected by the effective alphabet constraint (see 17.6), and to see when octet-aligned fields are or are not used for character string encodings. Again, we see differences between the ALIGNED and the UNALIGNED variants, but the encodings are what you would probably expect, or have invented yourself!

Each of the known multiplier character string types has a canonical order defined for the characters, based on the numerical value in the BER encoding (the ASCII value for IA5String, PrintableString, VisibleString, and NumericString, the UNI-

CODE value for BMPString, and the ISO 10646 32-bit value for characters outside the Basic Multilingual Plane for UniversalString). These values are used to provide a canonical order of characters. The values used to encode each character are determined by assigning the value zero to the first abstract character permitted by the effective alphabet constraint, one to the second, etc. The last value used is n-1 if there are n abstract characters permitted for the type (using only PER-visible constraints in this determination). There are a minimum number of bits needed to encode the value n-1 as a positive integer, and in the UNALIGNED variants, this is exactly the number of bits used to encode each character. For example:

```
Type definition                            No of bits per char

My-chars1 ::= IA5String (FROM ("T"))               Zero

My-chars2 ::= IA5String (FROM ("TF"))              One

My-chars2 ::= UniversalString (FROM ("01"))        One

My-chars2 ::= NumericString (FROM ("01234567")     Three
```

Note that the actual base type being constrained could be any of the known-multiplier character string types, and the result would actually be just the same encoding! You effectively design your own character set, and PER then assigns an efficient encoding for each character.

For the ALIGNED variants, the number of bits used is always rounded up to a power of 2—0, 1, 2, 4, 8, 16, 32, to ensure that octet alignment is not lost within the string.

There is one small exception to this mapping of values to new values for encoding. The original set of characters has associated values with some "holes" in the middle (in general). If remapping the original values to a compact range from zero to n-1 does **not** produce a reduction in the number of bits per character in the PER encoding (for whichever variant is in use), then the remapping is **not** done, and the original associated value is used in the encoding. In practice, this means that remapping is more likely for UNALIGNED PER than for ALIGNED PER (where the number of bits per character is always a power of two), except in the case of NumericString, where the presence of "space" means that for both variants (even with no constraints), remapping takes place, reducing the encoding to a maximum of four bits per character.

Thus, with

```
My-Boolean ::= IA5STRING (FROM ("TF"))(SIZE(1))
```

the encoding would be a single bit in a bit-field (with no length encoding)—in other words, it would be identical to the encoding of a BOOLEAN!

17.14.2 Padding Bits

When do we get padding bits in the ALIGNED case? Here we need to look at the combination of the effective size constraint (which restricts the number of abstract characters in every value) and the effective alphabet constraint (which determines the number of bits used to encode each character). If the combination of these is such that the total encoding size for a value of this constrained type can never exceed 16 bits,

> No padding if the size is constrained so that an encoded string value never exceeds 16 bits.

then there are **no** padding bits. The character string value is encoded into a bit-field. If, however, there are some values that might require more than 16 bits, then the encoding is into an octet-aligned bit-field, and no character will cross an octet boundary (in the ALIGNED case).

Some examples of character strings whose encodings do not produce padding bits:

```
String1 ::=   NumericString (SIZE (0..4))
String2 ::=   IA5String (FROM ("TF")) (SIZE (0..16))
String3 ::=   IA5String (SIZE (0..2))
String4 ::=   BMPString (SIZE (0..1))
```

Again, this rule of "16 bits" maximum is another example of PER being pragmatic. The limit could just as well have been set at 32 or 64 bits. The philosophy is that for short strings we do not want to force alignment, but that for long strings doing alignment at the start of the string (and then maintaining it) is on balance the best decision.

17.14.3 Extensible Character String Types

The encoding of an extensible (by PER-visible constraints) known multiplier character string type follows the normal pattern—an extensions bit set to zero if in the root, one otherwise, then the optimized encoding described above for root values, and an encoding of the unconstrained type (with a general length determinant) if we are not in the root. (Note, however, that mapping of associated values to produce a 4-bit encoding still occurs for an unconstrained NumericString).

This all applies only to the known-multiplier types. For the other character string types, there is **never** an extensions bit, the general encoding always applies for all values.

Finally, note that there is no concern in determining encodings of whether a known-multiplier type is extensible for alphabet or for size constraints. All that matters is whether or not PER-visible constraints make it

> No surprises here: an extensions bit, the optimized encoding if in the root, the general encoding otherwise—but only for the known multiplier types.

extensible, and what then are the effective alphabet and effective size constraints for the root. The encoding is totally determined by that.

17.15 Encoding SEQUENCE and SET Values

For a SEQUENCE without an extension marker, earlier text (17.9) has described the encoding. There is up front a preamble (encoded as a bit-field, not octet-aligned), with one bit for each element that is OPTIONAL or DEFAULT, set to one if there is an encoding present for a value of that element, and to zero otherwise. Then there is simply the encoding for each element.

> There is so little to say here—you know it all already—whoops! Not quite true—we need to discuss how the encoding of extension additions is handled. That is the only complicated part.

We have also discussed earlier the use of tags to provide a canonical order for the elements of a SET, which then encodes in exactly the same way as a SEQUENCE.

We are left here to discuss when and whether encoding of values equal to a DEFAULT value are required to be present, or required to be absent, or whether we have an encoder option. We also need to discuss the way extension additions are encoded.

But first, we have an example of encoding a value of a simple sequence type. The example is shown in Figure 17.12 and the encoding in Figure 17.13. The OPTIONAL/DEFAULT bit-map is preceded by "B:", contents by "C:", length determinant by "L:", and one or more padding bits by "P", as in earlier examples.

It is worth noting that the total length of this PER encoding is seven octets. In BER (assuming the encoder takes the option of encoding default values and always

```
my-sequence-val
    SEQUENCE
        {item-code    INTEGER (0..254),
         item-name    IA5String (SIZE (3..10))OPTIONAL,
         urgency      ENUMERATED
                        {normal, high} DEFAULT normal }
          ::= {item-code 29, item-name "SHERRY"}
```

Figure 17.12   A sequence value to be encoded.

using a 3-octet definite length field, both for the sake of simplicity), we end up with a total of 24 octets. If the encoder is more bandwidth conscious and omits the encoding of the default value and uses short definite lengths (which suffice in this case), BER will produce 13 octets.

17.15.1 Encoding DEFAULT Values

Here we find some differences between CANONICAL-PER (which is fully canonical), and BASIC-PER (which has encoder's options in complex cases that rarely arise).

For both encoding rules, if the actual value to be encoded equals the default value for "simple types" (defined as anything that is not a SET, SEQUENCE, SET OF, SEQUENCE OF, CHOICE, EMBEDDED PDV, EXTERNAL or unrestricted character string type, then the encoder is required to omit the encoding in both CANONICAL-PER and in BASIC-PER (both are canonical).

However, for these types, CANONICAL-PER again requires omission if the value equals the default value, but BASIC-PER leaves it as an encoder's option, making it unnecessary to do a possibly complex run-time check for equality of a value with the DEFAULT value.

17.15.2 Encoding Extension Additions

The general principles of encoding extensible types applies: we have an extensions bit up front (before the bit-map of OPTIONAL or DEFAULT elements), which is set to zero if the abstract value is in the root, and one otherwise.

Extension additions tend in practice to be marked OPTIONAL (or DEFAULT), but this is not a requirement. If in version 2, one addition was not so marked, then version-2 systems would always have to encode additions, and would always have the extensions bit set to one. Only version-1 systems would set it to zero.

```
B:10          (item-name present, urgency missing)
C:00011011    (value of item-code)
L:011 C:P534845525259    (length and value of item-name)
```

Figure 17.13   Encoding of the sequence value.

Values for extension additions are always encoded at the position of the insertion point, and a decoder expects such encodings if the extensions bit is set to one, not otherwise.

First, we must recap on extension additions in a SEQUENCE. These may be either a single element (called an extension-addition type), or a group of elements contained in version brackets (called an extension-addition group).

The easiest way to describe the handling of an extension-addition group (and the way it is described in the specification), is for the reader to mentally replace the entire group of elements and the version brackets with a single OPTIONAL SEQUENCE, whose elements are the elements of the addition group. There is just one rider: if all elements of the group are to be omitted in the encoding (they are all marked OPTIONAL or DEFAULT), then there is no encoding for the entire SEQUENCE, and the outermost OPTIONAL bit-map would record its absence. (An example of this is given later.)

We have now reduced the problem to a simple list of extension-addition types, some or all of which may be marked OPTIONAL, and hence may be missing in an encoding. As with elements in the root, a decoder needs to know which elements are present in the encoding, and which are not, and once again a bit-map is used. The problem in this case, however, is that version-1 systems will not know how many extension-addition types there are in the specification, and hence will not know the length of the bit-map. Moreover, such systems will not know whether an extension-addition type was marked optional. This produces two differences from the bit-map used for the root elements:

- The bit-map contains one bit for every extension-addition type, whether or not it is marked optional, recording its presence or absence in the encoding;

- The bit-map is preceded by a count giving the number of bits in the bit-map.

The count for the bit-map length is encoded as a normally small whole number.

The effect of encoding the count as a normally small whole number is that there is again provision for breaking the extension additions bit-map into 64K fragments if the number of extension additions exceeds 64K. With the presence of version brackets, where additions are unlikely to occur at less than about one-year intervals, a "not supported" response from a tool would be wholly appropriate!

Following the bit-map, we encode the value of the extension addition types, but in this case a version-1 system does not know the actual types involved, and would not be able to find the end of the encoding of an extension addition, so each of the extension-addition types is "wrapped up" with a preceding length determinant. The situation is slightly worse than this, however. What should be the length determinant count, given that the decoder does not know the type that is wrapped up? Clearly, the only possibility is bits or octets, and octets was chosen.

So each extension-addition type is treated as if it were an outer-level type being encoded. If it is present, but has zero bits (not likely to arise—a NULL, for example), then it encodes to a one-bit. It then has zero padding bits added at the end to make it up to an integral number of octets and is then added to the encoding preceded by a general length determinant (which, remember, is octet aligned).

This "wrapping up" then can be quite expensive on bandwidth, and it was for this reason (mainly) that "version brackets" were introduced. Because all the elements in a version bracket encode (optimally) as the elements of an OPTIONAL SEQUENCE, which is treated as a single extension addition, we get only one "wrapper" instead of one for each element.

The "wrapping up" also has a significant implementation cost in that it requires the complete encoding (or at least the first 64K octets thereof) of the extension addition to be produced **and any necessary padding bits inserted,** before the length wrapper count is known and can be encoded. (This is similar to the problem of the use of the long definite form in BER to encode the length of a SEQUENCE, rather

```
my-sequence-val
   SEQUENCE
      {item-code      INTEGER (0..254),
       item-name      IA5String (SIZE (3..10))OPTIONAL,
       ... !1 -- see para 14.6 for exception handling --,
       urgency        ENUMERATED {normal, high} DEFAULT normal,
       [[ alternate-item-code      INTEGER (0..254),
          alternate-item-name      IA5String (SIZE (3..10))OPTIONAL ]] }
            ::= {item-code 29, item-name "SHERRY",
                 urgency high, alternate-item-code 45,
                 alternate-item-name  "PORT" }
```

Figure 17.14   An extended sequence value for encoding.

```
E:1                          (extensions bit SET)
B:1                          (item-name present)
C:00011011                   (value of item-code)
L:011 C:P534845525259        (length and value of item-name)
L:000010  B:11               (length - normally small whole number
                              and value of extensions bit-map)
L:P0000001 C:10000000        (general length and
                              padded value of urgency)
L:P00000011                  (general length of version bracket addition)
C:00101101                   (alternate-item-code)
L:001 C:P504F5254            (length and value of alternate-item-name)
```

Figure 17.15   The encoding of the extended sequence value.

than the indefinite form.) There is, however, no alternative to this wrapping up if we want interworking between version-2 and version-1 systems (unless we go back to a TLV approach for everything.)

Now for an example of encoding an extensible SEQUENCE with one extension-addition type and one extension-addition group added. (We base this on the earlier sequence type example.) Figure 17.14 shows the value to be encoded, and Figure 17.15 shows the encoding (the notation used is the same as in earlier examples of encodings).

This gives a total of 18 octets. Again, if we take the worst-case BER encoding as described earlier, this gives 37 octets, and the best case gives 25.

17.16 Encoding CHOICE Values

The encoding of choice indexes for both root alternatives and for those outside the root has been fully described earlier. The only remaining point to note is that here, as for sequence, if the chosen alternative is outside the root a version-1 system will not be able to find the end of it, so we again have a "wrapper", encoded in exactly the same way as extension additions in a SEQUENCE or SET.

Here we give one example of each of these cases.

Note that version brackets **are** permitted in choice-type extensions, but they do not affect the encoding, and serve purely as a documentation aid for humans. What matters is simply the list of added alternatives, each of which must have distinct outer-level tags, even if they are in different version brackets.

The values to be encoded are shown in Figure 17.16 (assume an environment of automatic tags) and the encodings are shown in Figure 17.17, where "I:" is used to introduce the choice index encoding.

```
Choice-example ::= CHOICE
        {normal    NULL,
         high      NULL,
         ... !2 -- see para 14.6 for exception handling --
         medium    NULL }
first-choice Choice-example ::= normal:NULL
second-choice Choice-example ::= medium:NULL
```

Figure 17.16   Two choice values for encoding.

In this example, worst-case BER encodes with four octets in both cases, and best-case BER with two octets. PER took three octets in the second. This is just one of a small number of cases where PER can actually produce worse encodings than BER, but this is not often the case!

17.17 Encoding SEQUENCE OF and SET OF Values

There is nothing more to add here. There is a length determinant up front giving the iteration count. The form of this (depending on any SIZE constraint on the SEQUENCE OF or SET OF) has been fully discussed earlier.

> There is nothing further to say—you know it all!

Note that these types may have a SIZE constraint in which there is an extension marker. As usual, values outside the root encode as if there was no size constraint.

Two examples are shown in Figures 17.18 and 17.19. The numbers have been kept deliberately small for ease of illustration. Note that in the example both the iteration count and the type being iterated are extensible. For a value of the SEQUENCE OF to be in its root only requires the iteration count to be within the root. The fact that the integer value 4 is outside the root of the INTEGER in the third iteration is flagged in the encoding of the INTEGER, and does not affect the extensions bit for the SEQUENCE OF.

> Length count in octets, CER encoding of contents

17.18 Encoding REAL and OBJECT IDENTIFIER Values

The box says it all! We have a general length determinant giving a count in octets, then for REAL (for both BASIC-PER and CANONICAL-PER) the contents octets of the CER/DER encoding of REAL (they are the same). For OBJECT IDENTIFIER

```
first-choice:     E:0  I:0  C:      (a total of two bits)
second-choice:    E:1               (extensions bit set)
                  C:000000          (index as a normally small
                                        whole number)
                  L:P00000001       (general length "wrapper")
                  C:00000000        (padded encoding of NULL)
```

Figure 17.17   The encodings of the choice values.

encodings, the specification actually references the BER encoding, but the CER/DER encodings are exactly the same.

17.19 Encoding an Open Type

We have discussed the form of an outer-level encoding, and of a general length determinant to provide a "wrapper" for extensions in sequence and set and choice types. Exactly the same mechanism is used to wrap up an Open Type (a "hole" that can contain any ASN.1 type). In general, the field of the protocol, which tells a decoder what type

> General length followed by a padded encoding.

has been encoded into the "hole"—into the Open-Type field, may appear later in the encoding than that field, but with PER a decoder will be unable to find the end of the encoding in the "hole" without knowing the type. (Contrast BER, where there is a standard TLV wrapper at the outer level of all types, and where no additional wrapper is needed nor used). So in PER the wrapper is essential in the general case, and is always encoded.

The inclusion of a wrapper in PER Open Types has been exploited by some applications to "wrap-up" parts of an encoding, even though it is not strictly necessary to do so.

> If you want to "wrap-up" an ASN.1 type to ease modular implementations, use an Open Type with a type constraint.

Consider an element of a large SEQUENCE consisting of:

```
security-data SECURITY-TYPES.&Type (Type1)
```

This is an example of a "type constraint" on an Open Type, and the reader was referred here for an explanation of its usefulness.

From the point of view of abstract values, this is exactly equivalent to:

```
security-data Type1
```

```
My-sequence-of SEQUENCE (SIZE(1..4), ..., 4) OF INTEGER (0..3, ..., 4)
            My-value-1 My-sequence-of ::= {1, 3, 4}
            My-value-2 My-sequence-of ::= {1, 2, 3, 4}
```

Figure 17.18   Two SEQUENCE OF values for encoding.

The PER encoding, however, will have a wrapper round Type1 in the first case, not in the second (type constraints are not PER-visible).

This can be useful in an implementation, because it enables the main body of the protocol to be dealt with in an application-specific way, leaving the security data unwrapped and unprocessed, passing it as a complete package to some common "security kernel" in the implementation.

It is generally only in the security field that specifiers use these sorts of construct.

17.20 Encoding of the Remaining Types

GeneralizedTime, UTCTime, ObjectDescriptor, all encode with a general length determinant giving an octet count, and contents the same as BER or CER (for BASIC-PER and CANONICAL-PER, respectively). Notice that this is the fourth occurrence where BASIC-PER is not canonical, for the sake of simplicity—the other three occurrences here are

> At last! The final text on PER encodings. I wish this book was a Web site, so that I could see how many people had read all the way to here! Well done those of you who made it!

- encoding values of a SET OF type,

- encoding GeneralString and related character string types, and

- encoding a DEFAULT element (which is not a simple type) in a SEQUENCE or SET type.

Canonical PER is, of course, always canonical.

That only leaves types that are defined using the "ValueSetTypeAssignment" notation, that is, notation such as:

```
MyInt1 INTEGER ::= { 3 | 4 | 7}
MyReal1 REAL ::= {0 | PLUS-INFINITY | MINUS-INFINITY}
```

```
My-value-1:
        E:0                     (extensions bit)
        L:10                    (iteration count of 3)
            E:0   C:01  (value 1)
            E:0   C:11  (value 3)
            E:1   L:P0000001 C:00000100   (value 4)
My-value-2:
        E:1                     (extensions bit)
        L:P00000011             (iteration count of 4)
            E:0   C:01  (value 1)
            E:0   C:10  (value 2)
            E:0   C:11  (value 3)
            E:1   L:P00000001 C:00000100   (value 4)
```

Figure 17.19   The encodings of the two SEQUENCE OF values.

These are equivalent to:

```
MyInt2 ::= INTEGER ( 3 | 4 | 7)

MyReal2 ::= REAL (0 | PLUS-INFINITY | MINUS-INFINITY)
```

Initially the PER standard overlooked the specification of these types, but a Corrigendum was issued saying that they encode using this transformation.

17.21 Conclusion

In a chapter such as this, it seems important to emphasize that neither the author nor any of those involved

> Caveat Emptor!

in publishing this material can in any way be held liable for errors within the text.

The only authoritative definition of PER encodings is that specified in the Standards/Recommendations themselves, and anyone undertaking implementations should base their work on those primary documents, not on this tutorial text.

Nonetheless, it is hoped that this text will have been useful, and will help implementors to more readily read and to understand the actual specifications.

The reader should now have a good grasp of the principles used in PER to provide optimum encodings, but tempered by pragmatic decisions to avoid unnecessary implementation complexity.

Some things may **appear** to be unnecessarily complex, such as fragmenting bit-maps if they are more than 64K, or encoding zero bits if an INTEGER is restricted to a single value, as such things will never occur in the real world. These specifications, however, result from applying a general principle (and general code in an implementation) to a wider range of circumstances, and are not extra implementation complexity.

We have also seen in the examples how PER encodings achieve significant gains over BER in verbosity, and even greater gains if sensible use of constraints has been made in the base specification.

There is just one more chapter to come in this section (very much shorter than this one!). It will discuss some other encoding rules that never quite made it (or have not yet made it!) to become international standard, status, and the advantages and (mainly) disadvantages of "rolling your own" encoding rules.

## CHAPTER 18

Other ASN.1-Related Encoding Rules

(Or: So You Have Special Requirements?)

Summary

This chapter briefly describes other proposals for ASN.1 encoding rules that have been made from time to time. None of these is currently on a path for International Standardization as part of the ASN.1 specifications, and this chapter can safely be omitted by all but the intellectually curious. It is of no interest to most readers concerned with "What is ASN.1, how do I write it, and how do I implement protocols defined using it"? But it does give an (incomplete) picture of other attempts to enhance the ASN.1 notation with different encoding rules.

The order of coverage is not time order (saying when the germ of an idea first appeared within a sometimes closed community is not easy), but is basically random! The following are briefly mentioned:

- LWER—Light-Weight Encoding Rules;

- MBER—Minimum Bit Encoding Rules;

- OER—Octet Encoding Rules;

- Extended Mark-up Language (XML) Encoding Rules (XER);

- Building Automation Committee network (BACnet) Encoding Rules (BACnetER); and

- Encoding Control Specifications (ECS).

No doubt there are others lurking out there!

18.1 Why Do People Suggest New Encoding Rules?

As a basic workhorse, it is doubtful if BER can be bettered. It is simple, straightforward, and robust. If you keep its basic "TLV" approach, there are few improvements that can be made.

> In the beginning there was chaos. And the greater gods descended and each begat a new Standard, and the people worshipped the Standards and said "Give us more, give us more!" So the greater gods begat more Standards and more and more, and lo, there was chaos once more!

But it was clear in 1984 that it should be possible to encode more efficiently than BER, and several attempts were made prior to or around the time of the introduction of PER to produce essentially PER-like encodings. To avoid a proliferation of encoding rules, PER should have been developed and standardized in the late 1980s, not the early 1990s, but it was not! So several "industry-specific" encoding rules emerged to fill the vacuum.

Currently, major tool vendors support only BER and PER. Support for other encoding rules for particular industry-specific protocols (supporting only the types used in those protocols, rather than all ASN.1 types) by a library of routines to perform specific parts of the encoding (not by an ASN.1 compiler, as defined and described in Chapter 6) does however exist.

Producers of new encoding rules often claim either less verbosity on the line than BER, or greater simplicity than PER (or both!).

But to date, the standardizers of ASN.1 have not considered any of the alternative encoding rule drafts that have been submitted to have sufficient merit to progress them as standards within the ASN.1 suite.

That is not to say that they are, for example, necessarily on balance inferior to PER—everyone accepts that if you started again with what you know now, PER could be improved—but providing another standard for encoding rules that was very similar to PER and only a marginal improvement on it would not make any sort of sense. Tool vendors would not want to support it, and of course existing implementations of protocols would have to be considered. The ASN.1 encoding rules have a high degree of inertia (the notation can be changed much more easily) because of the "bits-on-the-line" that are flowing around the world every minute of every day.

Nonetheless, there continue to be attempts to provide slightly different encoding rules to support a particular protocol for a particular industry, usually proposed by some consultancy or software house associated with that industry, in the hope that those encoding rules will become the de facto standard for that industry. Such encoding rules rarely, however, achieve the market demand that leads to their incorporation in the main ASN.1 compiler tools, or ratification as international standards for ASN.1 encoding rules for use across all industries.

It is, perhaps, a sign of the success of the ASN.1 notation that many industries new to protocol design are choosing to use ASN.1 to define their messages, but perhaps it is the NIH (Not Invented Here) factor that so often leads to desires to cut down the notation, or to produce different encodings for it. Who knows?

18.2 LWER—Light-Weight Encoding Rules

Light-Weight Encoding Rules were first proposed in the late 1980s when ASN.1 compilers started to emerge, and were from the beginning the subject of much controversy, with the Deutsches Institut für Normung (DIN) strenuously opposing their development as international standards.

> Standards work was approved, but was eventually abandoned— too many problems!

Suggestions for LWER predated work on PER, and the concern was not with the verbosity of BER, but with the number of CPU cycles required to do a BER encoding. They were approved as a Work Item within ISO, and were being progressed up to the mid-1990s, when they were abandoned (the reasons follow).

18.2.1 The LWER Approach

The basic idea was simple, and was based on the observation that:

> Just ship the contents of the memory holding your ASN.1 value from your machine to another machine (standardizing the in-core memory representation). A very simple approach.

- an ASN.1 compiler generates the pattern for an in-core data structure to hold values of an ASN.1 type (it is usually a whole series of linked lists and pointers to similar structures), defining that in-core data structure using a high-level programming language;

- run-time support tree-walks that structure to generate encodings (at some cost in CPU cycles) that are then transmitted down the line; and

- a decoder reproduces a (very similar) in-core structure at the other end of the line.

Why not simply ship the contents of the in-core data structure directly? That was in essence the LWER proposal.

18.2.2 The Way to Proceed Was Agreed

> Agree on a standard in-core representation of ASN.1 values, and agree how to ship it to another machine. Easy.

Early work agreed on several key points:

- the first step was to agree on a model of computer memory on which to base the definition of in-core data structures;

- the second step was to standardize a memory-based in-core structure for holding the values of any ASN.1 type; and

- the third step was to standardize how such a structure was to be transmitted to a remote system.

18.2.3 Problems, Problems, Problems

Serious problems were encountered related to all these areas.

> Computers are actually very different in the way they hold information and pointers to other locations—the simple "set of pigeonholes" model just does not hold up!

As far as a model of computer memory was concerned, at assembler language level (which no one uses today anyway), memory is made up of addressable units capable of containing integers or pointers to other addressable units or strings of characters (a simplification, but it will do). But the size of those addressable units—bytes, 16-bit words, 32-bit words—hardware varies very much.

And if a structure is defined using such a model, how easy will it be to replicate that structure using the features available in particular high-level languages such as Java?

More significant was the little-endian/big-endian problem. (Named after the characters in Jonathan Swift's *Gulliver's Travels* who fought a war over whether eggs should be broken at their "little-end" or their "big-end".) But in computer parlance, you look at basic hardware architecture and proceed as follows:

- Assume byte addressing, and draw a picture of your memory with two-byte integers in it.

- Put an arrow on your picture from low addresses to high addresses. (Some people will have drawn the picture so that the arrow goes left-to-right, others the reverse. This is not important, it only affects the depiction on paper.)

- Now write down whether, for each integer, the first byte that you encounter in the direction of the arrow is the least significant octet of the integer (a little-endian machine) or the most significant octet of the integer (a big-endian machine).

Little-endians will probably have drawn the arrow going left-to-right, and big-endians will probably have drawn it going right-to-left, but that is not important (both could have drawn a mirror image of their picture). What matters is whether the high-order octet of an integer is at a higher or lower address position than the low-order octet. And remember, what applies to integers also (invariably) applies to fields holding addresses (pointers).

Unfortunately, both big-endian and little-endian machines exist in the world!

And if you have an in-core data structure representing an ASN.1 value on a little-endian machine, and you copy that to a big-endian machine, decoding it into a usable form will certainly not be lightweight!

So we need a big-endian and a little-endian variant of LWER, and you will only be able to use LWER if you are transferring between similar (endian-wise) machines, otherwise you go back to BER or PER.

But that was all assuming machines with byte addressing, and 16-bit integers and pointers. Now consider the possible permutations of 32-bit integers, or machines that can only (easily) address (point to) 16-bit or 32-bit words ... .

Suddenly we seem to need rather a lot of variants of LWER!

This was the basic reason for the DIN opposition to the work—even if standards were produced, they would be useful only for transfers between very restricted families of machine architecture. Add the problems of mirroring those low-level memory-based architectures in high-level languages. Throw in the **fact** that tool vendors can, if they wish, define an LWER (separate ones for each machine range that they support) to be used when their own tool is communicating with itself on the same machine range, and what do you get? Probably as much interworking as you would get with LWER!

What LWER demonstrated was the importance of defining encoding rules (whether character-based or binary-based) that were independent of any given machine architecture—the idea of having something like BER or PER was vindicated. (And of course character-based encodings are also architecture-independent.)

18.2.4 The Demise of LWER

Even if the preceding problems were sorted, there would still be issues about what to ship down the line. If the total memory the linked list structures occupied was shipped, empty memory within that total hunk would need to be zeroed to prevent security leaks. If empty memory was not shipped, then some form of garbage collection or of tree-walking for transmission would be needed, none of which seemed very lightweight.

> There were other problems with producing an LWER standard, but basically, PER did the job anyway!

But what eventually killed the LWER work is something that no one had expected. Implementations of PER began to emerge. While it was expected that PER would produce about a factor of two reduction in the length of an encoding (it did), it was wholly unexpected that it would encode and decode twice as fast! It did the job that LWER was trying to do!

Once you know, it seems obvious. All the complexity and CPU cycles in PER relates to analyzing the type definition and deciding what should be the encoding. This is either a hand-implementor's brain-cycles, or is the compiler phase of a tool. It does not affect run-time CPU cycles.

At run-time, it is a lot quicker (assuming code has been generated) to pick up an integer value from a known location, and add the bottom three bits, say, of that integer value to a bit-position in a buffer than it is to generate the T and the L and the V for BER (probably using subroutine calls).

There were also gains because if you reduce the size of the encoding you reduce the CPU cycles spent in the code of the lower layers of the protocol stack.

And finally, LWER was conceived in the mid- to late-1980s, but machines got faster year-by-year. Gradually the CPU cycles spent in encoding/decoding became insignificant and irrelevant (the application processing for actual protocols also became more complex and time-consuming by comparison).

LWER was dead. Too many problems with developing it, and what it was trying to achieve seemed no longer necessary. It was finally abandoned in 1997.

18.3 MBER—Minimum Bit Encoding Rules

Proposed in about the mid-1980s, MBER was never approved for the Standards path. Many of its principles were, however, adopted when PER was produced.

The idea behind MBER was to make full use of bounds information, and to produce encodings that were "what you would expect".

So a BOOLEAN would encode into one bit, and the type INTEGER (0..7) would encode into three bits.

> Hey, ASN.1 is great! But what about our legacy protocols?

MBER never addressed the encoding of all possible ASN.1 types (and in particular did not address the problems solved in PER by a choice index and a bit-map for OPTIONAL elements).

The main thrust of the MBER work was to make it possible to produce an ASN.1 definition of a type which, if MBER was applied to values of that type, would produce exactly and precisely the same bits on the line as some existing handcrafted protocol was producing.

Typically, the aim was to move from protocol definitions using the techniques described in 1.5.1 (pictures of octets) to ASN.1 specifications **with no change to the bits on the line.**

(The reader may well ask "Why?", but this was a rather flattering recognition that use of the ASN.1 notation was quite a good (clear) way to describe the fields in a protocol message.)

MBER was never progressed internationally, but the idea of "minimum bit encodings" had a long-term influence and was included in PER.

18.4 Octet Encoding Rules—OER

At the time of writing this text, the future of OER remains unclear, nor is its final form fully determined. This text merely gives an outline of what this specification appears to the author to look like in the (very) late 1990s.

It has been proposed as the encoding rules for a particular industry sector in the USA, and perhaps for international standardization for use with protocols in that sector. The industry sector is concerned with "intelligent highways". The sector is using ASN.1 to define protocols for communication between devices on the road-side and between them and control centers. In some cases the devices are large general-purpose computers (where BER or PER could certainly be easily handled). Some devices, however, will be more limited, and may not be able to handle the (alleged) complexity of PER, but where much of the efficiency of PER is required.

> PER (with bits of BER)—with a difference!

(In relation to "alleged", remember that all the complexity in PER is in the compile phase to analyze what the encoding should be. Once that is done, the actual encoding in PER is less code and simpler than in BER. Given a good cross-compiler system, even the simplest devices should be able to handle PER.)

OER was originally developed around the same time as PER, but in ignorance of the PER work (which was later folded into it). At the time of writing, it is a mix of BER (using BER length encodings) and PER.

The name **Octet-aligned** Encoding Rules stems from the fact that all elements of an OER encoding have padding bits that make them an integral of eight bits. So INTEGER (0..7) will encode into eight bits (no tag, no length field), and BOOLEAN will encode into eight bits (no tag, no length field).

Apart from the use of BER-style length encodings, OER is very much like PER, but omits some of the optimizations of PER, producing a specification that is (arguably) simpler.

These encoding rules were considered by a joint meeting of the ISO/IEC and ITU-T ASN.1 groups in 1999, and the idea of providing a "FULLY ALIGNED" version of PER received some support. This would in some ways complete the PER family, going alongside the existing UNALIGNED (no padding bits) and ALIGNED (padding bits where sensible) variants.

In discussion, it was felt that there was as yet insufficient customer demand to justify a "FULLY ALIGNED" version of PER, and that in any case such a version of PER would not in fact be OER-compatible because of the multitude of differences (less optimization and use of BER features) between OER and PER.

At the time of writing, international standardization of OER is not being progressed within ASN.1 standardization.

18.5 Extended Mark-up Language (XML) Encoding Rules (XER)

XER is a relative newcomer (in 1999) to ASN.1 standardization. Work on it is proceeding with great rapidity through electronic mailing groups, and serious consideration of it will occur within ISO/IEC and ITU-T soon after this text is put to bed! The outcome of that discussion can not be predicted with any accuracy, but I have a feeling that any second edition of this book may contain a substantial section on XER!

> You are an XML believer? This is for you!

Many readers will be aware that XML has a strong head of steam and many supporting tools. A marriage of XML with ASN.1 will undoubtedly be a good thing for both. But XER is VERY verbose!

XER is character-based, and carries XML start and end mark-up (tags which are usually the names of the elements of ASN.1 SEQUENCES or SETS or CHOICES, which are frequently very long) around ASN.1 items.

XER appears to hold out the promise of being able to send an XER encoding to a database system that has only been configured with a schema corresponding to the fields of an ASN.1 SEQUENCE, and to use code that is independent of the actual ASN.1 SEQUENCE definition (and which is part of the database vendor's software) to automatically insert the received values into the database. This may prove to be worth the price of the verbosity of XER (perhaps!).

18.6 Building Automation Committee Network (BACnet) Encoding Rules (BACnetER)

> Perhaps one of the first industry sectors to decide to use ASN.1, but to also decide to "roll their own" encoding rules.

These encoding rules are quite old, and were a very honest attempt to produce PER before PER ever existed! They were never submitted to the ASN.1 group for international standardization, and have largely been overtaken by PER (but are still in use).

They are again an industry sector de facto standard in the USA for messages used in "intelligent buildings" (compare the discussion of "intelligent highways" in 18.4).

BACnet encodings are used to control elevators, lights, central heating systems, and so on.

From a technical point of view, there are some ASN.1 constructs for which BACnetER does not provide unambiguous encodings, and they have no real advantage over the now standard PER, so it is unlikely (in the opinion of this author) that they will have further impact on the international scene.

18.7 Encoding Control Specifications

During 1999, largely resulting from consideration of requirements for variations of encoding rules such as OER, text was produced for extensions to the ASN.1 notation called "Encoding Control Specifications".

> If everyone is changing BER and PER, let us have a metalanguage to formally specify the changes they want. Good idea?

The idea is that the definition of an Encoding Control Specification (using a notation very distinct from ASN.1) could be associated with an ASN.1 module in much the same way as a stylesheet can be associated with a page of HTML or XML. The Encoding Control Specification could vary the way certain types were encoded, selecting (for specified types or all types) PER or BER styles of length, including or omitting tags and/or padding bits, and so on.

At the time of writing this text, this work was very much in its infancy. Could the result be a metalanguage (that a tool can be built to use) which is powerful enough that a suitable Encoding Control Specification could be applied to an ASN.1 module with the effect that types in that module are encoded with BACnetER or OER (or perhaps even XER) encodings?

This is broadly the aim of the work. But five years from now you may never have heard of it, and it may be as dead as LWER, or it may be supported by many tools and give important added flexibility to ASN.1. Don't know! Get the second edition (if there is one!) of this book! (But it is not yet even a formally approved Work Item in ISO, so this stuff is just glints in the eyes at present.)

History and Applications

## CHAPTER 19

The Development of ASN.1
(Or: The Ramblings of an Old Man!)

Summary

This chapter is somewhat different in style from the rest of the book. (This summary is not a list of bullets, for a start!) While it does contain **some** facts, it is not so much a formal record of the stages and dates in the development of ASN.1 (Olivier Dubuisson's book is better for that—see the link via Appendix 5) as my own personal recollections of the various events that occurred along the way.

Unusual for an academic text, in this chapter I blatantly use the "I" personal pronoun in several sections. It seemed appropriate.

I was involved in ASN.1 almost from its earliest days (I think that only Jim White—I talk about Jim in the first part of this chapter—can claim to have seen it through from its start, but he "retired" from Standards work in the late-1980s) through to the present day. I have been active in a number of areas of Standardization within ISO, but ASN.1 has probably taken up the largest part of my time because of its time-span (at the time of writing this text) of close to 20 years.

There were many other people who gave a great deal of their time to the development of ASN.1, and if you list some of them, you are in very great danger of being unfair to (and offending) those who just drop off the end of the list, but who nevertheless made important contributions to the work. There is no easy criterion on who to mention, and there are some of my past fellow workers whose names I can no longer spell with accuracy, and have lost the attendance records!

And, of course, there are the current participants in the ASN.1 work that seem larger than life simply because they **are** the current drivers. But I am ignoring most of them! I hope nobody takes offense at being left out.

The structure of this chapter is not a simple time-line. Rather, certain themes have been selected for the major subheadings, but within those subheadings the material is largely presented on a time-line basis. I hope that this will ensure rather more continuity in the text and easier reading than a pure time-line treatment, but the reader is advised that the major subheadings are largely self-contained, and can be read (or skipped, or omitted) in a more or less random order depending on YOUR interests.

One major part of this chapter contains the history of the development of character encodings that was promised in Chapter 9.

19.1 People

Jim White played an active part (perhaps a leading part—I am not sure) in the development of the Xerox Courier Specification, on which ASN.1 was eventually based.

> Let's get this one out of the way first!

Courier was part of the "XNS" protocol stack. It represented, I think, the first recognition in protocol architecture of the value of providing a notation for the definition of protocol messages that was supported by well-defined encoding rules and tools within high-level language systems to enable **users** (not just computer vendors) to define their own protocols and to have an easy implementation path for those protocols.

White (as Rapporteur in CCITT responsible for developing notational support for the X.400 work) was largely responsible for bringing the Courier principles into international standardization and in due course for the production of X.409.

Doug Steedman was also very active within both CCITT and ISO in the early days, and was (I think) the first person to author a full-length tutorial text on ASN.1. This is still read today, but unfortunately was never updated to cover the work beyond 1990, as Doug also "retired" from Standards work in the late 1980s.

I was ISO Editor for the early ISO texts (and after X.409, CCITT texts were copies of the ISO texts). Bancroft Scott came onto the scene in the late 1980s, when (due to other "retirements"), I became Rapporteur for the ASN.1 work in ISO, and

Bancroft, having volunteered to be Editor for **one** part of ASN.1, found himself Editor for **all** the different parts (now six parts in ISO and six corresponding ITU-T Recommendations), a role that he continues to occupy at the time of publication of this text.

In more recent years, Olivier Dubuisson has played a very active role in the development of ASN.1, and is the author of either the second, third, or fourth major book on ASN.1. (He can claim prior publication to this text with a French version of his book—making his the second text, but at the time of writing this I hope his English version will be later than this publication, making him also the fourth—but he could make third as well! Friendly rivalry!)

There are many, many, others that I could and perhaps should list, particularly colleagues in BSI that have provided much support for ASN.1 over the years, but then I should also mention colleagues operating within AFNOR and from Sweden, and colleagues in the USA who produced course material for ASN.1 that is still used throughout the world today, and ... I could go on, but will stop the "people" discussion here.

19.2 Going Round in Circles?

There are so many areas of notational and encoding support for computer communications where understanding has emerged only slowly. (Support for "holes", described earlier, is one of these, as are mechanisms to ensure interworking between implementations of "version 1" and "version 2" of protocol specifications.) Sometimes developments are clear steps forward (as was the case when ASN.1 was introduced in the early 1980s), and sometimes we take backward steps in some areas to make progress in others.

> We see through a glass darkly. What is the "right" notational support for people trying to define messages for computer communication? ASN.1 has much to offer, and has recognized many of the problems (and provided some good solutions) but the world has a way to go yet.

When ASN.1 was born in the early 1980s, Open System's Interconnection (OSI) Standards were "the best thing since sliced bread", and meetings to develop these Standards within ISO and CCITT often involved several hundred people. But in all the ISO groups defining OSI Standards for applications, there was at that time a doubt, a debate, about what notation to use to clearly specify the messages (including their semantics, and their bit-patterns) to be used to support the application. Every group was doing its own thing, with different approaches and different notations.

Use of a Bacchus-Naur Form (BNF) style of specification was common in most early OSI drafts, often with an encoding based on strings of characters (much as many Internet protocols are today).

When the first ASN.1 text (and it was not called ASN.1 in those days—that is another story—see following text) was sent as a liaison from CCITT to ISO, it was almost immediately welcomed by every single application layer standardization group in ISO as

- great to have a common and standard notation for all to use in specifying protocols, and

- great to get away from verbose text-based exchanges.

(Note the latter point. Despite later strong criticism of the verbosity of BER, and the eventual emergence of PER, both are far less verbose than text-based encodings.)

ASN.1 became the notation of choice (and BER the encoding) for all the Application Layer OSI Standards (and for the Presentation Layer as well).

But it was in the mid-1980s when ASN.1 started to become widely used outside of the OSI stack. There was even some adoption (usually in a cut-down—some would say bastardized!—form) within the Internet community, but the real expansion of ASN.1 was among the telecommunications standards specifiers.

A great many telecommunications standards (for mobile phones, for intelligent networks, for signaling systems, for control of electric power distribution, for air traffic control) use ASN.1. (See the next chapter.)

But today we still see a battle between those who prefer text-based protocols and the supporters of ASN.1. The emergence of XER (Extended Mark-up Language—XML—Encoding Rules) for ASN.1 has in some ways married the two camps; XER is based on ASN.1 notation for defining types, but is totally character-based (and verbose!) for the transfer of values of those types. However, you will hear people today (with some justification) saying:

- HTML (with Netscape and Microsoft) made provision for write-it-once, read-it-anywhere **Web pages;**

- JAVA made provision for write-it-once, run-it-anywhere **programs;** and

- XML makes provision for write-it-once, process-it-anywhere **data.**

And, of course, there is still CORBA (with its IDL notation and IOP protocol as an encoding) as a communications-specification-language contender!

Also, we still have many Internet Engineering Task Force (IETF) specifications choosing to use BNF and character-based exchanges as the preferred definition mechanism for messages.

It may be some time yet before the world homes in on, understands, or recognizes the "right" way to define and to encode computer communications (and that may or may not be ASN.1 in the form we know it today). We have progressed a lot (in terms of understanding the issues and problems to be solved) from the early 1980s, but we have progressed rather less far in political (lowercase "p") agreements, with a still (alarmingly large) number of contenders for notation to be used in defining protocols. And still people continue to suggest more! (I guess it is no worse than the programming language scene.)

So, I look forward to the next decade with interest! What notation will we be using in 2020 to specify protocol standards? I regret that I may not be around to find out! Some readers will!

19.3 Who Produces Standards?

Over the years and up to the present, there have been five main sets of actors in the production of standards related to computer communication, and in the adoption of various forms of notation to support those standards.

Who are the five?

I would suggest the following:

> There has always been a difficulty over de jure and de facto standards for computer communication around the world. National Standards Institutes often think/hope they wield the power. But the real power over deciding how the world's computers communicate is largely not in their hands, but has shifted over time between many actors.

- mainframe computer vendors in the 1970s, but largely now unimportant;

- CCITT (renamed ITU-T at the start of the 1990s) in the 1980s and 1990s, and still the dominant force in the specification of telecommunications standards today;

- ISO, working largely in collaboration with CCITT/ITU-T, but with its major influence limited to the OSI developments of the 1980s, and perhaps not being a dominant force today except in isolated areas;

- the IETF, its task forces and working groups, now responsible for the development of Internet standards, which have (for many applications) become the de facto standards for computer communication between telecommunications users (while ITU-T remains dominant for standardizing the protocols that make telecommunications possible); and

- with increasing influence today various consortia of manufacturers and other groups, including the SET consortium and the World Wide Web Consortium (W3C), and the CORBA grouping.

The importance of computer vendors in protocol definition had largely declined before ASN.1 entered the scene, with the notable exception of XEROX, which (as stated earlier) gave birth to the original ASN.1 concepts.

ASN.1 as an international specification started life within CCITT as X.409, entitled "Presentation Transfer Syntax and Notation". (Note that the "transfer syntax" was placed first in the—English—title, not the "notation!" Today, we would probably see the notation as the more important part of ASN.1.) The work leading to ASN.1 was originally intended only to provide notational support for the definition of the X.400-series e-mail protocols. However, it very rapidly moved into ISO, and during the early 1980s, although the work was collaborative, it was largely ISO National Bodies (they were then called "Member Bodies") through which most of the input was provided.

In the late 1990s the pendulum swung back (partly due to the decline of OSI, and partly due to reorganizations within ISO), with what had by then become ITU-T making most of the running in progressing new work on ASN.1.

Within IETF, take-up of ASN.1 was always very patchy. This was probably at least in part due to the fact that most of the movers in IETF wanted a specification language that had support from publicly available (for-free) tools. BNF-based text-encodings satisfied this requirement; ASN.1 did not, and does not to this day (1999). So most use of ASN.1 in the IETF world was (and is) using a cut-down version of ASN.1 that was (is) easily capable of being encoded without the use of any tools.

By contrast, ITU-T telecommunications specifications use the full power of ASN.1, and the telecomms and switch vendors implementing those specifications make full use of available tool products for easy, rapid, and (largely) bug-free implementation of protocols that are highly efficient in terms of bandwidth requirements.

19.4 The Numbers Game

The ASN.1 specifications have gone through a variety of designations.

The first published specification was X.409 (1984). X.409 pre-dated the use of the term "Abstract Syntax Notation One (ASN.1)", and was part of the X.400 series. It was seen, quite simply, as a notation (and encoding rules) to aid the specification of protocols in the X.400 (OSI e-mail) suite.

> A boring list of the identifications of ASN.1 specifications over the last twenty years—skip it!

Later, it was completely rewritten (with no technical changes—see later!) and published (with some additions) by ISO as ISO 8824 and ISO 8825 in 1986, and the same text (again with some additions) was then published by CCITT as X.208 and X.209 in 1988. There was a later version of this text (with minor corrections) published jointly by ISO and IEC in 1990 as ISO/IEC 8824 and ISO/IEC 8825. This became known as the infamous "1990 version of ASN.1".

The "1994 version of ASN.1" (with very major extensions to the 1990 version) was published jointly by ISO/IEC and CCITT as a whole raft of new documents with identical text. These were:

ITU-T X.680	ISO/IEC 8824-1
ITU-T X.681	ISO/IEC 8824-2
ITU-T X.682	ISO/IEC 8824-3
ITU-T X.683	ISO/IEC 8824-4
ITU-T X.690	ISO/IEC 8825-1
ITU-T X.691	ISO/IEC 8825-2

Still later, there was a joint ISO/IEC and ITU-T "1997 version" (with only relatively minor changes and additions to the 1994 version). However, while the "final" text was approved in 1997, neither ITU-T nor ISO has yet produced a published copy that people can purchase (current date early 1999)! But watch this space, it is imminent! (Later correction—you can now buy it from ITU-T!)

Readers should note that in 1994 (and in 1997) X.680 was roughly the old X.208 with some extensions, mainly in the character set area. X.681 contained extensions related to the Information Object concept; X.682 was the table and relational and user-defined constraints; X.683 was parameterization; X.690 was the old X.209 with CER and DER added; and X.691 was the PER specification.

Phew! I **hate** numbers! 'Nuff said.

19.5 The Early Years—X.409 and All That

19.5.1 Drafts Are Exchanged and the Name ASN.1 Is Assigned

The first drafts of X.409 were produced in CCITT. In those days both ISO and CCITT had a "7-layer model" for OSI, and they were totally different texts (technically very similar, but largely developed independently). The era of strong collaboration between the two groups was yet to come, and most communication was by written "liaison statements", usually accompanied by a draft of some specification.

> What's in a name? What's in a "dot"? Actually, an awful lot. Without a dot confusion reigns, add the dot, and all is hunky-dory!

This is how (during 1982) X.409 first reached ISO TC97 SC16 (Technical Committee 97—responsible for the whole of computer-related standards, Subcommittee 16—responsible for the OSI model and for all work on OSI standards above the Network Layer). At first, it was unclear how these X.409 concepts fitted into the OSI model, and an ad hoc group (chaired, I think, by Lloyd Hollis) was set up to consider the draft. It rapidly became apparent that this work should be slotted into the Presentation Layer of OSI, and a liaison statement was dispatched welcoming the work.

This X.409 draft came into an ISO vacuum—or perhaps I mean a primordial plasma! There was anarchy, with all the various application layer standards wondering what notational mechanisms to use to define their protocols, and all having different approaches. The new notation was accepted extremely rapidly accepted by every single Application Layer standards group as the means to define their protocols.

It was at this time that a name was considered for the notation, and the ISO group suggested Abstract Syntax Notation One, or "ASN1". The CCITT group replied "OK, but never talk to us about ASN2". Although ASN2 was never proposed, there are those who have argued that ASN.1 (1994) should have been named ASN.2 (see later text).

Notice that in the last paragraph there was no dot after "ASN". This was not a typo! The original proposed name was indeed "ASN1". However, within six months it became apparent that people were frequently mistyping it as "ANS1", and/or misreading it as "ANSI"—the American National Standards Institute. Considerable confusion was being caused! I remember the day when the head of the USA delegation (also Chairman of SC16!) came to the ASN.1 group and said, "Look, I know it **isn't** "ANSI", but it is so close that it is causing problems, can't you change the name?" Uproar! Explosion! But when the dust settled, the "dot" had been inserted and we had "ASN.1". Thereafter no one ever mistyped it or confused it with ANSI!

The "dot" is not without precedent—all CCITT Recommendations are written with a dot—X.400, X.25, V.24, so ASN.1 was readily accepted.

It was at this time that the term "BER" (Basic Encoding Rules) was coined. But in this case there was recognition in both ISO and CCITT that other and perhaps better encoding rules could be produced, but it took ten years before PER (Packed Encoding Rules) eventually emerged.

19.5.2 Splitting BER from the Notation

There were some difficult moments in these early years. It was ISO and not CCITT that had a very strong view on the importance of separating abstract specification (Application Layer) from encoding issues (the first published X.400 specifications were a monolithic protocol directly on the Session Layer, with no Presentation Layer). The X.409 draft, and the eventually published X.409 (1984), contained, interleaved paragraph by paragraph, a description of a piece of ASN.1 notation and the specification of the corresponding BER encoding.

The first thing that ISO decided to do was to rip these pieces apart, and completely rewrite them (in theory with no technical change) as two separate documents, one describing the notation (this eventually became ISO 8824) and one describing BER (this eventually became ISO 8825).

> ISO was serious about the Presentation Layer. Encoding details should be kept clearly separate (in separate documents) from application semantics. A great idea, but CCITT was not quite as evangelical about it. But without ASN.1 the concept would probably never have reached reality.

As closer and closer collaboration occurred between ISO and CCITT in the following years (and on the ASN.1 work in particular), the question of course arose—would CCITT adopt the ISO text for ASN.1 and drop X.409? After some agonizing, it did, and in 1988 X.409 was withdrawn and there were two new

CCITT recommendations in the X.200 series, X.208 and X.209. Recommendation X.200 itself was (and is) the CCITT/ITU-T publication of the OSI Reference Model—eventually aligned with that of ISO but leaning technically far more towards the original CCITT draft than to the OSI one—but that is a separate story! (See my book *Understanding OSI*, available on the Web.) Putting the ASN.1 specifications into the X.200 series was a recognition that ASN.1 had become a general tool for the whole of OSI, having outgrown X.400. I like to think that its move to the X.680 and the X.690 range in 1994 represented its outgrowing of OSI, but I think it was due more to the fact that it now needed six Recommendations, and there was no suitable space left in the X.200 range! (ISO does not have similar problems—a single part Standard like ISO 8824 can grow into ISO 8824 Part 1 (ISO 8824-1), Part 2, etc., without changing its number.)

X.409 was written in a fairly informal style, but when it was rewritten within the ISO community, the rather stilted "standardese" language required for ISO Standards was used. For example, "must" must never be used—use "shall" instead (this was due to claimed translation difficulties into French), do not give examples or reasons, just state clearly and exactly what the requirements are—you are writing a **specification** of what people must do to conform to the Standard, not a piece of descriptive text.

I often advise those who want a gentle introduction to ASN.1 to try to find an old copy of X.409 (1984) and read that—it is written in more informal language, and because the encodings are specified alongside the notation, I believe that it is easier for a beginner to grasp. But I was interested to see that in Oliver's book he claimed that 8824/8825 were more readable and better specifications than X.409! I guess we all have our own views on what makes a good specification!

19.5.3 When Are Changes Technical Changes?

> Correct a spelling, remove an example, trivial things. No problem. Don't you believe it!

Genuinely, ISO attempted to rewrite X.409 without making technical changes, but two crept in. The first was to do with the type "GeneralizedTime". These were in the days when people had human secretaries to do their typing and not word processors. X.409 had been authored in the USA. The ISO text for 8824/8825 had a UK Editor (mea culpa), and the secretary (another name—Barbara Cheadle!), unknown to the Editor, corrected the spelling to "GeneralisedTime". This went unnoticed through all the formal balloting, but was eventually corrected before 8824 was actually published! Irrespective of arguments over what is "correct" English, the term "GeneralizedTime" had to stand, because this was a formal part of the notation, and any change to its spelling represented a technical change!

The second change was only noticed in the early 1990s! Far too late to do anything about it! There was a point of detail about the character string type TeletexString that was only indicated in X.409 in an example. The example was lost in 8824, and the point of detail lost with it—I am afraid I have forgotten the precise details of the point of detail!

19.5.4 The Near-Demise of ASN.1—OPERATION and ERROR

The final incident I want to describe here about the early days is one which almost completely derailed ASN.1.

At that time, CCITT was locked into a four-year time-frame called a **Study Period** where at the start of the four years "Questions" (capital Q!) were formulated. (Each Question generally gave rise to a new Recommendation or to an update of an existing one.) At the end of the Study Period, a complete new set of CCITT Recommendations was published (with a different color cover in each period). In 1980 the color was Yellow, Red in 1984, and Blue in 1988.

(1988 was the last year this complete republication occurred, so if you have a set of the Blue books in mint condition, keep them—they will be valuable 50 years from now!)

> Easy wars are based on misunderstanding or lack of understanding (difficult ones are based on real clashes of self-interest). This was an easy war, but the short time-scales for achieving peace amplified the conflict.

It took time for the administration to prepare these new texts for publication, and in those days CCITT went into a "big sleep" about twelve months before the end of the Study Period, with the new or amended Recommendations finalized, and with only "rubber-stamping" meetings during the following year. It was in mid-1993, with the "big sleep" about to start— we were at five minutes to midnight—when the CCITT ASN.1 group sent their latest draft of X.409 to the ISO group.

Mostly it was only minor tidies, but a whole new section had been added that "hardwired" into the ASN.1 syntax the ability to write constructions such as

```
lookup OPERATION

      ARGUMENTS name Some-type

      RESULT name Result-type

      ERRORS {invalidName, nameNotfound}

  ::= 1
```

and

```
nameNotFound ERROR ::= 1

invalidName ERROR

        PARAMETER reason BITSTRING

                {nameTooLong(1),

                illegalCharacter(2),

                unspecified(3) }

      ::= 2
```

If the reader has read the earlier parts of this book, and in particular Chapters 13 and 14, that syntax will look rather familiar, and the meaning will be perhaps fairly obvious. But to those in the ISO group faced with a simple liaison statement defining the revised ASN.1 (and with absolutely no understanding or knowledge about even the existence of the ROSE work), there was utter incomprehension.

What had this to do with defining datatypes for an abstract syntax (and corresponding encoding rules)? How were ERROR and OPERATION encoded (there was no specification of any encoding in the draft)? What on earth was an "operation" or an "error"? Rip it all out! Had there been more time...! But the ISO group decided that in no way was this stuff going into the ISO Standards that were planned. Agonies within CCITT. Keep it in and risk different Recommendations and Standards for ASN.1?

It was one minute to midnight when the next draft of X.409 reached ISO. The offending OPERATION and ERROR syntax had been removed (deep sigh of relief) but a new Annex had been added defining a "macro notation". This Annex was **very, very** obscure! But many programming languages had a "macro notation" to support the language. (These usually took the form of some template text with dummy parameters that could be instantiated in various places with actual parameters—what was eventually introduced with the parameterization features of ASN.1.) And it **was** one minute to midnight. And the CCITT group **had** agreed to withdraw the OPERATION and ERROR syntax, and deserved a favor in return. The

ISO group agreed to accept the macro notation Annex. Peace had been achieved and ASN.1 had been saved!

In retrospect, this whole incident was probably a **good** thing, although it had reverberations into the late-1990s and beyond. If OPERATION and ERROR had remained hardwired, and there had been no macro notation, it would have been **very** much harder for ASN.1 to develop the concepts related to Information Objects (and it was quite hard anyway!). More on this subject follows.

19.6 Organization and Reorganization!

When the idea of Open Systems Interconnection was first considered in ISO, it came from the work in TC97 SC6 on HDLC (High-Level Data Link Control) from the question "Who is going to define— and how—the formats of what fills the HDLC frames?" At a meeting in Sydney of TC97 it was decided to create a new subcommittee, SC16, to be charged with the task of developing a model for OSI. At its first meeting, about six different proposed models were submitted from each of the major countries, but the submission that most nearly resembled the eventual shape of OSI was that from the European Computer Manufacturers Association (ECMA). The USA voted against the establishment of a new subcommittee, but by some rather interesting political maneuvers (again beyond the scope of this text!), became the Secretariat and provided the Chair for SC16.

Organizational structures matter a bit, but the technical work can often go on despite reorganization above. But sometimes too much turbulence can make it difficult to progress the work formally (and hence to reach publication status). Fortunately, with a joint project between ITU-T/CCITT and ISO/IEC, if you can't progress it in one forum, you can probably do it in the other!

SC16 became one of the largest subcommittees in the whole of ISO, and in its heyday could only meet by taking over a complete large university campus. ASN.1 became a relatively self-contained group within the Presentation Layer Rapporteur Group of SC16.

On the CCITT front, ASN.1 became a part of Study Group VII, and has had a relatively calm (organizational) life. When CCITT changed its name to ITU-T, it had little organizational impact at the bottom levels, the main change being that SG VII became SG 7! This is the home of ASN.1 to this day (within Working Party 5 of SG 7).

On the ISO front, there was a top-level reorganization when ISO agreed that standardization of computer matters was a joint responsibility with the International Electro-Technical Commission (IEC), and formed, with the IEC, a new "Joint Technical Committee 1" to replace TC97. (There has never been, and probably never will be, a JTC2.) This had zero impact on the ASN.1 work, save that the cover-page of the Standards now included the IEC logo alongside that of ISO, and the formal number became ISO/IEC 8824 instead of ISO 8824. JTC1 inherited exactly the same SC structure and the same officers and members as were originally in TC97. It was at this time that the name of contributors to the ISO work changed from "Member Body" to "National Body", but they were still the same organizations—BSI, ANSI, AFNOR, DIN, JISC, to name just a few.

A slightly more disruptive reorganization was when SC5 (programming languages and databases) and SC16 (OSI) were reshaped into a new SC21 and SC22, but the transition was smooth and the ASN.1 work was not really affected.

In the late 1990s, however, the Secretariat of SC21 decided it could no longer resource the subcommittee, and it was split into an SC32 and SC33. ASN.1 was placed in SC33 as a fully fledged Working Group (it had had the lower status of a Rapporteur Group within a Working Group for all its previous history), but it never met under this group as there was no National Body prepared to provide the Secretariat for it, and SC33 was disbanded almost before it ever existed. ASN.1 (together with other remnants of the original OSI work, including the continuing X.400 standardization) was assigned to SC6 (a very old subcommittee, responsible for the lower-layer protocol standards, and with a very long history of a close working relationship with CCITT/ITU-T SG VII/SG 7). This is likely to prove a good home for ASN.1 within ISO.

This last transition was less smooth than earlier reorganizations, and the formal progression of ASN.1 work within ISO was disrupted, but at the technical level the work nonetheless continued, and formal progression of documents was undertaken within the ITU-T structures.

19.7 The Tool Vendors

Of course, when ASN.1 was "invented" in the 1980 to 1984 CCITT Study Period, there were no tools to support the notation. While it drew on Xerox Courier for many of its concepts, it was sufficiently different that none of the Xerox tools was remotely useful for ASN.1.

It was the mid-1980s before tools began to appear, and these were generally just syntax-checkers and pretty-print programs. In the late 1980s, tools as we now know them started to emerge, and the ASN.1 tool vendor industry was borne. (See Chapter 6 for more about ASN.1 tools.)

Of course, in the early days, all those working on ASN.1 were essentially "users"—employees of computer manufacturers or telecommunications companies (sometimes universities), and usually with strong interests in some protocol that was using

> The tool vendors. The Traders of ASIMOV's "Foundation". A law unto themselves, but vital to the success of the enterprise and contributing immensely to its development in the middle years.

ASN.1 as its notation for protocol definition. But at the last meeting in 1999 of the ASN.1 group, the majority of those around the table had strong links one way or another with the vendor of some ASN.1 tool—ASN.1 had come of age!

There was an interesting transition point in the late 1980s when tool vendors were beginning to appear at Standards meetings, and were complaining that there were some features of the ASN.1 syntax that made it hard for computers to read (the main problem was the lack of a semicolon as a separator between assignment statements—eventually resolved by introducing a colon into the value notation for CHOICE and ANY values). At that time, there were strong arguments that ASN.1 was not, and was never intended to be, a computer-processable language. Rather it was a medium for communication between one set of humans (those writing protocol standards) and another set of humans (those producing implementations of those protocols). That view was rapidly demolished, and today ASN.1 is seen as very much a computer language, and many of the changes made in the early 1990s were driven by the need to make it fully computer friendly.

19.8 Object Identifiers

19.8.1 Long or Short, Human or Computer Friendly, That Is the Question

Object identifiers (I will use the informal abbreviation OID in what follows) predated the "Information Object" concept by at least five years, although today they are closely associated with that concept.

It was in the mid-1980s that it became apparent that many different groups within OSI had a requirement for unambiguous names to identify things that their protocol was dealing with, and which could be assigned in a distributed fashion by many groups around the world.

A similar problem had been tackled a few years earlier in SC6, but with the narrower focus of providing a name-space for so-called "Network Service Access Point Addresses"—NSAP addresses, the OSI equivalent of IP addresses on the Internet. If the reader studies the NSAP addressing scheme, some similarities will be seen to the Object Identifier system, but with the very important difference that the length of NSAP addresses had to be kept relatively short, while for application layer protocols long(ish) object identifiers were considered OK.

Around 1986 a lot of blood was spilt over the OBJECT IDENTIFIER type, and it could easily have gone in a totally opposite direction (but I think the right decision was eventually taken). This was not a CCITT vs. ISO fight—by this time the two groups were meeting jointly, and divisions between them were rarely apparent. (That situation continues to this day, where at any given meeting, the various attendees can often claim representation of both camps, but where

> Again, what's in a name? Well the length might matter if you are carrying it in your protocol!

if they **are** delegates from one camp or the other, discussion almost never polarizes around the two camps.)

To return to OIDs! The argument was over whether an OID should be as short as possible, using only numbers, or whether it should be much more human friendly and be character-based, with encouragement to use quite long names as components within it.

The eventual compromise was what we have today—an object identifier tree with unique numbers on each arc, but with a rather loose provision for providing names as well on each arc. In the value notation for object identifiers, the numbers always appear (apart from the top-level arcs, where the names are essentially well-known synonyms for the numbers), but the names can be added as well to aid human beings. In encodings, however, only the numbers are conveyed.

A further part of the compromise was the introduction of the "ObjectDescriptor" type to carry long human-friendly text, albeit text that was not guaranteed to be world-wide unambiguous, and hence which was not of much use to computers. As stated earlier, the "ObjectDescriptor" type was the biggest damp squib in the entire ASN.1 armory!

A very similar battle raged—but with pretty much the opposite outcome—within the X.500 group a year or so later. X.500 names (called "Distinguished Names") are an ASN.1 data-type that is (simplifying slightly again) essentially

```
SEQUENCE OF
    SEQUENCE
        {attribute-id      TYPE-IDENTIFIER.&id,
         attribute-value TYPE-IDENTIFIER.&Type}
```

Remember that "TYPE-IDENTIFIER.&id" is essentially a synonym for "OBJECT IDENTIFIER", so it is clear that X.500 names are considerably longer than ASN.1 names.

There was pressure in the late 1980s (from groups outside of X.500) for X.500 to support use of a simple single OBJECT IDENTIFER (a so-called "short-form" name) alongside its Distinguished Names (so-called "long-form" names), and I believe it was formally agreed within SC21 that this should happen, but I think it never did happen!

19.8.2 Where Should the Object Identifier Tree Be Defined?

Another problem with the definition of the OBJECT IDENTIFIER type is that it is not just defining a data type, it is implicitly establishing a whole registration authority structure.

This went beyond the remit of the ASN.1 group (a separate group in OSI

> Demarcation disputes. Ugh!

was charged with sorting out registration authority issues, and produced its own standard). This was a source of continuing wrangling over almost a decade. Initially (mid-1980), it was within ISO that people were saying "The description of the object identifier tree should be moved from ASN.1 to the Registration Authority Standard", but the CCITT people were saying "No way—ASN.1 users want to be able to read that text as part of the ASN.1 Standard, and control of it should remain with the ASN.1 group."

It remained in the ASN.1 Standard until (and including) the 1990 publication. But in the early 1990s, the roles were reversed, and there was pressure from ITU-T (largely from outside the ASN.1 work) to move the text from X.680 (ISO/IEC 8824-1) to X.660 (ISO/IEC 9834-1). There was some opposition within the ASN.1 group itself, but the move happened, and relevant text was deleted from X.680/8824 and replaced by a reference to X.660/9834. Ever since then, there have been various liaisons between the keepers of the respective standards to try to ensure continued consistency! Fortunately, however, the work on the object identifier tree itself was completed long ago and is very stable. (But see 19.8.3!)

19.8.3 The Battle for Top-Level Arcs and the Introduction of RELATIVE-OIDs

The change of name from CCITT to ITU-T was a simple top-level name change, yes? But remember that two of the top arcs of the object identifier tree were "ccitt" and "joint-iso-ccitt".

> Everyone wants to be at the top of the tree, but in this case for good reasons—it reduces the verbosity of their protocols.

ITU-T proposed two new arcs (with new numbers) for "itu-t" and "joint-iso-itu-t". Those who have read the text associated with Figure 16.10 will realize that while it was not wholly impossible to accede to this request, it would be very difficult! Eventually, the new names were accepted as synonyms for the existing arcs (keeping the same numbers).

Shortly after this, the demand increased from international organizations for object identifier name-space using a top arc. Organizations realized that object identifier values they allocated (and used in their protocols) would be shorter if they could get "hung" nearer the top of the tree. ITU-R, the International Postal Union, and IETF were among organizations expressing (with various degrees of strength) the wish to wrest some top-level arcs from ISO and ITU-T (who were surely never going to use all the ones allocated to them).

This issue looks today as if it has been defused by the addition of a new type called RELATIVE-OID. (Yes, at the time of writing it **is** OID, not OBJECT IDENTIFIER.) A RELATIVE-OID value identifies parts of the object identifier tree that sits below some (statically determined) root node, and the encodings of these values only contain the numbers of the nodes beneath that root node, omitting the common prefix.

This rather simple proposal was a very much cut-down version of an earlier proposal that would have allowed the common prefix to be transmitted in an instance of communication, and then be automatically associated with particular RELATIVE-OID values that were transmitted later in that instance of communication.

(It is always very difficult when writing books to avoid them becoming rapidly out of date—you either do not talk about things like RELATIVE-OID, or you do, with the danger that a few weeks after publication you find it has either been withdrawn or has been dramatically changed. But in this case, I am fairly confident that it will be added to ASN.1 much as described.)

19.9 The REAL Type

The REAL type might seem innocuous enough, but was also the source of controversy around 1986.

Everyone agreed we had to have it, but how to encode it? (The actual encoding eventually agreed on is fully described in 9.3.5, and the interested reader should refer to that.)

There were several issues, of which binary vs. character encodings was one. As usual, the easy compromise was to allow both, but that produced problems later when canonical

> Probably just an academic exercise—nobody uses REAL in actual protocols! But it produced its own heated moments.

encodings were needed, and the dirty fudge of saying that base 2 and base 10 values that are mathematically equal are regarded as distinct abstract values, and hence encode differently, even in the canonical encoding rules was taken.

But the main problem was with the binary encoding format. There was a (fairly new) standard at that time for floating point formats for computer systems, and it was generally used by people handling floating point in software, but not by existing hardware (later it was implemented in chips). Naturally, there were those who advocated use of this format for ASN.1 encodings.

The counterargument, however, eventually prevailed (and again I think this was the **right** decision). The counterargument was that we were some time away from a de facto standard for floating point formats, and that what mattered was to find a format that could be easily encoded and decoded with whatever floating point unit your hardware possessed.

This principle dictated, for example, the use of a "sign and magnitude" (rather than "two's complement" or "one's complement") mantissa, because "sign and magnitude" can be easily generated or processed by hardware of the other two forms, but the converse is not true. It was also this principle that gave rise to the rather curious format (not present in **any** real floating point hardware or package) involving the "F" scaling factor described in 16.3.5.2.

Finally, there was a lot of pressure at the time to support specific encodings that would identify "common and important" numbers that otherwise would have no finite representation, such as "3.14159..." and "2.7183...," and also values such as "overflow", and "not-a-number", but in the end all that was added was encodings to identify PLUS-INFINITY and MINUS-INFINITY, with plenty of encoding space for identification of other things related to type REAL later. The pressure to provide these additional encodings evaporated, and no extensions have been made, nor do any seem likely now.

19.9.10 Character String Types: Let's Try To Keep It Short!

> You were promised the history in Section II, so here it is! There are probably better histories around on the Web—go look for them!

The history of the development of encodings for "characters" (and discussion on just what a "character" is) is much broader than ASN.1. ASN.1 has not really contributed to this work, but rather has done its best to enable ASN.1 users to have available notation that can let them reference in their protocols, clearly and simply, these various character encoding standards.

The result, however, has been a steady growth in the number of character types in ASN.1 over the years, with a lot of fairly obsolete baggage being carried around now.

Chapter 9 promised that we would here provide a description of the history of the development of character encoding schemes, and the impact this had on ASN.1 over the years. What follows is the main parts of that history (but detail is sometimes lacking, and it is not a complete history—that is left to other texts), with the impact on ASN.1.

19.10.1 From the Beginning to ASCII

The earliest character coding standards were used for the telegraph system, and on punched paper tape and cards. The earliest formats used five bits to represent each character (32 possible encodings), with an encoding for "alpha-shift" and "numeric-shift" to allow uppercase letters, digits, and a few additional characters.

Later, the use of seven bits with an eighth parity bit became the de facto standard, and this eventually became enshrined in the 8-bit bytes of current computers. The ASCII code-set is the best-known 7-bit encoding, with essentially 32 so-called "control characters" (many of whose functions related to the framing of early protocol packets) and 94 so-called "graphics characters" (printing characters), plus SPACE and DEL (delete). (DEL, of course, is in the all-ones position—127 decimal—because on punched paper tape the only thing you could do if you had made a mistake was to punch out all the rest of the holes—you could not remove a hole!).

> Five-bit codes, seven-bit codes. And to come later, 16-bit codes and 32-bit codes! I doubt anyone will EVER suggest 64-bit codes . . . but on second thoughts, how many bits does Microsoft Word take to indicate fonts, etc.? (OK, that is usually per paragraph not per character, but in the future . . . ?)

ASCII has formed the basis of our character coding schemes for close to 40 years, and is only now being replaced. ASCII is in fact the American variant of the international standard ISO 646, which defines a number of "national options" in certain character positions, and many other countries defined similar (but different) national variants. The UK variant was often called (incorrectly!) "UK ASCII".

19.10.2 The Emergence of the International Register of Character Sets

Early computer protocols used 7-bit encodings, and retained the use of the eighth bit as a parity bit. That is why we find today that if you wish to send arbitrary binary over e-mail, it gets converted into a 7-bit format, and more or less doubles in size! More modern protocols

> Providing encodings for all the characters in the world—first attempt, and not a bad one.

(such as those used to access Web pages) provide what is called "full 8-bit transparency" and the eighth bit is a perfectly ordinary bit, which can carry user information.

As protocols developed, the use of a parity bit was very quickly dropped in favor of a Cyclic Redundancy Code (CRC) as an error-detecting code on a complete packet of information, and character coding schemes were free to move to an 8-bit encoding capable of representing 256 characters.

There were two developments related to this: The first of these was developed as early as 1973. This was ISO 2022, which established a framework (based on ISO 646) for the representation of all the characters in the world. (I am afraid the following description is of necessity somewhat simplified—the so-called multiple-byte formats and the dynamically redefinable character sets of 2022 are not mentioned in what follows.)

The way ISO 2022 worked was to identify the first two columns (32 cells holding control characters) of the ASCII structure as cells that could contain (represent, define) any so-called C-set of characters, and the remaining 94 positions (keeping the SPACE and DEL positions fixed as SPACE and DEL) as cells that could contain (represent, define) any so-called G-set. Moreover, within the C-set positions, the ASCII ESC character would always be kept at that precise position, so a C-set of characters was in fact only allowed to be 31 control functions.

The old parity bit could be used to identify one of two meanings (one of two character sets) for encodings of C-sets, called the C0 and the C1 set. If one of the C-sets in use included control characters for "shift-outer" and "shift-inner" (which affected the interpretation of G-set but not C-set codes), then the combination of using these together with the old parity bit enabled reference to (encodings of) up to **four** G-sets, called G0, G1, G2, and G3.

Finally, there was the concept of a register of C-sets and G-sets that, for each register entry, would assign characters to each position in the ASCII structure. At any point in time, up to two C-sets and up to four G-sets could be "designated and invoked" into the C0, C1, G0, G1, G2, and G3 positions. The ESC character (required to be present in the same position in all C-sets, remember) was given a special meaning. Each register entry contained the specification of binary codes that could follow the ESC character to "designate and invoke" any register entry into either a C0 or C1 position (for C entries) or into one of the G0 to G3 positions (for G-entries).

All that remained was to produce the register entries! This became the "International Register of Coded Character Sets to be used with Escape Sequences", commonly referred to as "the international register of character sets".

The register was originally maintained by the European Computer Manufacturer's Association (ECMA), and grew to well over 200 entries covering virtually the entire world's character sets. Today, it is maintained by the Japanese Industrial Standards Committee (JISC), the Japanese equivalent of BSI and ANSI and AFNOR and DIN. Both ECMA and JISC provide free copies and free updates to interested parties, but JISC now maintains a website with every register entry on it. (See Appendix 5 if you want to access this site.)

ASN.1 provides full support for ISO 2022, with GraphicString and GeneralString, and relies on the International Register for the definition of many of its other character string types.

19.10.3 The Development of ISO 8859

ISO 8859 arrived much later (in 1987), and came in a number of "parts".

The problem with the 2022 scheme was that because of the inclusion of ESC sequences to make new designations and invocations, encodings for characters were not fixed length.

ISO 8859 was designed to meet the needs of European languages with a fixed (eight bits per character) encoding. Each part of 8859 specified ASCII as its so-called "left half"—the encoding you got with the old parity bit set to zero, and a further 94 printing characters in its "right-half" designed to meet the

> Giving European languages full coverage with an efficient encoding—a standard ignored by ASN.1! Who cares about Europe in International Standardization? (President of the European Commission, please do not read this!)

needs of various European languages. So 8859-1 is called "Latin alphabet No.1", and in addition to ASCII provides characters with grave, circumflex, acute accents, cedillas, tildas and umlauts, together with a number of other characters. 8859-6 is called "Latin/Arabic", and contains arabic characters in its right-half.

ASN.1 never provided any direct support for 8859, although 8859 encodings were quite often used in computer systems in Europe.

19.10.4 The Emergence of ISO 10646 and Unicode

19.10.4.1 The Four-Dimensional Architecture

A very major development in the early 1990s (still, almost a decade later, to work its way completely into computer systems and protocols) was the development of a completely new framework for encoding characters, wholly unrelated to the ASCII structure. (But of course capable of encoding ASCII characters!)

> Probably the most important development in character set encoding work EVER. It is hard to see a likely change from this architecture at any time in the future. Wow! At ANY time in the future? Yup.

Here you must look at Figure 19.1. (Yes, the first figure in this chapter—you must be feeling deprived!) This shows a four-dimensional structure (compared with the ASCII two-dimensional code table).

Figure 19.1 shows a street of 256 houses. Each house has 256 "planes" in it (positioned vertically, and running left to right within the house on the street). Each plane has 256 rows in it (running top to bottom within each plane of each house), and each row has 256 cells in it (running from left to right within each row). Each cell can contain (define, represent) a different character. (Actually, the correct technical term for a house is a "group"—"house" is not used, but I prefer to call them houses!)

The very first plane (number zero) of the first house (number zero) is called **the Basic Multilingual Plane** or "BMP". The first row of that plane contains Latin Alphabet No. 1 (8859-1), and hence contains ASCII in its left-half.

(In the early drafts of ISO 10646, the other parts of 8859 occupied successive rows, and hence ASCII appeared multiple times, but this was removed in the "fight" with Unicode (see 19.10.4.2), and the other parts of 8859 only have their right-hand halves present.)

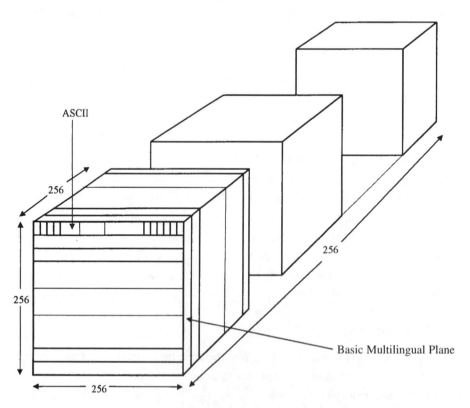

Figure 19.1   256 houses each with 256 planes each with 256 rows each with 256 cells.

Notice that any cell of any row of any plane of any house can be identified by four values of 0 to 255, that is to say, by 32 bits. So in its basic form ISO 10646 is a 32-bits per character encoding scheme.

Notice also that the numerical value of these 32 bits for ASCII characters is simply the numerical value of those characters in 7-bit ASCII—the top 25 bits are all zero!

Now, it is a sad fact of life that if

- you take all the characters there are in the world (defining things like "a-grave" and "a-circumflex" and even more complicated combinations of scribbles used in the Thai language as separate and distinct characters requiring a fixed length encoding), and

- you admit that glyphs (scribbles) in the Chinese and Japanese and Korean scripts that look to a Western eye to be extremely similar are actually distinct characters that need separate encodings, and

- you include all the scribbles carved into Egyptian tombstones and on bark long preserved in deepest Africa, and

- you include ASCII multiple times by putting the whole of each part of 8859 into successive rows of the BMP, then

you find that there are nowhere near 2 to the power 32 "characters" you would want to encode, but that there are very significantly more than 2 to the power 16.

The ISO 10646 structure permits all such characters to be represented with a fixed 32 bits per character, but is this overkill? Can we manage with just 16 bits per character if we do some judicious pruning?

19.10.4.2 Enter Unicode

(For a pointer to Unicode material on the Web, see Appendix 5.)

While the ISO group JTC1 SC2 was beavering away trying to develop ISO 10646, computer manufacturers were independently getting together to rec-

> The manufacturers flex their muscle. 32 bits per character is not necessary or sensible for commercially important character sets! 16 bits can be made to work.

ognize that neither the ISO 2022 nor the ISO 8859 schemes were adequate for the increasingly global communications infrastructure and text-processing requirements of the world, but they jibbed at going to a full 32 bits per character. Can't we make 16 bits suffice?

Well, we can reverse some of the earlier decisions. Let's ignore Egyptian hieroglyphs and anything of interest only to librarians. Let's also introduce the concept of **combining characters** with which we can build scribbles like a-grave etc. (this does not save much for European languages, but saves a lot for Eastern languages such as Thai). Of course, from one point of view, use of combining characters means we no longer have a fixed-length encoding for each character, but that depends on your definition of what is a character!

Finally, let us perform "Han unification" or "CJK Unification" to produce a "unified code" or "Unicode". CJK Unification means that we look at the scribbles in the Chinese (C), Japanese (J), and Korean (K) scripts with a western eye, and decide that they are sufficiently similar that we can assign all three similar scribbles to a single cell in our street of houses.

Now we have cracked it! There are less than 2 to the power 16 (important) characters in the world, and we can fit them all into the Basic Multilingual Plane and use just 16 bits per character to represent them.

Of course, when the final balloting to approve the ISO 10646 draft occurred, there were massive "NO" votes, saying "replace it with Unicode!"

19.10.4.3 The Final Compromise

ISO 10646 was published as an International Standard in 1993 (about 750 pages long!), and the Unicode specification was published in 1992 by Addison-Wesley on behalf of the Unicode Consortium, with version 2 appearing in 1996.

> And the amazing thing about international standardization is that compromises ARE often reached, and standards agreed upon.

Unicode and ISO 10646 were aligned: the CJK unification and the inclusion of combining characters was agreed, and the Basic Multilingual Plane of ISO 10646 was populated with exactly the same characters as appeared in the Unicode specification, and close collaboration has continued since.

However, important differences remained in the two texts. The ISO text describes three "levels of implementation" of ISO 10646. In level 1, combining characters are forbidden. Everything is encoded with the same number of bits, 32 (UCS-4) bits if you want the whole street, or 16 (UCS-2) bits if you just want the characters in the Basic Multilingual Plane. In level 2, you can use combining characters, but only if the character you want is not present in a populated cell (this forbids the use of "a" with the combining character "grave" to get "a-grave"). In level 3, anything goes. Unicode does not describe these levels, but it is in the spirit of Unicode to use combining characters wherever possible.

There are also other differences between the texts that do not relate to character encoding (and hence are irrelevant to ASN.1): the Unicode specification contains some excellent classificatory material that says what characters should be regarded as numbers, upper/lowercase mappings, and so on; such text is missing from ISO 10646.

After the initial publication of version 1 of Unicode and of ISO 10646, work continued. There **are** now characters in cells outside of the BMP, but both groups have agreed on a mechanism for referencing them within a 16-bit encoding scheme (called UTF-16—Universal Transformation Function 16) by using reserved characters in the BMP as escape characters to effectively designate and invoke other planes into the BMP position (although that is not the terminology used).

Another extremely important development was the definition of UTF-8, briefly described in 9.12 and described in more detail in 16.3.15. This provides a variable number of octets per character, but with all ASCII characters represented with just one octet, with their normal ASCII encoding (with the top bit—the old parity bit—set to zero).

For in-core handling of characters in programming languages (and operating system interfaces), computer vendors are supporting 16 bits (usually) or 32 bits (some) or both representations of characters. But for storage on disk or for transfer, UTF-8 is proving a very popular format.

19.10.5 And the Impact of All This on ASN.1?

Current ASN.1 support for character sets has been described in Section II, and it should now be possible for the reader to relate that text to the development of character set standards. The history of character set work in ASN.1 has, however, been a long uphill struggle to try to meet the demands of its users. It has not always succeeded in keeping everybody happy!

On the character set front, ASN.1 has just rolled with the punches. It has not seriously contributed to either repertoire definitions or to encodings. What it HAS tried to do is to provide simple notational support for referencing character set standards.

X.409 made no use of any of the ISO character set standards apart from ISO 646 (equal to CCITT International Alphabet #5), which it used in the definition of ISO646String (no control characters) and IA5String (control characters included). "ISO646String" is still a permitted type, but the synonym "VisibleString" is preferred. NumericString and PrintableString were also present in X.409, but with the character repertoires and the encodings hardwired into ASN.1 (as they still are today).

The only other two character string types in X.409 were T61String (with the preferred synonym today of TeletexString) and VideotexString, which were defined by reference to what was then Recommendations T.61 and T.100 and T.101.

In the early 1980s, writers of ISO standards had to get special permission to reference any specification that was not an ISO standard. So TeletexString and VideotexString posed some problems. The decision was taken (when the rewrite that produced ISO 8824 and ISO 8825 was done) to recast the definitions (with no technical change!) in terms of references to the international register of character sets described earlier, and this was successfully accomplished (by adding some new register entries!).

At the same time, GraphicString and GeneralString were added to provide full support for the International Register.

There were two problems with this: first, new entries were being continually made to the register, so it was very unclear what implementation of GraphicString and GeneralString really meant—these were open-ended specifications. Second, and perhaps more importantly, recasting TeletexString as a reference to particular register entries effectively "froze" it at the 1984 T.61 definition, but many countries made (successful) attempts to get their scripts added to the teletex Recommendations and were (perhaps not surprisingly!) annoyed that they were still not part of the formal definition of TeletexString in ASN.1!

Eventually the political pressure to change TeletexString in ASN.1 became just too great, and in 1994 a whole raft of new register entries was added as permissible entries to designate and invoke within a TeletexString encoding. What about existing implementations of existing protocols? Political pressure is no respector of such minor technical matters! The formal definition of TeletexString changed!

There was another change that also caused some upsets. Formally, VisibleString and IA5String referred to register entry #2, which was the so-called "International Reference Version" of ISO 646 (but virtually everyone—incorrectly—interpreted that as "ASCII"). But ISO 646 was changed in the late 1980s to introduce the "dollar" character—present in ASCII, but not in the International Reference Version of

ISO 646. So ASN.1 changed the reference to register entry #6 (ASCII). At the same time it changed the default G0 set at the start of all GraphicString and GeneralString encodings from #2 to #6. This caused great anger from the X.400 group, who now recommend that in these encodings the G-sets should be specifically designated and invoked by escape sequences, and a default should not be assumed.

Then ISO 10646 came along, and the ASN.1 group listened to the discussions between the ISO workers and the Unicode workers with interest, but from the sidelines. When a compromise was reached and ISO 10646 was published, it looked easy: ASN.1 provided two new types, UniversalString (UCS-4 32-bit encoding), and BMPString (UCS-2 16-bit encoding) for characters in the Basic Multilingual Plane; UCS-2 and UCS-4 provided escapes into encodings using the International Register—effectively the ability to embed GeneralString encodings in UniversalString or BMPString. In the interests of simplicity ASN.1 locked these escape mechanisms out in ASN.1 encodings, again causing complaints today from sophisticated users!

A more serious problem was that just after the ink was dry on the 1994 ASN.1 publication, UTF-8 (and UTF-16), described earlier, arrived as amendments to ISO 10646 and to Unicode. UTF8String was added to ASN.1 in the 1997 version, but at the time of writing there is no support for UTF-16, but some pressure to provide it!

In an attempt to "get out from under" in this character set and encoding debate, ASN.1 introduced "CHARACTER STRING" in 1994, supported by JTC1 SC2, which included an annex (but only an informative one!) in ISO 10646 that specified object identifier values to be used to identify character repertoires (including restrictions to level 1 or level 2 as already described) and encoding schemes (UCS-2 and UCS-4).

The type "CHARACTER STRING" was originally intended to be very efficient, with the object identifiers used to identify the character abstract and transfer syntaxes of character strings within a "SEQUENCE OF CHARACTER STRING" being transmitted only once. Unfortunately, the mechanism used to provide this turned out to have some fatal bugs in it, and was withdrawn. A later mechanism of "dynamic constraints", or "run-time parameters" attempted to provide equivalent support, but foundered because the power to complexity ratio was found to be too low. (This is discussed further in 19.16.)

ASN.1 also provided mappings from the names of "collections" of characters in ISO 10646 into ASN.1 (sub)type names, and provided (sub)type names corresponding to the different "levels of implementation" of ISO 10646, and value references for each of the characters in 10646. (See Chapter 9.)

That is the history to date, but watch this space. The saga of character sets and encodings is probably not over yet.

19.11 ANY, Macros, and Information Objects— Hard to Keep That Short (Even the Heading Has Gone to Three Lines)!

Maybe we can keep it short—the information object concept has been well and fully discussed earlier, and ANY and macros were withdrawn from ASN.1 in 1994, so perhaps there is not really much more to say!

> Much of this (if you are reading from front to back!) you already know. Let's pull the historical threads together.

The story starts with the attempted introduction of the OPERATION and ERROR syntax into ASN.1 in 1982/83 as described earlier.

This attempt failed, and macros were introduced. It turned out that what the macro notation really provided (forget about what it appeared to provide!) was the ability to define arbitrary syntactic extensions (but with no semantics to relate those extensions to other ASN.1 constructs) to ASN.1. Until 1986, there were only two macros defined. These were defined in ROSE and (surprise, surprise!) were called OPERATION and ERROR; they provided for any ASN.1 module that imported these macros to write precisely the OPERATION and ERROR syntax described earlier.

Of course, what was really happening (but this was only realized about five years later) was that the syntax was being provided to give ROSE users a reasonably friendly syntax with which to provide the information needed to complete the ROSE protocol—ASN.1 types and values associated with the definition of operations and errors that would be carried in ROSE messages. In other words, Information Objects. But while the macro notation gave ROSE the ability to define the syntax it wanted, the underlying information object concepts were missing, and the use of that syntax (to define information associated with an operation or error) had no formal link with the ROSE messages.

Around 1986 there was a sudden explosion in the writing of new macros. It seemed that almost every group using ASN.1 found the need to add new syntax to the ASN.1 notation. What were they all doing?

No one really knew, in terms of a global picture. The uses of that new syntax were many and varied, and had nothing to do with operations or errors. Moreover, tool providers were beginning to complain about the macro notation.

It became clear that (at least formally) it was possible to write new notation that claimed to define an ASN.1 type, but which totally failed to define the type unless accompanied by value notation (such as value notation in a value reference assignment, or use of DEFAULT in an element of a SET or SEQUENCE).

There were two other major problems.

The first was that ASN.1 users were given (via the macro notation) the power to define arbitrarily complex syntactic extensions to ASN.1 using the Bacchus-Naur Form (BNF) notation. BNF is an **extremely** powerful notation that is often used to define the syntax of programming languages (and is indeed used to formally define the syntax of the ASN.1 notation itself). However, it is well known to definers of programming languages and other users of BNF that if the resulting syntax is to be computer friendly (easily parsed by computers), then some moderately sophisticated and complex restrictions have to be adhered to in the BNF definition. No such restrictions were applied to its use in ASN.1.

The second problem was that it was generally not possible to find the end of a new piece of syntax introduced by a macro without knowing the details of that macro. But the definition of the macro could well follow the first use of the macro name and hence of the new syntax.

Whoops! Tool vendors did not like it! Some of the better tools hardwired into their tool knowledge of the syntax defined by macros in most known international standards, and then simply ignored the actual syntax definition (macro definition) supplied to the tool. It worked, but ... .

Around 1988, the USA campaigned strongly within SC21 for an embargo on the writing of new macros, and succeeded in getting a resolution passed forbidding such new macros until "either the macro notation was replaced, or the problems with it were resolved". It took about five years for this demand to be satisfied with, in fact, replacement.

Most of that time was spent trying to determine just exactly what the different groups were using macros for, but eventually light dawned, and it became apparent that in almost all cases the definition of extensions to the ASN.1 syntax was (as with ROSE) there to provide users of a protocol full of holes with a human-friendly but formal notation to specify the contents of those holes. Use of the macro notation was (almost) always associated with use of "ANY" (and later "ANY DEFINED BY") in ASN.1-defined messages. (There were important exceptions, such as the ENCRYPTED macro in X.500, where the new syntax was being used to provide a real extension to ASN.1 that was later satisfied using the user-defined constraint and parameterization, described earlier in this text.)

Around this time (late 1980s, early 1990s) the problems with "ANY" became more widely recognized (although they had been flagged as early as 1985, with attempts to shore up "ANY" with "ANY DEFINED BY").

The attempt to understand what macros were being used for and to define an appropriate replacement for macros and ANY went through many iterations and false starts over several years. "Nonencodable types" and "table types" were terms that were invented and discarded.

Eventually something was almost ready, but it was complicated, and the terminology was not clear. There was a critical meeting (I think in Seoul, Korea, and I am pretty sure it was Bancroft Scott's first international ASN.1 meeting) in which it looked as though we could not find a replacement for macros—the earlier work was just too complex. But after a night of no sleep, solutions began to appear. The next day we started to discuss the Information Object Class concept, and to keep things simple, we agreed to allow just (eg):

```
OPERATION.&Type
```

without any constraint applied to it. (Something I still regret!)

But the Seoul meeting was a good one. What looked (at the start) like the abandonment of several years of work ended with the Information Object Class terminology and associated concepts pretty well as we know them today.

Slightly later, another crucial meeting (at which probably no one really understood the magnitude of the decision taken) occurred around 1991—Washington, DC, I think (I remember the room, but can't remember the location!). The decision made at this meeting was to **withdraw** from ASN.1:

- The entire macro notation.

- The ANY and ANY DEFINED BY syntax.

These were to be replaced by the notation for defining information object classes, objects, and sets, and the associated "information from object class" notation and the application of table and relational constraints.

There was around this time a popular UK television series about UK Government in which a civil servant would often say to a Cabinet Minister, "Minister, that is very brave of you." The Minister would wince, and almost instantly attempt to withdraw what he had been proposing.

No one told the ASN.1 group that they were being "very brave" in withdrawing the macro and ANY and ANY DEFINED BY notation, but someone should have done so! I don't know whether they (we) would have backed off even if told, but I am sure that the extent of the adverse reaction was not anticipated.

This was the first (and only) non-backwards-compatible change to ASN.1 in its 20-year (to-date) history, and gave rise to the "ASN.1 1990 problem"—see 19.12—which lingered on for a decade and more.

19.12 The ASN.1 (1990) Controversy

When the 1994 version of ASN.1 was published, there was an accompanying campaign to get people to change their specifications from use of ANY and ANY DEFINED BY and macros to use of the information object concepts. I think the ASN.1 group felt that as this would not change any "bits on the line", it was not a big deal. But of course **any** change to a specification (even to add a single comma) that is

> Never, never, never produce a specification that makes illegal what was previously legal. If you do, you will regret it! But maybe sometimes it is the only way to get rid of a bad feature?

"stable" and not immediately about to be reissued in a new version is actually a costly exercise. The gains must be apparent.

The ASN.1 group had no doubt: there were so many flaws with the macro notation and the use of ANY, and the information object concepts and associated notation were so much better. Everyone should make the transition. A transition plan was agreed. A lot of the use of macro notation was in the original ROSE OPERATION and ERROR macros. So it was agreed that ROSE would change in 1994 (it did—keeping the old macro definition as an informative annex) and that users of ROSE would change no later than 1998.

New specifications (such as SET—Secure Electronic Transactions), did not, of course, like the readers of this book(!), have any problems in adopting the new concepts—they provided important clarity in the specification of protocols with holes in them.

Specifications such as X.400 and X.500, which defined their own macros and were still in the process of being extended, also bettered the agreed timeframe. They recognized the greater clarity of the new notation, and switched to it early in the 1990s.

However, there were some groups that found the change more difficult, and resisted it for longer. Interestingly, the embargo that the USA placed on writing new macros led one group whose protocol was almost 50% "ANY" (of course I exaggerate!) to define (in English) their own notation for specifying the information objects (as we now call them) that would complete their protocol. This notation is called "Generic Definition of Managed Objects" (GDMO), and is today supported by its own set of tools specific to that application and that notation. This group had the least incentive, and took longest, to make the transition to the 1994 version of ASN.1 (i.e., removal of uses of "ANY" from their protocol).

It is normal in ISO for a revised Standard to automatically replace an earlier version. It replaces it in the sense that the older version can no longer be purchased, is no longer recorded in the catalogue of available ISO Standards, and new Standards are not allowed to refer to the old version.

Because the definition of the ASN.1 notation in ASN.1 (1994) was not fully backwards compatible with the ASN.1 (1990) definition (and because everyone knew that time was needed for standards referencing ASN.1 to update their specifications to conform to the 1994 versions), there was strong pressure to "retain" ASN.1 (1990). ISO Central Secretariat agreed to this, provided a resolution to that effect was passed by SC21 at each of its annual plenary meetings.

Of course, these resolutions became the focus of a battle, with each year the ASN.1 group increasingly strongly proposing withdrawal of ASN.1 1990, and each year some group or other saying "we are not ready yet." The battle continues!

This has been a salutary lesson, and if in an ASN.1 meeting anyone dares to propose a change that would make illegal anything that could reasonably be interpreted as legal under the current wording, there are howls of "1990, 1990", and the proposal fails! Even if changes do not affect the bits on the line, the **notation** is now sacrosanct—too many people use it, and existing specifications can **not** be made retrospectively illegal.

19.13 The Emergence of PER

19.13.1 The First Attempt—PER-2

Pronounce that "PER minus 2"!

Work on producing better encoding rules started at about the same time as work on understanding how macros were being used, and on mending or replacing macros, and was for a long time overshadowed by that work, with only a small number of people really contributing to work on new encoding rules.

The original work (let me call this "PER-2", pronounced "PER minus 2"!) was based on using BER and "improving" it. The recognition was that BER often transmitted octets down the

> It took three attempts to get PER to where it is today—PER-2, PER-1, and finally real-PER.

line that a decoder (provided they had knowledge of the identical type definition to that being used by an encoder) could totally predict. This was what **had** to be sent at that point. Therefore it did not need to be sent.

It was also recognized that if the length field of a constructed encoding was changed to provide a count of the number of TLVs in the encoding of the contents rather than a count of the octets in the contents, then further octets could be removed. And finally, it was recognized that if there were constraints on the length of a character string field or on the size of an integer, then length fields could be omitted.

Accept these changes to BER, and then examine Figure 19.2, a (slightly contrived) example of a type to be encoded, and Figure 19.3, the BER encoding of that type.

Looking at Figure 19.3, we have 22 octets in the BER encoding. But all except octets 5, 10–11, 13–18, and 22 (a total of 10 octets) are completely known by a decoder, and need never be transmitted! PER-2 said "delete them!".

(Interestingly, while the final real-PER specification was totally different from this early approach, it is just these 10 octets that the current real-PER will transmit!)

The PER-2 draft said essentially:

- Do a standard BER encoding (slightly modified to provide counts of TLVs rather than octets for constructed encodings).

- Apply the following rules to delete octets from the encoding.

- At the receiving end, apply the rules in reverse to reconstruct the original BER encoding.

- Do a standard BER decoding (again modified to use TLV counts).

```
Example-for-encoding ::= SEQUENCE
    {first-element            INTEGER (0..127),
     second-element          SEQUENCE
         {string OCTET STRING (SIZE (2)),
            name   PrintableString (SIZE (1..8) ) },
     third-element  BIT STRING (SIZE (8) ) }
```

Figure 19.2   An example sequence to be encoded.

```
1         T=[Universal 16]
2         L=3  (TL   count)
3              T=[Universal 2]
4              L=1
5               =what-ever
6              T=[Universal 16]
7              L=2  (TL   count)
8                   T=[Universal 4]
9                   L=2
10-11                =what-ever
12                  T=[Universal 19]
13                  L=5  (say)
14-18                =what-ever
19             T=[Universal 3]
20             L=2
21              1=0  (no unused bits in last octet)
22              2=what-ever
```

Figure 19.3   The 22 octet BER encoding of Figure 19.2.

Some of the rules for when you could delete octets were obvious and straightforward, others were quite complicated. The reader might like to try to formulate precisely the rules that enabled us to delete (not transmit) 12 of the 22 octets in the encoding of Figure 19.3.

PER-2 was really a sort of "expert system" approach to encoding. There were a whole raft of rules to be applied to determine when you could or could not delete octets (with reinsertion on receipt), and these were very ad hoc and somehow looked as if they were not complete and not founded on any good general principles. (To be honest, they **were** ad hoc, and were not founded on any general principles!)

But the text was eventually deemed complete, and sent for ballot. The editing meeting to consider ballot comments was in New Jersey, and was scheduled to last for one week (this being the only business under consideration). Something went wrong with the administration, and the copies of the formal National Body responses to the ballot only became available by fax at 9 am on the first day of the meeting.

Faces dropped. Everyone knew their own country's response, but until then they did not know what others had said. Every, yes every, National Body had voted "DISAPPROVE." And none of the comments were in any way helpful for further progress. They more or less all said "This is just too complicated, too ad hoc, it will never work." **None** of them suggested anything that could be done to change the PER-2 draft to make it acceptable.

The meeting broke up for lunch that day at about 11 am, with many delegates (there were about a dozen present representing five or six countries) ringing their airlines to find out how much more it would cost to fly back that day rather than on their scheduled flight at the end of the week. Other delegates (myself included) retired to the bar to drown their sorrows.

After enough beer had been consumed, people started to think the unthinkable. Why not just abandon the TLV principle and start from scratch? Forget interworking between different versions of a standard (PER-2 didn't really provide that anyway)— how would we encode stuff, using maximum human intelligence, to produce minimum octets on the line? The "back of a cigarette pack" (actually, it was a paper table napkin) design started to take shape. (I wish now that I had kept the napkin, but I think it was consigned to the WPB (English) or round file (American). So much for important historical documents!) Come 2 pm, the chairman (Bancroft, the Editor, I think) said, "Shall we convene and get this meeting wrapped up?" "No", was the response from the then mildly intoxicated bar group (drunk—never!), "we might be getting somewhere." I think the meeting eventually resumed that day at around 4 pm. PER-1 (PER minus 1), almost PER as we now know it (but not quite) had been born.

The principles were in place:

- Forget about tags—abandon them! (You had to be pretty drunk to make **that** statement—TLV was a sort of mindset that it was hard to break out of.)

- Make full use of knowledge about constraints on integers and on lengths to remove length fields whenever possible.

- How to solve the problem of SET elements being in a random order? Fix the order! (You had to be a little drunk to say that too!)

- How to identify a chosen element of a CHOICE? Encode a choice index.

- How to identify missing OPTIONAL elements in a SEQUENCE or SET? Use a bit-map at the head of the SEQUENCE or SET.

- How to encode a BOOLEAN—well, of course, use just one bit!

- But ... octet-alignment? Recognize that it is good to have padding bits at times so that later material that is a sequence of elements that are an integral number of octets will lie on an octet boundary, but use the minimum number of bits without worrying about octet alignment where that looks sensible.

There were still some elements of the "expert system" approach to this design (as there are with current PER). It is a fairly ad hoc decision on which fields should encode into bit-fields (no padding bits) and which into octet-aligned-bit-fields (with padding bits).

Many details remained to be solved, but the meeting continued for the rest of the week, drafts were produced and considered, and PER-1 became a reality, with later editorial work being done to produce good text over the next few months.

And then it fell apart again!

19.13.2 The Second Attempt—PER-1

When PER-1 was balloted, it got a much more favorable response than PER-2, but there was still a very strong "DISAPPROVE" vote from the USA which said "Regrettably, after much discussion, we have to disapprove of PER-1. With PER-1 there is no way a version-1 system can interwork with a version-2 system (you can't even find the end of an encoding unless you are both working with an identical type definition). This stuff just isn't going to work for International Standards. Kill it."

> Nope—you must go back to TLV. Only TLV can provide interworking between version-1 and version-2 systems. It is a tried and true technique. Well, the last sentence is true, but is the second? We know now that it is not. In 1992 we were less sure!

This meeting was less traumatic than the last, but this "interworking" (or "extensibility" problem as it became known) delayed the production of the final real-PER for just over 12 months.

19.13.3 And Eventually We Obtain Real-PER

A lot of trees were cut down to provide paper for people to describe what sorts of additions or changes they would want to make between version 1 and version 2 of a protocol. The consensus that emerged was essentially "We only need to add things at the end."

> The ellipsis goes into the notation (and the exception marker with it), and the extension bit goes into PER. We have got there!

The ellipsis was provided for people to indicate this, and the extension bit in PER provided the encoding support.

The real-PER approach is to say essentially:

- If parts of the specification are **not** flagged as extensible, then encode them in an efficient manner.

- If parts are marked extensible, but the values are values of the version-1 specification (in the root), provide one bit to say so, but still encode them efficiently.

- If extensible parts have values outside of the root (version-2 additions), set the extensions bit to one, and provide a length wrapper.

It is unlikely that this approach would have been developed if we had not been starting from a design (PER-1) that did efficient encodings, with no concern for interworking. The various traumas on the path to PER were probably necessary to break the in-built tradition of TLV encodings as the only way to provide version-1 to version-2 interworking.

This is not quite the end of the story! Later, there was strong pressure to be able to add things in the middle of sequences and sets, and version brackets were added.

There was also pressure from the air traffic control people to get rid of the padding bits and to forget about octet alignment, which produced the UNALIGNED version of PER.

But these were minor problems. The path from PER-1 to the final PER has left us with text that is not always as precise as it should be, and in particular the integration of the extensibility and extensions bit concept into the PER-1 text still poses some problems today, with arguments (and probably eventually corrigenda) related to obscure uses of the extensibility notation (which fortunately no one has yet written, and perhaps never will!). Many of these problems were uncovered by Olivier and myself when we started writing our books! Fortunately, we both agreed on what the answer **should** be, and I think our books both tell the same story!

19.14 DER and CER

(Sounds familiar? Yup, I've used that box before—sorry!)

The major "option" in a BER encoding is the use of definite or indefinite

> Engraven on the hearts of standardizers: Your job is to produce standards. If you can't agree, make it optional, or better still, another standard. After all, if one standard is good, many standards must be better!

lengths for constructed encodings. There was never agreement on which was best, and both are allowed in the BER specification. There have been all sorts of rows over the years when some profiling groups attempted to mandate one form or the other.

Roughly speaking, for short messages, the definite length form is probably the most sensible, but for long ones the indefinite form is to be preferred. Leaving the option to an implementor seems like a good idea, but of course it means that decoders have to handle both forms.

If, however, you want encoding rules with no options for the encoder (to minimize the testing problem and to help with security-related problems, as discussed in 15.10) then you have to bite the bullet!

X.500 first produced (as about a 20-line specification) the rules for producing a canonical encoding of BER and called it a "distinguished" encoding. It did enough of the job to cover the types they wanted to apply it to, but it was not complete. It also (arguably) did not make some choices in an optimal manner.

The ASN.1 group decided to produce a standard for a canonical version of BER, which it decided to call "Distinguished Encoding Rules," taking the name from X.500.

The major difference between the ASN.1 specification and the X.500 specification was that X.500 mandated use of definite length encodings, and the ASN.1 group went for indefinite length wherever they were possible!

Major liaison statements, etc., etc. Meanwhile, workers on another standard—ODA (Office Document Architecture)—who had very large messages to ship but who also needed canonical encodings, liked the draft of the ASN.1 group!

The eventual upshot was effectively two separate standards, one for DER (totally aligned with the early X.500 text, and using definite length encodings), and one for CER ("improving" on the original X.500 work, and using indefinite length encodings whenever possible). Both "standards" are, of course, published alongside BER in X.690 (ISO/IEC 8825-1).

The X.500 use of DER is mainly for certificates, becoming now heavily used in the development of e-commerce. (Most e-commerce activity is based on X.509 certificates, which use DER encoding.) By contrast, the ODA work has not been widely implemented. So whatever their relative technical merits, DER has become the de facto standard for canonical encodings of BER, and CER is probably dead!

19.15 Semantic Models and All That—ASN.1 in the Late 1990s

There have always been questions about the legality of certain ASN.1 constructs where things were syntactically permissible, but might or might not really be something you should allow. The main area of these problems is in "type matching" rules between a value reference and its governor. For example, with

> Humans only write simple and obvious ASN.1. But stupid dumb computers want to know about the legality of the most abstruse expressions that the syntax allows. And the computers have an important voice in the tool vendors! They have to be listened to!

```
intval   INTEGER ::= 7
```

You might ask whether you can legally write as an element of a sequence

```
[27] INTEGER DEFAULT intval
```

or

```
INTEGER (0..127) DEFAULT intval
```

Of course, you would expect these to be legal, yes? But "[27] INTEGER" and "INTEGER (0..27)" are certainly not exactly the same type as "INTEGER". All three types do not contain exactly the same values, and the encoding of their common values differs in either or both of BER and PER.

Again, if a value reference is defined using a certain (fairly complex) type definition, and that value reference is then used when governed by an identical (but textually distinct) type reference, is that legal? And if the second textual occurrence is not **quite** identical to the first, by how much can it deviate before the text becomes illegal ASN.1?

Add to these examples use of the extension marker ... .

These are the problems that are being grappled with in the late 1990s, and which have led to the inclusion in the standard of models (pictures) of types as buckets containing values, and of "value mappings" between types that are defined by textually separate pieces of notation. Similar models/pictures are needed to cover types that have an ellipsis, and/or extensions.

The guiding principle in all this work is to make things legal if they make any sort of sense (rather than a tight specification that makes only the most obviously correct things legal), but also to end up with a very complete specification of what is legal ASN.1.

Of course, the reader will guess that the pressure for this work comes from tool vendors. They have to write code that is required to make judgments on the legality or otherwise of stuff that no protocol specifier in their right mind would ever write!

19.16 What Got Away?

There have been a few features of ASN.1 development that have not made it into the current standard. They may get resurrected, but probably won't!

The Light-Weight Encoding Rules (LWER) were fully discussed in Section III, Chapter 18, and will not be referred to again here.

> Could ASN.1 be even better? There are certainly further improvements that have been discussed. But is the added complexity worth the gains? The consensus is "NO."

Probably the major loss was in not providing an efficient encoding for SEQUENCE OF CHARACTER STRING, and for the encoding of a table where each column can be the choice of a number of possible types.

In the case of CHARACTER STRING (which, if you remember, carries two object identifier values with each encoding of this type), the original concept was to permit chains of encodings of type CHARACTER STRING, where each encoding in any given chain had the same object identifier values. These values would be transmitted at the start of each chain, and then, rather like virtual circuits in network protocol, there would be an abbreviated identification to link each encoding into its chain. Unfortunately, serious bugs were found in this chaining concept (because of interaction with extensions), and it was withdrawn within days of its initial publication.

At the time, it was felt that another feature "run-time parameters" (also called "dynamic constraints", because the run-time parameters could only be used in constraints) could support the same efficiency requirement, but run-time parameters (dynamic constraints) were eventually abandoned.

The approach was abandoned not because of any inherent problems, but simply that the marketplace (ASN.1 users) did not really seem to be demanding it, and adding a further fairly complex feature to ASN.1 did not seem worthwhile.

What were these run-time parameters? The idea was that a type could be a parameterized type, but the actual parameters would be transmitted in an instance of communication rather than being specified when the type was referenced. This would enable any information that was common to a SEQUENCE OF (for example, the object identifiers of SEQUENCE OF CHARACTER STRING, or the identification of the types for each column of a table) to be transmitted just once, rather than with each element of the SEQUENCE OF.

Another abandoned feature was "global parameters". If you have a parameterized type, it is quite common for parameters to be passed down from the abstract syntax definition through many levels of type definition to the point where they are eventually used.

The global parameters work was intended to improve clarity and reduce the verbosity of specifications by providing essentially a direct path from a parameter of the abstract syntax to the point where it would be used.

If you rather like some of these ideas, get into the standardization game and see if you can bring them back! If you don't want to get into the standardization game, then just agree that ASN.1 is great as it is, and we can end this chapter!

END OF CHAPTER.

## CHAPTER 20

Applications of ASN.1

(Or: Are You Using Software That Does ASN.1 Encodings?)

Summary

This chapter

- tries to provide an indication of the application areas in which ASN.1 has been used,

- tries to identify some of the organizations that have used ASN.1 as their chosen specification-language.

- uses a partial historical framework for the discussion of applications and organizations

20.1 Introduction

This brief chapter outlines some of the areas in which ASN.1 has been applied. It in no way claims to be exhaustive, and if some groups feel offended that they have not been mentioned, I apologize!

Equally, I have seen Web pages that say they will include their ASN.1 definitions, only to be assured by people I trust that use of ASN.1 for that particular application was abandoned! I hope there are not too many errors in what follows, but I am sure there are serious omissions.

> There are more of you left out than are included—Sorry!

While the emphasis is on different applications, the treatment is partly historical, showing the gradual extension of the use of ASN.1 from a single application (X.400) to a wide range of applications today.

Thus this chapter complements the previous historical chapter.

The chapter does **not** contain a detailed list of ISO Standard numbers and ITU-T Recommendations and Internet RFCs, but rather gives a broad outline of application areas with the occasional mention of an actual specification as an illustration.

For anyone interested, a more complete set of detailed references to specifications using ASN.1 can be found via the URL in Appendix 5, or in the companion text by Olivier Dubuisson (also referenced via Appendix 5).

Most of the acronyms and abbreviations in this chapter can be used as input to Web search engines, and will usually result in hits on home pages for the relevant organizations or specifications. This is the best way to obtain more information if Appendix 5 does not work for you! (Web URLs have a habit of changing!)

There are also Web sites (access via Appendix 5 or do a search) for ITU-T and ETSI and ECMA that will give you much more information about their specifications, and in the case of ITU-T a list of the Recommendations that use ASN.1. (If you get interested in any of the ITU-T Recommendations, beware—they can all be purchased and delivered online, but it will cost you serious money!)

This chapter inevitably contains **many** acronyms—every protocol and every organization has its own acronym. I try to spell out the acronym if it has not been used in earlier text, but sometimes it seems hardly worth the effort, because the acronym is often far better known than the full title!

In many cases you will find that a document you locate via a search uses the acronym without giving the full name. Many, many people know these acronyms, but would have to think hard to give you the full name, and would probably then get it wrong! (In some cases, different Web and other documents give different full names for the same acronyms—but clearly intend to identify the same thing!)

So, we do our best. But if you want a challenge, see what you can find out about the following acronyms (in the ASN.1 context). They are given in no particular order. Some are mentioned in this chapter, most are not. It is believed that they all relate to protocols or organizations that are using ASN.1 as a specification language. Test yourself on the following:

SET, SNMP, TCAP, CMIP, PKCS, MHS, ACSE, CSTA, NSDP, DPA, TDP, ETSI, DMH, ICAO, IMTC, DAVIC, DSS1, PKIX, IIF, LSM, MHEG, NSP, ROS(E), FTAM, JTMP, VT, RPI, RR, SCAI, TME, WMtp, GDMO, SMTP.

If you don't get 100% (although some could of course be mistyping!), you are not a network guru, and can't charge big bucks for your advice on network matters!

If you commute between Europe and the USA and are active in both communities, you stand a better chance of meeting the challenge than those operating on only one side of the Atlantic pond. Of course, ASN.1 tool providers CERTAINLY know what all these acronyms mean, because they are selling their tools to support them. But will they tell?

Well, I honestly admit that after a fair bit of research I can give full names for about 95% of the list (I have described a lot less than 95% in this chapter), but certainly not all!

If any reader can cover the lot (and preferably give a URL for further info) then an e-mail to my address via the link in Appendix 5 would be welcomed (too late for this book, but perhaps for the second edition?).

20.2 The Origins in X.400

X.400 was originally a related set of CCITT Recommendations covering (with gaps) X.400 to X.430. The X.400 specifications were intended to become the (OSI) de facto e-mail system for the world.

X.400 started off with many advantages over the Internet mail protocol (at that time it was Simple Mail Transfer Protocol (SMTP), with no frills—frills like Multipurpose Internet Mail Extensions (MIME) were added later).

> Everything has a beginning!

From the start X.400 supported a variety of different types of "body part", permitting multimedia attachments to mail, and in its 1998 version incorporated virtually all the security features of the Military Message Handling Systems (MMHS) specifications (security features in SMTP are still very much poorer).

However, SMTP was enhanced with the MIME extensions to provide for the transfer of arbitrary attachments (albeit at about twice the bandwidth of X.400) and Internet mail implementations today generally do not accept mail from outside their own domain, reducing (but not eliminating) the risks of masquerade. (None of this work is ASN.1-based.) But whatever the technical merits or otherwise, we all know that SMTP-based e-mail is now the world's de facto standard, although X.400 still plays a roll in gateways between different mail systems, and in military communications, and has other minority followings.

Originally produced to support just the X.400 specification, ASN.1 is of course still used in all the ongoing X.400 work.

Another important specification originally produced to support just X.400 was the Remote Operations Service Element (ROSE) specification—originally just called "ROS". Like ASN.1, this became recognized as of more general utility, and moved into the X.200 series of Recommendations. (ROSE is discussed further in Chapter 13). ROSE was (and is) totally ASN.1-based and is the foundation of many, many applications in the telecommunications area. Its requirements were very influential in the development of the Information Object concept and in the recognition of the need to handle "holes". (See the previous chapter on the history of ASN.1.)

20.3 The Move into Open Systems Interconnection (OSI) and ISO

In the early 1980s, papers at conferences would have titles like "OSI versus SNA" (SNA was IBM's "Systems Network Architecture"), with most people believing that the OSI work would eventually become the de facto standard for world-wide networking, but would have a battle to unseat SNA. Again, historically, OSI as a whole never really made it, but it was the intro-duction of ASN.1 into mainstream OSI

> Rapid expansion to take over the world through OSI—supposedly! But also take-up by several other ISO Technical Committees.

that moved ASN.1 from being a single-application language into a tool used by many protocol specifiers.

Very soon after it was introduced from CCITT (as it then was) into ISO, ASN.1 was adopted as the specification language of choice by every single group producing specifications for the Application Layer of OSI and for many other OSI-related stan-dards. Although implementations of most of these standards are still in use today, it is fair to say that, in most cases, use of OSI protocols for any given application area is a minority use.

Most of the OSI applications of ASN.1 were for standards in the so-called "Application Layer" of OSI, developed by ISO/JTC1/SC16, and then (following a reorganization) by ISO/JTC1/SC21. These covered, *inter alia*, standards for remote database access, transaction processing, file transfer, virtual terminals, and so on.

The ASN.1 concepts of a separation of abstract and transfer syntax fitted very well with the so-called "Presentation Layer" of OSI for protocols running over the OSI stack and using the Presentation Layer to negotiate the transfer syntax to be used for any given abstract syntax.

Interestingly, however, ASN.1 was also used to define the Presentation Layer pro-tocol itself—probably the first use of ASN.1 for a protocol that did not run **over** the OSI Presentation Layer (many others were to follow).

There was even a draft circulated showing how the OSI **Session** Layer (the layer below the Presentation Layer) could be defined (more clearly, and in a machine-readable format) using ASN.1. This was accompanied by a draft of a "Session-Layer-BER", which was a minor change to BER and which if applied to the ASN.1 definition would produce exactly the bits on the line that the Session Protocol Standard specified. But with the Session Layer specifications complete and stable by then, the draft never progressed.

A similar situation arose with the Generic Definition of Managed Objects (GDMO)—see 20.8, where an equivalent notation using Information Object Classes and "WITH SYNTAX" was identified in a circulated draft (from Japan) but was never progressed because the GDMO work was by then stable and quite mature.

ASN.1 has been used in many other ISO Technical Committees, in areas such as banking, security, protocols for control of automated production lines, and most recently in the development of protocols in the transportation domain for "intelligent highways". These protocols are often (usually) not carried over the OSI stack, and have served to show the independence of ASN.1 from OSI, despite its early roots in the OSI work.

A recent example of such use is for the definition (by ISO/TC68) of messages passing between an Integrated Circuit credit card and the card accepting device.

20.4 Use within the Protocol Testing Community

As well as protocol specifications, the OSI world started the idea of standardized tests of protocol implementations. These test sequences are, of course, protocols in their own right, where a testing system sends messages to an implementation under test, and assesses the responses it gets. The Tree and Tabular Combined Notation (TTCN) is the most commonly used notation for this

> You don't just want a standardized protocol, you want standardized tests of implementations!

purpose, and ASN.1 is embedded within this notation for the definition of data structures.

Closely related to the TTCN application is the use of ASN.1 within another ITU-T formal description technique, System Description Language (SDL).

The European Telecommunications Standards Institute (ETSI) has been a major actor in the development of testing specifications using these notations.

20.5 Use within the Integrated Services Digital Network (ISDN)

In the 1980s, Integrated Services Digital Network (ISDN) was the great talking point. It grew out of the digitization of the telephone network.

The telephone network in most advanced countries is now entirely digital apart from the so-called "local loop" between homes and the local telephone exchange, which in the majority of cases remains analogue.

> Probably the first application of ASN.1 outside of the main OSI work.

ISDN provided, using the existing local loops between homes and a local telephone exchange, two so-called "B-channels", each capable of carrying a telephone call or a 64 Kbps data connection, and a "D-channel" (used for signaling between the subscriber and the exchange). It became widely available to telephone subscribers, but its main application was (and remains so) the use of the two B-channels together to provide a 128 Kbps data channel for video-conferencing over the telephone network.

Within ISDN, many so-called "supplementary services" (for example, Call Back to Busy Subscriber) were implemented using the D-channel, and ASN.1 (with BER encodings) was chosen to define the protocol for these services.

20.6 Use in ITU-T and Multimedia Standards

> Widespread use of ASN.1 throughout many parts of ITU-T continues to this day.

ASN.1 was, of course, first introduced to ITU-T through X.400 and OSI, but was rapidly taken up by many other standardization groups within ITU-T (then CCITT).

Uses of ASN.1 within ITU-T can be found in

- The G-series recommendations for speech encoding and silence compression.

- The H-series for multimedia (audiovisual) communications, including moving video coding for low bit-rate communication, and specifications being implemented by the Interactive Multimedia Teleconferencing Consortium (IMTC).

- The M-series for test management in ATM.

- The Q-series for a host of specifications related to ISDN and Intelligent Networks (IN).

- The T-series for group 3 facsimile and for MHEG communications.

- The V-series for audiovisual terminal communication.

- The Z-series for use within SDL (already described) and within GDMO (to be described in 20.8).

- And of course, in the X-series for Recommendations that originated in the OSI work.

Regarding the H-series, the most important of these Recommendations is perhaps the H.323 series for audio, video, and data communication across the Internet (including video-conferencing, interactive shopping, network gaming, and many other multimedia applications—check out the H.323 Web site for further details). Other specifications in the H.320 series address multimedia communication over both narrowband and broadband (ATM) ISDN and PSTN communications. These Recommendations seem set to become de facto standards for multimedia communication that will operate over a wide range of network infrastructures.

It is these Recommendations that cause many familiar products to have ASN.1 (PER in this case) encoders embedded within them, so if you use any of these products, **you** are using ASN.1 (encodings)! Examples of such products are Microsoft NetMeeting, Intel VideoPhone, PictureTel software, and so on.

20.7 Use in European and American Standardization Groups

There are three European standardization groups worth mentioning where ASN.1 has been quite heavily used (no doubt there are others). The first two carry the name "European" in their title, but they all contribute standards to the world-wide community. These are the European Computer Manufacturers Association (ECMA), the European Telecommunications Standards Institute (ETSI), and the

> Many subinternational (to coin a phrase) groups that are really international actors have used ASN.1.

rather more recent Digital Audio Visual Council (DAVIC). (DAVIC is Europe-based, but would justifiably claim to be a world-wide consortium.)

ECMA has long worked on OSI-related standards for input into OSI (but also in broader areas, for example, it had significant input into the initial IEEE 802 Standard). It has also produced the ASN.1-based Computer Supported Telecommunications Applications (CSTA) specification for communication between telephone switches and end-user computers. Initial deployment of CSTA has been in support of large Call Centers—an important development in communications in the late 1990s. As is normal with ECMA specifications, the work has been input to ISO for international standardization.

ETSI is primarily concerned with European variants of ITU-T Recommendations and with the development of telecommunications specifications for input into ITU-T. It has also been active in the development of specifications based on TTCN (which has ASN.1 embedded within it). There is close liaison between ECMA and ETSI on telecommunications standards, and with ITU-T.

DAVIC is a consortium of 157 companies and government agencies from 25 countries promoting video-conferencing. Its specifications are input to ISO for international standardization.

There are also a number of standards groups and consortia in the USA that have used ASN.1 in their specifications. Frequently, but not always, such work feeds into international standardization.

Worth mentioning (but this list is very incomplete and a bit random—these are the ones I have heard about) are:

- The ANSI X9 committees concerned with Financial Industry Standardization (Funds Transfer and EDI, for example), feeding into ISO/TC68.

- The American Chemical Society (ACS) for the exchange of chemical information and DNA sequences (for the Web site, see links via Appendix 5 to the National Centre for Biological Information (NCBI)).

- Many Federal Information Processing Standards (FIPS) concerned with security matters, for example, FIPS PUB 188 on Standard Security Labels for Information Transfer—the Standard Security Label is defined as an ASN.1 type: "SET OF NamedTagSet" where "NamedTagSet" is ... etc.

- The SET consortium (see 20.9).

20.8 Use for Managing Computer-Controlled Systems

Another major "invention" from the OSI work was the concept of "managed objects" (devices that are interrogated, tested, configured, reset, etc. by remote communications). This came out of the work on Common Management Information Services/Protocol (CMIS/CMIP), which produced a model of such objects (identified by ASN.1 object identifiers) with attributes

> If it's controlled by a computer, you probably manage it remotely using ASN.1-based exchanges.

(which were ASN.1 types identified by further ASN.1 object identifiers). "Management" was essentially performed by reading from or writing to these "attributes" (using CMIP) which were, as it were, on the surface of the managed objects, and provided external visibility and control of the object.

When the CMIP standard was first published, it was a protocol full of "holes"—not a single managed object and its attributes had been defined at that stage! A notation was clearly needed to allow people to define (preferably in a machine-readable way) managed objects. An ASN.1 macro might well have been used to define that notation, but by then there was an embargo on writing new macros, and the replacement Information Object Class work was still in its infancy. So Generic Definition of Managed Objects (GDMO) was defined (in English) as a notation for specifying the necessary details about managed objects, with ASN.1 as an embedded notation within GDMO.

In the Internet world, the concepts of CMIS/CMIP were adopted, and while work was still continuing on the development of CMIS/CMIP, an RFC was produced for Simple Network Management Protocol (SNMP). Initially, this was stated to be a temporary solution until CMIS/CMIP matured, but like most temporary solutions, it became rather permanent, and has today a greater market share of management of remote devices than does CMIS/CMIP.

Like CMIS/CMIP, SNMP also uses ASN.1, but in a very cut-down form, and with considerable restrictions on the form of ASN.1 types that can be used to define the values to be set or read on managed objects. This did, however, represent the first real penetration of ASN.1 into the Internet standardization community.

CMIS/CMIP was originally designed to control implementations of the OSI stack in network switches and remote hosts, but (like SNMP) it is increasingly used today to manage remotely anything that is computer controlled. So applications of management protocols can include the steering of telescopes or radar dishes, or even the switching on and off of washing machines or ovens! (But I am not sure the latter are yet a reality.)

20.9 Use in PKCS and PKIX and SET and Other Security-Related Protocols

To get the acronyms and abbreviations in the title out of the way: PKCS is Public Key Cryptographic Standards, PKIX is Public Key Infrastructure (X.509), and SET is Secure Electronic Transactions (a little more detail on these follows).

X.500 is one of the OSI Standards that still has significant support, and its use of ASN.1 in the OSI work has led to adoption of ASN.1 in almost all security-related protocols.

X.500 was (and is) an ISO and ITU-T Standard and Recommendation, but the Light-Weight Directory Access Protocol (LDAP), which is a functional subset of X.500, is an Internet RFC, and is rapidly becoming the de

> The widespread adoption of X.509 (ASN.1-based) certificates has made ASN.1 the dominant specification technique in security work.

facto standard for access to Directory services, leaving X.500 proper for use "behind the scenes" to link local LDAP servers to provide a world-wide Directory service. LDAP uses the ASN.1 notation to define its messages, but specifies a text encoding for values of the (limited) subset of ASN.1 that it uses (see later discussion in 20.10 on preferences for text-based protocols among Internet specifiers).

While X.500 was primarily designed to provide a world-wide Directory service, allowing look-up of a very wide variety of information with a world-wide search, it also provided the first standard (X.509) for **certificates** (which were and are, of course, an ASN.1 type).

The basic certificate concept is that a Certification Authority (CA) will provide a public and private key pair (usually for some commercial fee) to an applicant, and will also provide an electronic bit-pattern (a certificate) that is encrypted using the public key of the CA. The certificate is an ASN.1 type that provides an association between the public key issued to the applicant and some property of the applicant (name, company registration number, etc.). Certificates cannot be forged provided the CA keeps its own private key secure. However, anyone knowing (for absolutely sure) the public key of the CA, can decrypt the certificates it issues and hence "believe" the public key of the organization or person that the certificate contains—and hence apply some degree of "trust" to that organization or person (and to messages or signatures that decrypt to produce valid hash values using that public key). Of course, the public key of the CA is usually obtained from another certificate issued by a "higher" CA, whose public key is obtained from another certificate issued by ... and so on, until, ... well, ... the Netscape public key is usually built into your Web browser software! (Which of course you obtained from a trustworthy source!)

This process of obtaining a public key from one certificate to unlock another certificate to get a public key that unlocks another certificate etc. is called certificate chaining, and originally people expected just one or two top-level CAs in the entire world, with their public keys **really** public—perhaps advertised daily in the newspapers!

But then just about every national government decided it wanted one of its agencies to be a top-level CA, and many companies also decided to be their own CA for internal use. And suddenly the problem of distribution of public keys and of degrees of trust got a lot more complicated.

PKIX stands for **P**ublic **K**ey **I**nfrastructure (**X**.509), and is a set of Internet RFCs and Draft RFCs that specify how CAs should operate. For example, PKIX 4 specifies the form of a Certification Policy Statement (CPS) that all conforming CAs should make available to the public. The CPS says, for example, that before issuing a certificate the CA should verify individual names by requiring a photocopy of a passport, or an actual passport, or a birth certificate, or (for a company in the UK) has checked that the Registered Office exists, as registered with Companies House, or ... . You get the idea. The certificate they issue asserts that there is some association between the public key it contains and some further information about an individual or company. How much trust can you place in that assertion? The CPS helps you to determine that.

Several parts of PKIX use ASN.1, fully and in a straightforward fashion.

The abbreviation PKCS stands for Public-Key Cryptographic Standards. These are standards produced by a consortium of RSA Data Security and its major licensees, including Microsoft, Apple, Lotus, Sun, Novell, and MIT. PKCS uses ASN.1 as its notation for defining data-structures and their encoding.

Another important security-related protocol is Secure Electronic Transactions (SET), produced by a consortium of MasterCard, Visa, and other parts of the computer and banking industries. This protocol is designed to support electronic commerce in a fully secure manner, and hence uses X.509 certificates, and is itself about 60 pages of ASN.1 (with many more pages of supporting text).

When SET certificates are stored on smart-cards (because of the limited memory available on smart-cards) **PER** encoding is likely to be used with an ASN.1 datatype called a **compressed certificate.**

In general, the use of ASN.1 in X.509 has led most security-related protocols to use ASN.1.

20.10 Use in Other Internet Specifications

We have already discussed PKCS, PKIX, and SNMP. ASN.1 (with PER) was considered for use in the latest version of HTTP, but instead an ASN.1-like notation called "pseudo-C" was invented.

In general, Internet specifiers try to keep protocol specifications as simple as possible and to make it easy for implementors to operate without specialized tools, or using only tools that are in the public domain.

> Yes, even here we see some use of ASN.1!

This tends to lead to protocols that in the end are simply lines of ASCII text (usually defined using BNF), or, if ASN.1 **is** used, to use of a subset of the ASN.1 notation.

The Web is very much part of the Internet, but the World-Wide Web Consortium (W3C) now has very much a life of its own.

It is within the W3C forum that work is ongoing to marry XML and ASN.1 through the definition of XML Encoding Rules (XER). This work is recent, and was mentioned also in Chapter 17, beginning on page 383.

20.11 Use in Major Corporate Enterprises and Agencies

It is known that a number of household name corporations and national and international agencies have made use of (and are still using) ASN.1 and its encoding rules to support communications activities within their corporations and agencies.

> Sorry—I can't tell you about these!

However, attempts to obtain more details for publication in this book met with an almost universal rejection, due to concerns about commercial confidentiality of the applications. With regret, therefore, I have decided to make no mention of any specific name of a commercial organization unless the information about their use of ASN.1 appears on the Web.

I will, however, mention one agency, and this is the International Civil Aviation Organization (ICAO).

ICAO is worth mentioning because it was the first organization to adopt (and to help in the development of) the Packed Encoding Rules. PER encodings were described in ICAO specifications long before the actual ASN.1 specifications were finally ratified, and use of ASN.1 and PER is fundamental to their Aeronautical Telecommunication Network (ATN).

20.12 Conclusion

ASN.1 has come a long way from the days when it provided support for just one application (X.400).

It is now used to a significant extent by all the main specifiers of protocols, and in some (but not all) cases is the dominant specification language. Usually use of the notation is associated with use of the ASN.1-defined encodings, with a few exceptions.

> We'll end with a tale of world-wide catastrophe!

If you were to wave a magic wand and eliminate from the world all messages that are encodings of ASN.1-defined values, disaster would certainly strike on a scale far beyond any that even the most pessimistic have described regarding the possible effects of the Y2K (year 2000) computer bugs. (Or any that actually occurred if you are reading this book post-2000!)

Aircraft would collide, mobile phones would cease to work, virtually all telecoms and network switches would be unmanageable and unmaintainable and would gradually die, electric power distribution systems would cease to work, and to look a little farther ahead before we wave our magic wand, smart-card-based electronic transactions would fail to complete and your washing machine might fail to work! But worst of all, your NetMeeting with your newly betrothed would suddenly collapse and your life would become a misery!

It is on that happy note that we will conclude this book!

Appendices

Appendix 1 The Wineco Protocol Scenario

Many of the examples in this book are based on the development of the "Wineco protocol." This is a fictitious protocol, used simply to illustrate various parts of ASN.1. The first parts of it appear in Figure 2.1, and a full copy of the final protocol is given in Appendix 2.

Wineco is a company that sells wine from a variety of outlets and owns two warehouses, one northern and one southern. Initially all outlets were in the UK only (where the name of an outlet could be supported by the ASCII character set), but later Wineco extended to overseas territories, where a larger character set was needed.

In Figure 2.1 we see one of the messages we use in the protocol, "Order-for-stock", to request a number of cases of particular types of wine with a specified urgency. We also see the form of a "Branch-identification" type.

In Chapter 3 we add the necessary module headers, and some extensibility markers with an insertion point not at the end. Later we turn it into a multimodule specification with "common types" in one module, the top-level type in another, and the ordering protocol message "Order-for-stock" in a third. We also introduced a second top-level message in Figure 3.8, "Return-of-sales", which provides for a report on the sales that have been made within the last period.

In Chapter 4 we populated the "Return-of-sales" message in a hopefully plausible way, but really solely in order to illustrate the remaining ASN.1 basic data-types! Exception markers and exception handling are introduced in this chapter. "Return-of-sales" and the "Report-item" type it uses are used as the main example for illustration of the output from an ASN.1-compiler-tool, given in Appendix 3 for C and in Appendix 4 for Java.

"Return-of-sales" is also used to illustrate the ASN.1 value notation in Chapter 4 (Figure 4.2).

The next use of our example is in Chapter 10, when we decide to define a "basic class" protocol as a strict subset of our "full class" protocol, both for ordering and for return of sales. Here we have also added a third top-level message as we enter the digital-cash age! We are uploading the contents of our electronic till using an enhanced protocol.

The final major extension is when we decide in Chapter 13 to change over to use of a Remote Operations metaphor, with four defined operations. This leads to two further modules—one to define the Remote Operations PDU (which in the real world would have been imported from the Remote Operations Service (ROSE) Standard), and one to define the Wineco OPERATION Information Objects.

Appendix 2 The Full Protocol for Wineco

This appendix gives the final version of the specification of the Wineco protocol in a form that is syntactically correct and complete.

```
Wineco-common-top-level
      {joint-iso-itu-t international-organization(23) set(42)
        set-vendors(9) wineco(43) modules(2) top(0)}
    DEFINITIONS
        AUTOMATIC TAGS ::=
    BEGIN

    EXPORTS ;
    IMPORTS Order-for-stock FROM
       Wineco-ordering-protocol
       {wineco-OID modules(2) ordering(1)}
          Return-of-sales FROM
       Wineco-returns-protocol
       {wineco-OID modules(2) returns(2)};

    wineco-OID OBJECT IDENTIFIER ::=
       {joint-iso-itu-t international-organization(23) set(42)
          set-vendors(9) wineco(43)}
    wineco-abstract-syntax  ABSTRACT-SYNTAX ::=
            {Wineco-protocol IDENTIFIED BY
                           {wineco-OID abstract-syntax(1)}
                             HAS PROPERTY
                             {handles-invalid-encodings}
                           --See clause 45.6 --    }
    Wineco-protocol ::= CHOICE
       {ordering  [APPLICATION 1] Order-for-stock,
        sales     [APPLICATION 2] Return-of-sales,
        ... ! PrintableString : "See clause 45.7"
        }

END
--New page in published spec.
Wineco-ordering-protocol
  {joint-iso-itu-t international-organization(23) set(42)
        set-vendors(9) wineco(43)modules(2) ordering(1)}
    DEFINITIONS
        AUTOMATIC TAGS ::=
    BEGIN

    EXPORTS Order-for-stock;
    IMPORTS OutletType,  Address,  Security-Type FROM
              Wineco-common-types
            {wineco-OID modules(2) common (3)};
    wineco-OID OBJECT IDENTIFIER ::=
            {joint-iso-itu-t international-organization(23) set(42)
                set-vendors(9) wineco(43)}
```

```
    Order-for-stock ::= SEQUENCE
        {order-no        INTEGER,
         name-address    BranchIdentification,
         details         SEQUENCE OF
                         SEQUENCE
                   {item       OBJECT IDENTIFIER,
                    cases      INTEGER},
          urgency        ENUMERATED
                   {tomorrow(0),
                    three-day(1),
                    week(2)}  DEFAULT week,
          authenticator Security-Type}


    BranchIdentification ::= SET
         {unique-id  OBJECT IDENTIFIER,
          details    CHOICE
               {uk   [0] SEQUENCE
                       {name          isibleString,
                        type       OutletType,
                        location   Address},
                  overseas [1] SEQUENCE
                        {name       UTF8String,
                         type       OutletType,
                         location Address},
                  warehouse [2] CHOICE
                        {northern   [0] NULL,
                         southern   [1] NULL} } }

    END
--New page in published spec.
   Wineco-returns-protocol
   {joint-iso-itu-t international-organization(23) set(42)
        set-vendors(9) wineco(43) modules(2) returns(2)}
    DEFINITIONS
        AUTOMATIC TAGS ::=
    BEGIN

    EXPORTS Return-of-sales;

    IMPORTS OutletType,  Address,  Security-Type FROM
                Wineco-common-types
            {wineco-OID modules(2) common (3)};


    wineco-OID OBJECT IDENTIFIER ::=
       {joint-iso-itu-t international-organization(23) set(42)
        set-vendors(9) wineco(43)}
    Return-of-sales ::= SEQUENCE
     {version        BIT STRING
             {version1 (0),  version2 (1)} DEFAULT {version1},
      no-of-days-reported-on  INTEGER
      {week(7),  month (28),  maximum (56)} (1..56) DEFAULT week,
```

```
    time-and-date-of-report   CHOICE
            {two-digit-year   UTCTime,
             four-digit-year GeneralizedTime},
            -- If the system clock provides a four-digit year,
            -- the second alternative shall be used.  With the
            -- first alternative the time shall be interpreted
            -- as a sliding window.
    reason-for-delay   ENUMERATED
          {computer-failure,  network-failure,  other} OPTIONAL,
            -- Include this field if and only if the
            -- no-of-days-reported-on exceeds seven.
    additional-information  SEQUENCE OF PrintableString OPTIONAL,
            -- Include this field if and only if the
            -- reason-for-delay is "other".
    sales-data  SET OF Report-item,
    ... ! PrintableString : "See wineco manual chapter 15" }
  Report-item ::= SEQUENCE
  {item                   OBJECT IDENTIFIER,
   item-description     ObjectDescriptor OPTIONAL,
        -- To be included for any newly-stocked item.
   bar-code-data         OCTET STRING,
        -- Represents the bar-code for the item as specified
        -- in the wineco manual chapter 29.
   ran-out-of-stock  BOOLEAN DEFAULT FALSE,
        -- Send TRUE if stock for item became exhausted at any
        -- time during the period reported on.
   min-stock-level      REAL,
   max-stock-level      REAL,
   average-stock-level  REAL
      -- Give minimum,  maximum,  and average levels during the
      -- period as a percentage of normal target stock-level-- }


   wineco-items OBJECT IDENTIFIER ::=
   {joint-iso-itu-t international-organization(23) set(42)
       set-vendors(9) wineco(43)stock-items (0)}
END


Wineco-common-types
      {joint-iso-itu-t internationalRA(23) set(42)
        set-vendors(9) wineco(43) modules(2) common(3)}
  DEFINITIONS
       AUTOMATIC TAGS ::=
  BEGIN


  EXPORTS  OutletType,  Address,  Security-Type;
--   IMPORTS Security-Type FROM
--       SET-module
--       {joint-iso-itu-t internationalRA(23) set(42) module(6) 0};
--Removed for this appendix to avoid needing the import,
--and replaced by the type below.
```

```
Security-Type ::= SEQUENCE{
        algorithm   OBJECT IDENTIFIER,
        encoding    OCTET STRING}

--OutletType is not populated in main text--
    OutletType ::=  SEQUENCE
        {type  ENUMERATED{mail-order,  retail},
        description CHARACTER STRING}

--Address is not populated in main text--
    Address ::= SEQUENCE
        {name   UTF8String,
        town    UTF8String,
        country UTF8String}

    END
```

Appendix 3 Compiler Output for C Support for the Wineco Protocol

This appendix contains the text produced by the "OSS ASN.1 Tools XE "OSS ASN.1 Tools" " product to provide support for a C implementation of "Return-of-sales" and "Report-item" in our Wineco protocol. (Some of this text is generated just for wineco, some is generic definitions obtained from an include file, for example "GeneralizedTime" and "ossBoolean"):

```c
typedef struct {
   short            year;    /* YYYY format when used for GeneralizedTime */
                             /* YY format when used for UTCTime */
   short            month;
   short            day;
   short            hour;
   short            minute;
   short            second;
   short            millisec;
   short            mindiff;  /* UTC +/- minute differential    */
   ossBoolean       utc;      /* TRUE means UTC time             */
} GeneralizedTime;

typedef GeneralizedTime UTCTime;

typedef struct ObjectID {
    unsigned short   length;
    unsigned char    *value;
} ObjectID;

typedef struct Report_item {
    unsigned char    bit_mask;
# define        ran_out_of_stock_present 0x80
    ObjectID         item;
    char             *item_description;  /* NULL for not present */
    struct {
        unsigned int    length;
        unsigned char   *value;
    } bar_code_data;
    ossBoolean       ran_out_of_stock;
            /* ran_out_of_stock_present not set in
             * bit_mask implies value is FALSE */
    double           min_stock_level;
    double           max_stock_level;
    double           average_stock_level;
} Report_item;
typedef struct Return_of_sales {
    unsigned char    bit_mask;
#       define       version_present 0x80
#       define       no_of_days_reported_on_present 0x40
```

```
#       define       reason_for_delay_present 0x20
#       define       additional_information_present 0x10
    unsigned char    version;
                        /* version_present not set in bit_mask
                         * implies value is { version1 } */
#       define       version1 0x80
#       define       version2 0x40
    unsigned short   no_of_days_reported_on;
                        /* no_of_days_reported_on_present not set
                         * in bit_mask implies value is week */
#       define       week 7
#       define       month 28
#       define       maximum 56
    struct {
        unsigned short  choice;
#           define       two_digit_year_chosen 1
#           define       four_digit_year_chosen 2
        union {
            UTCTime         two_digit_year;
                    /* to choose, set choice to
                     * two_digit_year_chosen */
            GeneralizedTime four_digit_year;
                    /* to choose, set choice to
                     * four_digit_year_chosen */
        } u;
    } time_and_date_of_report;
    enum {
        computer_failure = 0,
        network_failure = 1,
        other = 2
    } reason_for_delay;
                        /* optional; set in bit_mask
                         * reason_for_delay_present
                         * if present */
    struct _seqof1 {
        struct _seqof1  *next;
        char            *value;
    } *additional_information;
                        /* optional; set in bit_mask
                         * additional_information_present if present */
    struct _setof1 {
        struct _setof1  *next;
        Report_item     value;
    } *sales_data;
} Return_of_sales;
```

Appendix 4 Compiler Output for Java Support for the Wineco Protocol

This appendix contains the text for Java support for the "Return-of-sales" and the "Report-item" types in the Wineco Protocol. This is a part of the output produced by the "OSS ASN.1 Tools" product when it is fed with the Wineco modules. This is a bit more bulky than Appendix 3—does that say anything? Whoops—BAD STATEMENT—no way can one appear to be criticizing Java! This is more than Figure 999 stuff! The Java code is bulkier because it contains all the methods for setting and reading fields and for inserting and deleting items in SEQUENCE OF, so it does rather more than the C code in Appendix 3. If you don't know Java, you will **certainly** want to ignore this appendix. Even if you **do** know Java, you will probably only want to look at a few sample classes and methods. Here is the Java code:

```java
package wineco.wineco_returns_protocol;
import com.oss.asn1.*;
import com.oss.util.*;
import wineco.*;
import wineco.wineco_common_types.*;

public class Return_of_sales extends Sequence {

    /**
    The default constructor.
    */
    public Return_of_sales() {}

    protected ASN1World getASN1World()
                { return wineco.Wineco.cASN1World; }
    protected int getTypeIndex()
            { return Wineco_returns_protocol.Return_of_sales_PDU; }

    /**
    Construct from a IAAPI  alue Reference.
    */
    public Return_of_sales(ASN1World world, int index)
            { ASN1Module.get alueReference(world, this, index); }
    /**
    Construct with components.
    */
    public Return_of_sales(
         ersion version,
        No_of_days_reported_on no_of_days_reported_on,
        Time_and_date_of_report time_and_date_of_report,
        Reason_for_delay reason_for_delay,
        Additional_information additional_information,
        Sales_data sales_data)
```

```
{
    Set ersion(version);
    SetNo_of_days_reported_on(no_of_days_reported_on);
    SetTime_and_date_of_report(time_and_date_of_report);
    SetReason_for_delay(reason_for_delay);
    SetAdditional_information(additional_information);
    SetSales_data(sales_data);
}


/**
Construct with required components.
*/
public Return_of_sales(
    Time_and_date_of_report time_and_date_of_report,
    Sales_data sales_data)
{
    SetTime_and_date_of_report(time_and_date_of_report);
    SetSales_data(sales_data);
}


protected void initComponents()
{
    mComponents[0] = new  ersion();
    mComponents[1] = new No_of_days_reported_on();
    mComponents[2] = new Time_and_date_of_report();
    mComponents[3] = new Reason_for_delay();
    mComponents[4] = new Additional_information();
    mComponents[5] = new Sales_data();
}


// Instance initializer
{
    mComponents = new AbstractData[6];
    mPresentBits = new java.util.BitSet(mComponents.length);
}


// Methods for field "version"
public  ersion get ersion()
{
    return ( ersion)mComponents[0];
}
public void Set ersion( ersion version)
{
    mComponents[0] = version;
    SetComponentPresent(0);
}
public void Set ersionToDefault() {SetComponentAbsent(0); }
public boolean hasDefault ersion() { return componentIsPresent(0); }
public boolean has ersion() { return componentIsPresent(0); }
public void delete ersion() { SetComponentAbsent(0); }
public static class  ersion extends BitString {
```

```
    /**
    The default constructor.
    */
    public  ersion() { super(new byte[1], 2); }

    /**
    Construct Bit String from a byte array and significant bits.
      @param value the byte array to set this object to.
      @param sigBits the number of significant bits.
    */
    public  ersion(byte[] value, int sigBits)
                  { super(value, sigBits); }
    protected ASN1World getASN1World()
              { return wineco.Wineco.cASN1World; }
    // Named list definitions.
    public static final int version1 = 0;
    public static final int version2 = 1;
} // End class definition for  ersion

// Methods for field "no_of_days_reported_on"
public No_of_days_reported_on getNo_of_days_reported_on()
{
    return (No_of_days_reported_on)mComponents[1];
}
public void SetNo_of_days_reported_on
    (No_of_days_reported_on no_of_days_reported_on)
{
    mComponents[1] = no_of_days_reported_on;
    SetComponentPresent(1);
}
public void SetNo_of_days_reported_onToDefault()
            {SetComponentAbsent(1); }
public boolean hasDefaultNo_of_days_reported_on()
            { return componentIsPresent(1); }
public boolean hasNo_of_days_reported_on()
            { return componentIsPresent(1); }
public void deleteNo_of_days_reported_on()
            { SetComponentAbsent(1); }

public static class No_of_days_reported_on extends INTEGER {

    /**
    The default constructor.
    */
    public No_of_days_reported_on() {}
    public No_of_days_reported_on(short value) { super(value);}
    public No_of_days_reported_on(int   value) { super(value);}
    public No_of_days_reported_on(long  value) { super(value);}

    protected ASN1World getASN1World()
            { return wineco.Wineco.cASN1World; }
```

```
        // Named list definitions.
        public static final No_of_days_reported_on week =
                        new No_of_days_reported_on(7);
        public static final No_of_days_reported_on month =
                        new No_of_days_reported_on(28);
        public static final No_of_days_reported_on maximum =
                        new No_of_days_reported_on(56);
        private final static No_of_days_reported_on cNamedNumbers[] =
                        {week, month, maximum};
        protected final static long cFirstNumber = 7;
        protected final static boolean cLinearNumbers = false;
        protected INTEGER[] getNamedNumbers() { return cNamedNumbers;}
        protected boolean hasLinearNumbers() { return cLinearNumbers;}
        protected long getFirstNumber() { return cFirstNumber;}
    } // End class definition for No_of_days_reported_on


// Methods for field "time_and_date_of_report"
public Time_and_date_of_report getTime_and_date_of_report()
{
    return (Time_and_date_of_report)mComponents[2];
}
public void SetTime_and_date_of_report
            (Time_and_date_of_report time_and_date_of_report)
{
    mComponents[2] = time_and_date_of_report;
}
public static class Time_and_date_of_report extends Choice {

    /**
    The default constructor.
    */
    public Time_and_date_of_report() {}
    protected ASN1World getASN1World()
            { return wineco.Wineco.cASN1World; }

    /**
    Construct from a IAAPI  alue Reference.
    */
    public Time_and_date_of_report(ASN1World world, int index)
{ASN1Module.get alueReference(world, this, index); }

    public static final  int  two_digit_year_chosen = 1;
    public static final  int  four_digit_year_chosen = 2;
    // Methods for field "two_digit_year"
    public static Time_and_date_of_report
            createTime_and_date_of_reportWithTwo_digit_year
                (UTCTime two_digit_year)
            {Time_and_date_of_report __object =
                new Time_and_date_of_report();
            __object.SetTwo_digit_year(two_digit_year);
            return __object;
```

```
        }
    public boolean hasTwo_digit_year() {
        return getChosenFlag() == two_digit_year_chosen;
    }
    public void SetTwo_digit_year (UTCTime two_digit_year) {
        SetChosen alue(two_digit_year);
        SetChosenFlag(two_digit_year_chosen);
    }
    // Methods for field "four_digit_year"
    public static Time_and_date_of_report
            createTime_and_date_of_reportWithFour_digit_year
                    (GeneralizedTime four_digit_year)
            {Time_and_date_of_report __object =
                    new Time_and_date_of_report();
            __object.SetFour_digit_year(four_digit_year);
            return __object;
    }
    public boolean hasFour_digit_year() {
        return getChosenFlag() == four_digit_year_chosen;
    }
    public void SetFour_digit_year
    (GeneralizedTime four_digit_year) {
        SetChosen alue(four_digit_year);
        SetChosenFlag(four_digit_year_chosen);
    }
    // Method to create a specific choice instance
    protected AbstractData createInstance(int chosen) {
        switch(chosen) {
            case two_digit_year_chosen: return
                                    new UTCTime();
            case four_digit_year_chosen: return
                                    new GeneralizedTime();
            default: throw
                    new InternalError("Choice.createInstance()");
        }
    }
} // End class definition for Time_and_date_of_report
// Methods for field "reason_for_delay"
public Reason_for_delay getReason_for_delay()
{
    return (Reason_for_delay)mComponents[3];
}
public void SetReason_for_delay(Reason_for_delay reason_for_delay)
{
    mComponents[3] = reason_for_delay;
    SetComponentPresent(3);
}
public boolean hasReason_for_delay()
            { return componentIsPresent(3); }
public void deleteReason_for_delay()
            { SetComponentAbsent(3); }
```

```
public static class Reason_for_delay extends Enumerated {
    /**
    The default constructor.
    */
    public Reason_for_delay() {super(cFirstNumber);}
    protected Reason_for_delay(long value) { super(value);}
    protected ASN1World getASN1World()
            { return wineco.Wineco.cASN1World; }
    // Named list definitions.
    public static final Reason_for_delay computer_failure =
                    new Reason_for_delay(0);
    public static final Reason_for_delay network_failure =
                    new Reason_for_delay(1);
    public static final Reason_for_delay other =
                    new Reason_for_delay(2);
    private final static Reason_for_delay cNamedNumbers[] =
            {computer_failure, network_failure, other};
    protected final static long cFirstNumber = 0;
    protected final static boolean cLinearNumbers = false;
    protected Enumerated[] getNamedNumbers() { return cNamedNumbers;}
    protected boolean hasLinearNumbers() { return cLinearNumbers;}
    protected long getFirstNumber() { return cFirstNumber;}
} // End class definition for Reason_for_delay

// Methods for field "additional_information"
public Additional_information getAdditional_information()
{
    return (Additional_information)mComponents[4];
}
public void SetAdditional_information
    (Additional_information additional_information)
{
    mComponents[4] = additional_information;
    SetComponentPresent(4);
}
public boolean hasAdditional_information()
            { return componentIsPresent(4); }
public void deleteAdditional_information()
            { SetComponentAbsent(4); }
public static class Additional_information extends SequenceOf {

    /**
    The default constructor.
    */
    public Additional_information() {}

    protected ASN1World getASN1World()
            { return wineco.Wineco.cASN1World; }

    /**
```

```
    Construct from a IAAPI  alue Reference.
    */
    public Additional_information(ASN1World world, int index)
            {ASN1Module.get alueReference(world, this, index); }


    /**
    Add an Element to the SEQUENCE OF/SET OF.
    */
    public synchronized void add(PrintableString element)
    {
        super.addElement(element);
    }
    /**
    Set an Element in the SEQUENCE OF/SET OF.
    */
    public synchronized void set
            (PrintableString element, int atIndex)
    {
        super.SetElement(element, atIndex);
    }
    /**
    Get an Element from the SEQUENCE OF/SET OF.
    */
    public synchronized PrintableString get(int atIndex)
    {
        return (PrintableString) super.getElement(atIndex);
    }
    /**
    Insert an Element into the SEQUENCE OF/SET OF.
    */
    public synchronized void insert
            (PrintableString element, int atIndex)
    {
        super.insertElement(element, atIndex);
    }
    /**
    Remove an Element from the SEQUENCE OF/SET OF.
    */
    public synchronized void remove(PrintableString element)
    {
        super.removeElement(element);
    }
    /**
    Create an instance of  SEQUENCE OF/SET OF.
    */
    public AbstractData createInstance()
    {
        return ((AbstractData) new PrintableString());
    }
} // End class definition for Additional_information
```

```
// Methods for field "sales_data"
public Sales_data getSales_data()
{
    return (Sales_data)mComponents[5];
}
public void SetSales_data(Sales_data sales_data)
{
    mComponents[5] = sales_data;
}

public static class Sales_data extends SetOf {

    /**
    The default constructor.
    */
    public Sales_data() {}
    protected ASN1World getASN1World()
            { return wineco.Wineco.cASN1World; }

    /**
    Construct from a IAAPI  alue Reference.
    */
    public Sales_data(ASN1World world, int index)
            { ASN1Module.get alueReference(world, this, index); }

    /**
    Add an Element to the SEQUENCE OF/SET OF.
    */
    public synchronized void add(Report_item element)
    {
        super.addElement(element);
    }
    /**
    Set an Element in the SEQUENCE OF/SET OF.
    */
    public synchronized void set(Report_item element, int atIndex)
    {
        super.SetElement(element, atIndex);
    }
    /**
    Get an Element from the SEQUENCE OF/SET OF.
    */
    public synchronized Report_item get(int atIndex)
    {
        return (Report_item) super.getElement(atIndex);
    }
    /**
    Insert an Element into the SEQUENCE OF/SET OF.
    */
    public synchronized void insert
            (Report_item element, int atIndex)
```

```
            {
                super.insertElement(element, atIndex);
            }
            /**
            Remove an Element from the SEQUENCE OF/SET OF.
            */
            public synchronized void remove(Report_item element)
            {
                super.removeElement(element);
            }
            /**
            Create an instance of  SEQUENCE OF/SET OF.
            */
            public AbstractData createInstance()
            {
                return ((AbstractData) new Report_item());
            }
        } // End class definition for Sales_data
    } // End class definition for Return_of_sales
public class Report_item extends Sequence {

    /**
    The default constructor.
    */
    public Report_item() {}

    protected ASN1World getASN1World()
            { return wineco.Wineco.cASN1World; }

    /**
    Construct from an IAAPI Value Reference.
    */
    public Report_item(ASN1World world, int index)
            { ASN1Module.getValueReference(world, this, index); }
    /**
    Construct with components.
    */
    public Report_item(
        ObjectIdentifier item,
        ObjectDescriptor item_description,
        OctetString bar_code_data,
        boolean ran_out_of_stock,
        double min_stock_level,
        double max_stock_level,
        double average_stock_level)
    {
        SetItem(item);
        SetItem_description(item_description);
        SetBar_code_data(bar_code_data);
        SetRan_out_of_stock(ran_out_of_stock);
        SetMin_stock_level(min_stock_level);
```

```
        SetMax_stock_level(max_stock_level);
        SetAverage_stock_level(average_stock_level);
    }
    /**
    Construct with required components.
    */
    public Report_item(
        ObjectIdentifier item,
        OctetString bar_code_data,
        double min_stock_level,
        double max_stock_level,
        double average_stock_level)
    {
        SetItem(item);
        SetBar_code_data(bar_code_data);
        SetMin_stock_level(min_stock_level);
        SetMax_stock_level(max_stock_level);
        SetAverage_stock_level(average_stock_level);
    }
    protected void initComponents()
    {
        mComponents[0] = new ObjectIdentifier();
        mComponents[1] = new ObjectDescriptor();
        mComponents[2] = new OctetString();
        mComponents[3] = new BOOLEAN();
        mComponents[4] = new Real();
        mComponents[5] = new Real();
        mComponents[6] = new Real();
    }


    // Instance initializer
    {
        mComponents = new AbstractData[7];
        mPresentBits = new java.util.BitSet(mComponents.length);
        mComponents[3] = new BOOLEAN();
        mComponents[4] = new Real();
        mComponents[5] = new Real();
        mComponents[6] = new Real();
    }


    // Methods for field "item"
    public ObjectIdentifier getItem()
    {
        return (ObjectIdentifier)mComponents[0];
    }
    public void SetItem(ObjectIdentifier item)
    {
        mComponents[0] = item;
    }


    // Methods for field "item_description"
```

```
public ObjectDescriptor getItem_description()
{
    return (ObjectDescriptor)mComponents[1];
}
public void SetItem_description(ObjectDescriptor item_description)
{
    mComponents[1] = item_description;
    SetComponentPresent(1);
}
public boolean hasItem_description()
                    { return componentIsPresent(1); }
public void deleteItem_description()
                    { SetComponentAbsent(1); }


// Methods for field "bar_code_data"
public OctetString getBar_code_data()
{
    return (OctetString)mComponents[2];
}
public void SetBar_code_data(OctetString bar_code_data)
{
    mComponents[2] = bar_code_data;
}


// Methods for field "ran_out_of_stock"
public boolean getRan_out_of_stock()
{
    return ((BOOLEAN) mComponents[3]).booleanValue();
}
public void SetRan_out_of_stock(boolean ran_out_of_stock)
{
    ((BOOLEAN) mComponents[3]).SetValue(ran_out_of_stock);
    SetComponentPresent(3);
}
public void SetRan_out_of_stockToDefault()
                    {SetComponentAbsent(3); }
public boolean hasDefaultRan_out_of_stock()
                    { return componentIsPresent(3); }
public boolean hasRan_out_of_stock()
                    { return componentIsPresent(3); }
public void deleteRan_out_of_stock()
                    { SetComponentAbsent(3); }
// Methods for field "min_stock_level"
public double getMin_stock_level()
{
    return ((Real) mComponents[4]).doubleValue();
}
public void SetMin_stock_level(double min_stock_level)
{
    ((Real) mComponents[4]).SetValue(min_stock_level);
}
```

```
    // Methods for field "max_stock_level"
    public double getMax_stock_level()
    {
        return ((Real) mComponents[5]).doubleValue();
    }
    public void SetMax_stock_level(double max_stock_level)
    {
        ((Real) mComponents[5]).SetValue(max_stock_level);
    }


    // Methods for field "average_stock_level"
    public double getAverage_stock_level()
    {
        return ((Real) mComponents[6]).doubleValue();
    }
    public void SetAverage_stock_level(double average_stock_level)
    {
        ((Real) mComponents[6]).SetValue(average_stock_level);
    }
} // End class definition for Report_item
```

Appendix 5 ASN.1 Resources Via the Web

This appendix provides a single link to an OSS Nokalva site that contains both links to other Web resources and extensions of this book. In particular, it contains:

- References to other publications (both Web-based and hard-copy) that are relevant to readers of this book.

- A glossary of terms relevant to ASN.1, including all the acronyms and abbreviations used in this book. (Most of those used here are also included in the index, which will provide you with a quick look over and perhaps a little more information.)

- Details of and/or links to other Web-based ASN.1 resources such as mailing lists, Olivier Dubuisson's site with his book, the Unicode site, my own site with my book *Understanding OSI*, the International Register site, ITU-T and ETSI sites, a site giving the allocations for some parts of the Object Identifier tree, etc.

- More details of specifications that are defined using ASN.1, with links to electronic versions of those specifications where these are known to be publicly available.

- Errata sheets for this book as and when they are produced.

- An electronic copy of this book.

The URL for the OSS Nokalva site is:

> http://www.nokalva.com

Please come and visit!

And just in case things might move—URLs have a habit of changing—a crosslink is also provided at:

> http://www.larmouth.demon.co.uk/books

Index

Related Titles from Morgan Kaufmann

Morgan Kaufmann

http://www.mkp.com

- **NETWORKED APPLICATIONS: A GUIDE TO THE NEW COMPUTING INFRASTRUCTURE**
  David G. Messerschmitt
  ISBN: 1-55860-536-3 $34.95

- **MULTIMEDIA AND HYPERTEXT: THE INTERNET AND BEYOND**
  Jakob Nielsen
  ISBN: 0-12-518408-5 $32.00

- **SMIL AND STREAMING MEDIA FOR WEBMASTERS**
  Joseph T. Sinclair
  ISBN: 0-12-645536-8 $44.95

- **THIN CLIENTS CLEARLY EXPLAINED**
  Joseph T. Sinclair and Mark Merkow
  ISBN: 0-12-645535-X $39.95

- **MULTIMEDIA SERVERS: APPLICATIONS, ENVIRONMENTS, AND DESIGN**
  Dinkar Sitaram, Asit Dan
  ISBN: 1-55860-430-8 $69.95

- **HIGH-PERFORMANCE COMMUNICATION NETWORKS**
  Jean Walrand, Pravin Varya
  ISBN: 1-33860-341-7 $74.95

More Related Titles on next page

Related Titles from Morgan Kaufmann

Morgan Kaufmann

http://www.mkp.com

- **C++ FOR REAL PROGRAMMERS, REVISED EDITION**
  Jeff Alger
  ISBN: 0-12-049942-8 $39.95

- **INTERNETWORKING MULTIMEDIA**
  John Crowcroft, Mark Handley, Ian Wakeman
  ISBN: 1-55860-584-3 $54.95

- **SWITCHING IN IP NETWORKS: IP SWITCHING, TAG SWITCHING, AND RELATED TECHNOLOGIES**
  Bruce Davie, Paul Doolan, Yakov Rekhter
  ISBN: 1-55860-505-3 $44.95

- **APPLICATION SERVERS: POWERING THE WEB-BASED ENTERPRISE**
  Jesse Feiler
  ISBN: 0-12-251338-X $44.95

- **XML FOR REAL PROGRAMMERS**
  Reaz Hoque
  ISBN: 0-12-355592-2 $44.95

- **TCP/IP CLEARLY EXPLAINED, SECOND EDITION**
  Pete Loshin
  ISBN: 0-12-455826-7 $39.95

More Related Titles on previous page